Praise for *Angel in the Forest*

"I am obstinately becoming more and more convinced that the books best worth our attention are not the "sweeping" and the "powerful," but those over which we may ponder. And I salute *Angel in the Forest* for being a work of this meditative sort."
— Kenneth Burke, *Kenyon Review*, 1945

"Readers looking for neatly swept sidewalks, road signs, traffic lights, will find themselves engulfed in a precolonial wilderness, a fertile abundance of many-faced trees and flowers-in the hollow of every tree, a man, on every treetop, an angel . . . The writing, from first to last, shows a dynamic force, stronger than the neat rules of literary perfection."
— Marianne Hauser, *Sewanee Review*, 1946

"A book of astonishing subtlety and brilliance . . . One of the truly notable writers of her generation"
— Marin Lebowitz, *The Nation*, 1945

Angel

in

the Forest

Other Books by Marguerite Young

Prismatic Ground

Moderate Fable

Angel in the Forest: A Fairy Tale of Two Utopias

Miss MacIntosh, My Darling

Inviting the Muses: Stories, Essays, Reviews

Harp Song for a Radical: The Life and Times of Eugene Victor Debs

Marguerite Young

ngel
in
the Forest

Introduction by Mark Van Doren

DALKEY ARCHIVE PRESS

Dallas, TX / Rochester, NY

First Dalkey Archive Press Edition, 1994
First Dalkey Archive Essentials Edition, 2024
All rights reserved.

Paperback: 9781628975512
Electronic Book: 9781628975567

Library of Congress Cataloging-in-Publication Data:
Names: Young, Marguerite, 1908-1995, author.
Classification:
LCC HX656.N5 Y6 1994
DDC 335/.977234 94008748
LC record available at https://lccn.loc.gov/94008748

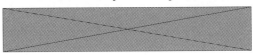

Support for this publication has been provided in part by a grant from the Addy Foundation.

Cover design by Justin Childress

Dalkey Archive Press
www.dalkeyarchive.com
Dallas, TX | Rochester, NY

Printed in the United States of America.

for
John and Faye Allison
Chester Young
Vivian Hall
Daphne Thomas
Lou Jon Thomas

Contents

Introduction

Marguerite Young is a poet whose prose, the longer it is looked at and listened to, becomes poetry also. This was true in 1945, when she published *Angel in the Forest*, just as it was true twenty years later when *Miss Macintosh, My Darling* made it so overwhelmingly clear that no reader of any page, let alone any chapter, could fail to be aware of the transformation.

The one book is history and the other is fiction, but again the distinction is no more than apparent. *Angel in the Forest* is excellent history, and at the same time it is a tale of such mysterious force, with such a rush of riches coming at us all the time, that we must wonder why so few other historians make the utmost of their subjects as she does of hers. The answer, doubtless, is that they are not poets, not story-tellers in the ancient tradition which assumed that nothing whatever is of merely neutral interest.

New Harmony, Indiana, the scene of *Angel in the Forest*, becomes in Miss Young's account a place of so rich and deep and wild and weird an interest that it can seem to us while we are in it a focal point where all the rays of human light and heat and sound somehow converge. We are in it only thirteen years, from 1814 to 1827; for the celibate community of Father Rapp was sold to Robert Owen in 1825, and Owen's socialist community, even though it lacked the handicap which celibacy entails, stuck it out but two years longer. Yet into that little space of time Miss Young has packed the essence, as it were, both of man's faith and of his folly. She has put both of these things inescapably there, welding them together in her imagination, and in her prose, so that with the best will in the world we are unable to pull them apart. The faith is real, the folly is real, yet each of them is an illusion too, as all things are in *Miss Macintosh, My Darling.* "Question—what is the nature of experience—what dream among dreams is reality?" These words from the earlier book could just as well be in the later one; and probably are.

Miss Young's unkillable concern with what she calls illusion is the secret of her power. Others, to distinguish it from reality, have called it appearance. Whatever its name, it is the surface that life presents. And what is beneath the surface? Miss Young, like Plato and many another, would like to know; and so she examines whatever she sees with eyes that make a passionate effort to pierce the veil of what, she is convinced, only seems to be there. Ultimately she fails, as we all do; but what is uncommon about her is the intensity of her trying. For her it is all drama, all excitement; and since she is witty too, and wise beyond the hope of truly succeeding, it is all fun.

Father Rapp, for instance, and his angel: the one he said he saw in old Harmony, Pennsylvania. Was the angel there, or was George Rapp, this madman out of Germany, deluded? Was he in fact a madman? Miss Young allows the question to float without ever coming down. Her Father Rapp is both grotesque and in his own way great: a mountebank, perhaps, and certainly a tyrant, but also unforgettable, and a man to be forgiven even for his monstrous theories of sex. So later on with Robert Owen, whom Miss Young finds it easier to admire, but whom she equally exposes to our skepticism; for he too was a fiasco, at any rate in New Harmony, and he survives with us only through his excellent intentions, which bore much better fruit elsewhere. Here, however, under Miss Young's remorseless burning-glass he and his disciples make a pretty sorry picture; "for by omitting all which did not come within the domain of reason, it seemed that they had omitted reason itself." An error both noble and absurd, like the pantheism of Frederick Rapp, the adopted son of George. "He believed that God is all, that God is everywhere—a huge animal without eyes, for there is nothing outside God for God to look on, not even one small, wet violet." There is Miss Young, perhaps, at her best. At the same moment that she seems to make fun of pantheism she shows that she completely understands it, insofar at least as it can be understood.

There are more people in the book, however, than Rapp and Owen. Indeed there seem to be millions of them, old and young, male and female, wise and foolish; just as there seem to be millions of objects that Miss Young desires to show us. They come in lists, in catalogues; they stream across our field of vision like particles of cosmic dust drawn here by some peculiar force. It is the force of Miss Young's concern with the surface she has set herself to explore. With or without illusion as to her chances of penetrating this surface, she incessantly strains to get all of it somehow in. And finally she does. No one sees the world as well as he who fears that nothing in it will be real.

MARK VAN DOREN

Angel
in
the Forest

New Harmony Today— A Glimpse in Summer, 1940

You come to old New Harmony by a creaking ferry. It has been operating for fifty years, according to the sign on the iron bell at the Wabash shore. This is a land of rolling hills on either side of the river. Sandpipers are continual migrants between two shores—primitive, they build no nests but holes in mudbanks, so that the hills seem coated with golden birds. Likely enough, there are two blind mules as other passengers on the ferry, and, tied to them like a cart behind them, translucent logs of the fallen birch. Likely enough, the ferryman will never speak a word. Far down the river, a barge turns toward the bend of the hills, the bargeman standing with his legs spread wide against a cloudless sky. Time passes, as the ferry creaks beneath a superfluous toll bridge, the government's extravagance, for few cross it. Ascending a path that seems to lead nowhere, you come at last to New Harmony, a disappointment. The past is an intangible in Indiana, you find, as in other parts of these abstract United States—a filling station where there were two Utopias, Mr. Babbitt where there was an angel. Surely, a Mexican town would be more flagrant in its tragic beauty, but this is a grayness, and the people are not picturesquely

3

blind, standing outside golden-domed cathedrals or kneeling before a Christ with Indian hair. Our ancestors, always hurried, left little evidence of their existence, if one discounts intangibles, a sundial, an apple a day, an angel in the forest.

New Harmony, once so supernatural, has subsided into easy naturalism, like that suggested by James Whitcomb Riley's poetry. This is, after all, the pocket country, hemmed in by two mighty rivers, the Wabash and Ohio, and some twenty miles, as the crow flies, from that large metropolis, Evansville, a pottery center and wharf for lazy steamboats, mostly imaginary. It is difficult to visualize this secluded area as once the scene of two Utopias, like the Cartesian split between body and soul—the Rappite, a Scriptural communism, founded by Father George Rapp, a German peasant, who believed his people to be future angels—the Owenite, founded by Robert Owen, an English cotton lord, who believed all men to be machines. The end result of Father Rapp's community, a celibate order, was heaven—and the end result of Robert Owen's, while also incalculable, was the British labor movement.

New Harmony has a charm escaping these and other categories. In 1940, it seemed like a good place to spend one's old age in or visit one's old Aunt Mary, the nonexistent character. School did or did not keep, and nobody cared, and the teacher was pretty, presumably. People did or did not wash on Monday, iron on Tuesday. There were old-fashioned flowers in abandoned lots and gardens—dusty blue morning glories trailing among stinkweeds, spires of yellowing lilies that seemed to flourish in neglect. There was a feeling of both tedium and voluptuousness.

Gradually, in spite of the ten-cent store, which was cobwebbed and insubstantial, the present faded, became of a texture with the past, as if today were only the conglomerate of all our yesterdays. Every item implied, however, desolation, since nothing lingers so like the memory of failure, especially if it has sought the extreme perfection. There were outhouses leaning with time, and a water tower covered with ivy, suggesting faerie lands forlorn, right in the heart of the green corn country. There was an abandoned Catholic church with a belfry where swallows had built their nests and fluttered back and forth like bells. There was nothing certain, but illusion in every facet, a feeling of the impermanence of man—for in New Harmony, he had always been a tramp—the impermanence of two Utopias as whimsical as himself. There was no commonplace of all mankind, but differentiation, mysteries unfathomable. Frame houses put up hastily by Sears, Roebuck looked out on a Hebrew and Greek maze symbolizing man's transience on this makeshift earth, also put up hastily. Others faced on the footprints of an abiding angel, big-footed.

Peculiarities multiplied, perhaps because New Harmony, which was the cradle of two Utopias, is literally, if not figuratively, cut off from the outside world and introverted as a nude drunk with memories. It is as if this pocket country were a little planet, whirling far out alone in space. Almost every citizen is aware of New Harmony's strangeness.

What far from average people have walked these streets, in old time! An angel like a hermaphrodite butterfly, a butterfly catcher, a Daniel Boone of the infinite, a finite Elijah, a herb doctor, Lot's wife, many pastorals, many mechanics, clouded dreamers, a celibate breeder of horses, poor Yahoos, the Spirit of Nature, rational man, irrational men, patriarchs, undertakers. Nor does this list, inclusive as it seems, exhaust the possibilities of nineteenth-century salvationism, as expressed by two Utopias—the first, forerunner of a New Jerusalem, exclusive and arbitrary; the second, forerunner of a New Moral World, to encompass all nations and all governments. Two Utopias comprehended, within a half-mile square surrounded by a vast wilderness, past, present, and future, however abstrusely—the burning of Rome, city planning, explosion of stars, a new calendar, anarchy, a New Jerusalem, repression, expansion, moneyless Eden, exaltation of pearls, a three-hour working day, exaltation of horses, infinite regress, the united nations of earth, the many, the few, Lucifer, lotus-eaters, the falling of autumn leaves, the myths of Narcissus, good dentistry, many fictions. So that such perfectionist orders, which would have excluded much of mistaken life, seem mistaken life itself, with all its infinite variety.

It was impossible, even in 1940, to visit at length in New Harmony without catching some of the "spirit" of the place— few who came were unappreciative of this rare gem, a frontier between eternity and time. Question—what is the nature of experience—what dream among dreams is reality? Man is the creator of those values by which he lives and perhaps dies. They are not handed down from heaven, usually.

On the banks of the Wabash, early in the nineteenth century, two Utopias attempted to erect, each in its own way, the character of the extreme perfection, socially considered. They were "gone but not forgotten" in 1940, like an advertisement in an obituary column. New Harmony has ever loved its dead. In shops on Brewery and Church Streets, golden rain tree shoots were for sale, six for twenty-five cents, and guaranteed to grow in any temperate latitude, unless high in the mountains—sign of the New Moral World envisioned by the Owenites, who believed that they had heard the death rattle of all competitive trades and conflicting systems. Sign of their predecessors and perhaps of their successors as well, two dolls, labeled "Father and Mother Rapp," looked out from under a bell-shaped glass, like saints or preserved flowers. Such pitiful dolls remind us only that man cannot exist in a vacuum, that the concepts which do not fit into his category are never really abandoned. How erect, even in heaven, to say nothing of earth, community without impedimenta, ties, relationships? How translate Mr. Babbitt into an angel who will not have the old attitude of man, or at least the many-faceted eyes of a fly?

There seemed, in 1940, except for the trade in rain tree pods and dolls, not much other business. Two Utopias could not account for New Harmony, an amorphous material. Perhaps as in similar river towns, the beauty operator added to her income by painting corpses after hours. If so, her idea of happiness was doubly complicated. The undertaker was a shepherd, almost Biblical, an apparition out of New Harmony's past. The undertaker's was the only dynasty in New Harmony now. He hoped that the old, sick sister would not go at lambing, which was his busy season—if death was his vocation, life was his avocation—he was always on the way from the grave to the cradle, so to speak. All of New Harmony depended, directly or indirectly, upon his many enterprises—and fortunately, he was the kindest man on earth, holding a string of mortgages he would not foreclose. He buried everybody. There were other antiquities. The Owenite chemical laboratory, with its Gothic spire awry, would have transferred happiness from the nonhuman elements to human society, a long time ago. It was empty now of any experiment but Caroline Dale's sewing basket, lined with blue silk, and pictures of fat Welsh pigs, in gilded frames carved with acorns—pictures, not hers, of the planets whose spirits are women in draperies of clouds, admirably adjusted—a few cobwebbed test tubes, also, to express the idealistic science of the vacuum which some had dreamed of filling up. The roof leaked.

Father Rapp looked forward to no twentieth century whatever. There would have been, if he had had his way, not a chance of Oscar Wilde's trial or other scandals in the late nineteenth century, not a chance of prize fighters and Mae West in the twentieth. The work of regeneration, according to Robert Owen, must be done immediately, else the people of the twentieth century could not be blamed for their characters being ill formed.

The events of this world are not admirably connected, or if they are, that harmony was not obvious in New Harmony. There were, in 1940, all kinds of contrasts—two Utopias like corn fields covered over with water. Families lived in the monastic Rappite houses—babies squalled where Rappite celibates had slept profoundly. There were to have been no wars, according to either Utopia, and an end to ethical confusions as well. In 1940, however, there was a rumor of oil under the peaceful corn fields— possibility of munitions blowing up the whole world, at which time every man would have a chicken in the pot, a good five-cent cigar, as Teddy Roosevelt had promised, or had he, and he was a great lion hunter; possibility of God's dissolving the world, at which time every man would have a star in his crown on the banks of the Wabash far away.

These, however, were matters to be engaged in during idle moments, when there was nothing to do but imagine the unimaginable. As a whole, regarding immediate prospects, the people were suspicious of violent change. New Harmony was New Harmony, a tautology—the same as to say that bread is bread—and a rose by any other name would never smell as sweet. Few, unless they were at death's door, gave more than a passing thought to the nature of ultimate happiness. Most people were happy enough if they could just keep the wolf from the door. Most people liked Franklin D. Roosevelt unless they owned real estate or aspired to. A man was lucky to own the ground under his feet. The majority in the pocket country were tenant farmers and did not reap the corn they sowed. They wanted little—enough to eat, enough to wear, a decent roof, a few of the things which are not of this world, and an automobile, which seemed unlikely. The few rich were sonorous Republicans with uniformed ebony chauffeurs—no other Negroes allowed— castles in Spain, private chapels in Oregon, manure on their boots when they came back home, but they never came. They were, in fact, problematical as angels. As for communism, nobody would object to it if it could be Christian, like the Society of Christ and the fishermen. There should be more pence for Peter the Fisherman and less for Peter the Pope, as the saying goes. Christ, it was well known, had struck water from the living rock and had fed the poor with quail. Quail shooting was still good in the pocket country—plenty of quail in the Rappite graveyard, for example. But where had a real communism ever been tried, outside the Bible? Millennium might be just around the corner, but as to man's making it, that seemed highly unlikely. Nobody could remove the flaws from the universe without destroying the universe, the undertaker said—and an old plow was better than none, and many a blind horse had its usefulness.

For most people, Hitler was not quite a menace as yet, not nearly so much as Haile Selassie, who had somehow contrived to capture their imagination. Stalin, in spite of propaganda, was sufficiently remote, like the Arctic or another planet. The barber objected to his lavender shirt—but otherwise, the Russian bear had little plausibility. A Gallup poll would have shown Gandhi as the most favored world character, a Christ-like man, who would let the grass grow high and the crows roost in his corn fields, and no old tax collector would ever find him out. Even Gandhi, however, would have come in second to Glaucas, the itinerant sewer cleaner, profane as the earth itself.

In general, they would leave the world as it goes. If they had not shared its fortunes, why should they share its misfortunes? Nobody wanted to change New Harmony, decay having its own remorseless attraction, and nothing so beautiful, in any season, as the autumn of man's soul, the sere, the yellow leaf. Even the Rappite maze had been more wonderful before restored to its approximate position, so that now boys and girls spooned there, most irreligiously, and the policeman under his tropical hat had that problem, on top of every other. Aged simplicity stood with its back against the wall, opposing every threat upon its own *status quo*. Even the mute could wax eloquent on the subject of New Harmony's cherry orchards and immunity to the blight of progress, discounting the W.P.A. housing project, discounting, too, the end of the world, which had long been looked forward to. While relief might be necessary, a health officer seemed excessive, in a valley populous with doves and men who had seen ninety summers. The health officer was a puny fellow, with moths in his stomach, and could not lift a ten-pound weight as Glaucas could—and Glaucas had never been to school. Besides, who had ever seen a germ? The one real improvement—granting even that President Roosevelt's intentions might be good, and the Secretary of Agriculture not too far off the track—would be for God to intervene, breaking off history like a rotted branch on the tree of life. At such a time, there would be white angels on white horses in Posey County, and not a tax collector or health officer in the entire creation, from star to shining star—perhaps not even a flea. And everything would be as it had been, excluding imperfections.

Meanwhile, for want of a better occupation, some bet on the horses which were running at Dade Park, this side of the Ohio in Kentucky, but it was a long trip—so they would just stay at home and bet on imaginary horses with imaginary money, which is a much safer sport. There was a fellow who owed another fellow a hundred purely fanciful dollars and skulked in shadows when he considered the immense debts he had piled up. Anyone would have thought he was the government.

New Harmony persisted—old, unresurrected, unredeemed perhaps, yet curiously, unreasonably wonderful. A whore where there had been an angel. Whisky where there had been prohibition.

It was good that the Rappites had left the black locust trees standing and that the Owenites had planted those golden rain trees, "the fastest-growing tree in the world," much used in Chinese graveyards because of their lantern-shaped leaves. Otherwise, both Utopias might have been forgotten, though advertised as remembered. Utopias of the past seemed, in spite of their shade trees, not so tangible, finally, as Miss Hobbie and Miss Duckie, old sisters carrying their feather pillows to the show where the seats were hard to set on—sneaking in to see Clark Gable. All mankind seemed not so real as one lonely, frost-bitten character, like the man who died with his feet in the ashes of the cold stove last winter, or was it winter before last? He was not missed until spring, when the saloonkeeper remembered him—that he had not been coming in for quite a while. New Harmony is full of such remarkable characters, each with a history. There was the man who stole the undertaker's hog last winter. He cut off the head and threw it into a well and dragged the body over the smooth snow, through a world of fairy crystal. That was how they tracked him right to his own door, a sheep's house in a field of ghostly thistle. They thought maybe a woman had been killed by a man from Illinois. It was only the undertaker's hog, though, as usual. So he spent six weeks in a nice, warm jail, repenting—and ate three hogs, the undertaker said, and read all the back numbers of *True Detective Stories*, the policeman said. There was also Old Thomas, a Kentuckian who got to New Harmony, God knows how. He slept in the room at the Tavern where Robert Owen used to sleep when this was Utopia. There was a hole widening in the floor. Everybody worried for fear Old Thomas would step through before the government could get around to repairing the floor, which was historical. He never did, and neither did the government. The hole is still there. He would go down and tell his secrets to the Wabash River, like a loudspeaker attached to a Ford. He was as mean as a woodpecker, but everybody pitied him, for he expressed what everybody felt. He was like a public voice of conscience. He drowned himself in a bathtub, one night when he came home from the river. There was also Old Joshua, famous for his teeth the length and breadth of Posey County—that, and the Republican party. He had seen those teeth pictured in a catalogue—inlaid with gold, smooth as pearls in a row, guaranteed to last a lifetime. So when he wrote for a harness and a currycomb, he put in his order, as a kind of afterthought—that they should send him along a pair of medium-sized human teeth. When they came, they did not fit. No teeth was made, he said, to fit his peculiar mouth, as hollow as a cavern. He carried his teeth ever after in his left-hand pocket, as if they were a watch to tell the time by—and would take them out and say, "What hour is it?" His teeth were a huge joke.

The fisherman sat weaving his hooped nets under the shade of the prickly hedge apple. He was glad to be where he was. He went to Chicago once and did not like it. He preferred the earth, which was turning on its axis, although slowing up, he said. As for himself, yes, he was happy, for happiness is the instinct of the universe. He didn't give a straw in the wind for all your Utopias. The corruptible had not yet put off corruption, nor had the hills dissolved like mist in fire. If things got too bad, there would be a grand Methodist revival, a new outcropping of stars and men. Meanwhile, the catfish were biting, just as many fish in the river as ever was caught. The same with human beings. Also, he heard that Charlie Chaplin was playing tonight on the screen, *The Gold Rush*, for which he would pay with a string of fish. He liked Charlie, a spider that crawls on top of a glacier—and when the glacier cracks, Charlie don't know the difference. Or if a mule comes to Charlie's dinner party instead of the lady who has been invited, why, he entertains the mule. Everything turns out all right, just because Charlie is so, so confused.

It was, all in all, a beautiful day, this somnolent August booming with the buzz of bees, the caws of crows, and spinsters numerous as hollyhocks. Life seemed to be able to take life in its stride, a merry bachelor observed. There was, on every street, the smell of honeysuckle and new-baked bread. There were prim little girls under parasols and little boys with the seats of their breeches torn, the brown skin twinkling through. There was a feeling that any man might become the subject of American mythology, for no reason but that he went barefoot or left his hat in a corn field.

Nothing seemed to run according to schedule. There was a pregnant woman, eating an ice-cream cone. "I don't know who done it," she said, over and over again, with the bewildered look of a large, gross child. But who could blame her, in a town which had been dedicated, in its Rappite era, to the extinction of that two-legged animal, man? Honestly, nobody could. Any humanity, everybody said, seemed better than none. At least, that was what the saloonkeeper said, speaking for a mythological everybody—and he had seen much life from his place behind the counter. Only this morning, a teamster from Haubstadt, a Jehovah's Witness, a moron, Old Doc, a geologist with his hat full of flowers, and a man who hated his mother, loved his grandmother, and cried at the mention of little children. What had they argued about but Republicans, Democrats, God, the housing project, the end of the world, Joe Louis, the best bull, the beginning of time, alfalfa, Mr. Willkie's chances—except that the man who loved little children just kept crying into his beer?

That night, there would be dancing at the saloon, and under the table, babies in market baskets, like sleepy papooses, and an old dog licking the slime of beer from the floor, and a tinny music in the slot machine. That night, on lonely Cut-off Island, a preacher would predict the second Coming of One, Jesus Christ, the King of Kings, Who cometh in a great cloud, with glory, and Who washeth away all sins, and Who maketh the old to be young as new-born lambs. Only a few would listen, feeling superior to their horse-betting neighbors, who did not know what was going to happen unless they could get on the W.P.A. housing project or something.

Father Rapp, long ago, said that there would be a poisonous gas like the dews from Jehovah, a conflagration covering the whole wide earth. No iota would escape destruction. Such was God's despair of man. Still, caught against the spikes of the thorn bush, a little goat cried and cried in 1940. For the world had never really

ended. It had not even been divided into two parts, good and evil.
The whorled milkweed multiplied with charming ignorance of
God's error in prolonging mortal history. Spiders ate flies, swallows
ate spiders, and the hawk ate swallows. Dusty hollyhocks grew up
high at the door of the Rappite fortress. Dust had gathered inside,
thick as flour in the flour mill. Rabbits ran in the Rappite maze, a
public park. The Rappite underground passage, which had spread
like roots of an infernal tree beneath these meadows, was covered
over by God's handkerchief, the green grass—signposts, however,
marking the approximate position of exit and entrance to these
Dantesque chambers. The Rappite sundial measured the shadow
on the Rappite wall, just next to a Bull Durham tobacco sign—but
no ironic juxtaposition, this, like the golden rose of the celibates
above a schoolhouse door where little children droned like bees.
Near a house where a few ruins of Pompeii were carefully sheltered, there were the footprints of an angel, who had descended
to Rappite Harmony and who left this evidence of his incorpo-
real extension, and a doctrine of heaven quite irreconcilable with
earth. There were fewer evidences of the Owenite. A stone's throw
from the angel's footprints, however, stood the tomb of Thomas
Say, Owenite, who sought nothing supernatural but the Spirit of
Nature, a stainless woman, revealed in the aspect of the black-
berry lily, the false foxglove, the orange trumpet flower. Perhaps
the two visions, Rappite and Owenite, supernatural and natural,
must merge into one indistinction by and by—like a maze where
lovers walk. Perhaps not.

Long grasses had grown in wheels and curves over the nameless graves of the Rappites, themselves in their gray gowns only
one layer above an Indian burial ground, its warriors, squaws,
papooses, pottery, and colored beads. When resurrection comes,
will both racial groups emerge, with tomahawks and hallelujahs?
There was no resurrection as yet, no winged being of air and light,
but only the shy quail in the long grasses behind a red-brick

cemetery wall, only the usual lovers in the maze. No sky rolling back, no coming of Christ on a golden throne upheld by cherubim, but only a lonely crow, monogamist bird—and an airplane on some mysterious mission of its own, the advertisement of Lucky Strikes, a writing in that sky.

Backward into Old Harmony— A Dissolving Vista

In old Harmony, sometime between the years 1815 and 1824, an angel descended to the earth. He stood in the fields of hop and barley, leaving his footprints impressed on a slab of stone. Throughout the nineteenth century, with all its ups and downs, these footprints endured, seemingly. By 1900, the right footprint was still complete, but the forepart of the left footprint had disappeared—weather taking its toll from the evidence of even a celestial being.

In 1940, an odd-jobs man, a berrypicker or builder perhaps of outhouses, was hired to do the work of community restoration, at fifty cents an hour. He could be seen squat on the lawn, chiseling—though always willing to exchange words with any stranger. He wore a hat with holes for ventilation. He chewed a straw, most somnolently. It would have been inconsistent with his character to contradict himself. If there had been no angel, then he would not be putting its footprints back into place, would he? Providence may have its reasons we know not of. He himself was grateful. As a nonunion laborer, having no steady employment, he found it hard to keep body and soul together, and was glad for this windfall, and would not look the gift horse in the mouth.

Carving an angel's footprints was better than berry-picking at twenty-five cents an hour and meant shoes for baby, whose toes were always sticking out. As to the authenticity of the footprints, he was in no position to say, being, as he was, a man from Mt. Vernon, twenty miles up the river, which is a long way. His one ambition would have been to own a bull and a few cows.

H. R. Schoolcraft described, however, these footprints as they appeared, in 1826, before deterioration. The learned ethnologist reported that they were, to all appearances, the impressions of a man who stood upright, the left foot a little forward, the heels turned inward. Distance between the heels, by an exact measurement, six and one-fourth inches, distance between the extremities of the great toes, three and one-half inches. These were not feet which had been accustomed to European shoes— the toes were pressed out and the foot flat, a condition commonly observed among those who walk barefoot. Probably, the impression was caused by an individual belonging to a race of men ignorant of the art of tanning hides, for whom shoes would have been themselves an extraneous miracle. Such a people must have existed in a much earlier age than the traditions of present Indians. This supposition was felt to be considerably strengthened by the extraordinary size of the feet. In another sense, the imprints were strikingly natural, the muscles being represented with minutest exactitude and truth. Thus was weakened the hypothesis that these footprints were the sculpture of men living in remote ages—history indicating no early people with tools of obsidian, porphyry, hornstone, flint, or such materials on the North American continent. Whatever else might be said, the man was a runner, who had stood forward on the balls of his feet, and not, evidently, of average height or build. The medium length of the human male footprint may be accepted as ten inches— whereas this amounted to ten and one-fourth inches. The breadth measured over the toes in a right angle with the first line was four inches, but the greatest spread of the base was four and one-half inches, which decreased at the heels to two and one-half inches.

Directly beneath these impressions was a scroll in the shape of a rectangle or square. The slab was of compact limestone, bluish gray, ten feet by five inches, five inches thick. Judging by the empirical evidence, as it presented itself to the senses, there seemed nothing supernatural, such as a thunder in the evening of the world, or the fiction of a realm of purposes.

But what of a nonscientific hypothesis, a psychic creation, an illusion whereby to face the unhuman universe? From the given figures, it would be possible to deduce the height and weight of the man, it is true, as if he were a murderer at large, a kind of Frankenstein monster. On the other hand, granting the presence of an angel, he might have stood with his left foot a little forward. This is the natural pose. Although most angels wear sandals and remain in a cloud, this was the barefoot angel who touched the ground—a fact which seems not unusual in the neighborhood of the Wabash, and taxes the imagination no more than if he had hovered in mid-air. Miracles have taken place in other dark corners, certainly—in Syria and Arabia and Asiatic old Kentucky, and wherever there is pitying and pitiful human nature, and wherever that question is asked: Why are we confined on earth and limited to this mortal frame, this dust? A teamster from Haubstadt saw an angel dissolving like snow. It had his mother's face, or almost hers. He was as drunk as a loon, of course.

Father Rapp was the sole eye witness to the authentic Posey County angel—who else but he, himself not an average man, but an imposing figure, almost six feet tall, his height accentuated by a peak-shaped hat, his white hair curling to his shoulders, and beard like the drift of snow upon his breast? Physically, he was well equipped to play a spiritual part—he looked like the patriarch he was, an object of veneration, the concentration of unusual powers. There is nothing so impressive as exaltation made homely, however. Father Rapp, vice-regent of the Deity, walked encompassed by stars like golden pomegranates, conversed with angels, yet kept his eye on the horse market, knew the price of oats, how to shoe a horse, the local situation, how to extract oil from nuts. He was apprised of both remote and immediate possibilities, however seemingly impossible, the virtue of deprivation of the flesh for the sake of the spirit in certain departments, wool combing, the moral law which dwells out of relation with average man, horse breeding, the subordination of the ruled to the will of the ruler, drainage, the soul equated to a mustard seed. As vice-regent of the Deity, Father Rapp left nothing to the Deity, in fact. He was nobody's fool, no idle dreamer. By means of the underground passage, which the workers themselves had built, he kept the workers within the range of his eaglelike vision, easily. Out of sight, he could never be out of mind. It was impossible to stand leaning on one's shovel. Fear was implicit. Father Rapp might be under the sweet-potato field or under the green corn—who knew where? Pushing his head through a strategic opening, he would seem, from a distance, to merge into the landscape, as only another rusted hay hillock or wintry thorn bush, only another rock. Impossible to say that the trees did not have eyes, and the grass did not have ears. Thus Father Rapp played on the superstitions of his people, as a harper plucks at the strings of a harp. To inherit heaven, they must give up earth, or at least most aspects of it. Not all acorns become oaks, Father Rapp said. Similarly, not all men become angels.

Father Rapp merely expressed what had long ago been accepted by his people, those placid German faces on which sorrow and time had left their mark. All were agreed, basically, as to the nature of this world, a poor substitute for the world beyond apprehension by man's sensory equipment, which was defective, as if he had been born blind, deaf, and dumb. Adam, it seems, fell from grace because he desired a helpmate. Adam, before he fell, was possessed of both sexual elements, the male and female conjoined. He was, in that pristine state, himself a horn of plenty, himself a receptacle, who might have reproduced without the adjunct of woman. It was only when he saw the beasts in pairs—ostriches, elephants, all kinds of living creatures—that he envied them and thus forfeited his godhead, which should have sufficed him undiminished throughout eternity. Like a sleeping Adonis, he had been disturbed, unreasonably, by the female spirit of the ever waning and waxing moon, by the sexual copulation of all beings but himself. From that mistaken urge in the beginning had come about this unstable fabric, man's mortal life. Man, therefore, and in particular the Rappite, must wrestle with that dark adversary, his own nature, his own instinct. "For in the resurrection, they neither marry, nor are given in marriage, but are as the angels of God in heaven." Thus would man be lifted from the flaming furnace, the lions' den, the bakery, the cocoonery. Imitating the Creator, the created, exalted and rejoicing, would come to that heaven populated by asexual angels only, by choirs of beings neither male nor female, but fire and light tincture both, a pure radiance without parts or odors. That state of everlasting harmony would be the only one—and this, a phantom in a forgotten past, an aberration best forgotten. No one would remember his father or his mother.

Father Rapp was crossing the field between the river and the piggery, let us assume. It was a fine day. The air was clearer after a heavy rain. This seemed more like spring than autumn with the leaves falling, as in Württemberg they also fell, according to the edict of final tragedy. There was no glint of hoarfrost on the ground, and there was this deception to the senses—that the old and crippled earth seemed young, even like a bride going forth to the bridegroom. Yet who escaped the pervasive quality of rottenness, and who escaped decay? The worm was mother of the man, the female spirit causing division of man from man, causing autumn, all wars, and even the competitive system.

Father Rapp was hardy and direct. He saw a marvelous angel, and the angel stood in the hop fields between the river and the piggery. Where had he come from? The leaves falling, they all stood still in mid-air. There was a suspension of the natural processes, as on that day when Elijah was caught up among the clouds, in everlasting denial of Newton and British rationalism. Evolved out of ether and air, tears and sorrow, an angel stood in the hop field. He was big, massive, corpulent. He carried a rainbow on his back. His head and his hairs were white, like whitest wool or cotton. He had seven stars in his right hand, and, in his left hand, seven golden candlesticks. His eyes were a flame of fire. Out of his mouth he had a two-edged sword. He was taller than an oak full grown, and of a diameter exceeding the oak, the beech, the sassafras. His shadow fell over the hop meadow, and over Cutoff Island, and over the scarred hills of Indian Mound. He was a kindly person. He wore a shift of finest linen. Girt about his paps was a girdle flashing heaven's light of ruby, sapphire, emerald, and clasped with a clasp of gold. He had both sexual elements, the fire and light tincture, the breast of woman, the head and feet of man. And yet he was angelic. He was grass and fire and homely as an old shoe. He was a farmer with a golden book in his hand—a honey in the mouth, a fire in the belly of him who ate the words of the Lord.

His voice was like the river Wabash, loud and wild, rolling between the buff-colored hills. His voice was like the wind. They shall not hurt in all my holy mountains, he said, and pointed toward Indian Mound. Pittsburgh was damned, he said. Philadelphia, a port of hypocrisy, would be destroyed. There would not be a blade of grass in Baltimore. Not only Pittsburgh, that old whore of Babylon in the wilderness, but also Württemberg in Germany would be destroyed by smoke and flame and poisonous gases raining down. Rome, London, Paris, Berlin, the high and mighty places—they would fall at the sound of a trumpet blowing in every corner of the sky, while the merchants stood far out at sea. The great kings would eat dust and crawl like lepers on an endless road. But unto the Rappites, a little people like the infant Moses hidden in the marsh, would come, when all else failed, the golden rose of Micah, the first dominion, that New Jerusalem which was ever promised, its ten gates of gold studded with rubies and diamonds, its peaceful grass. Not even an insect would flourish in Pittsburgh, vast, empty, melancholy, a scorched earth, the very floor of hell. In Württemberg there would be likewise desolation, and the bees would make honey in the skulls of the dead, strewn thick as daisies in a field.

Man, the angel said, is very helpless without God in this green forest, for without Him it is a desert and fruitless enterprise—sour grapes. God gives not a straw for civilization in cities, not a straw for Rome, not a straw for pale Madonnas and Madonna-worship, no more for these than He gave for Pharaohs powdered with pollen. Long ago, He destroyed Sodom and Gomorrah—as also, He shall destroy the cities of Europe and America, the cities spawning humanity, the cities of whoremongers. He shall shake them down like rotted apples from a tree. Yea, in His good time. That majority have not, as have the Rappites, the discipline of God over them. God, therefore, has loved a little people, dwelling outside this world, as it were, and He knows the number of the hairs of their heads, and He knows their rising up and sitting down, and every sparrow that falleth. God is apprised by His ambassador of all their interests—the cocoonery, the boot factory, the pastures for the brood mare in foal. The eyes of God are searchlights, playing over the dark fields, lighting a dark-green sky. When hailstones as big as apples fall on Germany, when England cries for forgiveness and sinks into the sea—then will this land on the Wabash be exempted, a pocket for the New Jerusalem, subtle as music of a conch shell, a city as measured by the burnished reed. There will be pain of neither birth nor death.

The lion will lie down with the lamb, and the old will not grow older. There will be pomegranates, peaches, oranges, and all manner of fruit trees. There will be sickles studded with diamonds.

Therefore, God has led the Rappites out of the valley which is the shadow of death, the angel said. Therefore, they have pitched their tents in the Wabash valley. Each day, as the earth turns on its axis, is a step nearer the end, and a simplification of existence. Yea, the sands of time run low. Though there is sorrow, an inner peace belongs to the Rappites. If they obey God's commandments, He will keep his promise. They will be lifted up like Elijah in the whirlwind and the fowls of the air. Until the flesh dissolves, the flesh must eat, God knows, and did not forget Elijah, but, when he hid near the torrent of Cherith, every day sent ravens with good bread and fat pullets. Lo, in Harmony the Rappites hide as behind a waterfall. Believing in angels, none will starve, for there are fat pullets, and none will go unclothed—until that time when this old world shall fall away like a garment. God and nature, the angel said, are thus everlastingly opposed, as they have been since Eve plucked of the forbidden fruit of the tree of knowledge. God would give to her knowledge, but He would not give her life. Nature, from that time forward, has been on a downward way—and only God's word can reduce truth to harmony again.

Evil being the woman, the angel said, let all men avoid her. Was it not written in old time that the carcass of Jezebel shall be as dung upon the face of the field, a banquet for hungry crows? "Who wants to bury her, will find no more than her skull, and her feet, and the palms of her hands." By her progeny, she would have separated herself out from the divine body, like the cream from the milk. But this cream was soured in the lightning of God's wrath. God, however, is a parent of great forgiveness. God will take the Rappites up into His arms like infants puking. Before a babe now born can reach maturity, the world will have ended, anyhow—some April day when the cherries are not ripe as yet, the apples green and sour and worm-bitten. Oh, how surprised all sinners will be, the world over! The angel came and the angel departed. Then did the sleet rain drip like rusted tears from the leaves of the oak, the beech, the sassafras, the cherry. There was a calmness in the darkening sky, the livid colors having disappeared, and only a lonely crow gliding homeward, and, in the fields, the glassy cry of a lost goat, caught on the spikes of the thorn bush. The basic facts may be just what they are, but there is always a deep human attempt to figure nature out in a way that is hardly possible. Belief, however fantastic, begets its consequence in action. That night after the angel's departure, the watchman passed between the rows of wooden barracks, on the empty streets of Harmony, under the locust trees where baby owls rustled—and cried as he had cried before:

Come unto me, all ye people,
Midnight sounds from the steeple!
Ten gates hath the city of gold,
So gather we now to the fold,

It's one step nearer the end.
Another day passes, the sands of time are running low—
It's one step nearer the end.

The Children
of the Ozarks, 1940

In 1940, there was a peculiar people dwelling at the outskirts of New Harmony—the children of the Ozarks, like the lost children of Israel.

They were twenty in number, including the females and infants, but not those who had perished on the asphalt road. They lived temporarily in yellow-stained tents down by the river and the birch forest, all, all alone, except for the wind sighing through the trees, which were not deeply rooted, and the stars, and the moon, fugitive like themselves. They understood what passed beyond their comprehension.

A woman looked out from her long black hair like a curtain. One leg was shorter than the other, and she leaned on a homemade crutch. Her quietude suggested no challenge to the outer world. There was a vacuous baby who stared at the sun, with watery eyes—its head, a huge mistake of nature, like perhaps every other head. A long-bodied dog switched at flies with his shaven tail. There was a ruddy young man lifting a heavy weight, for no particular reason. Grandpap sat with his broken fiddle on his knee, fumbling to find a tune on two strings. There was a feeling that love is not expressed by sterility or bungalows. There was a feeling that man is in himself valuable, as man, though here denuded of many of his characteristic accompaniments.

God did never deliver these people out of any wilderness, real or unreal. No sea divided for them, and no river appeared as dry land unless it was in Oklahoma. The Ozarks were not His holy mountains. God did never feed these people with manna like the dews falling from heaven. God did never rustle up the quail for their sake. Once some poisoned blackbirds fell. There was a great distance between God and these people—no miracle but the absent relative, a son who became a salesman of washing machines. There was a black kettle always boiling. There was an old ham bone always. There was a lamb's head thrown out among half-peeled branches of the fallen birch. Old tin cans were piled in pyramids among the orange trumpet weeds. Old clothes, the color of many roads, hung stiff as scarecrows on a line between two rusty maples. These were almost all the earthly goods.

Nobody cared which party was in power, Republican or Democrat, because nobody knew the difference between them, and because Washington, D.C., was farther away than heaven was. When Roosevelt's voice came over the radio, down among the battered chicken coops, they just turned it off. Maybe he was talking about a city more beautiful than Eden, where there would be a bathtub and happiness. Maybe not. Nobody cared because nobody cared. They were unshaken and unconcerned and all-sufficient.

They knew what they knew, and that was not much. They knew of Kansas City, the bleak mountains, the dark valleys, the long stretches without a filling station. They knew of the circumstances as old as earth or man, a flat tire, a wheel broken at the cistern, a dust storm, a cradle of bulrushes, a spoiled can, a nail in the lung. There was a son in St. Louis who never wrote a letter, so they never answered it. There was a daughter who dropped out of sight in a ditch, twenty-odd years ago. Their vote would not mend broken pieces, not even an old slop jar or Grandpap. The fragments were more wonderful than the whole was, anyhow. What was the use to try to change your skin and the color of your eyes? It was always too late. The last time anybody voted was for Hoover, who said prosperity was just around the corner, a New Jerusalem. Their old Ford was a skeleton, its curtains flapping like a blackbird's wings. Only, when they turned the corner, whatever it was they were looking for, it wasn't there—it was Razorback, Missouri, or it was Kansas.

Grandpap could play on a fiddle with two strings, once he got himself wound up. He knew all the tunes by heart, which was two strings—and two and two make four. He used to ride a blind mule in the moonlight when he went to dances. Over his back he had a fiddle, nobody knew how many strings. His brother blew a trumpet. They put that trumpet blower in the ground at Springfield, Illinois, after he died from the shoulders up and the shoulders down. Grandpap's old woman once was young, and she had yellow hair, and her picture taken in a kodak, but the man did not ever send it to her—and then she was wrapped in canvas and dropped into a dusty well. There was a time when the boys zoomed around her like bumblebees. She had a quick tongue, a small foot, a ready hand. That was long ago, nobody knew how far back. It must have been before Garfield was shot. Grandpap could not remember yesterday, though—he thought it was always here, with no effect of deterioration but his own toothless head.

Grandpap still hoped to see a League of Nations and the triumph of Eugene V. Debs.

The Children of Israel

The fire in the breast of hysterical Ann Lee, the founder of the Shaker celibate communities, had been kindled in the breast of Moses on Mt. Sinai. The fire in Father Rapp's breast had emanated from the same original light, evidently. For both Ann Lee and Father Rapp, as for many a sultry pioneer, America was a promise, not merely of the physical conquest but of the New Jerusalem, a city above and beyond this world of shopkeepers, marriage beds, scarecrows, and other evidences of mistaken nature. Ann was the Holy Mother, as Father Rapp was the Holy Father. Both had communities of worshipful followers—but there the resemblance ends, for the marriage of true souls admits impediment. Ann built several cities, merely by shaking like a poplar tree whose leaves are silvered in wind. When she shook, her followers shook—all ceasing to consider the where, and why, and whither, and what of things. Among celibate communities, Ann's seems the least frost-bitten, the freest from secondary aims, the most truly enthusiastic, as if no reason at all was necessary—God shaking, Ann shaking, everybody shaking. By comparison, Father Rapp's project fails both in grandeur and mysticism, becomes the acme of prudence.

Father Rapp's true life and its consequences may have been a drama of which he was unaware, just as he was oblivious to God's affinity with Ann, though Ann was the receptacle of divinity, too, and sprouted most miraculously, as Father Rapp withered from the shoulders downward. His loins were girt with faith. He, with his mind fixed on an eternal purpose, could not afford to consider that his position was perhaps more average than eccentric—how many ambassadors of God there were, how many bearded patriarchs and lost tribes of Israel, how God had spoken out of every burning bush in that part of America which had been explored, how many New Jerusalems were being hatched, how many others were carelessly spoiled like ostrich eggs in Brazil. It was necessary that Father Rapp, like other leaders, feel his loneliness and his differentiation from an accursed mankind. In Germany, he was a successful farmer. Yet he would have preferred America, this land of Biblical promise, if he had had to live like the wild boar who eats roots.

Father Rapp's cradle, Württemberg, had nurtured many clouded dreamers, many who aspired, like Faust, for infinite space, infinite power, and oranges in winter. He believed himself in league with God, however, and not with the Devil, representative of an obtrusive and detailed reality. His imagination, all the same, did not run away with him. While influenced by Jacob Böhme and Jung-Stilling—"ever the mystics farthest removed from this world"—he liked to buy cheap and sell dear. He had both his feet on the ground. He was far divergent, for example, from another under the influence of German romantic idealism, William Blake, who saw angels swinging upside down from apple trees, who saw the antinomies of heaven and hell reversed, who saw that the fly was his little brother and chief glory of God. No such raptures for Father Rapp, the strong man. Let other German schismatics from the Lutheran order seek other frontiers on eternity—such as Russian Tartary, near the Caspian Sea, where God's snowy stars looked down, but where there were few opportunities for practical expansion. Let poets dream what they would. Father Rapp chose America first—not because he believed that God's voice would speak out of the marsh more clearly than it had spoken out of the vineyards in Württemberg, but because the land was fierce and cheap. Father Rapp had a Bible in one hand and an ax in the other—and thus far seems the average pioneer, a far from average being, a Daniel Boone of both the infinite and finite, an adventurer. The picture, however, is deceptive. Most of the violence, unlike that of Daniel Boone or Andrew Jackson, was verbal. Father Rapp's entire adventure, though posited on angelic beings, was the working out of an almost infallible machinery. Serious as were the perils attending this negative spirit, the conquest of the American wilderness could hardly have taken place without it.

Factually stated, Father Rapp's saga differs from that of the average pioneer, who possessed only two hands, two feet, one head, and a perhaps limited imagination. All too frequently for most, millennium was an unorganized way of life, a hollow tree but recently vacated by gregarious hornets or the grizzly bear. All too frequently, their only real estate was the ground they were buried in, if they were buried at all. Not a few were buried in the bellies of great birds. Father Rapp had untold advantages in the age of city building. He was, from the beginning, head of a corporation whose members held gilt-edged shares in the stock of a New Jerusalem, a perhaps imaginary wealth. His fantasy was thus public-minded. He held at his command seven hundred people, an unquestioning, automatic body, greased by the soul, as it were. Seven hundred multiplied by two would make fourteen hundred hands and feet—the heads, except that they were agreed on a few fundamental assumptions, were comparatively unimportant, almost spurious. The erection of a purely negative goal made possible the avoidance of the schism. All shared, in fact, the irrationality of absolute obedience to the will of a supernatural authority—Father Rapp, who unified scattered chimeras as a theory of reality to displace reality, and out of whose spidery being was spun the web of possible human relations.

Thus at fifty, when many men think of retiring, Father Rapp was ready, in spite of his philosophy of nature's corruption, to act as a pioneer in America—where the suppressed dream would emerge as an unhooded reality, an angel in the forest.

Father Rapp, as befitted his position of exclusive power, which had been handed down from God's throne, came to America in advance of his people, to choose a correct site for the community of angelic beings and butchers. In January and February, 1804, he crossed the Atlantic, accompanied by his son John, who was not strong-minded, and a Mr. Haller, agent for another flock of dissenters. It was a holy mission, a renunciation of instinct for the sake of the future, where there would be no adversary among the lower elements. Gabriel's foghorn blew in the night, doubtless. But whatever the savage wilderness surrounding him, Father Rapp would cling to a wintry concept—that nature is an inconsequential thing, a loon, but money talks.

In Germany, mapping his course by pins, Father Rapp had believed Louisiana to be the farthest removed from corrupting influences, the damned majority. That site he rejected, once he realized the utter vastness of America, a continent more terrifying than infinity, a continent crisscrossed by erroneous buffalo tracks—a maze, indeed, but neither Biblical nor geometrical. There were few, if any, cherubim riding on lions. There were many sporadic wars. Father Rapp, a peace-loving man, dutifully explored parts of Pennsylvania, Maryland, and Ohio, a territory as yet little influenced by the aridity of rationalism. He determined on a large tract of land some twenty-five miles west of Pittsburgh, where it might be possible to insure survival of the fit by trade with the unfit. God's agent must do business with the Devil, even in America.

Frederick Reichert, Father Rapp's most faithful disciple, and
yet most intelligent, had remained in Germany, as shepherd
to the flock of gray Millenniasts until the date of their release
from materially barren pastures. They were the chosen people,
indeed—though few were representative of most German peasants at that time. The average German, that is, the small farmer,
had turned his eyes away from the things of this earth, in expectation of a city in the sun. The new religion of rationalism, so cold,
so correct, so lonely, could make little appeal to a people accustomed to a more glorious thinking, at a lower level. Where were
God's thunderbolts, and where were the showers of locusts, and
where was the promise of paradise? The King of Württemberg, a
rationalist, had dismissed Father Rapp when brought to trial for
preaching his strange faith in the end of the world. The Rappites,
like eels with eyes enlarged, seemed a harmless group intent on
suicide—it was their business, he thought, infringing not at all
on his, and he could afford to lose them. Their crime was not evident. He believed them to be a minority. In view of the fact that
the Rappites, aberrants though they were, represented so many
others or at least their aspirations, it was probably the king who
was in the minority, a lost soul, a gentleman leaning on his cane
like a three-legged insect, and doomed to die an insect's death
when God spoke out of the saffron clouds. At any rate, he was
reasonably happy.

To Frederick, Father Rapp wrote a conservative estimate of the
new land, as if it were, however, a beast which could be tamed.
Using the funds of his congregation, as instructed, he had purchased five thousand wild, lavish acres. Frederick should urge
no one to come, however—it was a "long and perilous journey,"
without possibility of turning back, once embarked upon, the
worker to be divorced from the means of production in a bar-
barian hemisphere, where there were more boars than people as
yet. Those who could not endure privation in God's name should

drop out—what was needed most was courage to try the body and soul. They might have to sleep on the bare ground at first. They would be surrounded, as in Germany, by every peril, every temptation.

Undaunted by promised difficulties, the chosen came, sure as of their noses that they were united by a contract to which God Himself, in a loft in Germany, had been co-signer. The great drama of change was lifting them out of an otherwise obscure existence where each had been the victim of meaningless chance. Untold riches beckoned them. Now those who were despised and lonely, a minority in Germany, would be a majority in America—and Father Rapp, who had been a careful farmer, would be a king of kings. Did not such an endeavor, in God's name, deserve the sacrifice which each must make, even the severance with memory? Surely, they would build a city of pearls, such as had been promised of old.

The ships *Aurora*, *Atlantic*, and *Margaretta*, having weathered many a rough-riding, fierce, implacable storm and waves ten feet high, docked in Philadelphia, that summer of 1804. They came straggling into port. Never were there more subtle pioneers discharged on rugged shores—seekers after the golden domes of Genghis Khan, and, what is more to the purpose, they would build that edifice themselves—the destruction within and the construction without. Father Rapp was down at the dock to meet them. The familiar values persisted like his beard. Nothing had changed. "And if thine eye offend thee, pluck it out, and cast it from thee: it is better for thee to enter into life with one eye, rather than having two eyes to be cast into hell fire." This group, moreover, would not taste of death, the sum total of all in nature but themselves, it was believed.

Actually, the Scriptural communism, as it was called, was not altogether miraculous, though founded on the assumption of many miracles, many escapes from the wheels of time. To transport themselves to America, the Rappite peasants had pooled their hard-earned funds, the result of sales of their property, the small farms, the wheels broken at old cisterns. In America, what uncertainties there had been in the past seemed multiplied. Organization was necessary as never before, unless the Rappites wished to perish—or sink to the position of the average pioneer, a weakling with one eye out. There was little alternative but to strengthen the bonds by which they had been united. Salt was hard to get. Besides, they were faced by the deceptive phenomena of all mortal existence and by boundless, cold immensity. At least, the wolves had been metaphorical in Germany. Father Rapp acted, therefore, as the spokesman of God and of perhaps an even harder taskmaster, blind necessity. The Rappites had to sleep at first on the bare ground, as had been promised. They were filled, however, with religious zeal. They were not tempted. They did not forget that they were related to the most sacred characters in sacred history—like Eli among the brambles, eating a raven. For God had chosen the things which are not, to bring to nought the things that are.

At the end of the first year, Harmony, Pennsylvania, had emerged—a town of sixty log houses, grist mill, barns, shops, houses of worship, sawmills, tannery, distillery. This was, however, civilization without its usual corruptions—the wilderness acting as an effective barrier between the Rappites and the mistaken world. There were street cleaners now where there had been wild pigs before, and a night watchman where the wolf had roamed, and a golden rose where the fox had slept in its hole, and a church where there had been a burning bush. No flesh should glory in the presence of God, Father Rapp said. There were ample, succulent crops. There were excellent horses. Within a few years, the Rappites could show a large surplus of agricultural and manufacturing products of all kinds. By fraternal love and internal unification, they had made a conquest over nature, this world of fugitive financiers, shopkeepers, and whoremongers. They had harnessed all the nonhuman elements, as well as human, it seems—but if they wore the bit in their mouths, they did so happily, as a matter of celestial habit.

The Rappite location was a strategic one, the point of evacuation for the West. Man, it has been said, was impelled westward in the era of discovery by no economic necessity but by the rotation of the earth eastward. The Rappites were not alone in strangeness. They seemed, if anything, the sanest group imaginable, at least by contrast with their competitors, many of whom were burdened with shrewish wives and droves of half-starved children. Their productions, when so many were unreliable, were absolutely reliable, the one certitude at a port where fantasy thrived, along with busy commerce in nonexistent townships and gunpowder. They provided shoes for energetic Americans, gun powder unalloyed by flour, and excellent whisky, enough to enflame the imagination of waning, evanescent men, poor adventurers. To the disorganized, they represented almost the climax of moral development. They were sure of a real city, of sticks and stones, when other men had nothing but an always fading prospect, a new Jerusalem under a coonskin hat. No merely average pioneer could compete with this society of homogeneous producers, united alike in life and death.

This was the German prototype of American Puritanism, compelled, as were the original founding fathers, by a sense of persecution and innate difference from the rest of mankind. Their only affiliations were with the past. They felt the greatest correspondence between, not themselves and others burning like the dry thorn in the wilderness, but themselves and God, Who had spoken out of the burning bush, themselves and the children of Israel, themselves and Saul, David, Solomon, Job, Job's turkey, and Tobit's dog. They were aristocratic. They converted, consciously or unconsciously, hallucination into fact and fact into hallucination, wherever they could. Their religion, while they grew fatter, was centered upon themselves, magnified unto eternity, as a body both male and female—which phantom seemed to them a virtue, not a vice, naturally. Their round red cheeks, their health, were deceptive. Purveyors of whisky, they realized no connection between themselves and crimes committed by enflamed Indians or anarchic pioneers, no connection between themselves and grizzled wife-beaters. They were self-isolated. Undoubtedly, few gave a thought to the poor Indian, who was already, like natural man, a dwindling order—though no celibate, for he had more papooses than imaginary pearls or onions on a string. After all, it is easier to comprehend eternity than the multitudinous operations of that vaster complexus, the experience of man. In honesty, it must be added that perhaps the Rappites were more interested in their cabbages than in eternity.

A bookkeeper in Pittsburgh, a future Mormon, must have observed, during the course of his business, the Rappite order—so that there is some generic relation between the polygamists and these celibates, the former springing from the latter like Minerva from the head of Jove.

In spite of dire prophecies to the contrary, with prosperity had come no decline to the individual way of life. Lo, the walls of communism were strengthened. Lo, the angelic order was not sacrificed. The Rappites renewed, by further contract, their agreement by which they had bound themselves before emigration from Germany. They would obey unquestioningly their superior officer, would give the labor of their hands, and would hold their children and their children's children, though nonexistent now and in futurity, to do the same. They would look on morality as that which transcends this world of shopkeepers. Father Rapp, in return, was to extend such education as would tend both to their temporal welfare and eternal felicity, and to support them and their widows alike in sickness, health, and old age unto the world's end. It had been intended that a member, withdrawing, might receive a refund in the amount of his investment, or in keeping with what his character had been. This section of the contract was abrogated, however, as comprising a tie with the mistaken world. Should anyone desire to leave this community, he must do so without reward and on his own responsibility—the dogs of hell hounding after him.

In an even profounder sense did pale Jacob triumph over his brother, red Esau. What was inconceivable to the average man happened. During a transport of religious enthusiasm, when all people seemed carried beyond the domain of their ordinary senses, for they had been considering the beauty of a ghostly erection, Father Rapp lifted his hand. Now, he said, the vow of celibacy should be taken in dead earnest—for there had been a fatal ambiguity before, with consequent embarrassment to this community and to the race of angelic beings, who see not as men see. Thus would be broken the last of all possible ties with a tired world—this vow to be as a seal upon the forehead and the lips, a sign of omniscience.

Some of the older members, according to a report which has come down, were startled. Should all men suddenly become converted to their faith in asexual angels, walls of crystal, and everlasting harmony, they realized, the earth would soon be stripped bare of people, like a dovecote from which all the doves have flown away. Still, theirs had been a lonely bypath, a way of thorns and brambles, they realized, as if they had eaten ravens like Eli. Other pioneers could be trusted to beget the usual sparrow-boned children—so that the world, even if mistaken, might go on somehow. A consoling thought, at least to a few sentimentalists. Besides, all saw the light of holiness shining in Father Rapp's uplifted face, that unusual glitter in his eye, as if he walked surrounded by stars like empty gourds where the oriole houses, as if he were in communion with the most distant powers. The fact

that all were to share in the deprival of the flesh for the sake of
the spirit made the burden only easier. None should escape. They
were indebted to Father Rapp, they knew. Had he not delivered
them out of the mouth of the lion? Had he not brought them
into a marvelous land, like Lebanon, where the eagle is perched
upon the topmost branch of the cedar? There was great rejoicing,
as the rafters shook. Old and young men, old and young women,
many fourteen-year-olds, all leaped and shouted, and the young
shouted louder than the old.

Perhaps most of these good people did not think at all, since
sudden emotion is more powerful an agent than prolonged logic.
There was, however, a sadly dissenting voice—a worm in the
green wheat—and lo, the worm lifted up its head, for it was a
cosmic dust. Father Rapp's son John, still in the prime of his
manhood, could not accept so readily the attitude of self-im-
posed sterility. He had his wife with him, those limbs he had
already clasped, that breast like honey and mead, that immediate
sense of her personal goodness, a thing more wonderful to him
than thousands of angels shouting hallelujahs. She was life, John
thought. Many months after the agreement on a universal celibacy, a strange thing happened—John's wife began to swell out
like the yeast of bread. It became impossible, by any subterfuge,
to conceal her condition under the immense skirts and draperies of shawls. The woman was with child. Acknowledgment of
secret sin was made glaringly public, by every slow movement
and wandering gesture, by the eyes dilated, the breath coming
short. She felt her shame, that she was Jezebel, that she was the
whore of Babylon who had walked with cymbals and tinkling
bells—indeed, she was the world's disaster. People stared at her,
unbelieving, for this was a greater crime than to steal a little
sugar. John, far from being cautious, was triumphant openly, as
if he had struggled with an angel and had come out with no part
of his thigh missing. He had established, obscurely, it is true, a

union between himself and the moths which are not motivated by the idea of God. He walked on a cloud, and he whistled like a mockingbird. He was happy, the poor fool. He had seen a droplet of milk on that fair breast. His wife, however, more melancholy as her time advanced, could hardly stoop to lift the turnips from the fields. The third part of the moon was already dark, and she was going down the sky with a third part of the moon. Her crime had brought its punishment. John, persisting in his ecstasy, thus differentiated himself from all the ghostly others, including his wife—he was not a tactful winner in the game of life, but boastful.

It was an embarrassing situation for the vice-regent of the Deity, the ambassador of God on earth—his own son, a father! What was more, there seemed to be no indication that John would ever desert his wife—for night after night, he went in to her. Was there to be an exception, an ignoring of the prohibition placed upon a depraved natural instinct, by which the individual withdrew himself from the residue of divine truth? Was at least one critic to stand outside the community with a cynic's leering sneer? Men who were, after all, merely human complained of the immense injustice. They had been temperate as cabbages, and what was the result? Father Rapp determined, sadly, that the malcreant must be punished. So Abraham would have sacrificed Isaac, was it not so, had not an angel of the Lord intervened? Community must be preserved, at any cost to the finite destiny of finite man. It would be like taking down the strap from its nail on the wall—he had beaten his son before, as a training for manhood. The evil part must be removed. Nakedness, a groveling, a howling, a mute repentance as the body learns its master, self-mastery. Better to strike at evil than let evil fester! Unfortunately, this was no flogging but emasculation, and the victim died, crying like a stuck pig—somewhere in the neighborhood of the piggery.

More than one murder had taken place undiscovered in the dense American wilderness. More than one man, it is recorded, had set out on a journey from which he had not returned, and no inquiries had been made, there being a gap between the man who departed and the man who arrived, and an impossibility of communication at such extremes in time and space. More than one had been swallowed up by the wilderness—a disembodied head in a burlap sack of corn shucks, like the head of John the Baptist, a headless body weighted down by stones in a distant river. Nobody caring.

As the Rappites were isolated and their own police, it seemed that a veil might be drawn across the macabre scene. After all, as so often happens, the only eye witnesses to this murder were the murderers. Rumor got out, however, that Father Rapp had killed his only son. There was just a little trickle of blood, and then there was a dead body. It was a tale told in all the taverns, both in America and Germany—how the old man had imposed his will upon his people. Half a century later, *The Atlantic Monthly* carried a few hints as to what had happened. Nothing was ever said as to the fate of the widow, whether her skull and palms were cast upon the turnip fields, or what became of her. Beyond doubt, an infant daughter survived the experiment and grew to robust womanhood, with a certain twinkling laughter in her eyes.

The death of John Rapp had at least the virtue that it marked an impasse and turning point on the road of Rappite history. Now, in 1814, Father Rapp was ready to abandon Harmony in favor of a second enterprise, much like the first—to move on, like Daniel Boone, seeking elbow room. A flawless opportunity, a magnet drawing the compass—thousands of people turning toward the sunset, and among these, the Oriental despot, Father Rapp, manufacturer of whisky and illusion.

The Rappite property was sold, in short, to a man named Ziegler for $100,000, a great sacrifice, although it represented

$85,000 profit over the original investment. Ziegler, by the way, had no notions as to the extinction of the human race, by mutilation or millennium. He put up FOR RENT signs everywhere and opened a puppet show, where little men danced on strings, and all their activities seemed the effect of invisible spiritual powers.

A Journey to the Wabash

Late in the year 1814, Father Rapp lifted up his eyes unto the hills, and a voice spoke to him out of the wilderness, that he should come to the wild West. Like any traveler, he proceeded with his party down the Ohio River in a flatboat. If he imagined that he existed in a vacuum, there was no hint of this either in his manner or his dress. He carried a rifle. From the Ohio, he entered the Wabash, and went up to the land that God had promised.

It was a situation which looked "desolate enough," he reported, although to the "eye of hope" there were "great and beautiful plans"—that golden rose, that first dominion, the whisky trade, the hattery, and yea, the bringing of the end of life into touch with its beginning. A fence here and a fence there would make for much improvement over the natural situation.

There was, to begin with, plenty of rolling pasture for sheep and horses and brood mares. There were plenty of encompassing highlands, well watered with flowing springs, brooks, and streams. The central lands were as level as a floor, yet with grade enough for drainage. There were trees of every kind, heavy timbers—the oak, the beech, the ash, the birch, three kinds of nut trees, three to four feet in diameter, with trunks fifty to sixty feet high—a splendid material for carpenter work. And every place where the soles of these people's feet should tread should be theirs, nearly thirty thousand acres in extent, and even the lands of Cutoff, and even the lands of Indian Mound. The lands were Biblical, showing no mark as yet of the Roman beast who wears a number in his forehead. The Wabash was like the river Euphrates, though not in Syrian deserts, fortunately for the prodigal sons of eternity.

Father Rapp and his party set to work, felling trees, building houses, planting corn. Everybody put his shoulder to the wheel. Corn in this valley should be the attestation of divine truth, as if God co-operated in building a world which, in short order, God intended to destroy. Not that they strained after paradoxes necessarily, but that these were inherent in their human situation.

Frederick Reichert, now Frederick Rapp, as he was Father Rapp's "adopted son" and legal heir, had remained as protector to the majority in Pennsylvania. When, one year later, he brought them out to the Wabash valley, he found Harmony, an enterprising settlement, everything in order—the golden grapes upon the golden bough, no discontented foxes. Frederick was filled with hope for the future of America, should it become a community of such industrious souls as this, where he foresaw the bones would flourish like tender grass, and where the altruistic ideal would transcend selfishness.

Their new situation seemed, to Frederick, an unbelievable one, a multiplicity within unity, a framework of permanence within transience. All men were acting in conformity to the purposes which were held to constitute the highest morality. All had accepted the duties of human intercourse, at a high level. Doubtless their community was not yet perfect, but what one was, even though practicing, as this did, a free co-operation of labor, and aspiring to be angels? In imperfection itself there might be many values—nothing so beautiful as trial and error, this side of paradise.

Frederick was, to tell the truth, in love with the Wabash valley, right from the start. Wheat was already tall that year, shining
above water as clear as a sea of glass. There were houses built to
endure as long as the earth did—with heavy timbers, with joints
mortised and pegged, a lining of straw, no cranny to let the
deathly swallow in. Yet the wilderness seemed almost a promise,
not a threat—its wild, high acres of gum trees, sycamore, persimmon, like music unheard but felt. Earth turned on its axis, imper-
sonally, as if there were no evil. There were peaches of an enormous diameter and size, this side millennium—a fuzz upon them
like a baby's cheek. Man had himself a capacity for a spontaneous
action—was not chained to any wheel. There were maple and
sugar trees, from which great quantities of sugar could be made
in each succeeding spring. There was no angel, nor even a way
to deduce one from such a primitive landscape. Sandpipers and
bobolinks, bluejays and woodpeckers were far more common.
Although there was no angel, there was a wild turkey, almost
as handsome, the male bird of which often attained a weight of
twenty-five pounds, quite good for eating. This was, in fact, a
land of natural resources, was something more than an abstraction deducible from it, was not devitalized, was not robbed of
integrated richness. In the shaded lowlands, there were very large,
magnificent cypresses, good for the articles made by the cooper.
    Where could there be more happiness on earth, if not in
heaven? Frederick felt, privately, a sap within his veins, as if he
were a birch tree himself, tapped by the butterfly's proboscis.
The ultimate goal might be necessary, but it omitted everything
significant—such as the furry-thighed hawk moth, the butterfly
which hibernates all winter long in hollow trees.
    There were deer peering through the leaves of many a burn-
ing bush from which God had not spoken as yet. Still, God
was the best working hypothesis, the best approach to the problem of decay. There were shy, light-stepping antelopes, and the

rumors of the bear which is the color of honey, and the mysterious groundhog few eyes had seen—for he was as shy as the mother of Jesus Christ. There were rabbits with great purple eyes, chattering and quarrelsome squirrels, delicate snakes in festoons upon leafless thorn trees. An infinite variety of complex sensations, and how exclude them? The dead tree stumps were filled with clumsy cocoons. Oh, how admirable was the work of God! Droves of wild pigeons would darken the sky, their wings rustling like surf on the shores of heaven. And oh, to have the wings of a dove, to be a part of nature. Oh, to have the bandages removed from one's eyes, to walk freely and without fear of judgment.

All in all, Indiana seemed an improvement over Pennsylvania, and a destruction of the distinction between subject and object, as if nature itself were a spiritual armor to put on. Frederick took great delight in observing nature, its many aspects, such as the leaves of a certain plant which were formed like a rat trap, to draw in any small moth which lighted on its surface, and bees confining their journeying ever to certain flowers, and those windflowers which were pollinated by the wind only.

To his friends in the outside world, Frederick wrote that, in a few years, Indiana might be, in regard to the cultivation of small grain, one of the most important parts of the nation, perhaps its breadbasket. While the trees did not bear pearls as big as goose eggs, fireflies darted above them, like a lower firmament. While no phoenix had arisen from its ashes on these shores, it seemed clear that the human spirit, like the phoenix, was a thing indestructible. "It decomposes but to recompose." Frederick hoped that Indiana would not be always so empty of people as it now was, so filled with nonexistent townships and barren fictions. He hoped that the Rappite example of co-operation would attract virtuous men as citizens in Indiana, a state which, under careful management, might well become a second Germany, or if not that, at least a terrestrial Eden, complete with apple orchards.

Perhaps, in future time, the Rappites would be remembered for their contribution, however small, to the idea of human progress. Already, their experience was becoming the subject of marvel among men under the individual system, who saw, by this example, how easily might be guaranteed the satisfaction of common wants and needs—without quarrel, without contention.

Store goods were scarce in this backward country, and so would sell very well—women would come in from the outlying districts to look at printed yardgoods. Silver, fortunately, was plentiful, in constant circulation. The Rappites were prepared to extend loans on mortgages at six per cent to the East. Their power was already too great for a limited circumstance, was spreading, required new populations, new frontiers. The Rappites showed a character not soft and crumbling like limestone, but as hard as granite or the rock of ages. No better people could have been chosen as pioneers of a brave, new world—but oh, that it had more people in it.

A Machine Like Clockwork

When Rapp the Harmonist embargoed marriage
  In his harmonious settlement which flourishes
Strangely enough as yet without miscarriage,
Why call'd he 'Harmony' a state sans wedlock?
  Now here I've got the preacher at a dead lock.

Because he either meant to sneer at harmony
  Or marriage, by divorcing them thus oddly;
But whether reverend Rapp learn'd this in Germany
  Or not, 'tis said his sect is rich and godly,
Pious and pure, beyond what I can term any
  Of ours. . . .

—LORD BYRON, *Don Juan*, CANTO XV

Lord Byron had a cynic's sneer, as might have been expected from
one in his corrupt bodily state, and one who held that man is naturally good. By way of footnote, he hinted that, prior to the edict of
total celibacy, babies had arrived among the Rappites at stated periods, in litters like hairless pigs—never at harvest, certainly, the impli-
cation being that Father Rapp's harmony was a form of economy.

Still, so many babies were bound to create confusion and a distraction from the true Rappite goal—for if community were to be preserved, the individual must be destroyed and his perceptions sink to the level of the general desire. Angelic asexuality and Adam's fall as a result of sexual copulation afforded an excellent excuse for the most drastic measures, even emasculation. Moreover, although the avowed enemy of rationalists and their coldly calculated view of life, Father Rapp had not forgotten the instructions of the preachers of the new light who had invaded the Lutheran pulpit—where, instead of discoursing on the broad highway to hell, the narrow gate of heaven, and God's thunderbolts, they had urged the consideration of such arid subjects as birth control and soil preservation. Father Rapp, who knew his oats, harnessed the new science to the old religion. From complete birth control it was possible to progress, by the shortest possible route, to the complete death of the individual will and to the simplified angelic state, its weakest echo. This was but one, however, of the many advantages offered by such a harmonious plan. Men who concurred with this would not be likely to raise objections on less important matters.

Man in this immaterial state of Harmony seems metamorphosed all too quickly into a material thing, as Emerson once remarked, but speaking of the average, the great rabble, for he believed each man should be his own eccentric star—many productions of wheat, bricks, tallow, gas, fats, linen, wool. The psychic reality is one thing, and the social order quite another. There are two forecasts for the future. The producer is forced to lop off his own branch of the tree of life, that the books of the corporation may show a steady increase in earnings. The producer has been promised an overwhelming reward, but in another sphere, and he makes his coffin at the least possible expense to the corporation. If of a very obliging nature, or if there is a gun pointed to his face, he digs his own grave and falls backward into it. The great mystery is that such a state may be one of utter happiness, as it provides opinions concerning things, but no knowledge of the things themselves. The discipline of God, or of some other "master mind," is over the inert producer—the blacksmith to be refined at the forge until he becomes, in his own time, a battering angel, and if not, who can report the experience which transcends experience? As for the young oak, the Rappite could not expect to sit in its shade when it was become the king of the forest. Both man and tree would have been felled by the mightiest axman of all, God, Who abhorred corrupted nature, kid gloves, bodily ease, puny moths, Greek freedom, new clothes, luxury, public education, Catholic priests, whisky drinkers, secret ballots, Thomas Jefferson, gamblers, suffrage, confusion of immensity, baby owls. God was, in fact, that true life which is the life uncreated—and toward which all men should aspire with all their strength.

There were, in the early nineteenth century, communities of American drunkards, communities of outlaws, cardsharpers, cutthroats, perjurers, liars, ancient mariners, Methodists. This was the strangest of all, a community of businessmen who acted like oiled saints. The Rappites had their stores in Vincennes, Shawneetown, St. Louis, their agents at Pittsburgh, Louisville, St. Louis, and other points. They sold their products throughout the Mississippi valley, wherever there were men, of any nature. Wheat, corn, oats, hides, furs, butter, wax, horses, cattle, hogs, shingles, sugar, linen, tobacco, cheese, flax, hops, hemp, logs. Every year provided a surplus of deerskins, hogskins, bearskins, wolfskins, horsehides, raccoons, otter, muskrat, beaver, mink, rabbits, pork, venison, hog fat, tallow, quills, feathers, eggs, bristles, bacon, gunpowder, cloth, bags, honey, geese, cider, apples, yarns, chairs, shoes. The products of a marvelously fecund nature, operated by celibates, who believed all things fleeting but themselves, the instrument of God.

Their barges laden with whisky barrels and illusion went down the Mississippi to lazy Creole towns, where nobody knew what time of day it was, and to New Orleans, a great port and center of depravity, where the only graybeards were cypress trees, and murder was a romantic profession, and few were not inclined toward gay, reckless content. Beauteous whores walked the shady streets of New Orleans—and though wearing skirts ornamented with gold lace, slippers of gold embroidery and gold rosettes, and hairnets of gold studded with pearls, were happily unaware of their approximation to the imagery of a New Jerusalem, which is not of this creation or sterile enterprise. Nor did the sleepy Rappite bargemen see that pearls and gold do not necessarily transcend, as shown by this example, mortal existence—may be, in fact, wherever they are found, the expression of mortal corruption. But such parallels are merely interesting lines, unavoidable in the maze of mortal life.

In 1823, the Rappite produce sold for $13,141.83, and, in the year following, for $12,441.83, a slight depression, but no sign of God's displeasure, as fluctuations in the market were necessary to His plan, seemingly. Harmony was stabilized, at least by comparison with the rest of the world. For it was a good land of hills and valleys, which drank waters of the rain of heaven—a good land for sheep and cattle and every living creature. In 1820, the evaluation upon the real property, lock, stock, barrel, and chicken coops, and on the Rappite trade, was placed at $1,000,000—no exaggeration. And an angel, an effect of moral consciousness crowned with pearls, had descended to the hop fields or perhaps the barley.

Rappite Harmony seemed, in fact if not in fancy, a hundred years ahead of its quarrelsome neighbors—Mt. Vernon, where the chief building was a prison; Evansville, a poor trading post of ragged scarecrows and no corn; Shawneetown, where few had the correct theory of the universe, unless it was "Judge Lynch," the hangman, for all or almost all were outlaws. When Fort Wayne was a place where white settlers had adopted the costume and manner of

Indians, and adorned their horses with necklaces of human scalps, Harmony seemed like a center of peacefulness. When Chicago, a straggling half-Indian village, offered no inducement to any settler because of its baneful birds, humid air, and maize which seldom ripened in the harsh lake winds, it seemed that Harmony might become, in spite of itself, the capital of the virgin West.

There was a church with a fragile steeple and belfry, its bells the largest which had been imported at that date. There were also a Greek cross, a dovecote, stone ovens, a peacock on a leash, gnarled apple trees, beehives, a ferryman, an iron bell at the river's edge, an iron key, a coffin of coins buried in one of numerous nameless graves, cucumber frames, God's will, suspension of human birth. An entire block was given over to harmonious business buildings—a cocoonery, where the worms worked, and a silk factory operated by Father Rapp's daughter Rosina, a brickyard, a brewery, woolen and oil mills, furnaces, shoe factories, a hattery, and several smaller concerns, the power of which was derived from a treadmill operated by castrated dogs. The golden rose of Micah was a seal upon the heart and the merchandise. The streets were laid out according to the cardinal points of the compass, to suggest an order in the universe. There was a tower of bees. There was everything but a maternity ward. God rested above all knowledge and subtlety, all joy and gladness, all fame and praise, creation itself, all things that He was not.

The one tragic flaw was that of which the Rappites were hardly aware—themselves, naturally. It would have been difficult to argue the case against their happiness. Were they not happy? Yet security seemed mortal's greatest enemy, according to numerous travelers who stood outside the charmed circle of Scriptural communism, so-called, and saw nothing but a system of prohibitions and repressions.

John Woods, of English Prairy, twenty miles up the Wabash on the Illinois side, had heard conflicting reports, that Harmony was both heaven and hell, both Raphael's order and Beelzebub's, the extremes of mortal destiny, both rose and canker. The combination seemed to him far from impossible in the nature of things.

In July, 1820, approaching the place, as yet unconvinced of any difference between Illinois and the Indiana shore, he saw what truly amazed him, however—the Rappite people. They were amazingly similar. The men wore jackets and pantaloons, very wide, of vivid Prussian blue, with coarse flat hats like pancakes. The women wore jackets and petticoats, a darker shade, with skullcaps and straw bonnets. To see how such harmony happened, it would be necessary to depart from reason altogether, with the realization that the sum of individual beings is somehow much more than a mere sum—something has happened to make it greater than all its parts. What Woods felt was sinister. The Rappite people, marching in unison, two by two, waved their sickles in distant greetings as they passed, as if they had been given a signal to do so. Woods counted eighty-seven milch cows going just then to pasture—at which point, the comparison could not be escaped, this community was like a drove of cattle. They looked on the world, moreover, as a field of stubble burning.

As the Rappites did not marry, and yet they suffered no visible reduction in number, Woods figured that replacement was by immigration from Germany, whose people had been adapted, through long experience, to such despotic views as these. Good Americans, he said, were unlikely to join them—there was "something repulsive" about their suspension of relations between the sexes which, if examined, would doubtless prove to be a brute fact like any other, and nothing divinely commanded.

Woods was correct as to the method of re-enforcement— new recruits from Germany replaced, periodically, the exhausted number. The number was always that of those who had died in the harness. The occupations were the occupations of those who had fallen. Thus, the great Scriptural communism was subject to none of the fluctuations which disturbed Cincinnati, St. Louis, or Knoxville, centers for Philistines, where there were many unsolved problems, such as housing, intoxication, labor shortage, mothers-in-law, wages, prodigal sons, and the tendency of mental life, like that of the Rappites, to escape derivation from the laws of nature.

There was, however, one exception to the usual method of replacing fallen members, which is worthy of record in the book of human character. A half-demented widower, moaning that he had lost his dear Sarah, came to the gates of Harmony, in a bleak, windy March. His circumstance was pitiful, indeed, as he carried, wrapped in a flour sack, a new-born baby in his arms, and was followed by his numerous progeny, of all ages short of adulthood, and as mournful as wet, windruffled owls. Oh, that the ghostly reaper had never cut his Sarah down! He offered himself and his motherless children as converts to the Scriptural communism, where there should be neither marriage nor giving in marriage, neither pain of parturition nor death. They were accepted, with gratitude to providence and other factors, and regarded, from that moment, as creatures of the moral law which escapes terrestrial claims. The new-born baby looked like a little old man, anyhow.

Morris Birbeck, of the Albion, Illinois, community of free-thinking English farmers, visited often in Harmony, drawn by his immense curiosity as to what made the clock tick upon the distant star of Scriptural communism, so-called. Why had Harmony succeeded when Albion seemed always ready to topple over like a rotted oak? His observation was that a system which produced so much happiness must have more of good than evil in it. Yet he abhorred, he said, the hypocrisy which governed the ignorant by nursing them in monstrous superstitions and fears of the unknowable.

Much depends on man, whose sensations provide, Birbeck recalled Hume, the one searchlight in an eternal darkness. Without man's sensory apparatus, as now given, there would be a totally different world reported. If man were endowed, for example, with microscopic eyes, he would see how color loses its color—color inhering perhaps only in man—how even the garden rose of Micah existed in relation to a certain kind of sensory apparatus, and not apart from it. Therefore, when the Rappites became all light and fire, how should the rose be golden? Perhaps such an obscure subject was of no importance—until one viewed the effects of absolutism in conduct. Too many people, the world over, were basing their expectations upon something which, when they were no longer what they were, would be no longer what it was. Too many did not realize that their ideas, even of the absolute, could be broken into particles without reference to any whole but man. A wheat field, much less God, does not come to us as an entity—but is many particles, is many sensations. How should a wheat field ever be lifted above the earth, above time and fluctuation? An analysis of God reveals, accordingly, our paucity. What were the shadowy images which had been employed to convey the idea of God, that greater despot—perhaps a footstool, perhaps a horse, perhaps a river flowing from under His skirt, perhaps pearls of the oyster. Men show their littleness, that they are never able to reject the physical, even in approaching God. Men are of the mechanical process themselves, and unable to lift their heads into a sphere of fixed harmonies, where roses are something more than the experience of sensation.

 Birbeck was not depressed to discover no fundamental law. The realization of the flowing of sensations like water had given to him a vast freedom from the artifice of laws imposed by stricter men. Where, in such a life-giving process, was the edict of celibacy, cold as snow water—where, the perhaps bodiless angel? At Albion, though their situation was precarious, and they walked on water, they were at least free, in love with progress. The truths, the many truths they saw pertained to humanity and sensation—that men should eat, sleep, reproduce, and be kind to one another. Education, they saw as the propagation not merely of goats and sheep—but of human society, though precarious. In Harmony, the individual was dwarfed and stunted in growth, for the sake of an immortal but purely problematical Leviathan, an imaginary wealth.

Slavish acquiescence, under a disgusting superstition, checked all desire of imitation, even though this community prospered, Birbeck said. Perhaps, indeed, the leaders were sincere, if somewhat limited in their idea of human good. The association of numbers, in the application of a good capital, accounted for the pecuniary success at Harmony. No other miracle would have been necessary. The "unnatural restraint" was, Birbeck said, prospective rather than immediate in its object—as this was a closed shop, a dwindling order, and there would doubtless come a time when the fallen would not be replaced. Of necessity, in the nature of things, even on this remote star, Rappite after Rappite would drop away, like the ripe peach which falleth—a local, but no universal extinction, in all probability. Sure as the clock ticks, there would be at least one predatory survivor, inheriting the work of all—one rich capitalist as the result of so many depressed Scriptural communists, one crow as the result of so many mourning doves.

Birbeck would place his faith, not in the New Jerusalem, but in Pittsburgh or Cincinnati, or down among the shanties of the Wabash, at the last gasp of his breath.

A City
Whose Ten Gates
Are of Gold

Harmony bristled with life and activity—there was no decadence of the state, evidently, although the individual may have seemed, from some perspectives, apathetic. Harmony was harmonious, although based upon an assumption of a schism in the universe, a barrier dividing men from men. Yet who escapes the power of a similar illusion, a skull which, rotted and rain-whitened, looks down on every mortal traveler?

An examination of the Rappite architecture reveals nothing so much as that trust was based on distrust, recklessness on caution, radicalism on conservatism.

The one luxurious private dwelling, like a feudal castle surrounded by huts, was Father Rapp's, a red brick mansion with turrets, gables, lace curtains, and privacy. It was provided, moreover, with two lightning rods—a measure which seems rather unnecessary for a man so well apprised of the intention of the Deity, even as to His last gilded dragonfly hanging motionless over a green-scummed pond. There were several barracks or dormitories, some for women, some for men, as the sexes were not trusted together. The smaller houses were built with no door facing any other door—an architecture to discourage gossip over the fate of the stallion, the black hen, the cheese head, and that waste product, the world, what was going to become of it all. The granary, smelling of wheat and innocence, was provided with loopholes, rifle racks, and ammunition—the hollyhocks, fat crows, gooseberry bushes, and peaceful atmosphere serving as a camouflage, a smoke screen in the eyes of the exterior enemy. Whereas the underground passage was a system to guarantee control from within, should there be a worm in the wheat.

There were, however, no exterior enemies—only a few lazy Indians and squatters, like so many Philistines, like so many grasshoppers for whom God had no plans whatever. The squatters were aware that Father Rapp held a monopoly on trade and perhaps on God. They did not resent such privileges, nor Scriptural communism, all of which were a little beyond their field, a watermelon patch. They did, however, object to celibacy as a practice among married people. It seemed to them uncalled for, a denial of impulse in contradiction to all they had ever experienced, an escape from responsibility, and an appeal to the baser passions of men. They expressed their objections by writing obscene words on the Rappite walls. Driven by desperation, a man rode into Harmony in his nightshirt astride a white horse, shouting hallelujah for the entire human race. Woe, he said, upon the infidel who builds an empty house! Woe upon the selfish heart! For God is a lover of little children and baby owls. However, as this reformer was slightly addled by Rappite whisky, he fell rigid from his chivalric mount, which eventuality was just another example of God's will, working in mysterious ways.

Perhaps the building which attracted most attention from outsiders other than squatters was one described as "problematical." Frances Trollope, when she visited in America, lamented the absence of German castles to enhance the Ohio, that primitive river which had so many characteristics in common, she felt, with the Rhine. On the banks of the Wabash, at that date, she would have found a cruciform church, the plans of which had been handed down from heaven during a thunderstorm, in black ink on a golden scroll. Mrs. Trollope, a sophisticated student of human nature and imperfectibility, would have been unimpressed, probably, by this celestial origin, as she was by Cincinnati, a strictly human concept, and by Nashoba. Of Nashoba, Frances Wright's community for the freeing of Negro slaves, she reported only, with acrid humor, that the cold starlight shone through the chinks in the roof, and the rats gnawed all night in the floor. And that was that.

Still, the Rappite church was, with its many aisles and stately colonnades, an "unusual building" for this region, a London gentleman, Mr. Herbert, affirmed. There were four entrances, closed by folding doors. The doors were about one hundred and twenty feet from each other—the upper story supported by twenty-eight pillars of walnut, cherry, and sassafras, the walnut pillars being six feet in circumference and twenty-five feet high—the others, twenty-one feet high, and of a proportionate circumference. The measurements suggested various arks of God and the architecture employed by the glorious Solomon. There, the similarity ended. There was an effect of grandeur, but no grandeur, nothing for the delight of the eye—no golden fretwork, no integration of material and spiritual riches, no company of Byzantine angels, not even a bright-eyed opossum, not even a groundhog hypostasized unto eternity. It was all a hollow immensity, a feeling of unutterable loss.

Although the cosmos might fluctuate, every day went according to rigorous schedule. Never a deviation from what was here the normal order. Each morning, when the cowsherd blew his ivy-wreathed horn, then out of their stalls in back gardens, the cows came marching toward greener pastures, two by two, their bells clanking. The cowsherd, known as Gabriel, no relation to the angel or a very remote one, drove a wagon on wheels, known as Noah's Ark. An old sailor on this prairy, he could measure his course by shadow and star, tacking due northwest past apple trees, due southeast past a knoll of locusts. Or he might follow that equatorial line, a rail fence at the edge of the angelic hop meadow. Gabriel had at least that power of choice. Gabriel blew the trumpet for the Rappites to awaken. On the side of Noah's Ark, they read the community newspaper, which contained no news but news from nowhere—though it was short and sweet. Lo, the Lord was with them, wherever two or three were gathered together, they were informed, day after day. Lo, they should go forth, as assigned, to the loom, hattery, apple picking, distillery, furnace, piggery. Lo, they were the heirs of salvation, though the earth should be destroyed, and the heavens, also—for they and the Lord should both endure, above time, above space, above accident. Two abreast, the Rappites marched to the appointed task, keeping time to a martial music which the band played from its shell on the hills—a mighty fortress is our God, Who moveth mountains by a mustard seed, and Whose word is sharper than a two-edged sword. The working day was twelve hours, excluding the time taken for meals, of which there were four—food being, in this community, an all-engrossing subject. On the other hand, they needed strength for their huge task. As many as a hundred acres of wheat were harvested by sickle in a single day. There was never an empty moment. Everybody did a little more than his share. Everybody was glad to see each day a step nearer the end.

There was an important ritual, a relief from monotony. Sometime before sunset, Father Rapp, wearing a cleric's gown which, slightly stiffened by flour, rattled accordingly, heard the confession of sin. It is difficult to guess what these good people imagined their sin to be. There were certainly no wife-beaters or horse thieves around. Still, there was always the interesting possibility of error. None should be puffed up. God despised above all things a double-headed man, Father Rapp said, and that vanity of vanities, the tongue. He urged discretion in the use of that little member, the tongue, which boasted great things—"Behold, how great a matter a little fire kindleth!" Nor must they let their thoughts wander far. Whoever would be the friend of the world was the enemy of God, Father Rapp said. They were ever endangered by their proximity to the United States of squatters.

Another important ritual. At sunset, in the presence of a few elders, who had no official function but to be eye witness to this and similar operations, Father Rapp performed funeral services when necessary. Dust to dust. God had laid in the beginning the foundations of the earth and the heavens. The earth and the heavens should wax old as a garment, but God should remain—ever the same, and His years should not fail. For the heirs of salvation, God had prepared a lodging, a space in Him. There would be not one feeble person among the tribes of the raised, but the soul made white as snow when from smoky distance the Son of God would ride with heron-winged angels, to put into subjection the world to come. "And then shall that wicked be revealed, whom the Lord shall consume with the spirit of His mouth, and shall destroy with the brightness of His coming." There could be, in view of such an immediate prospect, no mourning for the dead. The open graves were filled with flowers—turkey beard, buckwheat, foxglove, wild oat—then closed, with a fitting gesture. Soon the grass grew over that place like a wave, and the quail rustled in the long grass. As the graves were not marked with stones—for these would be a sign of individuality even under the long grass— the exact locality of the dead was soon lost in cloud and mist. Mr. Wolfgang, for example, could never tell where Mrs. Wolfgang was. A chart was kept in the company archives, however—a series of rectangles, some marked, some as yet unmarked—along with the various columns of "Profit and Loss."

After sunset, the band played hymns, while the men dozed on the door-stoops, and the women busied themselves with their housework, as women have done from time immemorial. At nine o'clock, as church bells rang, all retired to their separate beds, like the caterpillar to its mud existence, every caterpillar to be a butterfly. All night long, the watchman walked the streets.

There were two suicides among the Rappites in Harmony—and that is a good record for any such impression of absolute order. The body of a fair-haired infant was found by a squatter in a cave on Indian Mound—and was attributed, however mistakenly, to the Rappite celibates.

Their adversary, like a roaring Devil, walked about, seeking whom he might devour—but none, or few, were devoured. Perhaps a few beat their heads against the earth. On the whole, however, all things were done decently and in order. No evil communications corrupted good manners. This community was framed, after all, on the word of God, Who had never told a lie. Besides, there was no gossip to exchange—it would have been impossible to engage in imaginary horse betting or boast of imaginary riches. Nothing wonderful could be told, as all obeyed from the heart that form of doctrine which had been delivered to them by the bright angel in the hop field, between the river and the piggery. He had pointed out this world's deficiencies. Besides, the mightiest fish that was ever caught would pale by the side of that immortal Leviathan, the New Jerusalem. For once in history, the pocket country lacked, it seems, its professional liars—at least, discounting the squatters at the gate of Harmony.

Life, for all its poetry, was made up of many prohibitions, usually imposed by the collective, a harder taskmaster than Father Rapp. It was considered an offense against the state to tear one's garments. Woe to the man who caught his trousers on a nail. Woe to the woman who slammed a door. Woe to the woman who disposed of a half-spoiled cabbage head. Such details were almost as

important as the hope for an eternal life—perhaps more important. For violation of rules, social ostracism was the most effective punishment imaginable. Conformity was the great good and
happiness—every Christian soldier exactly equated with every
other. How sad that one should be toothless and that another
should have teeth! Yet all were members, as they knew, of Jesus
Christ's body, the spiritual state. If they did not die in it, they
could not live in it.

On July 4 of each year, at a table groaning with food, the
Rappites celebrated their escape from Germany to the United
States, where they had found freedom to worship as they pleased.
There were three or four other feast days, among these, the Lord's
Supper, in the autumn of each year, when the pumpkins had
ripened.

Except as migrants from one community site to another, most
of the Rappites did not set foot off their estate, of which the
boundary lines were marked with white flags, to announce both
to themselves and others the difference between the heavenly
within and the earthly without. Only Gabriel, the cowsherd, had
freedom of motion within bounds—and seemed peculiar, the one
deviate, and likely to be engulfed by a sense of his own importance. Others walked the beaten path. Their exclusive use of the
German language furnished another barrier between themselves
and their neighbors. All they could see, from their restricted area,
was the hard life of the average pioneer, who was, as likely as not,
whisky-drinking, tobacco-spitting, undernourished, a scarecrow
at the border line of this Utopia.

In state elections, Father Rapp cast the ballots for the citizens
of Harmony. He fought, in their name, for banking laws and the
law of primogeniture. He opposed, in their name, Negro slavery,
a rival order. There was never a dissenting voice among them.

Of Harmony, the poor squatter said, considering his own hard
lot and the smallness of his onions, "I studies it and I studies it."

He could see only the granary, the wharves, the shining vats, the horseshoeing department, the very real prosperity. He could see only what met his eye, more or less. Hearing of the angel Gabriel, who had not so much as scared a hen from its roost, he said, "Well, I never. Well, I'll be gosh-danged." He asked Dusty, one of the numerous Indian chieftains without tribes, and other sad relics of former glories in the pocket country—did anyone see an angel in the forest anywhere, a tall man with wings outspread like an eagle's and maybe a dove in his mouth? Nobody ever had, though some were drunk with whisky, though some had no confidence in the flesh. He went home with his hands empty and told his wife, who had just got through having another baby in the pork tub. She was plumb sick and tired, she said, of his empty hands and his empty talk, the way he had promised her this and the way he had promised her that, a side of bacon, and all he had ever brung her was a gosh-danged opossum and a roasting ear. If this was Injianny, she wished she had stayed in Tennessee, where there was plank sidewalks and churches, and she could have wrung off the hog's head herself, and could have been a lady in a straw hat, and could have sung in the choir. They went to bed and argued the whole night long, never thinking of Jacob Schrieber, because they did not know him, and who can think of what he does not know of? If they had heard his story, they would have said, "Well, I never. Well, I'll be gosh-danged"—and let it go at that.

Jacob Schrieber was one Rappite filled with the surging health of a newly discovered puberty, sufficiently mystifying. He saw a Rappite girl distinct from the others, full-blown, her hair the color of barley in a green light, her eyes like the eyes of the shy doe in the forest. She was coming through the pasture gate one day when he noticed that she had a pair of feet. For some reason or other, he began to shake. He stopped her, so that she could not go forward without running into his arms. When she moved backward, he followed her. He all but drove her off into the forest. There was a wild light in his eyes. What was Jacob Schrieber thinking of? Perhaps God had visited him with His light? Yes, it was God, Jacob Schrieber said—and put out his hand and touched her on the shelf of her bosom. It was this way a bee landed on a flower. Could they not join hands? For, he said, 'twould be the greatest happiness for the greatest number! And God had often appeared to the daughters of men, as when He took Hagar by the hand in the deserts of Egypt—"Weep not, Hagar," God had said. "For thy son shall be as a wild ass among men." But the maid dwelled beside the untrodden ways. She threatened to scream. She ran straight to Father Rapp, reporting all that had been said—how Jacob Schrieber had approached her, and how her blood had turned to ice.

Father Rapp, although it was not like him to lose his temper, for he was ordinarily calm in the face of disaster, was mad enough to kill a hog. If Jacob Schrieber so much as thought of a reversion to decayed natural man, he would turn him forth without so much as the bag upon his back. Or he would call down the thunderbolts from heaven. Or he would chain Jacob Schrieber like a dog to the treadmill at the bottom of hell. He would stamp him into a thousand pieces and cast him upon the four winds—so that, on resurrection day, he might never be assembled with the others. Or crows would peck out the eyes of Jacob Schrieber, high on Indian Mound. Jehovah was a mighty archer and would bring the wicked down. Yea, verily.

A comic touch may enliven the macabre banquet. Their property being shared in common, even their coats not their own, yet the Rappites retained one item as strictly pertaining to the individual—their chickens, of whom they made the greatest pets. There were quarrels, alas, when a chicken got over into somebody else's garden and pecked at alien corn—a great scolding back and forth among irate neighbors. All the old animosities were thus displayed—the pent-up emotions, the sense of a perhaps basic injustice in even the perfect arrangement. At such moments, faith seemed to waver like a wave driven by the wind and tossed. Father Rapp was regretful. Frequently, but not in the pulpit, he brought up the problems of chickens, as if on its solution depended the future of community, both on earth and in heaven above. He proposed that hens and roosters should be impounded as community property, too, like their eggs. It was wrong that one item should be exempted. Chickens were, besides, indiscriminate and cold-blooded, loving no man better than another, and might as well be put into one pen. Thus would be avoided unseemly conduct among the brothers and sisters who had broken the frost on the ground and had entertained an angel unaware. How grieved Gabriel would be ever to arrive in the middle of a war over chickens! Balaam's ass, who saw an angel, had been wet, at all times, with heaven's dew. So should the Rappites be.

Father Rapp's proposal was coldly, stonily ignored. He might have authority on all other matters, even the stars in their courses, the most remote contingency, the river of the water of life, clear as crystal, flowing out of the throne of God. But as to this, he was helpless, just an average man among men. Each rooster strutted, lord of his kingdom. Each old hen cackled—the eggs in the nest were oval, white, and warm—warm under the breast of the brooder. It seems that the poultry yard was the one province beyond the powers of a Scriptural communism, that New Jerusalem, a city as measured by the burnished reed, growing by little streams.

ℱrederick Rapp,
the Lord Temporal

A short distance from the cruciform church was that famous horticultural design, the Rappite maze—"arranged with such intricacy," according to an early report, "that without some Daedalus to furnish a clew, one might walk for hours and fail to reach a building erected at the center." This maze, symbolic of mortal life, even of the uterus, had its origin at the dawn of history. There were mazes at Nineveh, Babylon, Athens, Crete, Alexandria, Württemberg, Hampton Court. The ancients danced in mazes, their faces smeared with the blood of bullocks or pigeons—Jehovah or Jove as tutelary deity, or an indistinction comprising both. The gray-eyed Athena, who had accompanied and sometimes merged into Zeus, was displaced, in Roman mazes, by our blue-eyed Lady of Salvation, where pigeons roosted. At Württemberg and Hampton Court, significantly enough, the Deity and His adjuncts were omitted. Our Lady of the Rappites, though nonexistent, would have been a colorful character, indeed.

Her face, the face of an American male squatter. Her feet, the feet of a blacksmithing asexual angel. Around her neck, a string of pearls as big as goose eggs, to indicate the New Jerusalem and New Orleans; and at her chest, a pair of moneybags, to indicate St. Louis and Shawneetown; and for her spear, an ax handle; and at her waist, a sheaf of flax for the hat manufactory, a painted arrow, a human skull in reminder of mortality; and on her brow, a seal, the golden rose of the whisky trade, expressed in mystic numerals. In her left hand, a live rooster. Withal, she wears a sunbonnet, three woolen petticoats, and cowhide boots. Her pockets, variously concealed, are filled with billiard balls, mortgages, horseshoes, fables, marked cards, chunks of coal, false premises, diamonds, inductive leaps, sleeping powders, dualism, a wheat field, lost causes, political campaigns, knitting needles, slogans, gold nuggets, manna, etc. Withal, she is not weighted down but is the palest abstraction deducible from herself, a realist who has been stung by bumblebees and who fights on both sides of every war, providing ammunition from a safe distance.

Our Lady of the Rappites is a continuance of certain functions, a cessation of others. The longer one observes her harmony, the more chaotic, the more temporal it becomes—to account for a tavern of cutthroats a little farther down the river, land sharks, liars, shrewd mystery, force, the exaltation of degradation, the sacrifice of the many for the sake of the few. She is a separation, an isolation, a deathly distinction, a middle-class ambition for static aristocracy and walls of crystal. An angel whose history is written in snow and water, yet she retains, even in flight, a mysterious affinity for turreted coach houses filled with plumed horses, aggression, pheasant and peacock farms, banking laws, straw-roofed beehives, power, a prenatal conditioning of the worker to accept his life on very dubious terms while she is stabilized, electricity, all manner of precious stones, all manner of materials. She is religion in alliance with capital.

Wheel within wheel, trade goes on, at any cost to the true virtues and capacities of man, a fact which Robert Owen long ago pointed out. Modern technicians have equated man with a hooded or white rat in a maze, and have ascertained that the rat, hooded or white, may be conditioned to turn toward food, water, sleep, and copulation, beyond which there is nothing, but that if confused by false signals, the rat becomes desperate, even suicidal, and withers from within. At some future date, they hope to bridge the gulf between rat and man, whose reactions to misfortune may then be more fully understood. Where sensual Greeks had danced in frenzy, battling imaginary cranes, the Rappite walked alone, little suspecting that the New Jerusalem would be a congregation of crows. It was easier to visualize that transparent city of glass and jacinth than to have guessed, in a million years, Chicago's Wrigley Building. Under the shade of trees where Indian papooses had swung like hornets' nests, the Rappite walked a mile and a half of serpentine paths contracted to a diameter of one hundred and forty feet. That was the circumstance to which his reflexes had been conditioned. There was no goal but one. There were bypaths which would lead him back to the periphery where God was not, but only emptiness. To reach the center, the Rappite must ignore the apparent short cut. Rabbits could go counter to the geometrical lines, but the Rappite could not. They could breed, but he could not. If he succeeded in his travels, he came, after an hour, to a little house which was the reward of his struggle—a pearl above price, a crown of rubies, a sling in the hand of David, a company of angels, a golden bowl unbroken, a wheel unbroken at the cistern. This humble building, made of rude oak logs and covered over with shaggy grapevines and convolvulus, was almost invisible under the semblance of its nature, yet a solution to every ill the flesh is heir to, promise of that greener pasture, when the weaned child shall lay its hand on the cockatrice den. It was the house of a wished-for death, really. The interior was furnished pleasantly. Blue silk curtains, stitched by Rosina, adorned the walls. The cupboards were well stocked with cheese and wine. There was a bench to rest on. There was a golden book on a higher shelf, but written in fine, spidery print, which no one had eyesight or patience enough to read. It was said to contain directions for the building of a city foursquare, the length, breadth, and height of which should be equal. Agriculture and manufacturing, astutely combined, had achieved this Arctic of the soul, finally. From this point, creation would always begin again, in one way or another.

Frederick Rapp, adopted son to take the place of one John, deceased, believed that life, to be life, cannot be stripped to the bone. He had seen far too many gravedigger spiders at work on the small bodies of birds. His efforts, though pitifully inadequate to change the Rappite system, were intended to introduce beauty into life before it reached the grave. They had resulted in various public luxuries—a military band, a harp, a vase of flowers on every machine, a golden rose carved on a slab of stone, and a maze. Had there been a maternity ward for humans as well as for sheep and goats, he might have considered that the Rappites had not received such a bad deal in the game of life—God being, as it was, the joker in the pack, of which all the cards were marked.

Frederick walked in a larger maze than any he had planned, the wilderness, both actual and political. He was a traveling salesman, purely mundane. In that capacity, he had run into all kinds and conditions of men—desperadoes, carpenters, anchorites, botanists, Indian chieftains without tribes, counterfeiters, ragged tailors, preachers without congregations, blacksmiths, prostitutes who looked like fallen angels and smelled like skunks, giants, dwarfs, a mannish bearded lady in a Kentucky tavern, men whose canes concealed swords, false millenniasts, robber barons quoting the work of John Wesley, pregnant women, Shakers, a Punch-and-Judy show, coffinmakers, teamsters, human imagination gone hog-wild. He had seen, during the course of his many travels, many a Lord's Supper—the fowls that fly in the midst of the heaven gathering themselves together, to eat of the flesh of men and the flesh of horses. At the same time, he had seen the endless multiplication of men, horses, and fowls of the air. There was nothing but an hourly life-and-death excitement. Yet there was something hopeful in the very confusion of the scene, something escaping boundaries—the future of the American nation, real or imaginary, the development of half-Indian Chicago, where Frederick doubted that ever on the thigh of an angel would be written the name of the King of Kings.

Frederick was a member of the convention which met under the famous elm tree at Corydon, to frame the first Constitution of the State of Indiana. A communist, a celibate, a slave of God, and a millenniast, he voted in favor of capitalistic banking laws, property laws, family arrangements, schooling, freedom from slavery black or white, the future world of imperfections, yea, of delusive hopes, of fountains yielding both salt water and sweet. He engaged in many charities. He helped to locate, at the center of the state, a new capital, Indianapolis—Tecumseh plus Socrates—its four avenues radiating from a circle, according to the cardinal points of the compass, and no immediate conflagration likely, where there were rivers and streams, wild ducks swimming among lilies, the kingfisher flashing light, and an abundance of water rats. What a world lay in even a drop of water—immense futurities.

There would be, in Indianapolis, both marriage and giving in marriage, both birth and death, many geraniums, many pear-shaped eggs, and many taproots. A drove of spotted cattle cropping the grass around the governor's mansion in the 1830s, visionary hermits, crows, a dry-goods store, virtuous spinsters, a schoolhouse covered with honeysuckle in the 1840s, a toll bridge, rumors of wars, wars, Abraham Lincoln's speech in the driving rain, Abraham Lincoln's funeral cortege, a funeral cortege of spiders, the forms of leaves packed into a waxen bud. How time marched on. Thousands of larvae, thousands of gnats. And many people whom science would not know how to place. President Roosevelt's speech in the mist blossoming with umbrellas in the 1930s, distrust of the W.P.A., distrust of the masses, swan song for rugged individualism, our first families, pioneers in evening dress, scrap iron for Japanese consumption, stuffed shirts, Mrs. Malaprop in a hat like the leaning tower of Pisa, a tear for China, a tear for the world in the 1940s, Jacob's ladder, parachutists, seraphim, bombers where the wild geese flew over.

A peace in the heart of war, a war in the heart of peace.

It may be asked—how could Frederick reconcile such conflicting purposes—but who has not been caught, like Hamlet, between the horns of a similar dilemma—and who has not played the part of both Banquo and Macbeth at the feast?

Frederick's character remains mysterious, a thing dwelling apart. Fifteen new-born opossums can be held in a silver spoon— and that is life, no holy city, no convention of shades on streets of gold above the world of time and fluctuation. Choosing between these two alternatives, Frederick would have chosen opossums, yet seemed to cast his lot with regal shades. Perhaps he saw no easy solution, no reduction of life to a tear. The Rappites were, after all, a part of the great stream, the great error. Death rides always with principalities and powers, whether in one world or another—many a gilded Pericles to lift his head in fog-colored Indianapolis, at the corset factory, the box or silk mill—many a gilded security to become, in 1929, as worthless as a certificate for soap flakes or a one-way ticket to the New Jerusalem. Many parachutists to blossom in the sky.

According to Frances Wright, when she visited Rappite Harmony as a student of Utopias, Frederick confessed that he was far from satisfied with the Aladdin's lamp he had rubbed. If he could effect no change, in time, for the emancipation of the Rappites, he intended to make his own escape at least, and to join

her, at Nashoba on the Fox River, in her work for the release of
the Negro slave. As God's spy on God's ambassador, he remained
at Harmony, hoping against hope—a carver of the golden rose,
a great player of the flute, and something of a sentimentalist. He
was to meet a violent death in 1832, just two years before the
supposed end of the world, as little squirrels leaped from bough
to bough, and ants formed battalions.

Frederick was, alas, in the heart of nature-denying celibates,
a pantheist, a lover of nature. He believed that God is all, that
God is everywhere—inhering in the feathery catkins of the wil-
low, the pyramids of the horse-chestnut, the black buds of the
ash, the locust leaves. The body of the entirety of the universe,
he had come to believe the body of the entirety of God—a huge
animal without eyes, for there is nothing outside God for God
to look on, not even one small, wet violet. Had not God warned
that an evil tongue might try to set fire to the course of nature? If
nature perished, it perished only in the head of man, the inveter-
ate dreamer. Man had believed his words to be things. But what
were words, finally? They flew through the air, but they could
not hurt the rock.

Frederick's world, he had furnished with the imperishable
riches—the Greenland whale which lives four hundred years,
the May fly which lives only for a day. Each new evidence of life
exalted him beyond measure. Maybe his eyes grew big with wonder, taking it all in—the butterfly with swollen joints, the flower
distended for the wanderer bee, the sexual juices, the harmony
larger than Harmony provided—the endless business of procre-
ation, the eternal weight of God's glory. Frederick's little golden
book was Seneca—"The true God has planted, not a few oxen,
but all the herds on their pastures throughout the world, and
furnished food to all the flocks; he has ordained the alterations of
summer and winter . . . he has invented so many arts and varieties
of voice, so many notes to make music. . . . We have implanted

in us the seeds of all ages, of all arts; and God our Master brings forth our intellects from obscurity."

A third part of the moon was already dark, and the earth, like Father Rapp, past its meridian, according to the Rappite theology of decline. To Frederick, however, the expectation of the world's end became, with each year, increasingly pitiful. He knew something of the true science of the earth and sky—the impossibility of an escape from continuity. He saw where the wild pigeons came to roost in the forest, like numberless moons. How should heaven be a pearl of the oyster, charming as that thought was? How should four angels be concealed at the bottom of the river Euphrates, if not at the bottom of the Wabash? But the skeptic was unfit to live in a state of everlasting harmony, Frederick recalled, with some happiness that he would be cast, finally, among dogs and whoremongers. In that sense, his vote was with the majority. "For he who shall defy, whom God hath not defied, his eyes shall be consumed, and there will be all terror over him, and his dead body shall fall in the wilderness, and the earth will cover him up, and he shall be no more upon the earth of men." He will leave some night on a journey with his leather case, his great-coat, his mortgages, his deeds, a bill of sale, a wedding ring, a half a bushel of oats for his horse, sample tobacco, a copy of the Constitution of the United States, a dream of fair women. He will not return, and nobody will ask what became of him. Lo, when his white horse wanders over the American prairy, nobody will ask who the rider was, as he was ever an excess—so it will be Jesus Christ's, the property of the man who can catch it.

What was the variety of nature—but a construct of the imagination, a public fantasy, a veering, Athena with the face of Mary, Mary with the face of a woman who squatted on the road, as the pod of her body opened? The erection of a conclusive system would probably be forever beyond man's powers, Frederick thought. There could be nothing simply and absolutely so—but many possibilities, alluring as bypaths, many visions, deformities, grandeurs, scandals, soldier kingdoms, overladen horses, warped glories, holy cities. The external world, on its entrance to the mind at Harmony, had been ferried from reality to the most fearful unreality—as if the kingdom of God cometh not with observation of nature. Suppose the gulf between the finite and infinite to be itself infinite, however? It would be better to accept the tangible reports of the sensations, wherever possible—parasitic tufts on the maple, a bird in the bush, hooked seeds, the zebra stripes of sunlight on dark grasses, orange trumpet flower, a woman's breasts. Better to have been a nomadic pioneer, wanderer like nature herself, who leaves her footprints in the marshes. Better to have slept all night in an Indian village, among cripples, babies, and old, flea-bitten dogs. Better to have taken a chance with the worst of men, even the gambler, if he gambled for the love of gambling and not for the false love of a false God. For then men would at least be undeceived.

This community was a more exacting master than chance would have been, yet was victimized by a cosmic imposture, fickle as chance. Was it for the sake of equality that the women worked in the fields, overdeveloped in some ways, like huge dray horses with bulging eyes? Was it for the sake of equality that they bore no children? Was it for equality that the men became each year more flute-voiced and vacant-eyed, as if they walked behind a Turkish veil? Was it for equality that they abused themselves? Was it for equality that this community, lost far out at sea, believed itself anchored to truth and hope?

Never were there, in one scene, so many ambiguities, so many first and second deaths, so much of life everlasting. Frederick was prone to laugh rather than cry. The world was not, after all, the complete mirror of their will. How could an angel supervise the conduct of the whisky business—an angel have traffic with St. Louis, Knoxville, New Orleans, such centers of patricide, fratricide, matricide, and legalized murder? Was a divine responsible for a swarm of drunkards, a celibate responsible for a bigamist and wife-beater? Was the angel as factual as one item, the elm like a flaming sword at the gates of the maze? Was not the angel merely the end result of a system of covetousness? Did he not favor the abuse of mankind? Why was the fortress constructed to last a hundred years beyond the world's end, and why an interest in the law of primogeniture? What avails a city made of glass to him who sleeps beneath unmoving hills? What man could rise beyond the status of man, even though he be translated upward among stars like crows' nests filled with strands of human hair and lost handkerchiefs? The fashion of this world would never change, Frederick believed, though the priest himself might be changeable.

Harmony would have passed away like dew when the fox's hole should be a house under the sycamore—but there would be other centers for the dispensation of merchandise. Philadelphia would be a great harbor, though not for winged creatures. The American coastline would be a mooring place for boats from Burma, Korea, Siam, Egypt, the Yellow Sea, the Sea of China, the Sea of Azov, the Sea of Kobe, the Gulf of Karabugaz. New York, not the New Jerusalem, would glitter like diamonds strung on gold threads in the sky.

Frederick considered the lilies, that they worked not, neither did they spin on the coasts of Decapolis. He considered the women of New Orleans, with their veiled faces, their tinkling bells, their odors and ointments—and the Song of Solomon, that my love is both black and comely. What was the significance of mysterious woman, with the sweet bundles of myrrh at her snowy breasts? Was there no balm in Gilead? If the third part of the moon was already dark, why should a woman never sleep with man, and the voice of the bridegroom and the bride be heard no more at all on earth? If owls were breeding, should man be sterile and dry? If the machinery of nature continued to operate, should man be clogged with dead cocoons and autumn leaves? Those stormy wooers, the bramble moths, achieved their copulation in three minutes, mid-air. And Abraham went in to Hagar, in the deserts of Egypt. God himself asked Sarah how her baby did. He looked into her tent and said, "Why are you laughing, Sarah?" And when she said, "I was not laughing," God said, "You were, too, Sarah. I heard you." Jacob toiled in the vineyards for Leah, Rachel, and numerous concubines the color of blackberries. The daughter of Pharaoh lifted the infant Moses up into her arms. Was not this the most beautiful act imaginable in time and space?

Yet what if that great end by conflagration came according to schedule, an annihilation almost universal, a scorched earth, and the sea perhaps giving up its dead—would it ever eradicate past beauties, even so? Man, recreating the world, can remember only his past experience with which to do so. Maybe God, too, must suffer from this basic limitation—and must make, even after the destruction of the world, fine linen to be the righteousness of saints. Maybe God loved His gooseberry bush, His jenny wren, His apples green and sour, a thousand variant details, even an old thimble, a tooth-marked spoon, a withered rose, a path across the pasture, a dairy house, a petticoat awry, and six per cent on a fabulous investment. If God really intended to cut the tree of life down, and board up the house of this earth, and hang out a FOR RENT sign, He showed no indication as yet of His quixotic plan.

Pittsburgh and Cincinnati seemed, in fact, curiously indifferent as to the destruction of the earth by fire and brimstone, the loosing of Satan out of his prison, the organization of thousands of Gogs and Magogs to compass the camp of saints in the last battle. They were getting along as best they could. They were building new hotels and sidewalks, with little inkling that their efforts were wasted on nothingness. Also, their women were the ornaments of existence—their skirts like bells, their feet like clappers, a music as of the spheres wherever they walked. Or if they were poor, they enjoyed kindness, a child's head, not merely the lamb at shearing time between their knees. What fearful toll gate was this at New Harmony, thus to rob a father of his father-hood and God of His potence? In sterility itself was decay, and the Rappites, aberrants from the true course of nature—old children in a green forest, less wise than fox or owl or Terre Haute, on which they held the mortgage at six per cent.

The Exodus
of the Rappites
from Harmony

"In the twenty-fourth of May, 1824, we have departed. Lord, with thy great help, and goodness, in body and soul, protect us." This was an inscription made by the Rappites in a dark corner under the stairs at Harmony. They had departed, in May, which is a beautiful season of flame upon the river and the hills, when the bumblebees plunder sleeping flowers, and the common thistle seems the eloquence of God.

Though by his works a man is justified, and not by his faith only, Harmony was effectively abandoned, was emptied as by a great plague of locusts, was stripped of every movable property but a fire engine, was left desolate, void, incongruous, a sad commentary, like a ghost gold town in the Old West. Great blocks of bullion and gold were carried from the Rappite fortress down to the barges on the Wabash—always at night. What concord had Harmony with Belial?

Strong reasons must have influenced Father Rapp to make a change. Removal meant the loss of trade with adjacent states, the abandonment of prosperous stores. Removal meant perhaps another wilderness. Surely, Father Rapp must have felt some tie with the many acres he had planted, where only thistle and mullein stalk had grown before—and some regret to leave the scene of future paradise, a city as measured by the jimson weed. Nobody knows for certain what his reasons were. They have been listed, over a period of time, however, as fever, ague, unpleasant neighbors, remoteness from business centers, depreciation of state currency, involvement of property in courts of law, Father Rapp's wish to have new real estate made out in his name, and the possibility that to cease being where one is attests the possibility to cease being what one is. True, many Rappites had died like flies during the first few years, when the germs of malaria were released by the breaking up of the bottom lands. Fever and ague had almost disappeared in 1824, however—that year, there had been only two deaths. A few cynics have suggested that this was the exact reason for Father Rapp's moving on— death of his members suited his purposes better than life did, as the removal of the original stockholders meant that there could be no rival queen bee in the social hive. Father Rapp, however, had long since had the property made out in his name. As to unpleasant neighbors, they would be a problem anywhere and an important aspect of martyrdom. The Rappites had ever been well armed against the exterior enemy, should he reveal himself. The Rappite books of finance showed an increase in earnings, a generally upward trend, nothing short of an earthquake could stop. The Rappite property was not involved in courts of law. There was ample money to defend it. The most probable of the reasons suggested concern the mental state. Perhaps the outside of the cup was bright, but the inside was corruption. Things were getting too easy at Harmony, and the state of Scriptural communism declining toward a state of luxury. All the wants but one were satisfied. In such a state, the Goliath of individualism might still raise his hoary head, or Esau might inquire of Jacob what had become of his corn fields. In fact, if life at Harmony was too harmonious, the Scriptural communism would have gone with the wind. The problem, however remote, had to be considered. There was the problem, a little nearer at hand, of boredom, even of inertia. The idea of power required expression, by continual conquest over the enemy, continual moving on. For this community's perpetuation, there had to be a wilderness proportionate to their objective and a feeling of nameless fears.

Woman, like a wild colt harnessed to a plow, comprised a bitter problem in early nineteenth-century American Utopias. According to a commentator of that period, a woman could not so easily divide herself between an individual and a universal love, when these two objects were opposed. Better a bird in the hand than two in the bush! The Rappite community was, moreover, an organization of married people who had abjured relations merely for the duration and might easily tire of counting the years. Not all were old when they took the vow. There were a number of hardy young people coming up. A community of hopeful bachelors and aesthetic spinsters might better have approximated the lost Atlantis, an island where gods copulated with the daughters of men until the daystar arose in their hearts.

Harmony, considered as real estate, is a study of paradoxes at this point, as it was to become almost immediately another paradise, on a plan not envisioned by the celibate builder—the Owenite community of rationalism, free love, and easy living. The German prototype of American Puritanism was thus to be followed by the French Revolution in miniature, the gaiety of nations, Rousseau or Bentham as prophet, the footprints of an Indian nymph wreathed with Grecian laurels, a nursery of babes and sucklings, the truth of the pen and not the sword—a challenge, finally, to death, diamond cutters, and country squires. Under the Rappite system, there were mazes of error, wilds of imagination, a God Who sends His people into woods and marshes, a God Who has no standard of reason, and Whose heart is gladdened when vials of poisonous gases are poured down upon all but His holy city, which may be only a bull pen or a promise. For He is likely to deal in nonexistent items. Under the Owenite, the world must be emptied simply of gross super-stitions and nameless fears, through an organization of society which will give a new existence to man by surrounding him with superior circumstances only. The Owenite order intended no mystery, no hieroglyphic writings on a golden scroll handed down from heaven—nor its corrupted version—but a system founded on what they believed to be the eternal laws of nature and human nature. Nor was it imagined that the greatest happi-ness may seem the greatest unhappiness.

Although selling Harmony at a sacrifice, Father Rapp prof-ited, in spite of or perhaps because of his pursuit of happiness, which he recognized to be unhappiness. From Robert Owen, of New Lanark, Scotland, he received, in 1825, a little less than $150,000 for houses, factories, lands, the goods in the store, stocks of horses, cows, steers, bulls, the fruit of the apple-, per-simmon-, cherry-, peach-bearing vineyards, a furnace, a fire engine, a wharf. All but the castrated dogs, which he took with him. The sale of Utopia was an excellent business deal for a cap-italist to have engaged in, although its purchase by a capitalist will be yet another history, symbolic as this.

Father Rapp had abandoned the old oaken bucket that hangs by the well, but not his ideals, not the overflowing bucket of the New Jerusalem. Once more, untormented by regret, he proceeded with a party of explorers in search of opportunity, another nest to befoul. Once more, Frederick and the majority remained behind. Before the first Owenites came, however, the last of the Rappites had departed, carrying their secret of happiness with them, like the bags upon their backs. The Owenites found no welcoming committee, as had been promised them. Harmony seemed only a gruesomely embalmed scene of German rustic architecture, from which all life had been ferried quietly away, just as the barns were half painted, just as the fields were half plowed. There was empty silence, broken only by the grunt of the wild boar in the streets where the sentinel used to walk. The fox had come out of its hole.

The direction of American energy was increasingly westward. Up the rugged slopes of the Alleghenies, and through the awesome Cumberland Gap, wound covered wagons like portentous caterpillars. Men, women, babies, seed, farm implements, cows, the Bible, memory, the works of Rousseau, the mind as a blank page, the rose of Sharon, innate depravity, innate innocence. All along the Santa Fe Trail, which was being opened, were the bones of people who had had the courage of their convictions. Many a city which had existed under a coonskin hat became something more than the exemplification of thought. Settlements appeared in far-flung places, often unpromising. Every salt lick was a future city. Following the impulse of expansion, there were communities of celibates, usually off-springs of older bodies. Not an eagle's flight from Harmony, an angel named Moroni would, within a few years, bless polygamy in the temples at Nauvoo.

Father Rapp, turning against what seemed the invincible tide of the nation's progress, went back to Pennsylvania. He was not so adventuresome in fact as Hebraic Joseph Smith, or even the least sun-bonneted woman with her unplanned babies on her hip. He was the arch-conservative, the savior of the sacred few. Woe to them that were with child, and woe to those who gave suck in those days of American expansion! For there would be great distress throughout the land, and wrath upon this careless people, and many streams dried up. Why build a world so soon about to end? These were the days of vengeance, and signs in the moon and stars—the world was about to end, not with a whimper but a bang.

With the proceeds of Harmony, Father Rapp purchased an estate in Beaver County, Pennsylvania, eighteen miles from Pittsburgh, on the Ohio waterfront. It was a strategic location, not far from where he had begun—and a point of evacuation for the West. The new town, Father Rapp called Economy—a name which has suggested to some a change of character, although this seems doubtful, as economy was always inherent in harmony, a fact suggested by Lord Byron. The great adventure was to build a town like that they had abandoned—and still to look forward to a company of immortals, still to live like angels for whom no mating season ever befalleth. Economy was thus laid out exactly like Harmony, or as near as it was possible to come. The streets were geometrical. All parts pertained to the whole, as arms and feet to body. A granary or fortress, studfarms, sheepfold, hen coops, hop gardens, warrens, pigstys, orchards, hat factory, manufacture of brooms which swept the wheat of the first bread from the first threshing floor, furnaces, distillery, the golden rose, autocracy, the book of heaven, birth control, God's will, Rosina.

While Father Rapp engaged in city building and city planning, and planted peach trees which would bear their fruit in paradise, as both heaven and earth would have passed away—there were disasters elsewhere, naturally, and woe upon the land. It is given to the many to cry out, but only the few shall be saved—this life being what it is. While Father Rapp pursued the even tenor of his days, Joseph Smith, the head of polygamists, was murdered at Carthage, and its temples and schools were burned to the ground. While Father Rapp continued as he had been, Brigham Young, new head of the Mormons, led a remnant people through the untrammeled wilderness, to a desert hemmed in by something more than metaphorical mountains. There, they would be saved from extinction by God's sea gulls who ate God's locusts. Gabriel and Moroni, at times no more than a crow's flight apart, were angels with separate versions of God's word. Gabriel, the Rappite, was abstemious. Moroni, the Mormon, emitted spores as big as those of the octopus, like purple grapes in autumn. He was productive in the grand, archaic manner.

In Economy, by and by, there was a maze, old pattern repeated as far as possible. In its center, however, there was now a round house, bearing upon its walls the inscription, "And the Devil took Jesus up to a high tower, and showed him all the kingdoms of the earth." There was, in addition to the maze, a grotto, conducted, it has been said, on the Chinese principle of pleasing contrasts. In its center was a little house of rough stone, covered over with wild grapevines and convolvulus—the gates to paradise. Certain shiftings, certain veerings like those of a sea gull in the wind, but the universe still held to its true course—and the symbol employed was mightier than the impoverished fact. The little house was furnished with statuary to suggest the trials and tribulations of the Rappite Christian soldier—walking through wilderness, pitching a tent in the desert, blowing a trumpet outside the walls of Jericho. The dates of the great events in the society's wanderings were engraved on the walls. Mt. Olympus, as it was called, looked more like a cattle shelter than a Greek temple, or might have been mistaken for an outhouse.

At Frederick's request, there was established, also, a capacious museum to house the things of this creation, perishing as it was—minerals, shells, stones, eagle feathers, stuffed birds and animals, Indian headdress, tomahawks, pottery, the anomalies of geography and geology, skulls, fabrics, buffalo jawbone shaped like a harp, beads, bearskin, cradle of the papoose, embroidered moccasins, a wampum belt, a pair of teeth. There was no way to infer from such relics a celestial city, which has no need of the sun or of the moon, but shines in a self-engendered radiance, as an independent entity. There was many a *rara avis* but no angel, no phoenix, not even an ostrich.

Father Rapp's house was, in Economy as it had been in Harmony, the only pretentious private dwelling. The end result of Moses in the wilderness and Gabriel in the hop field, it was like the menage of a prosperous German farmer, one who had not struggled in vain. There were walks winding through a wilderness of all the flowers which could be cultivated in that latitude. Flowers from the old Jerusalem, flowers from Württemberg and Harmony, made the more enticing by the sign, *Verboten*. There were fruit trees, apple, peach, pear, cherry—swollen pigs' bladders, filled with pebbles, tied to their boughs, to scare away marauding birds.

Except for its relation to Scriptural communism, as apex of the social pyramid, the Rapp family would have seemed merely the average upper middle class. They differed not so much from prosperous people in other cities as from the Rappite workers, a drove which slept in warrens. Their house was furnished tastefully. The dining table was set with good china and heavy silverware, under a large portrait of Christ healing the leper. The bread, meat, and wine were of the best. There was a correct servant. Father Rapp's daughter Rosina was a charming hostess, exceedingly well bred—if somewhat colorless, as she was always concerned with the cultivation of silkworms. Frederick found refuge in her detached peacefulness and the delicate music of her harp. It was as if all their fathers were under the cloud, and all had passed through the sea, and all had drunk of the spiritual rock—and there was no one in the world but himself and Rosina, "dearest sister," in a silk dress, with her hands moving among the strings. Besides Father Rapp, Frederick, and Rosina, there was a fourth. A bouncing girl, daughter of the son who had died under such plaintive circumstances, brightened the household. Though in view of her origin she was perhaps a heresy, this fact seemed forgotten. She was the flower of Father Rapp's old age, it was said.

A few years in Economy, and Father Rapp was able to retire from his earlier strenuous labors, such as walking an underground

passage between church and granary. His estates seemed to operate of their own accord, wheels turning within wheels. He enjoyed
tours of inspection through his large factories, but merely as a
sign of his continued interest. Whenever he entered a workshop,
the young Rappite girls fluttered around him, like moths around
an old apple tree. He expressed his pride in their achievements
and productions. He promised paradise, not far distant. He was
less interested in the girls, however, than in his greenhouse, where
he cultivated orange trees, maintaining the temperature of summer even in the worst blizzard. It was a gentleman's hobby, a type
of honor, an indication of six per cent, a reward for his protracted
labors, and perhaps their symbol. He had also a compound of
wild deer, which he fed with his own hands, as he had once fed
slop to pigs—would thrust spoiled lettuce heads or roses through
the bars. The wild deer were graceful, stepping out like dancers,
nuzzling against him like little children, their eyes almost like the
eyes of luminous angels. A light footstep which scarcely touched
the ground.

There were not many visitors to this remote kingdom, but
the few important guests, especially the members of European
royalty, would be greeted by uniformed heralds with horns and
trumpets, and the band playing music in the church tower. The
Rappites were proud of their great leader, who seemed to them
more important by far than the King of Württemberg, a withered
spider. He had plotted a moral map, and he had been a good
surveyor in the wilderness—though the great event, of course,
was that which had not happened as yet. They awaited, with
quiet cheer, the second Coming of One, Jesus Christ, the King
of Kings, Who should lift them all up into the society of imperishable angels. There was little else to look forward to. Their
peacefulness, however, was to be disturbed by an unexpected
event, indeed, the Coming of One.

The Coming of One

The time was July, 1829; the place, Economy, Pennsylvania. Regally embossed, weighted with the look of importance, came a letter from Frankfort-on-Main, addressed to the "Aged Patriarch George Rapp and his Associated Superintendents and Society, etc."—signed John George Gantgen, "Private Secretary of Count Maximilian de Leon" and "Chief Librarian of the Free City of Frankfort, and Doctor of Philosophy and Theology."

The contents were even more impressive. The Count was, according to his Secretary's confidential report, none other than "the Great Ambassador and Anointed One of God," descendant from "the Stem of Judah and the Root of David." His inheritance dated back to the oldest names in sacred history. A genealogy like pearls on a string. He was the child of Moses, Abraham, and Isaac, child of harpers harping on a sea of glass, child of the architect Solomon, child of every imaginable patriarch in the deserts of Egypt, the vineyards of Damascus, the armed cities of Edom and Ethiopia. His forefathers had been most productive, ere the evil days came on us, and their ramifications as many as the grapevine and word of God on high. The Count was, moreover, the enemy of Cain, Philistines, painted Pharaohs, Herod especially, Pontius Pilate, Belial, etc. He was a Samson in the house of the enemy, an avenger, a wild ass among men, a mighty archer, a despiser of the Epicurean sty. He was not the light but was sent to be witness to the light.

To the Architect of two Harmonies, Economy, and a New Jerusalem, this child of the ancient kings of Judah extended his greetings and felicitations. He would have been himself a Jacob wrestling with dark adversaries, a Judith carrying the head of lecherous Holofernes in her bag of meats. But what could he do? Although he had put off his coat of emblazoned armor, his breastplates, his shield, and his spear, yet Europe was a Goliath who could not be blinded by the few pebbles in his hands, and Europe, a Saul who was deaf, yea, an indifferent Pharaoh, eating no heart out but its own. In the quarter of a century since Father Rapp's withdrawal from monarchical Europe, the measure of corruption was at last become full, a cup running over, a progress of degeneration to which he had been eye witness, sterility in the place of the tree of life, unequal struggle, exploitation of the many for the sake of the few, monstrous system, denial of grace, seven years of lean, the murder of Abel, pit of hell, men blinded like dogs, the dark of rationalism, the superficial sphere of knowledge which separates the heart of man from the heart of the child, glorification of evil, slaughter of the first-born. The Count was prepared, therefore, to come to America, as a last hope for salvation, spiritual body, spores which will bear their fruit in paradise, shepherd, harper, rose of Micah, green valley, peace, retirement, white angel riding a white horse, asexual, balm in Gilead, golden book, fatted calf, progress, regeneration, harmony, the New Jerusalem. He was, fortunately, provided with ample funds, the sum of his inheritance, by which he would be able to transport other souls who burned like the dry thorn, like Daniel in the furnaces of Europe. Would Father Rapp advise him on the founding of a Scriptural communism, giving the benefit of his long experience in America, a few practical suggestions as to the steps he should take, initial outlay, correct location, number and kinds of workers, number and kinds of tools? Too long, the European aristocrat had played with God as if He were a billiard ball, to be struck in every direction. The Count was aware, however, of one almighty and abiding truth—that this world is not a billiard table.

Father Rapp, who had had no knowledge of his fame in Europe, was pleased by a plea for help from so distinguished a convert, in Europe his superior. He would welcome, he replied, a visit from the Count Maximilian de Leon, child of the ancient kings of Judah, who walked not as others walked. His house, though small, was filled with the glory of God like a cloud. He would share his last crumb with one who, like himself, was fixed on the eternal purpose. He was the Count's most humble servant, in the eyes of God, and ever would be, even to the end of time. He could undoubtedly provide helpful hints on markets, real estate, malaria, attitude of the American people, uses of waste products, problems of transportation and communication, selection of fit subjects, legal systems, banking laws, climate, distance, the bewildering maze of this new world. Louisiana seemed, at the moment, the best of all open countries.

It took two years for the Count to wind up his transatlantic affairs. The voyage over was a long and perilous one. His ship came near going down in a storm at sea, which accident would have deferred forever the consummation of divine purposes, no doubt. Finally, however, as God works in mysterious ways, news arrived that the Count had disembarked and was on the road to Economy.

It was late Indian summer, 1831, a day when the yellow leaves were falling, and the first glint of hoarfrost had lighted up a dark ground. Oh, ineffable rose of heaven! It fadeth not among the dreamers of dreams, the seers of visions, time having in this one realm only no passage, no effect of deterioration. The Rappite men and women, with offerings of late autumn flowers, stood lining the narrow streets of Economy, as the band played martial music from the church tower. Father Rapp, wearing his black, embroidered gown, seemed more the priest than the retired farmer. Frederick, lord temporal, stood by his side, expectant. Rosina was only a pale face at the window—she could not come down, as she was busy with her worms. The day was brisk and fine, enough to put color in the cheeks, enough to make the breath come short. The Rappites, like one body, experienced a surge of excitement. On such a day, Jesus Christ had come riding on an old ass colt—and He had healed the halt, the lame, the blind. Yea, Mary Magdalene had washed His feet and dried them with her hair.

The Rappite herdsmen blew three times upon their horns, as if they would welcome, indeed, a heavenly host, that shepherd with the wooly lamb in His arms, accompanied by a few thatched fishermen of souls like Himself. But what was this—a cortege of carriages, as at a funeral or a wedding? Never had there been such a stir in any Rappite town, not even when, long ago in Harmony, Gabriel descended.

Out of the first carriage stepped an emblazoned herald, with a trumpet at his cherubic mouth, announcing, in singsong tones, the Private Secretary to the Count Maximilian de Leon and Doctor of Natural Philosophy. Out of the second stepped the illustrious Private Secretary, clothed like a minister of justice, in a sable, flowing gown, with a golden sword uplifted like a sickle in his hands. He, in turn, in singsong tones, announced, at great length, the Count Maximilian de Leon, the Lion of the Tribe of Judah, the Branch of the Tree of Life, the Lazarus who creeps out of his tomb, the confidant of Gabriel, Israfel, and others. From his curtained carriage, finally, at an auspicious moment, stepped forth the Count Maximilian de Leon himself, the long-expected one—a corpulent, fat gentleman, nothing ethereal, in a suit of purple and green broadcloth, with his blond curls draped over his coat collar, and a golden book open in his green-gloved hands.

Was this the promised Coming of One or angel of another dispensation? This was Bernard Mueller, a traveling salesman, having no means but the borrowed clothes on his back and the idea of happiness.

Undoubtedly, Father Rapp must have been surprised at the grand show, the number of the Count's party, lace collar, plumes, bells, golden sword, golden book, slightly faded luxury, fat face with three chins, female hips, peacock struttings, kid gloves, and general spirit of infirmity. Equal to any situation, even this, he showed his guest the way to the pulpit—for he could not afford to disappoint his people at their greatest hour. Instead of preaching, as he had promised, the Count gasped that he was filled with an emotion too deep for words, for never in his entire life had he experienced such sensations of happiness, so that his heart fluttered like moths in his mouth, and he was aware of the ultimate paradise which would be, yea, verily, the first dominion, a thing not of this creation. All tongues, he said, should then vanish away. He begged to be excused, for the moment, from further use of his tongue, a tired member.

Father Rapp ascended into the pulpit, since speech was necessary. He spoke, however, haltingly, without his usual command of thunderbolts. Such hospitality as he now offered, he said, had been given in the fenced cities of Judah and the cities of Ephram. The Rappites knew that mortal dogmas occupy the idle reason. If a stumbling block should be laid before them, they should not stumble over it. The inner man was the only man. God had been good to them. To the carpenter, God had been a door. To the farmer, God had been a plow. To the drover, God had been a herd of cattle. To the doctor, God had been the greatest surgeon. To the brick-layer, God had been a plumbline dropped from the wall. To the weaver, God had been a cloth. To the sinner, God had been one who washes away the sins of the world. God had been simple. God had despised, in His heart of hearts, counterfeiters, false prophets, perjurers, and patent-leather shoes. The Rappites must be patient, as they had ever been, and receive with meekness, like trees, the engrafted word, which was able to save their souls— the word of God, Who hated bodily ease, kid gloves, and feather plumes. He who saves his soul must lose his body. For himself, Father Rapp had wanted nothing. He did not own the coat on his back. He was as poor as Job's turkey. Many a night, he had set up trying to make both ends meet. God had been with him. Father Rapp spoke, finally, of him who dwelleth in the lonely rock, that though he mount as high as the eagle over the Wabash, yet Jehovah will bring him down. Pride goeth before destruction. Whoever beholds his natural face in a mirror, preferring this to God's word, is doomed to be the food of dogs. Whoever imagines a space outside of God is doomed to occupy that space.

The Count, although forewarned, seemed in no hurry to depart from Economy. There were not beds enough for so many unexpected guests—but the Count was quite happy to share accommodations with his Secretary, who had become accustomed to such little inconveniences in the past.

Weeks passed—and the law of the Count's mind, he said, warred not against the law of his physical members. Smooth-cheeked as an egg, he seemed not at all impressed by the chilly distance between himself and the representative of the Deity, that single basic reality on which all other things depended. In fact, the Count preferred association with others, on the friendliest terms. He was not aloof. To the Rappites, so long without news or excitement, he seemed like a messenger from both God and the world itself. He had visited in Rome, Paris, Moscow, Cairo, Constantinople, had been in great capitals—and everywhere had battled against evil, on which subject he was an authority. He insisted that he had a golden thigh, a mind invulnerable to attack. He insisted that he had associated with angels. So he was able to draw to light what had not been revealed before. Many were able to speak thoughts which they had not suspected themselves of having entertained, even remotely. Why were so many of the original investors now dead? Why had they lost touch with their relatives in Germany? Why was Rosina never called on to do any of the heavy labor? Why had Father Rapp a granddaughter? Why were the graves nameless?

The Count was sufficiently cautious, though sympathetic. Every man has a right to his day in court, the Count said, and drew from under his hat, like a rabbit, a copy of the Constitution of the United States. Here was a most mysterious document, passing human understanding, as do the ways of God. It permitted, however, to every man the pursuit of happiness and to every man an orange tree. It permitted to every man the fruits of his loins. As all men were created equal, God had lifted Father Rapp up as He had lifted ancient Pharaohs, merely to show his weakness, his littleness, his fears—else why two lightning rods, else why a cane? The Count proposed other questions, most of which had already been asked. What had become of Abel's gardens? Who would carry on the family name of Schrieber? Where was Mrs. Wolfgang now? Where were the unborn children? The Count thought it better to slide back into the cradle than the grave, better to put on the long clothes of infancy than be the food of dismal worms. For that matter, why were the Rappites never shown the books of this mysterious corporation—why had these been kept in the dark?

The Count—himself a celibate and one with a golden thigh— seemed a judgment on economy. He explored every detail of Economy, such as the purplish beans in glass jars, a lonely woman, a man who could not sleep at night, a pair of baby shoes, a lamb between the knees of the shearer, a dry thorn bush burning in the wind, a nest of naked robins, the price of corn, a litter of pigs, an empty doll's cradle, a bracelet of hair, an iron key, the price of wheat, peach and apple orchards, molasses kegs, the breeding of silkworms—a million dollars of industry. The facts spoke for themselves.

When, after six hectic, embittered weeks, the Count ascended into the pulpit, he had at hand not only the history of community but of every individual. Each man had emerged, as different from every other. The Count knew how some would have given up the New Jerusalem for a watch like Frederick's, a dress like Rosina's. With utter confidence, with great joy, therefore, he made known his doctrine of dispensation. There were men in New Orleans, Pittsburgh, Philadelphia, men in London, Berlin, Warsaw, men in the deserts of Egypt, men at the antipodes of each other. And God had created them all. More wonderful was man than woodpeckers in Elysium or flotsam on the shores of Atlantis, where the skull is used as a vase for flowers. Lo, every man was the world shut inside himself, onion skin within onion skin, mystery within mystery, which only God could peel off. Until the day when God should peel the onion, none should do so. The Count, sent as God's messenger to God's ambassador, was appointed to restore the Rappite women to their pleasant firesides and the Rappite men to their green fields and orchards—not merely at a remote period when the universe of matter dissolves, and there is a loud gnashing of teeth, but here and now. The Count, as God's messenger, proposed a continuation of the good works accomplished by God's ambassador—but with this one exception, that the Rappites should enjoy the restoration of marriage, that they should be no more pressed down. The Count, who had seen so many mistakes, feared that the Rappite was blown off his course, far, far from that happy shore, the New Jerusalem—but he had come to take the wheel, at God's express command.

It was a difficult winter for the spiritual brotherhood. It was, by all odds, the hardest winter in American history. The earth

enlarged its baldness like the head of the eagle. Lightning struck
an old horse in the white meadow and tore off the roof of the
whisky distillery. Trees broke and fell under the weight of armo-
rial ice. Pennsylvania seemed like the North Pole, and every man,
a seal with bright eyes, observing the white, effulgent beams of a
new universe, a new deal. In the intense cold, the Count made
converts, as easily as if he had been a snake in the grass. Those
who had anticipated millennium, a tide that comes to shore, were
most cruelly disappointed at this strange turn of affairs. There
was a loud gnashing of teeth, a lamentation of the Children of
Israel, as the fire on Mt. Sinai wavered and seemed ready to go
out. Those who had considered millennium as by no means a
certainty, as an ever-receding goal, were ready to join the Count's
party, without so much as a tear of regret. It all happened so
quietly. There was no argument, but only a division of the odd
from the even, the fat from the lean. Father Rapp seemed forgotten—as if he had never been the power of this community,
but only its sign.

Of seven hundred members, two hundred fifty deserted the
ranks of the faithful, brother and sister taking opposite sides,
husband and wife retiring to separate camps. Father Rapp said
that the tail of the old serpent had drawn down a third part of
the stars from heaven and had cast them into the deep sea. How
were the mighty fallen, he said, and they should never wear the
crown of life.

Frederick, throughout the conflict, had held to the adage that
the apples of speech are silver, but the apples of silence are golden.
Yet he had listened with the utmost intensity to the Count's
remarks—and, in the act of listening, came almost to fraternize
with that very Devil, almost to greet him with a mild affection.
He seemed to agree, in fact, that there would not he only the
voices of young lions in New York, only the grass in the empty
streets of Philadelphia, the crying of the panther in Boston. Had

not God been always compassionate, a dog whose bark was worse than his bite? Silently, he seemed to give up his will to the will of another. It was his silence and a slight wink of the eye which betrayed him.

After a winter of dissension at the heart of harmony, an agreement as to business matters was reached—the Count and his suite to withdraw from Economy within six weeks, his adherents to withdraw within three months, the third part of the moon to receive a compensation of $105,000. All other claims to property were by this contract ceded. The Count and his community were to leave the neighborhood immediately and the state of Pennsylvania within six months. Thus, it seemed that Economy might continue undisturbed by new assaults.

The seceders were to be considered only as beasts who should perish in their own corruption, Father Rapp said to the chosen few.

The Count, in violation of his promise, remained in the Rappite neighborhood, however, like an old dog sniffing at a bone. He was always on the verge of becoming an apparition from another sphere. Not twenty miles away, he set up his rival plan for salvation, a community of honeymooners, a primitive garden of Eden, where the instincts blossomed, and everybody was happy to sleep on the bare ground. The Count, a confirmed bachelor, was very happy. Within six months, he had spent, apparently, all of $105,000, and was down to his last suit of clean underwear, as the Secretary to the child of Judah could not be expected to do their washing in the brook. Loving creature though the Secretary was. Unfortunately, when poverty flies in at the window, love flies out. There was not even a window. Winter was coming on, and several women were with child—so it seemed that even this plan for happiness had its fatal defects. The fallen Rappites, or Leonites, as they called themselves, looked like squatters, and they had the attitude of squatters. Their former

experience had not prepared them for the hard life of the individual pioneer, nor for the flight of the individual soul to God.
The Count, far from being a father to the human race, was interested in no one but himself and, it may be, his Secretary. While
the Leonites sat recalling their former glory, the Count and his
Secretary discoursed, among the bushes, on the fortunes they
had lost at gaming tables, cock betting, etc. When told that there
were many babies about to be born into the world, the Count
looked vapid and blank. The first great whirling snowflakes had
already fallen, and there was not a roof above their heads. Soon
the Leonites, like an army of scarecrows, were ready to descend
on the citadel of the crow.

Father Rapp, a watcher from a high tower, had foreseen exactly
this eventuality—the Leonites like dark angels rising from the
flood. At the first sign of invasion, his men retired to the woods,
as Father Rapp had instructed—for he wished to avoid bloodshed in the streets of Economy if possible. When the Leonites
arrived, they found an apparently empty city, the doors locked,
the shutters drawn, a deathly silence, not so much as the cackle
of a hen. With mighty effort, they battered down the doors of
storehouses which, they knew, were furnished with hams. Much
were they taken by surprise, however—as the women, who had
remained on guard, greeted them with showers of hot water,
brickbats, brooms, coals, loud scoldings, and many a kick in the
pants. The Leonites withdrew, completely beaten down by their
Amazonian ex-sisters in Jesus Christ. No use trying to get the
best of a woman. They scattered to the four winds, taking their
women with them. One or two groups joined celibate communities elsewhere, it must be admitted, and perhaps they cannot
be blamed. The Count absconded with his Secretary in a boat
to Alexandria, on the Red River, where he perished soon after of
cholera—for Jehovah always had the highest card up his sleeve,
and all Jehovah's cards were marked.

Economy's rampart, Father Rapp said, was like the vast sea, invulnerable to attack. The Leonites, he said, were like locusts, like swarms of grasshoppers, which encamp in the hedges in the cold day, but when the sun rises, they are gone, and nobody knows the place where they have been.

Jacob Zundel, who had followed Father Rapp in every divinely guided exodus, had followed the Count's party, also. On the Count's death, he joined the Mormons at Nauvoo. Thus he would encompass within one lifetime celibacy, monogamy, polygamy—going from extreme to extreme. He infinitely preferred the state of polygamy to the state of celibacy, it seems. He spent the rest of his life urging the Rappites to join the Mormons, for though these suffered greatly and lived in tents under the open sky, they had something which his older friends lacked, if only he could convince them. Zion was with the Mormons, not with the Rappites! Zion was theirs. The Rappites should not look upon the Mormon joys as playthings, he wrote to the Rappites, even when they were old and waning and only the hope of death could light up their sky—"If only I could impress the truth on you, I would count myself happy. I am now happy already, of course, but without you this happiness is not so complete. I am your best friend, the best you ever had, whether you believe it or not, for I am concerned about the welfare of your soul, for I know exactly what you are still lacking, if only I could tell you." It was not only their money that he wanted for the Mormon cause. Father Rapp always read these letters from the pulpit. Meetings with the Mormons were arranged, but none transpired. Perhaps they could have reached some kind of agreement, as both orders sacrificed, necessarily, the family.

From the time of the Leonites, if report can be trusted, Frederick's spirits drooped, "a broken spirit soon ushering in a broken body." There was a "breach unhealable" between the elder and the younger Rapp, an irreconcilable difference of opinion, an army of seraphim against seraphim, a state of perpetual war. It was written in prophecy—"For he who shall defy, whom God hath not defied, his eyes shall be consumed, and his spirit shall pine away, and his dead body shall fall in the wilderness. . . ." An April day of wind, the world ends. Either Frederick was killed by the falling of a rotted oak tree in the forest, or he was murdered, like Absalom, and the tree placed, as a deception, over him. The hat was his, and the gold watch, and the riderless horse, but the fox had eaten his limbs away. What happened may have been an accident, but the world was inclined to accept the hypothesis of murder—and this was a tale told in taverns, both in America and Germany. Frederick had many friends in the outside world.

Father Rapp was, of course, the chief mourner in the funeral procession which moved slowly through the streets of Economy. Rosina watched from her window—she was busy with silkworms, out of whose bodies would come the strands for her own shroud. She had walked for a long time down a darkening sky. She was all alone. Under the apple trees of an old orchard, Frederick was buried, and his grave left nameless like the others. Soon the grass had covered over it, and the quail rustled in the long shadow, and no one could have told the police where it was. No one but Rosina.

The Fading of the Golden Rose

Unto thee shall come the golden rose, the Erst dominion.
—MICAH, 4:8, LUTHERAN TEXT

After Frederick's departure, Father Rapp became more and more the mystic, giving himself up to the dream of the past. Like any other old man, he would sit in his garden with his blanket drawn up to his chin, motionless. In his garden, within view of that chair, he caused to be erected a colossal wooden statue of Harmony— like the figurehead of a ship, not male, not female, a journeyer over grass like surf, a graphic statement of his war against the evil world. Economy, the present scene, had slipped from its moorings.

He studied the maps of seas and the boundary lines in Canaan, Syria, Ethiopia, where the refulgent image of measureless cubits was the universal architecture. He traced the wanderings of all old prophets. He was sure of a path through the Red Sea, a division of water like the stone walls of a lane in Württemberg. He was sure of a tent on Mt. Sinai, a pillar of cloud by day, a pillar of fire by night, a spiritual rock to drink of. There were fishgates at the City of David, peach and cherry trees by the walls of Jericho. He

was sure of a hat factory at Nineveh, a shoe factory at Tyre, barley
and hop fields in the neighborhood of Babylon, yea, an angel
in the wheat, a crown of diamonds. There was balm in Gilead.
Certain shiftings, certain veerings, but the universe tacked true
to its one course ever. Edom, Moab, Ramoth-Gilead—they were
familiar to him as Harmony, Economy, his own old shoe.

Father Rapp's reminiscences suggested a vaster experience than
any he had had. He spoke of the lake of Sodom, the waters of the
East, as things nearer at hand than Economy. He knew the exact
well where Joseph was cast by his envious brothers, the tree where
Absalom was caught by his hair among the oak boughs. Various old
property laws. He spoke of grain markets at Corinth, as if it were
Shawneetown. He remembered Egypt as a very fair heifer, and her
hired men and eunuchs like fatted bullocks, and the night watchmen of Babylon, how they had sung at curfew, and a hiding place
in Ethiopia where the Rappites could go. The Wabash seemed now
the river Euphrates, now the river Ahava, its trees not cherry but
dusty olive, his own people the children of Senah or the children
of Pashur, their black hair sleek as crows' wings, their feet shod in
fire. Had not his ark taken grain, venison, poultry, pork, and flour
down to New Orleans? Had not the raven fed the prophet? Orphel,
the place over against the water gate to the east, where the tower
stands out in the sky, and there is a gate for horses and sheep—was
it not Harmony, down to the last butter keg?

God's children had been poor in Germany, Father Rapp
recalled, yet had become rich. They had escaped bondage,
bubonic plague, the slaughter of the first-born, Napoleonic wars,
starvation, Philistines, the two-party system, locusts, corruptions
of all kinds. They had built their tabernacles by rills of sparkling
water in America, the New Jerusalem—for God had never led
them to a stream dried up.

Most wonderful of all characters, it seemed to Father Rapp,
was Noah, whose ark had contained two of every beast and bird,

from the elephant to the silkworm, and eight people besides. Father Rapp and Noah had much in common. Another favored father was Moses, whose one program, like his own, had been to choose the lesser evil. The many unborn Rappite infants, Father Rapp felt, had escaped evil entirely. How shrewdly he had beaten the Devil at his own game. Father Rapp was beautifully confused, considering that the Monroe Doctrine was his work, that he had despised the Russians in Alaska, and that he had outwitted both Nebuchadnezzar and the British crown. He had favored, he announced, the acquisition of California and Texas, which had been in the hands of futile Catholics. He had favored, all his life, by similar conquest, the acquisition of Asia Minor, Syria, Damascus, Crete, Balbec, Tyre, Hong Kong, India, the islands, the lands of Gog and Magog.

As Father Rapp's body failed, his mind increased, even to the last. His mind traversed the earth and time, in the flicker of an eyelid. He spoke increasingly of the ways of lions, wild asses, and slave traders, the ways of the horse, hawk, eagle, and Wall Street, God's power as depicted in the hippopotamus, crocodile, and Alexander Hamilton, the treasures of the earth and St. Louis, the far places, African chieftains, Brazilian ostriches, the Missouri Fur Company with its forts on the turgid Mississippi, iron ore in the neighborhood of Economy, the fluctuations of markets at Philadelphia, New Orleans, and Ur of the Chaldees. Evidently, all existed contemporary with him.

From Father Rapp's point of view, as he sat in a rose garden looking out on asexual Harmony, Thomas Jefferson seemed the most decadent dreamer, eating grass like Nebuchadnezzar— whereas Andrew Jackson had slain a hundred Philistines with the jawbone of an ass. And Andrew Jackson's father was buried in a nameless grave. America, Father Rapp said, would be the first of the great industrial nations, a center for iron, oil, and high explosives. The American empire would comprise the entirety of earth. He predicted a foundry in the neighborhood of Pittsburgh, a pit of fire, and mortal faces blackened with smoke and terror. God, the principle of power, was secretly concerned, he believed, with the manipulation of electricity and a symbolic ark, when the world should be destroyed by fire.

Meanwhile, Father Rapp's luggage was always packed, his best clothes folded in a box of cherrywood like a coffin—though doubtless, the moths had long inhabited them, as they had inhabited the skull of Ozymandias. At any rate, Father Rapp was ready, on the least sign from above, to start out for the New Jerusalem, which seemed to be of this creation, after all, and an excellent real estate, complete with lustrous fig trees. He kept busy checking on sailings, routes, horses, camels, supplies, expenses, ways to cut corners, lesser evils such as the British at Gibraltar. Oh, how he yearned to drink of the spiritual rock! As to the world's end, however, he experienced, toward the end, new revelations—"In some far distant geological cycle the universe of matter, which, like the universe of spirit, has been distorted and diseased through the fall, will be restored to its former beauty and happiness, and sin and suffering will finally be banished." There were a few more years. As his face waxed pale, and his bones groaned with cold, he thought constantly of the fig tree shaking its ripe fruit down into the mouth of the eater. To have a fig tree was his one ambition, worthier than a thousand hats in the hat manufactury. A mere orange would not satisfy him.

At times, he seemed reconciled to an island off the coast of Florida. Again, he believed that Florida would be the New Jerusalem, a place where the old do not grow older. Alas, he could not move unaided. Lying still in bed, he commanded that Rosina should play her harp for him, and think no more about the cultivation of worms. "The worm, Rosina," he said, "will care for itself."

In August, a sultry day, 1847, Father Rapp roused himself out of a coma and appeared once more at his window, as preacher to his people. He was ninety years in age and insubstantial. He repeated, however, his old promise, as if it were new, that the decayed states must dissolve, and the sinner must perish, for this was ever God's will—and then the falsehood by which man had lived would be destroyed forever, in a city transparent as glass. Had he not been assured, by that great God in heaven above, Who sees all things, that he was destined to lead his people to the land on the banks of the river Euphrates, a city of everlasting harmony, where there are harpers harping, he might believe that this was the very hour of his interior death. It could not be. The voice of Jehovah had spoken out of a cloud, assuring him that he should reach a hundred summers in the valley of Sharon, where there are honeycombs, and there are strawberries. His lips thinned to a translucent line. His head rolled back. He never spoke again.

Mourned greatly by all his people, who felt that God had somehow miscalculated and gone astray, Father Rapp was buried in a plain wooden coffin, under the shade of the ubiquitous apple tree. In respect to his wishes, no monument was placed above his grave. Soon, the purple-headed clover and grass had covered it over, and no one could have told the place where it was, in an orchard a little beyond the stud farm, beyond the upland pastures and the piggery.

Father Rapp had lived thirteen years beyond the promised Coming of One. In that expectation disappointed, he had seen, however, Indian and other wars, the growth of national unity, the moving frontier, multiplication of slaves, carelessness of human life, the rise of rugged individualism, the rise of high finance. He, in his long career, had committed, at most, two murders.

Twenty years after Father Rapp's death, a writer in *The Atlantic Monthly* observed, "It needs no second thought to discern the end of Rapp's schemes." Scriptural communism was ever a type of graft, the very thing which it opposed.

Two or three strong-willed managers converted the machinery of Economy into a powerful money-making agent. Through them, Rappite Economy kept a hand on the world or, more accurately speaking, on the market. Pipe lines were constructed to connect Economy's oil fields with industrial centers. Coal and gas businesses flourished, though at some distance from Economy, a placid village, an almost deserted one. Outside Economy, the many industries were enlarged, with as many branches as an octopus. The Rappites were perhaps the first great business concern to import droves of labor from the lotus-scented Orient. Japanese laborers worked in the silk mills, at a slavery of a few cents a day. On these sons of heaven, the joys of celibacy were not imposed. In Rappite Economy, celibacy continued unabated, perhaps because most of the Rappites were in the late autumn of their lives. Father Rapp's granddaughter, a musician, enjoyed for many years, however, the sheeplike devotion of a Rappite manager. They believed themselves to be brother and sister in Jesus Christ. They looked forward to no marriage but the marriage of the Lamb. This was their strange, sad, unerring romance. The Rappites were truly a dwindling people, as had been predicted, although worth something more than a million dollars, as had also been predicted. No new converts were brought out from Germany. The financial corporation passed, with each year, into the possession of fewer and fewer hands.

Like peaceful grandparents, this little people sat on their door-stoops in the late evening light of day and their lives, exchanging a few words. Their new masters permitted smoking, as a reward for many years of tobacco growing. Perhaps the New Jerusalem seemed still a promise which would be fulfilled—a renunciation of the flesh, a reunion of the human family in heavenly mansions. Perhaps Father Rapp was sure to greet the immigrants when they reached that regal shore, the world which lies always beyond our grasp. Perhaps not. They were a ship of state which had been dry-docked and left to rot. Grass grew high in the streets. Bats flickered in a ruined doorway. There was an atmosphere of cherished decay. Apparently, not one peaceful Rappite, with red eye of his pipe burning in darkness, suspected what had been his part in the building of America—a smokestack where there had been an angel. Nor would any think of claiming a reward in the flesh, naturally—for the flesh had waned, and the individual had long ago been lost.

No Rappite was acquainted, it seems, with Walt Whitman's barbaric yawp over the rooftops of the world, his surging affinity with nature and natural man—his invitation to the world to take its clothes off and come out under the sky. Nor was Whitman acquainted with the Rappite order. Listing the census of the nineteenth century, every human, every grass blade, he omitted the negative aspect, the golden rose of Micah, the thousand hats for nonexistent customers. Maybe the Rappites were the profounder thinkers. Maybe the unreality sufficed where reality would have failed.

The facts of the case are these, finally—that the country churchyard was converted over to the uses of the Bethlehem Steel Corporation, of which it thus provides the shadowy background, and that the nineteenth-century dream of a New Jerusalem resulted in the twentieth century's dream of organized death. Had the Rappites survived as an entity, they might have rivaled Rockefeller or Henry Ford, it has been said—a model factory, a model community, no labor problems. They perished, presumably, and in that fact lies their chief charm. Only New Harmony would retain, dilated and at large, the memory of these founding fathers, whom God had stirred to build a city in the wilderness.

Another Coming, Another Dispensation

New Harmony, a summer day in 1940.

The rust-browed farmers stand on the streets, talking of rain. It is a good year when the river does not rise and, overflowing its banks, bury the fields and Cut-off Island. This is a bad year, as there has been little rain to speak of. The brooks are as dry as dust, only the thistle flourishing.

Only the undertaker can make a decent living, they say. He owns the islands that are buried under the river and rise in the dry seasons with trees and singing birds. He owns all this pasture land, far as the eye can see, every grass blade, apple orchards, vineyards, new-painted barns, a drove of fine cattle, a house with turrets, a prize bull, sheep and goats, a stone pit, an Indian battle-ground, sows like dancers with high heels, a brick kiln, a granary, a stud farm, all but the swallows and the Rappite graveyard. All but the golden rose of the New Jerusalem and something else lingering in this neighborhood, though nobody knows what it is—perhaps a mere idea afloat in the sky. Indeed, however, as the county records will show, he owns the earth and what is under the earth, that vast lake of oil, that Sodom.

The undertaker is a man worthy of admiration, all agree, and is always ready to give a helping hand. He began at the bottom of the ladder, but he has not forgotten how the other half lives. That is why he is so daft on building houses and barns, so daft on plumbing facilities and soil conservation. It happened this way. He saw so many dead people that he began to think more and more of the living—for there was no way he could improve on the real condition of the dead, which was God's work or nobody's. Seeing so much disunity, he felt more and more the need of unity. He puts a geometry book under the head of every man who dies in New Harmony. Geometry, of course, has no significance—it is merely a cheap pillow, by which to adjust the head in its coffin. Geometry is just another of life's numerous accidents. He bought geometry dirt cheap at an auction sale in the freight station at St. Louis, along with several battered tins of salmon. It might have been Greek just as well as geometry, which is Greek to him. To the dead, it makes no difference what the story is, whether how to grow two grains where there was one before or how to tame wild horses. If a man has no eyes in his head, he cannot read—and besides, all books are erroneous, and of the writing of books there is no end. That is why the undertaker would rather bury books than put them into libraries. The undertaker is about the best Republican anybody ever saw around here. He is always talking about the birth throes of humanity and lambs. If the world ends, everybody knows, it will be quite a disappointment to him, just when he is so busy tearing down old houses and putting up new ones with flowered wallpaper and cross ventilation.

The only man who ever goes down and comes up again is Glaucas, the sewer cleaner. All Glaucas ever found down there to be afraid of was a toad with eyes like headlights. Pretty soon, he got to be friendly with it. First thing you knew, he had it in his pocket. When he isn't down under the ground, he is up above it. You can count on that. If he wears a bright blue shirt, that means he has got himself a new wife, though where he gets her from, nobody knows. There is such a scarcity. So almost every Saturday, sure as sin, he wears a bright blue shirt, with a price tag still on it, and no one would think of asking, What became of that last girl, Glaucas? Glaucas would never be able to tell. They all look alike to him. Maybe she went to Vincennes to visit her mother, and maybe the fishes ate her. Glaucas is carefree. He has nothing to bind him to himself—no memories, not even the petrified bird's egg he carries in his pocket. He is always barefoot, with his long hair hanging in his eyes, and his eyes like a toad's with a light in them. When anybody asks him what he thinks, no matter whether it's politics or weather, he says, "Oh, horsefeathers." Somebody ought to discover Glaucas before it's too late.

The farmers talk of rain's possibility, price of corn, this old world putting off its sinful garments, hog breeding, oil, the undertaker's dynasty, Byrd's expedition to the Arctic, or was it the Antarctic, prosperity which is just around the corner, the impossibility of Greta Garbo, great adversaries, the high cost of living, sheep's lice, Homer Hamm's broken back, the history of every field, the year of sweet white Dutch clover, the Secretary of Agriculture's belief in spiritual beings. They say the oil is made up of the melted bodies of dinosaurs who used to roam these hills, snorting around. That was a while back, but the preacher says it is propaganda against the word of God, and not half so important as what is going on in old Homer Hamm's head right at this moment, the memories. There could not have been a garden of Eden and dinosaurs, too, and glacial ages. Monkeys could not have been our ancestors.

Still, if the dinosaurs really melted and left such huge deposits of oil under the corn fields, it looks as if poor New Harmony is doomed to witness a great misfortune. There will be fountains of oil spouting as from a whale's back where there were corn fields before, and the leaves of the trees will be eaten away, and a man won't be able to relax. The town will be run over with strangers coming from afar, like lice on a dead horse's body—shifty-eyed geologists, working for Rockefeller, and how secretive they are, and how much at odds with each other. Not only these, but there will be many cowboys from Texas and Oklahoma—wearing high-heeled shoes and embroidered hats and shooting each other. The jail won't hold all the cutthroats then. The old ladies with memories will never open their mansions to take in modern roomers. There will be men sleeping in granaries, with the dust of wheat up to their chins, or sleeping in hog houses. The hog houses down the road to Mt. Vernon are already filled with men, for the most part. The watchman at the maze will have quite a problem. The rich will get richer, and the poor will get poorer. There will be nothing left of New Harmony but the footprints of an angel. The kids played hopscotch on it last Hallowe'en.

Maybe truth riding a white horse with feathers will get here before the oil boom does. His eyes will be a flame, and on his head will be many crowns, but not those of the oil companies, and he will be followed after by all the armies of heaven, and he will make war against evil. Then the earth will really go up in smoke and fire, and every man will have a star in his crown. And the sinner will be washed away in the waters of paradise, the way Old Thomas was.

Meanwhile, if it would only rain in Posey County, as the paper said it would, that is all a man in his senses could ask for, and a good five-cent cigar, and maybe a beer in the shade of the golden rain trees, and something to look forward to for his old age and period of uselessness. There ought to be a way to get rid of bunions. Maybe Roosevelt will do something. Hoover tried, but it was the old, old story—his Congress was against him.

Pilgrim's Progress

Newtown in Wales, 1771. It was announced that a new son had arrived at the Owen household. The squalling brat was to become father of the British labor union and father of the human race, both unguessed of as entities.

The Elizabethan Renaissance had made scarcely an impression in that green valley in Wales. There had been little change to speak of, within the memory of even the most aged. The ownership of one cow indicated prosperity—two cows, an enviable wealth. Every lawn was cropped by fat sheep. Newtown in Wales, like Goldsmith's Auburn before the Industrial Revolution—or like New Harmony in 1940—was an idealized portrait, a sleepy village of typical eccentrics, a steady-going humanity unstained as yet by international politics, foreign trade, or luxury. Factories were two-legged animals themselves, without help of any machinery but the most primitive. Their webs of linen were laid out to bleach upon the grass, or spread upon the hedges. Woe to the thief who stole these in the gloaming. His punishment was death. Elastic was not, and china buttons were not. Needs were simple and few. The imagination was parochial. There were many holy-minded shepherds, drovers, saddlers, carpenters, under no mortal leadership but the power of old customs. Life was accepted as hard. A face pitted with smallpox might be met within half an hour on any country road. Embarrassing questions were not asked of God. All illnesses were mysterious and purposeful. Heaven and Wales seemed more real than the outside world, from which few messages ever arrived. It would have been easier to conceive a real connection between heaven and Newtown than between Newtown and New Harmony, though this would be its offshoot in time and space.

The elder Owen was a postman, saddler, farmer, and man of much importance in his community. He stood godfather to many babies and observed no rationality in the corporeal nature of things. Little could he have suspected that from the mouth of his youngest would come the true science of society, like the diamond which the prince spits out in the fairy tale.

At an early age, however, Robert Owen had begun to entertain a new view as to the organization of human nature—he had picked, like daisies in a field, ideas which were to change the course of man. The child argued with withered Methodist spinsters, defending what he believed to be the plain light of reason, what they believed to be the arid light. Aside from this precocity, which had its origin in a rapid reading of the Bible, *Pilgrim's Progress*, *Robinson Crusoe*, various popular works, a few unpopular medical treatises, and floating impressions gathered from life itself, the "little preacher," as he was called, was happy—a great rider, dancer, and player of the flute. A model of good behavior, he escaped punishment, except in so far as he was of a sympathetic nature. For he occasionally heard, emitting from the upper regions, the goatlike bleatings of his brothers and sisters—it being a maxim of the elder Owen that as the twig bent, so the tree is inclined. Robert decided that punishment should be expelled from the earth. We are all the victims, as he later expressed it, of the impressions which are made upon us, by our mistaken parents, our monstrous nurses, and our ignorant teachers. There is no original tendency toward sin. The mind comes into this world a blank page, where any writing can be placed, even the most erroneous—as witness Mrs. Malaprop, miscalling everything, and other fictitious characters, all the creatures of circumstance. Other than such observations, there is little to tell of his early life—except that he narrowly escaped being trampled to death under the hoofs of his pony, and that his stomach was scalded by an overdose of hot flummery, for which reason he would never be a great eater. Also, he could not tell a lie.

Like the Prince Rasselas, Robert Owen was unwilling to remain forever even in that green valley of innocence and happy childhood. He wanted to see the world of two-headed men outside Wales—for he had been reading geography, according to Daniel Defoe, who had spent, however, much time in a London pillory but none in darkest Africa, where such two-headed men abounded. Four years before Edward Cartwright invented the power loom, which would change what had seemed the stabilized face of nature, Robert Owen announced his desire to go to London, where he might be self-supporting, and where there were, he believed, so many two-headed specimens of humanity. In 1781, at the ripe old age of ten, he put on his hat and, figuratively speaking, never took it off again, as he was to be the world's greatest spokesman of Utopia, a society achievable through the suppression of the irrational, the excessive head. Now, at the age of ten, as a second-class passenger, exposed to wind and sleety rain, he rode all night on the top of a whirling carriage—dimly aware of how far he would travel, yet sympathetically considering the plight of all mankind, a two-legged Friday which, like himself, was exposed to the elements and injustice, because of nothing fixed in the nature of things, but only the power of custom, only that old, white-bearded man, God or Robinson Crusoe in an advanced state, who refused to share the compartment with his fellow traveler. So the rain drove, significantly enough, in the little boy's wizened face. Until all human beings should ride in one compartment, Robert Owen would never rest content. Inequality was never, from his point of view, destiny.

He was destined to become, like Robinson Crusoe, a builder of empire, but also its first great critic and destroyer. As a cotton lord, he would advocate the destruction of cotton lords and the unfair system they represented—"Civilization! How the term has been misapplied! The affairs of the world carried on by violence and force, through massacres, legal robberies, devastations, superstitions, bigotry, and selfish mysteries. And yet this gross conduct of rank insanity is called civilization."

We see Robert Owen as he appears in his eightieth year—a patriarch with flowing beard and hair, Moses to the British labor union, united world state, race of man, excluding not even the Zulus who have been recently conquered by Queen Victoria. He is returning for the first time to the place of his birth by the river Severn. Having lost his money on that vast speculation, or series of speculations, Utopia, a bubble, he is still a second-class passenger. And happy to be so. He has crossed oceans, continents, deserts, mountains, has pitched his tent in strange valleys, has forded dark rivers, even Wabash and Lethe—and has preached always, over and over again, with deadly monotony, one message, that happiness is the instinct of the universe, that happiness is attainable through the union of workingmen in a rational order. "That old bore intruding upon the dancers," Macaulay called him. He is "pertinaceous as a mole," according to one report. Others say that he is an Ancient Mariner, a King Lear, a loon. Miss Harriet Martineau complained that he had never read the Bible—and he, that she had never read *Hamlet*. "Word comes that Robert Owen walks the earth again," *The Times* (London) reports, cheerfully, as if he had been dead and is now but temporarily resurrected, a ragged phantom in the cosmic storm, a bramble-whipped nonentity. It seems that he has failed, at least in the more important political sphere—and what he may achieve in the universe is nobody's business. "Owen," Bentham said, "begins in vapour and ends in mist. . . ."

Robert Owen, however, is alive, although cut off from direct communication with others. Even at this last hour, he plans to rebuild, if not the world, at least Newtown in Wales. His valise is filled with mortality rates, newspaper clippings, and blocks of human populace. In Newtown, he displays these blocks to children, who believe them to be playthings like their marbles and quoits. He who has handled facts is spokesman for fancy, seemingly. Under the weeping-willow trees, to wide-eyed, solemn children, he lectures for the last time on happiness, a thing to be attained in this, the human sphere. That certain classes grow with as much precision into pickpockets as others into preachers cannot be traced to the capricious temper of heaven. Only man is responsible for man. These blocks are representative, he says, of the total edifice of society to date, but entirely out of proportion, top-heavy, as fickle as a dream—the apex, ghostly aristocrat—the base, the powerless working class of homeless colliers, farmers, and all the men submerged on land or sea. These blocks, he says, are no more playthings than standing armies, navies, paper money, wealth, disease, sectarianism, high tariff, and riots in the Afghan hills. The road to the golden domes of Ghenghis Khan is brutally finite, and the goal itself a false one, either dream or reality. Robert Owen hopes that, among his little audience, there are some who will put away childish things—that out of Wales will come a united labor front, to encompass all men in all nations of the earth. The true patriot is the patriot of the world.

When the children go off to their spinning tops—the apex upside down—Robert Owens turns to speak with others, whose twitterings he hears always around his head, like starlings settling on a barren tree. These are spirits of the light and air, departed friends—members of stillborn British labor unions, children who perished in cotton mills, black slaves of the American South, soldiers of every army, nameless men innumerable as the sands of the sea. Among those present, too, are Shelley, the Duke of Kent, Elijah, Thomas Jefferson, a sea captain off the Bahamas, an Indian bishop in the High Sierras, the elder Owen, an old physician of Wales, a pony. These comprise a council very different from that which sits at the feet of Queen Victoria at Windsor, this year of 1857. These are concerned, not with the romance of big business and the dwarfing of multitudes but with the science of human society and redemption. They speak not of the ammunition exhausted, the treasuries of India, the Christian population of Agra facing slaughter, and other projects for the expansion of empire at any cost. Rather, they tell of errands they are doing in the name of all mankind, to dissolve barriers, customs, capitalistic interests, capitalistic myth, prestige, the very dream of death.

In the room of his birth, Robert Owen lies down to die or maybe to sleep, as he is convinced of future life, a fact brought home to him by his waning senses. His last words are, "Relief has come." Who fails to love this man fails to love humanity.

Even as a boy clerking, in the 1780's, in the McGuffog drapery establishment at Stamford, Robert Owen had begun to see sectarianism as the root of evil. He noticed the conjugal bliss of his employers, that although Mrs. McGuffog went to High Church and Mr. McGuffog to Low Church, they drank water from the same well, and the well was not poisoned. Why, then, should men be split asunder by abstruse considerations, such as the nature of the body of Jesus Christ? It seemed to Robert Owen, in the dim light of reason at McGuffog's, a gross mistake that the Jews should be held to blame for the death of a Savior who may have existed by report of mouth only. Why should millions of Jews, who had not been present at Christ's murder, be subjected to an everlasting persecution? Moreover, who had ever chosen to be born a Jew? No one selects the place or manner of his birth, his parents, or his nationality. Christ had come into the world a blank page—and Barrabas, likewise. Christ deserved no praise—and Barrabas, no blame. They had been, in fact, but two aspects of the same circumstance, which was Janus-faced, with one face looking toward heaven, the other toward hell—when all that was necessary to do was to look at the McGuffogs. Both Jew and Catholic were excluded from many walks of life in England, and all because of something which had happened such a long time ago, and all because of a body which no undertaker could ever examine. Strolling through Burleigh Park at twilight of each day, the lad carried with him a little book of Seneca—and perhaps, in the words of an early biographer, there has never been, since the death of Rome, a more momentous convert to the stoic charity of the human race.

From McGuffog's, which was by comparison an ivory tower, Robert Owen went, at the age of seventeen, to Flint & Palmer, large retail drapers in an overhanging shop at London Bridge. Here he worked from fifteen to eighteen hours a day, after which he must spend two hours powdering his wig, a foolish aping of the rich, before he could throw himself half clothed into a bed shared by two other clerks, both asthmatic. What a life! The wig became a mark of social oppression, one with the old gentleman in a carriage going out of Wales. Robert Owen, in spite of his hardships, was fortunately placed, as Flint & Palmer was a meeting place for the aristocracy of the kingdom. Every day saw a long line of heraldric carriages. Every day saw a mania of buying silks, perhaps as the result of some subtle emotional malady, the disintegration of the world. All eyes were concentrated on a mirror. What fashionable, tired customer could have guessed the interest of the big-headed clerk with the narrow shoulders, the rather absent-minded air? He merely measured out their cloth, was no one to carry away a picture of. Yet beyond the pageantry of pomade, hair powder, satin floods, brocades, hats like harps or bird cages, and other excesses, the look of distance, the hands transparent as autumn leaves, Robert Owen could always detect a human being, not different from himself. When the lord mayor of London coughed, he was reminded of a poor thief at the gallows who had coughed when a rope was put around his neck—who had asked for a rag to blow his nose with. Therein lay the humanity. The rich seemed miserable, and the poor certainly were. Both lord mayor and his poorest thief were the direct result of circumstance—the difference being that the lord mayor was the greater thief, having had the greater opportunity in this mistaken world.

All the values and vehicles of values were mistaken! There were too many ways of concealing tragedy, too many artifices, too much embroidery.

Robert Owen observed, without praise or blame of individuals, the great shadow play, the stagnant procedure. Poor Pamela, who had only five pounds, laughingly signed her death warrant rather than face another arid social season. Iris-necked pigeons with pink feet were much happier than she, for they lived according to nature. The bishops, too, were overclothed, wearing too many petticoats, too many lace aprons for comfort of body or mind. Yet were not the congregations naked? So much was purely arbitrary and conventional, the mere product of an environment. Few people could afford the luxury of integrity. Note that George III, in 1788, his mind having departed from him, imagined himself to be a farmer—yet the farmer, each day, was being driven off his land, with nothing but the bag upon his back. Note that there was too great a difference ever between the dream and the reality. Under the overhanging shop of silks, each day a bargeful of boys and girls passed up the Thames, and what was their picnic? They were going to certain death in a cotton town. They would be themselves the crumbs thrown out to fatty birds. Meanwhile many withered citizens, one foot already in the grave, argued on the body of Jesus Christ made bread.

The more Robert Owen observed and heard, the more dissatisfied he became with the haphazard growth of past history—the division of the human race into nationalities, classes, sects, and families. In his opinion, men were all cut off the same bolt. Not all were silk or satin, but all were cotton. He began to write a Bible of his own, in plain, simple language, without mystery, wigs, or parrots. He began to set down what he considered to be the indispensable laws of human nature. One and all religions, he was convinced, had emanated from the wild imaginations of our early ancestors, when men knew not what they were, and did those things which they should not have done for their happiness. Illusion must be dispensed with. By no wild stretch of his imagination could he conceive that God had contracted Himself into a little bush to speak to Moses. The word could have no weight without deed.

Note that this is not the best of all possible worlds, Voltaire said—but that it may be improved immeasurably, Robert Owens said. And that the improvement should be visible. What is now the apex of civilized life? It is a well-managed dinner party with blackbirds baked into a pie, crystal goblets, the most cunning artifices, the savor of beauty and wit, not the least suggestion of violence. Yet in preparation for this event, a boy of six or seven, a poor chimney sweep with stripes upon his thighs, was sent up the chimney in a blaze to put out the fire, and did not come down again. No one at the dinner party knows of the toasted child somewhere above the roof. Besides, what is that incidental, necessary death, compared to the charm of the spectral hostess, a lady the color of laburnum in twilight? Human life is cheap, durable material—easily replaced. One sends the bereaved mother a few shillings—and asks for her next son in line, a poor, sniffling fellow exposed to justice. The England of this day has many Mr.

Badmen and innumerable agents of death, all most highly polished, and many quite unconscious of their destructive mission.
This is also the situation in the world at large. Note that the
world is a vast insane asylum, as Jonathan Swift said—though
by a few simple, easy steps, it would be possible to arrive at the
sane, irreproachable truth, Robert Owen said.

From Flint & Palmer, Robert Owen, in his late teens, went
to work for a Mr. Satterfield, with whom he remained a year,
studying human nature. His first enterprise on his own was a
partnership with a wireworker named Jones. As he did not like
Jones's character, he soon sold out for three of the "mules" they
were making for the advancement of the cotton industry. At the
end of the first year, his books showed a profit of fifteen hundred dollars—no small sum, in those days, for a ripe old man of
twenty. Though an excellent, unconfused bookkeeper, he continued, after business hours, to cipher the dark, chaotic pages
of human nature. Why it was that the few succeeded and the
many failed. Man's proclivity to attribute injustice to Moloch,
ignoring nearer origins, like the stout financier who had to have
a curve cut out at his dining table, to accommodate his abnormal
obesity. Or a cadaverous wireworker, one Jones, who believed all
men were wire.

Robert Owen's life would be a series of revelations and gen-
eralities as to human nature and the artifices of civilization. The
old washwomen of Glasgow Green, with their skirts pinned
unashamedly up to their knees, would not be so much themselves, Martha and Jeannie and Ann, as a stratification of the
social rock of ages, which should be dissolved. A gatekeeper at
a toll bridge in Scotland, who refused a gold coin, not knowing
that this substance had any value whatever, for he had seen nothing but a few pence before, would prove the thesis that money,
like the social rock of ages, is not an absolute, is an artificial
wealth. Similarly, the eyes cut out like grapes on a platter can

never see the edifice of crystal. How illusion can be destroyed, though far from destroyed as yet. Robert Owen was no enemy to the Catholic Church but to civilization itself, as then understood. A Mexican bishop, half Indian, would show that man, even at this extreme, even though surrounded by the skulls of pregnant nuns, is capable of understanding the basic laws of human nature and society. Among Protestants, too, there would be many Popes of Rome, and all double-headed, due to the vast difference between the spiritual and the material spheres at that date, the soul to be saved, the body to be destroyed. How the weaving sheds of Manchester and Leeds would be emptied as by a great plague when the cotton lords found cheaper labor in the ruined cities of India.

Meanwhile, it was a golden age, extravagantly prosperous— not an era to breed cynics among businessmen. The rush to the cotton centers was, it has been said, like the rush to the Klondike. Fifty per cent return on an investment was not extraordinary. Any man with a little capital and horse sense could put himself on the proverbial easy street—much to the despair of the true British aristocrat, who was apt to be confined to a tapestry with hunting dogs. There was no ceiling to the possibilities of mercantile profit—not even the sky was the limit. This increase in the power of the few brought with it, of course, almost insurmountable difficulties to the many. Machinery was supplanting man, at a rapid rate—a dredge where there had been a pearl diver. Thousands, willing to work, were reduced inevitably to the most terrible pauperdom. There being nothing so dirt cheap as labor, wages were cut to the bone, as profit boomed like cannon balls. The cotton towns were filled with scrofulous workers, looking for heaven. The watering places were filled with cotton lords looking, however, for imaginary cures.

By strange coincidence, or perhaps not strange, the enslavement of the English working classes came at the very time when ideas of political and economic freedom were everywhere in the ascendant—for such was the extreme of misery. At the moment when man was being employed for his own destruction, humanism was experiencing one of its multiple births.

At twenty-two, Robert Owen became superintendent of a Mr. Drinkwater's cotton mill in Manchester. Within a few years, having studied both machinery and human nature, he was able to show a great increase in profit. His yarns were sought by all the best houses. He was what is known as a success in life. He could have enjoyed, certainly, a gentleman's concept of heaven as a billiard table, God as the ball which may be shot in any direction. He could have forgotten his lowly origin. He could have spent his evenings at cribbage with Manchester husband-hunting ladies—and certainly, a number were after him. He gave himself up instead to moving statistical counters on a cosmic chessboard—the workers in cotton mills. He was not indulging, however, in cold-blooded abstractions or a forlorn sense of power. He had seen the mill workers in other mills than Drinkwater's— big-headed dwarfs, aged seven, whose fingers had been cut off in machineries. The progress of industry was making obsolete all old customs, proverbs, maxims, fables, nursery tales, religions. Who expected apple trees to grow at the North Pole?

There was, at Manchester, the great cotton center, a new philosophical society, whose members were spokesmen for what is usually known as the "modern spirit." Robert Owen, during his twenties, had the benefit of association with this group, made up of older and perhaps wiser men than he. Erasmus Darwin, grandfather of Charles, wrote a scientific poetry, in which flowers breathed Platonic intelligence. Robert Fulton was engaged in drawing up a plan for a steamship, which should contribute much to world unity, it was thought. There were various learned economists, both Malthusian and anti-Malthusian, various statisticians, a sprinkling of astronomers, a few bishops in shovel hats, a number of Unitarians who were always busy sweeping out angels, a number of utilitarians. Members of the Manchester group, heterogeneous though it was, were agreed that a twenty-mile channel could not divide England from the progressive outlook of the French Revolution. Manchester, the whole of England, must be bombarded by the long-range idealism of the French coast. Already, in America and England, where the old political edifices and institutions had been shattered, a social as well as political millennium was hourly expected. England alone seemed as lethargic as an Egyptian mummy covered with gold dust. England must be awakened from her ancient stupor, must accept responsibility for the resurrection of the abused working classes. Saint-Simon, Fourier, Babeuf, and other social reconstructionists had removed, the Manchester group felt, the veil from the face of human nature—and what they had seen was ultimately beautiful.

Among these Manchester explorers of the finite, however, there was a wobbling explorer of the infinite, a queer fellow as yellow-skinned as a mummy, and nostalgic for distance, one Samuel Coleridge, poet—"very difficult to classify, but at that time considered a genius," as Robert Owen recalled in later life. Robert Owen and Coleridge held many debates on the subject of human nature, its various aspects, whether rational or irrational, the universe, whether orderly or disorderly, status of earth in same, whether the soul exists after death in a refined material, perhaps as a fume, and related matters. Coleridge had planned a Pantisocracy on the banks of the Susquehanna, in North America, but never to be realized, as he was already lost in a wilderness of metaphysical speculation—the shooting of the albatross may be considered his shooting of the material world. He could accept, in fact, no limitation of the human spirit, which was whirled by every ether. Spiritual beings had often perched upon his four bedposts. There were such things as miracles—the supernatural natural—and caverns measureless to man. Elijah, a phantom neither mist nor cloud, could find a loophole of escape, even through the Newtonian sphere, sealed as it was supposed to be—could exist apart from any process of events. Thoughts might walk above our heads. Coleridge disliked, in fact, the causal nexus, the law of gravity, any prediction whatever about the future course of this planet, all abstract generalizations as to human nature and subhuman nature. There would always be, for him, a cloud surrounding every factual statement, a penumbra of uncertainty—and a voice rising from the unhuman deep. There would be a populace in every solitude. Dead souls manned the painted shrouds in painted oceans. No system of measurement could be precise, man being the measurer. There might be water everywhere nor any drop to drink. An albatross must be hung around the neck of the best of men—for we murder what we love, compelled against ourselves to do so, and our sense of guilt compels the world. The Church of England should be resurrected. Robert Owen, Coleridge said, was a reasoning machine, because he "made man a mere reasoning machine and made to be so by nature and society." Man, Coleridge said, must go forth to the bride who is death, there being no other way to resolve polarities, and even this might be ineffectual. All constellations existed in the warped mind, as well as unsuspected whirlwinds, gulfs, streams, and Seas of Sargasso. Jonah might even swallow the whale. The one law was ever to love all things, both great and small—though the islands fled away, and the mountains were not found, and there remained only the soul of man, which was perhaps the entirety of experienced reality, to begin with.

The quarrel was an engagement between two mystics, religionist and scientist. Where there was not a human body, there was not a man, Robert Owen believed. The mind without body would be unthinkable. Theologians in all ages had wanted to show man as a privileged being, free of the conditions which

move a planet in its necessary orbit. What they had sought was
not purely haphazard, the purely free—but to make room for a
foursquare New Jerusalem and other concepts of being which,
long ago, were exploded by the astronomical sciences. Labor,
while chained to the wheel of causality, had been taught to expect
an imaginary reward, to fear an imaginary punishment. There
was, however, no life but this, here and now. As the situation
really existed in England then, the rich man lived for the increase
in his capital—the poor man, to satisfy the cravings of his stomach. The mystery, unlike the fog, could be dispelled. Man, Robert
Owen said, is the best of all possible machineries, the most delicate,
but is still a machine, of whom all the parts may be known and
studied, and whose requirements are simple and few—food, water,
shelter, clothing, the love of our fellow beings—beyond which, there
is nothing but the dance of the golden atoms in the void. To change
human character, it is necessary only to change the circumstance.

Life at Manchester had, after all, its charms, and no catastrophe but one, when a mercenary suitor sought both the hand of
Mr. Drinkwater's eldest daughter and the management of Mr.
Drinkwater's cotton mill. Robert Owen, hearing of the proposed
alliance of marriage with finance, resigned immediately, and
perhaps a bit prematurely, for the lady gave her hand to a less
ambitious gentleman. The change, however, was advantageous—
Robert Owen continuing to climb the financial ladder, by leaps
and bounds. Was not the world his apple then? There need have
been nothing to disturb his peace. He might have hung around in
the Manchester clubrooms the rest of his life, theorizing, arguing
with ghosts. As he acquired prestige in cotton circles, however,
he began to urge publicly that Parliament should investigate the
condition of labor in cotton mills, their sad kingdom within the
kingdom.

In 1799, in his twenty-ninth year, walking on Glasgow Green
one day, Robert Owen had no eye for any husband-hunting lady,

but only for an old washwoman with her skirts pinned up to her knobby knees. Gently, he played at moving this figure on the social chessboard—a mere shift of circumstance, and she would have been seated on a throne of ebony with her skirts extended like a satin flood, or like the river of Lethe—and a queen would have been bent double, beating clothes. And no one the wiser. Yet how prove his thesis, that man is solely the creature of his circumstance? He might become, in spite of himself, another helpless visionary, a poet spouting beautiful words.

As Robert Owen was wrapped in this somber, disquieting thought, however, reality touched him on the shoulder—in the person of a Miss Spears, who had long since rejected him as a possible husband. Generously, she introduced him to her companion, a lady clothed in funereal black from head to foot, yet charming. This was Caroline Dale, daughter of David Dale, the well-known merchant and owner of New Lanark cotton mills and various banking institutions, preacher, also, at dissenting churches throughout the Scottish kingdom. Robert Owen was perhaps more interested in the father than the daughter, at this point—knowing little of women except as "customers in business."

They met often on Glasgow Green, through a series of happy accidents well planned by Caroline. Unfortunately, or so the lady thought, Robert's only subject of interest was cotton—though to her, there was nothing so simply and austerely effective as black silk. Besides, she was always in mourning for somebody. Romance seemed to lag under a burden of the most awful statistics—the number of cotton bolts, the number of workers, the number of dead souls at New Lanark. Caroline was vague. She could not say what the winters were like at New Lanark—she always fled to Glasgow like the birds in autumn. Her father had cared for the soul of man, which must be exercised—but the body was a more difficult matter, and he was not God. She did not know the number of beds and whether they were occupied both day and night by shifts of workers. She could have spoken, more specifically, of cages of evil birds in Babylon. Not that her heart was narrow! Discouraged by this man's everlasting interest in business, and more business, Caroline sent Miss Spears, finally, as her emissary, to convey the delicate information that her heart was intricately involved. Should he not pursue his suit, she must remain a maid unwedded forever, mother only to her little sisters, whom she had always mothered. A rose unplucked, a song unsung!

The idea of marriage had not occurred to Robert Owen, who thought himself unattractive to ladies. Losing no time, he went to New Lanark to inspect the business, and was unfavorably impressed by nothing but a church steeple on the mill wall, most precariously balanced, and the condition of the workers. David Dale had refused to take on any partner who objected to his church steeple—for if they did not see eye to eye on that, they would agree in nothing else. David Dale had been, though superior to the average cotton lord, much absent, far too busy riding from church to church. Robert Owen purchased, in company with his partners, the New Lanark cotton mill.

It was a strange ceremony, involving bride, church steeple, and mill, when in the Charlotte Street mansion in Glasgow, September, 1799, Caroline Dale, daughter of an Old Scots fundamentalist, became the wife of Robert Owen, Unitarian and perhaps atheist. David Dale united the two. To this unbeliever, who was now in possession of his mill, his church steeple, and his daughter, he said, "Thou needest be very right, for thou art very positive." It was his first and final word of warning.

On their wedding journey, as they passed a thatched cottage where chickens scratched at the door, Robert Owen informed his bride that he was taking her to a place like this. For there would be no ghostly powers in the world to come. Caroline was relieved when their carriage stopped at Greenheys—the house planned by the elder De Quincey, who had not lived to see the last nail driven. There were ivory cherubim, who might have been billiard balls, chasing velvet butterflies down endless corridors—and in a small office, among mortality rates, Robert Owen lived. Caroline thought much of the disappointed builder, the elder De Quincey. At idyllic Greenheys, they spent their honeymoon, discussing the erection of a new moral world from which society's unhappiness would have been removed forever. To be consistent with his objective, Robert Owen said, they must go to New Lanark. Mere theorists were clouds without water, carried about by every wind, trees without fruit. The word without the act was nothing.

In January, down a bleak road over the Scottish moors, an unpopulous district, where the gorse stood out like dead men's bones, they came to New Lanark, and the spacious Braxfield, a house blackened by clouds and whitened by snow. This house, of which the interior was becomingly appointed, had been built by none other than the murderous Lord Braxfield, the "laughing hangman." Robert Louis Stevenson depicts him in the mad character of Weir of Hermiston. The "laughing hangman," the king's servant, had sentenced every petty culprit, every pilferer of ribbon, every pilferer of fallen twigs, to be hanged by the neck until dead—and the more corpses there were, the merrier was he. As for the former hostess, Lady Braxfield, Mrs. Weir, although her husband was a rotund murderer, and disdainful of all nature less coarse than his own, she had put on the texts of her divinity in the morning with her clothes, as a kind of protection against the ways of Cain in Abel's garden. Braxfield was destined now to be the scene of even greater cosmic and domestic rifts than these. Where formerly a skeleton had dangled from every tree would be effected a program for the regeneration of the human race, but in the flesh.

It was not necessary that Robert Owen be eye witness even to the visible sorrow, the "gruesome" sight of children filing through the mill gates at gray dawn, with their cold coffee mugs clutched in their hands like bird claws. He might have dwelled at a safe distance from the tragic mills. Immediately, he declared his needs, however—before he could take his hat off, he would have to have five hundred bathtubs, toilet facilities for a large population, many beds, ample bedding, a chair at every machine, and all the externals necessary for the improvement of an environment.

He would demonstrate visibly, he said, the connection between universal happiness and practical mechanics. He would erect immediately a cosmos to rival the flickering light on Mt. Sinai. He would show that man is the best of all possible machineries, a being responsive to the best care. Human confusion seemed to him not necessary in the nature of things—nor death a fountain of youth, from which the dying man rises as a golden dove covered with silver paint. He would believe no more than what his eye could see. Reality of the fact that the enslavement of the masses was accepted by the cheerless, cheerful manufacturers, as a principle handed down from the garden of Eden. Reality of the fact that the cotton mills were receptacles for living human skeletons, almost disrobed of intellect, where, as the business was now conducted, they lingered out a few years of miserable existence, acquiring every bad habit which could be disseminated throughout the body of society. The united cotton lords, although perhaps divided on every other subject, were busily signing the death warrant of the strength, morals, and happiness of an entire population, including themselves. Christian justice had been strangely blind and deaf, allured by harpers harping on a sea of glass, and other nonexistent items, to ignore the suppression of a large percentage of human beings forever. It was an old story.

New Lanark was to be conducted on humanitarian principles only. From the beginning, Robert Owen used the word "government" instead of "management," as he had no wish to be enthroned himself, being in the act of disenthroning all despotic powers. His partners, fortunately, seemed interested in that all-engrossing topic, profit. As long as the golden tides came in, they were willing, apparently, to give free reign to his imagination. If he liked, he could visualize the world upside down and the North Pole at the South—while the *status quo* was not disturbed, of course.

Robert Owen had, however, to overcome the distrust of the workers themselves. Why should they have faith in the promises of any cotton lord? They felt that they were being destroyed in the race for power. As change had disrupted their lives previously, they were suspicious of change. They were without hope of any improvement, in fact, but the second Coming of One, Jesus Christ, the King of Kings, Who would take into His arms the maimed, the halt, the blind, the desecrated, even the drunk. Because they had been forced by terrible circumstance, because they had not meant to be what they were, because they would have been themselves in a greener valley. There were, in all, two thousand souls at New Lanark—to the world, Robert Owen said, nothing but indentured paupers, deserving of the whip, to themselves, the last of Scottish pride, the last of the old Border warriors. Some, as immigrants from the Isle of Skye, had survived shipwreck, only to be confronted by death-in-life. Almost all were suffering from those characteristics which usually attend extreme poverty and despair of any good. To their enemy, they seemed their own worst enemies, deserving of extinction—yea, suicidal.

Robert Owen wrote, for the New Lanark community, a constitution to guarantee life, liberty, and the pursuit of happiness to all. They should think charitably of their neighbors regarding differences of creeds and opinions. Argument, drawn from the pages of Robert Burns, a drunk with a vision, "A man's a man for a' that"—and the wee, sleekit, trembling field mouse is the glory of God.

Robert Owen sought out the leaders among the workers and explained his plans to them. Gradually, step by step, he was able to enlist their cooperation and confidence in his motives. When he came, the village was like a pigsty, the streets muddy, dunghills piled in front of every lowbrowed door, parts of buildings torn away. He instituted first of all a cleanup program. The streets were paved, the dunghills removed, and doors provided where the old ones had been used as firewood. Every night, watchmen walked the streets, reporting those who were drunk or disorderly. As bathtubs had been installed, all were urged to bathe at least once a week—for cleanliness is next to godliness, though this is not always the case. A committee performed a weekly inspection of houses—in spite of the loud lamentations of women who objected to the prying eyes of "bug hunters," as they were called, and washing their dirty linen in public. There were other disciplines. Children were not to be beaten—the prying eyes of "bug hunters," who knew no reticence, inspected these along with pots, pans, and sheets. The greatest catch on the marriage market, throughout the British industrial kingdom at that date, was a widow with a brood of children. With as many children as he could get into his clutches and their income from the mills, a man could take a little swig to forget his sorrows, could drink himself to death if necessary. At New Lanark, both lovelorn adventurers and pigs were ejected from the widow's parlor. Here, if nowhere else, the old pub was about to be boarded up, about to be covered over with vines. A constructive employment was found for all adults. Infants were purchased from their parents, at the salary they had had before—and turned loose into a meadow. Not even Rome was built in a single day, however, and for a while the population seemed, in spite of many changes, to persist unchanged—big heads, stooped shoulders, pendulous stomachs, spindle legs, dim eyesight, and a general inclination to die before the age of forty. But only for a while.

A curious device was used to encourage co-operation at New Lanark—no passage underground nor maze, but it achieved a good result. A block of wood was hung in front of every worker at his machine, each side a different color, which would announce what had been his conduct during the previous day. Black was bad, blue was average, yellow was good, white was excellent. Each department kept a book of character, the books changing six times a year, but permanently preserved in the company archives. The act of setting down the number of color in the book of character, never to be effaced, might be likened, Robert Owen said, to the supposed recording angel marking the good and bad deeds of the poor, disparaged human nature, which was, however, the subject of neither praise nor blame. As time went on, the black and blue gave place to yellow and white—for the character of the people of New Lanark had improved, visibly. There was, according to one report, "a gradual evolution of his [Robert Owen's] wooden flowers, from the Satanic to the angelic hue."

To suspend wooden blocks by wire threads was harmless and might contribute to the flow of their profit, the partners believed. To reduce working hours from thirteen to ten and three-fourths, when the average mill day was seventeen hours, and to increase wages above any high water mark ever heard of, seemed both paradoxical and dangerous. The partners, Lancashire men, presented their junior member with a silver salver, in recognition of a return on their investment, but suggested that he give up his many charities. Two or three years, and Robert Owen purchased the mill, with Scottish associates whom he believed to be friendly to the cause of labor. They showed themselves to be less generous than their predecessors. They objected to the liberal scale of wages, shortened hours of labor, schoolrooms, bathtubs, and other airy projects as yet unrealized by this pale Don Quixote. Perhaps their suspicions reflected the disruptions caused by that great challenger to the *status quo*, Napoleon. The old order seemed threatened—and in their terror, the partners did not know but that there might be some charmed value in the most insignificant thing, such as a silver spoon or salver. Should all the scattered forces be united, what would become of England and the old way of life?

Ireland had always been a bone of contention, for example, but profitable to English interests. Because of the everlasting quarrel between Irish Catholics and Irish Protestants, internal unification had been impossible. In 1798, these bodies had coalesced, in a movement of rebellion against the English. The argument as to the nature of Jesus Christ's body soon reasserting itself, Catholic and Protestant betrayed each other. Lord Edward Fitzgerald, disguised as a woman, was betrayed by a perceptive woman named Reynolds. Such Irish extravagances had contributed to English national welfare. With Ireland ready to join France, England would have been open to invasion.

Napoleon, the dark angel, had risen from the flood. The suppressed elements were now emerging, with the result of a perpetual chaos. In 1805, the redoubtable Mr. Pitt, in alliance with the deity, was made Secretary of War, to pursue Napoleon by land and sea, wherever he should have the temerity to show himself. Soon the poker-faced Beelzebub, the Prince of Darkness, appeared at the dinner table of the poor Queen of Württemberg, daughter of George III of England. She had to seem, in spite of herself, a charming hostess. She complained that he was not so much Beelzebub, a fallen angel, as an indigenous devil. A mad dog! Though mad George III barked like a dog at Windsor, it was said that Napoleon was the mad dog loose in Europe. Near Cairo, he had gained the battle of the Pyramids, where Pharaohs slept through it all, and was always storming empty citadels, and caused much suffering, and left not even a blade of grass in parts of Germany. He knew no bounds. He had exalted himself to be emperor of a new Roman Empire and king of kings—at a

magnificent ceremony, had placed upon his head a wreath of
hammered laurel leaves, while the poor Pope of the True Church
had had no function but to be a spectator. This seemed, to the
Protestant English, the last insolence, the last straw.

As Napoleon's armies, ever on the march, surrounded many
a sultan, many a king in Europe, George III continued to whine
like an old dog kenneled at Windsor, for perhaps the dog was
harassed by fleas, as he by spirits. Mr. Pitt's war cry, "King,
Church, and Constitution," was heard in every drawing room
in England. Civilization was at stake. Mr. Pitt, apologist for
Malthus, died within a year of Napoleon's triumph at Austerlitz,
as did Mr. Fox, his great rival, who had embraced the principles
of Rousseau. It was necessary to change horses in the middle
of the stream. Two new men were soon in harness, and both
allied to the gilded carriage of the gilded past—the able Lord
Castlereagh as War Minister, the able Mr. Canning as Secretary
of Foreign Affairs.

The war progressed, disastrously, our world affording more
material for Dante's Hell than for Dante's Heaven.

Napoleon, having in mind an heir to his mortal glory, abandoned Josephine, who was sterile and loved him, in favor of Marie
Louise—and his seed assured in futurity, was off to Moscow,
where he was greeted by tongues of fire and every rooftop ablaze.
Impossible to stay there. Through blinding snowstorms, dogged
by Cossacks, Napoleon's armies retreated from Russia—an entire
regiment was devoured by red-eyed wolves. Prussia, encouraged
by Russian victory, rose to its feet, and France was tired of wars.
Napoleon's power seemed broken, at last. Napoleon was dis-
patched to Elba, there to live as the most illusory despot surrounded by stars like golden pomegranates—there to imagine
what worlds he pleased.

The new map of Europe was being drawn, to maintain what
was called the balance of power—and France was sending back

to their owners the marble statues which Napoleon had carried off with him—when full in the midst, like a thunderbolt out of the blue, came the news that the little Emperor was landed on the French coast, and was rallying his old legions around him.

The war, with all its inconveniences, was not over—the celebration, a bit premature.

While King George accompanied the music of the spheres, Europe was made once more a charnal house. Twenty-six workers in the arsenal at Woolwich combined their resources, such as they had never had in peacetime, to purchase equal shares in a bull and a cow. This was a notable attempt at socialism, perhaps the very beginning of the British labor movement. Otherwise, industries other than munitions being closed, the workers were starving acutely. Lord Castlereagh worked fourteen hours a day to win not only the foreign war but the war against the workers at home.

The nation prospered, and victory came. When the Duke of Wellington's news of victory at Waterloo was sent, it was couched in such shy, hesitant, unboastful language, composite clubmen were stunned into silence—believing it was "Noney" who had won the day. Wellington having been ascertained, however, the victor, he was showered with massive pearls—it being enough to make the head swim when one considers the contribution of oysters to this world's progress. The ladies of England sent him a bronze statue of Achilles without the large heel.

Apparently, Robert Owen's was a much smaller concern than either Napoleon's or Wellington's—for what duller than, during the great struggle of deadlocked powers, to be shut inside a model mill town or lecture to empty halls? Even George III, on whom the outer world could make but little impression, for he was his own harassed star, seemed less remote from reality than this manufacturer of durable cloth and moth-eaten philosophies of human progress.

When his second set of partners attempted to destroy the constructive program at New Lanark, and to return the mills to serfdom, Robert Owen offered to purchase the property. They refused to sell—partly because they knew a rich vein, partly because they believed him to be Napoleon's partner. Robert Owen, as he could make no compromise, was forced to resign. Immediately, he drew up plans for the further development of his schemes at New Lanark and its purlieus, the surrounding earth, as if, most sinister thought, he intended to return. The years 1813–14, he spent in London—urging, in the middle of a war-torn world, the complete reorganization of society, in all the business and pleasure of life. For the moment, it is enough to say that he succeeded in interesting new investors, a flock of pacific Quakers, and not one money-worshiper in the lot—William Allen, John Walker, Joseph Fox, Joseph Foster—and Michael Gibbs, who was to become lord mayor of London. Jeremy Bentham was a silent, perhaps sardonic partner.

During Robert Owen's absence in London, the partners at New Lanark had spread abroad a vicious rumor that the New Lanark mills were gone to rack and ruin, so far as profit was concerned—for such had been his quixotic management, sacrificing business to loutish human nature. By this device, they hoped to buy the property in at half its value, when they should then be in a position to take the chairs away from the workers and to fill the schoolroom with bolts of cotton. They had already arranged a dinner party at which to celebrate Robert Owen's defeat. The persistence of Robert Owen's bidders, however, resulted in victory—the partners giving up at $650,000.

Great was the rejoicing, throughout that countryside, when first word came that Robert Owen was to continue his good work at New Lanark. All people awaited, in fact, the second coming of one, Robert Owen, who would have his crown of diamonds in heaven above—or at least his reward. According to the account in a Glasgow newspaper, the Society of Free Masons, and almost all townspeople, met him in the burgh of Old Lanark, where nearly every house was lighted with a candle at the window, as on Christmas Eve. The people took the horses from his carriage and, a flag being draped in front, drew him and his astonished Quaker partners along, amid the wild plaudits of multitudes, until they reached his house at Braxfield, where his lady, dearest Caroline, awaited him with her accustomed smile. Robert Owen, when he spoke, objected that the workers had tried to harness themselves to his carriage—the workers of the world had been treated like horses long enough, he announced. For days, the report continues, there was animation at New Lanark—the one mill town where machinery had been employed for the benefit of the laborer as well as the investor, the one mill town where had been adopted a positive view of human life, its origin and destiny.

Dearest Caroline had all she desired. Her Robert was a good man, and if he would but walk in the straight and narrow way of God, which was indeed a maze with harmony at its center, then her happiness would have been a cup full and overflowing, both loaf of bread and rose of Sharon, both heaven and earth. She found herself in dangerous straits between the Devil and the deep blue sea, in view of her creed as a Calvinist and her love of that godless man, Robert Owen.

Dearest Caroline

How small, of all that human hearts endure,
That part which kings alone can kill or cure!

—OLIVER GOLDSMITH

There was, for all its well-managed quietude, no real harmony in Caroline's house, but a cosmic schism, dividing heaven from hell, herself from her husband. Dearest Caroline! She would have understood the Fool of Nature, the lamentations of the Pears family, and that happiness which was never happiness anywhere, not even in sad New Harmony. She could have prophesied the whole thing, the dissolution. Indeed, she did not object to a new moral world—but what mere human could create it, permanently, or even for a few precarious hours? The corruption of a body might well be only its movement toward divinity.

It was good that cattle, swine, poultry, and dogs should be expelled from the houses of New Lanark. It was good that human pigs should sleep no longer in the widow's parlor. These were practical, needed reforms. Yet could any act of Parliament cure all the evils the flesh is heir to? Old Jamie would still be blind as a bat, Caroline thought. Old Saul would still be toothless. No

man could remove the bandages veiling even her own bright
eyes, which detected every speck of dust. How could poor man
determine the course of natural events, if such events made up, as
her husband believed, the great part of his character? As well ask
the blind to lead the blind. They would both fall into the ditch,
like a drunk poet riding on a wild horse. Far from believing that
all men were endowed the same, Caroline affirmed that each
had his peculiar gift, one after this manner, and another after
that. Thieves, atheists, and whoremongers should not come into
God's kingdom, unless they be born again, and supernaturally.
Oh, how sacrilegious to assume that man should not survive the
complete annihilation of his body. "What? know ye not that your
body is the temple of the Holy Ghost which is in you, which
ye have of God, and ye are not your own?" French atheists and
English freethinkers had taught a godless dogma which would
wither every field, blast every oak, every blossom. There would
be nothing but an infinite desolation. Caroline tread carefully,
as if she were gathering her skirts in a thorny bypath—for there
was danger that she might lose her way in the midst of so much
natural, unnatural philosophy.

Caroline would agree—threading her needle, with one eye
on the punctual clock—that the New Lanark system should be
extended, perhaps discreetly, and at the behest of the owners, to
other cotton mills. She had heard, with her husband, the reports
of unbiased surgeons, as to the mutilations, murders, midnight
burials in cotton towns. She was not heartless. No one despised,
more than she did, the race for power. She could not agree, however, that sin may be attributed to the effect of institutions only.
All sin had its origin in the individual heart, each man being born
into this world as a poor, erroneous being, the inheritor of the
sins of his fathers. There had been no progress but toward decay.

If New Lanark was the microcosm in which her husband
saw the pattern of the cosmos, yet did it not confirm that man

was fallen? There were many Beelzebubs, numerous as lice on a
dead horse. From such a dual nature as man's, it was impossible
to predict a completely decent behavior. If human nature was
basically good, as her husband believed, why had not the rational
situation existed from the beginning, without his help? It was
late in the world's history to begin the world's reform. There was
not much time left.

Life would escape machineries, as Caroline had, merely with
a smile, a turning through the door. The definition of human
nature was inadequate to account for reality. Surely, the one truth
of truths was God, keeping a book of character on every human
soul—listing who was clean, who was loathsome, who was Mary,
who was Martha, who was capable, who dawdled at his work, who
was glutted with pleasure, who crushed a toad with his shovel,
who watered her garden with tears. None could open that book
but the Lion of the Tribe of Judah—a heavy volume, indeed,
where every dry hiccuping sob, every gesture of the soul would
be recorded, in the entire history of all peoples, no matter what
zone they lived in. On the last day, a judgment should be made. So
that, when the scroll of the skies was unfolded, blind Jamie might
have immaculate vision—for worthy is the lamb that was slain
to receive power and ineffable riches.

Caroline was grateful to her Maker, who was somehow
involved, though she scarcely realized it, with the slate roof over
Braxfield, her chipped straw bonnet, her garden shears, her dairy
house, her jars of pearl-sized onions, her thread mits, her clean
linen, her fruit wall where little green pears came to maturity
each harsh October, her apple dumplings, the continuity of her
race. The Lord had given to her a flock of handsome children,
whom it was her duty to convoy as nearly straight to heaven as
she could. Her humility was immeasurable, like her pride. She was
no better than her cook in her kitchen, who might be, she realized,
stars and stars above her, and at some date in the near future, too.

Both her husband and her father had started at the bottom of the social ladder—but a more important ladder was Jacob's, which one climbed without reference to class or condition. Meanwhile, was there not a lesson to be learned from battling insecurity? The fact of a black silk dress did not signify security. So long as spiders caught flies in their webs, or until the spirit was caught up among the clouds, there could be no expulsion of sorrow from the earth. The tragic spirit seemed to Caroline a thing most fine, most needful to progress—for without it, what would there be but blank faces, nasal slumbers, sheepdogs, hobnailed routine, damp earth, graceless graces, old bones, old rags? If her husband's system could produce so much happiness with so little care, yet the adoption of it would make man a race of beings but little removed from the brute creation, shut behind ramparts whom God could not bombard with memory or love. The poet Pope, though mistaken about most things, had written that man envies the polar bear his fur but is only a little lower than the angels— caught on the isthmus of this middle state, ever betwixt and between. No Christian, with thirst unassuageable, could wish for a well of dust—nor for that supposedly rational order when men would be as bears, and angels nonexistent items or exploded, along with a devoted conscience, tasks taken up and willingly performed, a sense of interior dignity, a shrine of honor, many recollections, many pots of mignonette, many jars of honey, the aura of human personality. Even a withered hand.

Was there not an innate knowledge upon which to rely—a consent naturally imprinted, perhaps before birth, to show man the difference between good and evil? Was not God the giver of moral laws, which it was within the power of every individual to apprehend, though whole nations should choose to ignore them? Was there no difference, Caroline asked, between herself and a cannibal, except a difference between the circumstances in which they had been placed from birth? For so her husband assured her, even when she was stepping forth to church with her beaming children, and all her antennae out to catch the Spirit of the Lord where He rode on the wind, and her prayer book in her hand. Yet would she not always, on the loneliest isthmus, have apprehended the earnest truth? How could she have eaten, under any circumstance whatever, the flesh of her own kind—be the graveyard of those she loved, as her husband seemed to think? From his point of view, to preserve the past was the nature of much religion—but Caroline had only the future in mind, that it should not be empty.

Usually, Caroline preferred not to speculate on remote possibilities. She was far too busy to indulge in the luxury of thought. She had little or no interest in the trackless sea, the clammy mist, the chunks of ultimate world stuff, the science of society. Any wilderness, even the deserts of Egypt, about which she had read so much in Christian history, would have been repugnant to a woman of her Christian tastes and interests. Although the poet Pope had praised the happy life in American caves, he had ridden in a curtained sedan through the streets of London, and had been a great frequenter of coffeehouses. To Caroline, Pope's employment of graceful words to describe such a graceless life in caves, which he himself could not have endured, for he had hardly the courage of a rabbit, was sinful. Oh, what a stumbling block was Pope in his brother's path, and what a sentimental creature was Rousseau, in all probability not dry behind the ears, and with no more brain than if he had been knee-high to a grasshopper.

Caroline was, of course, not only busy, but tactful—a woman who spoke rarely except between stitches, and whose comments were always mild—"God so loved the world that He gave His only begotten Son," or "What shall we do for our little sister, in the hour when she shall be spoken for?" She could convey almost all her thoughts, even as to the most practical matters, by Biblical quotations—"She bringeth butter in a goodly dish." Oh, and she had a purple distaff. She desired only that her husband confine his interests to New Lanark, which was achievement enough for one lifetime. She preferred, as a fact which she could adorn with a wealth of proverbs, her own house to any model community whatever, this side the New Jerusalem, where there should enter no abomination or lie. All else was vulnerable. She would not give her thimble for a parochial farm in Kent, figuratively speaking, or a spoon for a house of industry on the Isle of Wight. She had so little to give. It would not improve the situation of all mankind if she left Braxfield and scattered joys which only she attributed value to, the small pears, the hedges, a tuft of withered primroses at the foot of a sunken marble slab in the old churchyard, a piece of ribbon, a fallen twig. Most Utopias could be found, not in the pages of nature, but in the pages of fiction, where they were still far from satisfactory, and quite as vacuous as the writer's mind. Better to dwell in a temple not made by human hands, not of this creation! As for herself, any Utopia would have been out of the question, no matter how exalted the goal, if it did not include the past, clean sheets, and moth balls.

Caroline told her children that death provided the only translation possible to a better life than this. Only by going beyond the purlieus of earth itself could they arrive at a perfection which would not be a type of imperfection, a type of loss. She told them that their teeth would drop out of their heads and they would become skeletons, barren as barren trees in a bleak wind. God, therefore, must be the subject of their utmost devotion—all other love, such as that of man for man, being a poor substitute. Without God, the farmer plows under his own heart, time and again. Without God, this life is a meaningless fluctuation, a long torture. They must worship the unseen power of powers, a man with a long white beard, who sat on a great throne high up in the sky, above blackbirds, above everything. God, thus circumstanced, knew every catastrophe long before it happened—as when Robert Dale, her eldest, had hit his nurse over the head

with a broomstick, quite by accident. Wherever they went, each
was accompanied by his recording angel, born into this world
with him, and who could ascend through the false ceiling of
heaven, in the twinkling of an eye, to make his report to God,
their true father. Every word was written in a little golden book
with perhaps a silver pencil. When Robert Dale had quarreled
with that carrot-colored errand boy, this fact had caused the
weeping of angels. Sin must be considered as not in the great
thing only, but in the small, like an oath upon the lips of the
shepherd at the sheep washing. If old Gavin had not sworn,
Napoleon might not have risen in Europe—for guilt cannot be
blamed on only the war lords of this world, all men being mortal.

Her husband's plea was for no domestic hearth, cut off from
the fate of the human race, but for the united family of mankind.
Caroline remained quietly unconvinced, solicitous of her own
brood, and fearful of the impression which rationalism might
make on their tender minds. Loyal as she was to her husband,
she undermined him. She pointed to the iron foundry over the
river and said it was like hell. A spear of distant grass, jeweled
with dew in sunlight, was like heaven, but seen through a mist
of tears. Good people were those who believed in the Bible, word
for word. They did not seek to overthrow the established order or
draw down the powder of stars from the heavens. They obeyed
God and their parents, implicitly. They were kind to their ponies,
the knife grinder, the chambermaid, and nature. They looked
upon their French dancing master with suspicion, as he had
long hair, revolutionary ideas, and a feeble ambition to marry
Caroline's little sister, somewhat above him in rank and station.
Caroline held, in fact, to her doctrine of innate differences—as
between men and angels, men and men, men and beasts—even
in the house of universal love.

The present system, Robert Owen believed to be the co-operation of institutions with mysteries—the result being that earth

was a pandemonium, such as could not be much longer supported by any man in his senses. The present system, Caroline
accepted as unfortunate but inevitable, this side of heaven, when
all men should be carried out of their senses. The little Owens
enjoyed, however, a fairly happy childhood. Prayers, catechism,
and atheism were taken for granted, like the old postman who
brought the mail. Mother was going to heaven, where there were
pressed rose leaves and fallen sparrows—and Father was going
to hell, which would be a great factory with clocks and wheels.
Now both seemed to be in the same house, Father at the head of
the table and Mother at the foot.

The little Owens played at hawk and hounds, archery, war,
and conquest, matching the strength of Hector with that of Ajax.
They chased their ball across the meadow, found harbors for
their ships in a grove of locusts under the bulging wind, rode on
lively ponies through the parks at Braxfield and Rosebanks, the
adjoining estate of David Dale. Braxfield, with its silvery fir trees
on a knob against the sky, its view of civil river and hills, drone of
honey bees, irruption of sheep, phantom horse hoofs which told
that the horse, if not the rider, that old Border warrior, was ever
on the homeward way. Rosebanks, with sunk area surrounding
it like a moat, sundial, a wilderness of roses, a bowling green like
velvet, graveyard, kirk, and ivy-clad mansion. The little Owens'
lives were like a series of illustrations in a fine old book. History,
their French dancing master told them, had always waltzed most
beautifully, from century to century, in a room lined with mirrors. God, he told them, had wept one perfect tear, the earth. It
would take a lifetime to learn a perfect step of the great waltz.
Under their mother's supervision, and their dancing master's, the
little Owens hardly suspected the existence of rival saviors. They
were as indifferent to rationalism as to the fate of the Russian
fleet, which could find no outlet except through the Arctic sea,
frozen half of every year. However, they were but little children.

It was Robert Dale, the eldest son, who first commented on the difference of vision in the Owen household—his father, a geographer, and his mother, a lover of God. God, he announced, was not obliged to create a man who was sure to be an unbeliever, and by not creating him could have prevented him from being wicked and from going to hell. God, therefore, should never have created his father, if he intended for him to be a sinner, and should never have created outlandish nations, such as seal-eating Eskimos, whom no bells ring to church. Caroline retired from the room in tears. She had always considered Robert Dale the most devout of all her children, the most thoughtful for the welfare of his immortal soul. As indeed he was. But she could not have guessed then that he would one day recall her from the bright regions of the upper world, that as a spiritual being she would convey, in the drawing room of a Neapolitan despot, by a series of raps, what oath old Gavin had enunciated at sheep washing. For who but herself, though dead, would remember this, across the years? Or that, when she was dead, her invisible spirit hands would move a silver pencil on the pages of a golden book mid-air—telling what she thought of an impending war between the American states. Caroline would not have liked that naughty performance, either.

Caroline was a good, Christian woman, as democratic toward her superiors as toward her inferiors. She entertained distinguished guests as if they were nobody in particular, was unimpressed by the most fabulous. She probably would have held even Gabriel in some suspicion, had he appeared visibly before her in her drawing room—all things visible being, as she knew, corruptible. "For the mystery of iniquity doth already work. . . ."

For example, there was Nicholas, Grand Duke of Russia, when, according to the report of Robert Dale, there was no indication that he would become the stern autocrat of his later years and reviver of mass capital punishment. He was, at this period of his youth, a mystic who wished not to destroy, but to create anew the human race. With marked attention, for he was acting as his mother's agent, he listened two solid hours to Robert Owen's plan for the formulation of a new moral world, from which all crime and all punishment would have been removed. He was struck by the deepest emotions. Alluding to the Malthusian theory that Great Britain, due to the multiplication of its reforms and reformers, was likely to be overpopulated, he urged that Robert Owen come with thousands of workers to Russia, an empty land. Russia, the Grand Duke said, needed only an influx of skilled populations to convert it into a literal paradise on earth, where spades, not men, would hang from trees. When this offer was rejected, as Robert Owen believed it impossible to carry on regeneration in collaboration with the Russian Orthodox Church, the Grand Duke begged that he might take an Owen boy, preferably David, who would be reared as a member of his court, with every advantage of the royal household, including a hobnailed crown. An offer which Caroline rejected, smiling.

The Grand Duke was a mystic, a primitivist, a sentimentalist, and something of a rationalist. He adored the simple life of peasants in mud houses, sheepshearing, horseshoeing, and such poetic activities for the exercise of his soul. His diet was cheese, of a certain sourness, and black bread, of a certain coarseness. He would have preferred rags in lieu of riches, had anyone asked him to choose the manner and place of his birth. As a child, it had been his greatest delight to play with the children of peasants in the royal stables. Caroline, if she had not been a lady, would have snorted. She mistrusted this Grand Duke and his smallpocked crew, to the extent that she was watchful of her silverware. He was a man capable, she believed, of any crime, from the smallest to the greatest. In the room which she had provided, with her own hands, he ignored the pleasant bed smelling of camphor and cleanliness, and slept on a dirty leather mattress stuffed with hay. This was not simplicity—it was affectation and deserved a

horsewhip. Outside his door, what was worse insult, he caused
a servant to stand guard, for fear of an assassin, as if he were not
at Braxfield, in civilized Scotland, but in some horrible den of
gross Tartars. A man who expected murder could well commit it,
according to Caroline's view of logic—and she was no logician,
as she knew. She was sorry to see her husband deceived by fine
visions, the beautiful philosophy to be maintained among archaic
brass founders, forgers, turners in wood and iron, an earthly
paradise in Russia, of all the forsaken places. More likely, Russia
would be the pit of hell. She was even sorrier when Robert Owen
handed over to the Grand Duke her most cherished silver dessert
set, as their crest was the double eagle of the Russian family. A
mere coincidence, she felt, and had no significance whatever. The
Owen butler cried when he had to part with it.

For a long time, incidentally, a memorial of the Grand Duke's
conversations with Robert Owen was preserved in the Russian
archives. Much was said of the materialism of the social order,
man as a machine, the new moral world, perfectibility—but not
a word as to the lady and her spoons.

However, she kept her peace unusually well, this dearest
Caroline—in spite of slight discrepancies, slight flaws in the
universe, let alone the heart of the best of men. She was agreeable and composed, a charming hostess, although she had begun
to suspect herself of an inner malignancy, which might spread,
as hers was a frail tenement, indeed, a house of clay. The older
she grew, the sadder and wiser she became, as she told herself.
Hearing of the duration of eternity, she clipped the dead rose pet-
als from the bush at her window, and thought of her hair which
was turning gray. She smiled when she heard of the princess who
had furnished her house with ten thousand yards of silk for the
relief of silk weavers—and scarcely changed her expression upon
mention of that harmonious adjustment of proportions which is
the secret of society's happiness—a large order, indeed.

An Eden of Children

While George III accompanied the music of the spheres on the harpsichord, as a diversion from metaphysical farming, and millions of others faced worse than imaginary death, Robert Owen conducted, at New Lanark, his infant school, to demonstrate the possibilities of a rational happiness. Twenty years of his life were thus spent. Education, he said, is the primary source of all the good and evil, misery and happiness, which exist in the world. The infant school at New Lanark he considered but the first step of a great program to accustom man to a better environment.

With his view, he could belong to no party, because in many ways he was opposed to all. He cared not, he said, for the miracles which have been performed in a dark corner of the earth—visitations by saints, ghostly edifices, negations of reality, destruction of the many for the sake of the few, destruction of the few for the sake of nothing. He could not recognize, even indirectly, that a dissertation concerning Pharaoh and his host had any bearing on his subject. He was unimpressed by the fact that Moses was born more than one thousand years before Pythagoras, Parmenides, Solon, Socrates, Plato, Xenophon, Zeno, or Seneca. The truth he considered to be always consistent with itself and every other truth in the universe. So long as a particular tribe of men should be permitted to impress upon society their own peculiar notions, without any right of reply, there was no belief, however monstrous, which might not be forced upon artfully degraded minds. An engine had pressed them down into the lowest depths of ignorance, for the express purpose that they should receive impressions convenient to their masters. Man had been beguiled from his true welfare by a concern with centaurs, griffins, the funeral rites of the Egyptians, the art of embalming, the glory of resurrection day, none of which had ever made the slightest improvement in his real condition or circumstance. Why manufacture such difficulties?

A government founded on the correct principles will attend, Robert Owen said, solely to the improvement and happiness of those governed. Its first inquiry will be the study of human nature. These are the things necessary for human happiness: the possession of a good organization, physical, mental, and moral; the power to produce whatever is necessary for the best state of health; and an education which shall cultivate, from infancy to maturity, the physical, intellectual, and moral powers of all the population; the means of enjoying the best society we know, the means of traveling at pleasure; a release from superstition, from supernatural fears, and from the fear of death; and lastly, to live in a society in which all its laws, institutions, and arrangements shall be in accordance with the requirements of human nature, well organized and well governed. All men will be on a perfect equality from birth to death. No individual will receive reward or punishment in this life or the next. No one will be condemned for any opinion, notion, or faith whatever, as man cannot be held responsible for his sensations. There is but one universe, for the division of which into two worlds, spiritual and material, good and evil, there is no ground whatever. There is but one human nature, for the division of which into races and creeds and classes there is no ground whatever. Man is not a rigid but a plastic material. The differences observable among the Quaker, Jew, and Indian, for example, arise solely from the differences in their external circumstances. Were we to take the infants of the Jews and give them to be brought up by Indians, they would make good Indians. Were we to take the infants of the Quakers and give them to be brought up by Jews, they would make good Jews. Similarly, a child may be brought up without reference to any race or religion whatever.

Hitherto, the book of nature had been sealed, but Robert Owen proposed to open it at New Lanark, for all the world to read. There was but one purpose—that children should be happy, and from this original goodness all other good would follow. Robert Owen had no fear that for man to be a happy animal would be to deny half his nature, no fear that he could not cast out the indescribable spirits which are said to haunt the regions of the human cranium. He attached no importance to the spiritual joys in a New Jerusalem, when tired soldiers should come to an unfading heritage in the presence of God, with the society of angels, principalities, and powers. Everything fabulous would be omitted, for the sake of the development of the human body in health and goodness. Nothing should enter which would contradict the nature of man.

The curriculum at New Lanark was that which would guarantee freedom of motion to the young. All were to learn of their own nature, through direct experience with the objects around them—birds, brooks, flowers, stones, trees. The younger children, as soon as they were able, received instructions in dancing, singing and play. The older children were set to learn the wheelwright's art, blacksmithing, mechanics, and other useful trades, but with great dignity, for in the world to come there would be no superiority assumed by students of Greek, Latin, and other mysterious tongues. All were to be educated, in fact, for the millennial state of existence on earth, when the King of England should have become what he now merely imagined himself to be, a farmer—and Parliament should be rational.

Visitors at New Lanark found it difficult to realize, even within its gates, that what they beheld was only a school for mill children, surely a defective material. How had Robert Owen managed to achieve this miracle of a new human nature—a thing outshining even wizened aristocrats? Here the children, in denial of the experience elsewhere, were happy animals, roaming graceful and free—like little lambs at play, and every babe wore heaven's dew. There were no quarrels, no cryings. The children were always at ease, their muscles excellently co-ordinated—and what a contrast between these and their older brothers and sisters, the heavy-headed, the pot-bellied, the bird-legged. They seemed unconscious of themselves. They exhibited no fear. They were unabashed by dukes and princes. It was as if a charm had veiled them from the savagery of nature. They, who should die young, according to the edict long ago handed down, or at least according to the present practice, were not only saved for posterity, but saved with clear eyes, round cheeks, dimples, laughter. Yet not one was insolent. They wore, at dancing, a costume of white cotton, in the style of a tunic, knee-length for boys, ankle-length for girls. They had three fresh changes a week. They were so clean, they smelled like rosebuds after a rain, according to the report which has come down. The Duke of Kent's physician, Dr. Grey MacNab, smelled them, one by one, and turned them around, and inspected them from head to foot, methodically. Never, he declared, had he witnessed so much happiness on earth as at New Lanark, where he had found that "nature unadorned is most adorned"—it would take "the pen of a Milton, the pencil of a Rubens" to describe this Eden of Children, a Paradise of Babes and Sucklings, a Paradise Regained.

The school building at New Lanark was a pleasant place, large, light, and airy—an improvement over the best schools of that

day. The classroom walls were decorated becomingly with representations of zoological and mineralogical specimens—quad-
rupeds, birds, fishes, reptiles, insects, many rocks, many shells.
There was a map of the world, each country a different color,
and rational, when papery tariff walls should have broken down
and when Russia should have found an outlet through the Arctic
sea, presumably.

An old admiral, who had sailed around the globe many times,
confessed that any six-year-old at New Lanark could triumph
over him in pointing out, with a ruler, the most obscure countries, and relating strange customs and beliefs. He was impressed,
too, by the children's adeptness in pointing out the ages represented on a much larger map, the Stream of Time. Yet he wondered that Robert Owen should have rejected polarities in the
realm of natural forces, as in the realm of morality. Also, although
it had been his experience to traverse the many waters of this
world, he had seen as yet no site naturally suited for the establishment of Utopia, a state which, he believed, like the society
of angels, must be forever a little beyond and above the many
streams of time.

The priesthoods and kingdoms of the world sent emissaries to
New Lanark, especially during its early years. There was a constant stream of sight-seers—members of royalty from almost all
nations, diplomats, ambassadors, bankers, economists, bishops,
novelists, utilitarians, and even a few brother cotton lords, and
an occasional American businessman, and an occasional mad
tailor. There were few who did not realize the significance of this
experiment to show man as a plastic material, a wax, where any
impression can be placed. Almost all approved of the project
within the gates at New Lanark—almost all would disapprove of
its extension and would reject its view of happiness. A London
lady sighed, wishing her son could enjoy half the advantages at
New Lanark. These children, unlike her son, were to be taught

nothing they could not understand—but that little gentleman was on his way to the House of Lords, a thing made up of ambiguities. If the choice was only between two systems of tyranny, as she believed it to be, she preferred the old to the new. Other conservatives reacted similarly. Most liberals, especially the exponents of *laissez faire,* smelled despotism.

Robert Owen himself displayed, it has been said, the candor and openness of a child. When he entered the schoolroom at New Lanark, the children rushed toward him in a swarm. They seized him by his coattails, climbed to his shoulders, kissed and fondled him. Infants who could not walk alone crawled toward him, crying to be taken into his arms. In the midst of a war-torn world, he would sit on the floor for hours, playing with wooden blocks, as children co-operated in building a toy village which was soon to be torn down. Robert Browning would have appreciated this wise, innocent man, this Ivan Ivanovitch. Caroline said that he loved the mill children better than his own, and the human family better than his own family. What had happened was the effect of her husband. Robert Owen denied, however, that his personality had been a factor in the success at New Lanark. The correct principles, he said, had been placed in operation and were operating. These children had "co-operated in the building of store houses and cells, storing them full of the necessaries of animal life, humming from flower to flower, under the influence of just knowledge and sound philosophy." Mankind itself could be a colony of bees like this and swarm to open flowers, if once relieved from needless superstitions and fears. Had not Socrates turned his face away from the cold starlight to consider the nearer problem of mankind and man's republic? The great good of the universe was ever man, and not some vague extension of him above the clouds where man is not.

The correct principles, Robert Owen believed, were like those of astronomy—children, like the stars in their courses, to be viewed as the subject of a rational order. Newton's mechanics could be made to pertain to the moral sphere. Both moral and celestial spheres should be considered as one—and the moral exclude, as the celestial did, miraculous compensations, such as a city of glass and jacinth above the system of factory wheels, or crystal wheels of stars. Theologians had pointed men's eyes away from earth to heaven. The brute facts of experience, they had said, would disappear by and by. But in heaven, either to come or coexistent with earth, a counter-earth, that which had passed away would be restored. Should all the ghosts of English dray horses be arisen, they who had died frothing at the mouth, and all the ghosts of English sparrows, they who had been shot down? What of England's many unloved children? Think of the traffic, the congestion, ye soothsaying Malthusians! Doubtless, such a counter-earth must exclude much of even the shade of reality, lest it should become itself the thing most fearful. Another factory. Man's one objective must rather be, Robert Owen believed, the improvement of our present life, without reliance upon a system of deportation to another star, which was but an aspect of the slave trade or penal colonization. Another Botany Bay. No past example could be looked to, really. There were dark specks upon the moral map of Moses and of all old prophets. Each had spoken for only a part of the human race. Each had imagined a singular destiny. The animal man, tired creature, time and again had been led into a Slough of Despond by the ethical man, an overwhelming angel—time and again had been led into a wilderness as if escape were possible. Man, in the coming age of the machine, must proclaim his solidarity with the entirety of mankind, and look no more for salvation to wandering stars, burning bushes, wild illusions of wild grandeur. He must choose whether the machine should be used for positive or negative goals. Already, it had uprooted whole populations—and the gravitation toward misery would increase with every year, should there be no consideration of world unity and the percipient creature. On him, the sky should fall, rather.

Distrusting traditionalists of every order, Robert Owen employed in his schools at New Lanark two teachers who could neither read nor write and thus were free from sophistry which denies natural man. These teachers were Molly Young, a girl of seventeen, vapid and bland as a milkmaid, though she had been herself a child worker in the mills, and old James Buchanan, a weaver of common cotton goods by hand, a kind of Silas Marner, though perhaps not so morose as that fictitious character. Past seventy, his trade having failed him as the new machine displaced the worker, old James had become, naturally and easily, a convert to the philosophy of Rousseau, a lover of little children, and a chaser after the immortal butterfly. He was dominated, alas, by his horse-faced wife after school hours. A Calvinist dipped and dyed, she held that happiness was never the instinct of an old, lame, blind, deaf, dumb, senile world like this. Fortunately, she was inarticulate, and so expressed herself by floor mopping and beating clothes at the brookside.

When asked whether the New Lanark educational system would work elsewhere, Robert Owen expressed his unswerving faith in it. He offered to farm out old James to a London charity school, where the founders, among them James Mill, a pioneer in associative psychology, had expressed their deep interest. Old James, while merely human, and a man who could not walk straight across a meadow without changing his course a little each time, knew the exact principles of social happiness, which were undulatory like himself. He would not falter. Reports from London were most gratifying. Old James had not swerved an inch too far, but ran true to his course, like a Newtonian planet in its social orbit. There was no doubt but that the universal good might be made operable in the human exemplar—the important one, as man does not exist detached from his sensations. Robert

Owen, while lecturing in London to empty halls, decided to walk over to the dark tenement where old James conducted his regenerative school. Expecting the best, he found the worst—a scene over which history should draw the veil—the determined Calvinist wife, a bundle of lively whips, a boy unbreeched at her capacious knees, many faces stained with dirt and tears, wild grins, wild grimaces, poor old James turned toward the corner.

The circumstance had been beyond old James' control. His wife was the representative of force and he of gentleness. He had averted his eyes and closed his ears. After that, he was never the same. He would have his day, however, in the spirit world, and his wife not present. He would be in the cloud with Elijah, Molly Young, the Duke of Kent, Thomas Jefferson, a reformed Napoleon—and still a chaser after the immortal butterfly at the edge of the human swamp.

Robert Owen's public proceedings caused his downfall, people said. As a rich man, his eccentricities would have been respected, verily. He might have had a paradise for mill children or a grove of marble Apollos, at his pleasure. The trouble was that he desired to make his wax museum the public order—that even the government should adopt his novel principles, the science of wax society. The trouble was that he impinged on others. His face was always turning up at every banquet, like the ghost of Banquo, although he represented, he said, no political party but the dead souls of England. He went around and talked to gravediggers outside the armed fortresses of cotton towns. He had no discretion. He publicized widely his findings as to the numbers of pygmy bones in public burial pits. The carnage of peace, he announced, was as terrible as that of war.

For two years, he waited in the anterooms of Parliament, to testify before a committee which was considering the problems of factory management. He was refused a hearing but was permitted to hand in his recommendations, which were for the government protection of labor. The cotton lords, realizing the dangers of such a proposal, got busy producing evidence to deny his morose findings. Physicians on the payrolls of cotton lords swore before Parliament that if children perished in the cotton mills, it was because their bodies were constitutionally weak to begin with. Due, in all probability, to the sins of Adam, who had yearned for a mate. For a child of four or five to work fourteen hours a day, in a closed atmosphere, breathing lint and dust, would not affect his health, unless he had been singled out by God for an early death. Big business, evidently, was assured that a certain aggregation of mankind was intended to populate the Slough of Despond, along with Christian. Cotton lords sent spies out to New Lanark, to see if there was not a skeleton in the Owen household. A Reverend Mr. Menzies, a sly, coughing gentleman, testified before Parliament that although he had seen no skeleton in the Owen closet, he had heard music coming from an unknown source. It was supernatural. He was dismissed, with wildest laughter, the House of Lords shaking, when it was ascertained that a choir of mill children had been concealed in a curtained gallery—it was not heaven but earth. For four years, the great debate was carried on, though much interrupted. When, in 1819, Robert Owen's bill was passed, it had suffered, at the suggestions of various committees, many amputations—was as ineffectual as a cripple without hands or feet. The cotton lords, though they seemed defeated, had won out in the battle against government control—for England's national life depended on the perpetuation of the cotton trade, though innocents be slaugh-tered in droves. The supervision of cotton mills was left to clerics who were, but this is of no importance, on the payrolls of cot-ton lords—like the surgeons, like the undertakers. The fine for violation of any article would not have purchased a new harness or bishop's shovel hat. So things continued, apparently, much as they had been—though this sick legislation was a first step in the emancipation of nations, Parliament barking at shadows all the while.

Robert Owen had, at this period, no public intercourse with the operatives and working classes themselves. He addressed his pleas, necessarily, to the ruling powers, blind, deaf, and dumb as they were. What he proposed was that England, which had grown unconsciously, should be covered with rectangular villages, the result of consciousness—that, as a wag put it, every mill town should be a paradise, but on earth. Upon a certain amount of land should be combined skill, labor, capital, and population. The people in the proposed rectangular villages would engage in both manufacturing and farming. Lords spiritual, lords temporal, middlemen, shopkeepers, and parasites should be excluded. The professions as such should be done away with, physicians and surgeons to be employed under new principles. Nor were there to be imaginary representations of wealth, such as gold, silver, or paper money—labor to be the one bank of real wealth. In such rectangular villages, Robert Owen hoped that, as pigeon fanciers may breed a better type of pigeon, so could men breed a better type of man.

Generally speaking, the proposed rectangular villages were considered a huge, perhaps sinister joke. It seemed inevitable or at least advisable that society should endure, within itself, that struggle for existence, the limitation of which was society's goal. The debauch of little children was fundamental to prosperity. "Oh! I see it all!" Lord Lauderdale exclaimed. "Nothing can be more complete for the poor and working class. But what will become of us?" Few were so generous as he. An ironic critic, observing that the mortality rate in a Glasgow cotton mill was only two per thousand, and yet this was no model community, suggested that they ought to build mills as public sanatoriums the length and breadth of England. These would be more practical than the proposed rectangular villages and less expensive, as they were already in operation. And what went on behind the scenes, it was intended no one should know—though many did know, among these, Mrs. Trollope, who publicized her findings. How the cold starlight shone through chinks in the roofs.

Everywhere, with childlike candor, Robert Owen displayed his plans for rectangular villages, to include bathtubs, happiness, shade trees, the science of society, libraries, public dining halls. In fact, the man was weighted down with impedimenta—among his articles of display, a set of building blocks, known as the cubes of human populace, which he hoped would help induce Utopia, as the lesson they conveyed might easily be understood by a child of three. The cubes of human populace, Robert Owen obligingly set up on a billiard table at Windsor, in the presence of a few feather-brained members of the royal family, perhaps even poor George III, with his crown somewhat awry—and all were amazed to see themselves dissolve in cloud and mist. For they were so much excess baggage on the ship of state. "It was a leveling exhibition," the Duke of York remarked, laughingly. These cubes of human populace showed, Robert Owen said, the accumulation of misery at the negative pole of society, the accumulation of monstrous wealth at the top. These cubes of human populace signified the true riddle of the Sphinx—and every nation which did not solve the mystery would be destroyed by the very monsters it had supported. Accordingly, as here shown, the working class was equal to the base of a pyramid thirty-one and five-sixth inches a side, whereas the apex, representing the royal family, the House of Peers, the Lords Spiritual and Temporal, measured, disproportionately to their power, three-sixteenths of an inch. The vast majority, now suppressed, must come to share in the real consumption of real goods, the works of their hands—if not by peaceful means, then by violence. Man interests himself little in forms of ideal government, being by nature not thoughtful— until he reaches a state of extreme desperation, cold and misery, with a package of dynamite in his hands. And then we see the insecurity of works of ages, the ghostly top blown off, the edifice dissolving.

Alas! Godwin's proposal of an ethereal Utopia in cactus-ridden Mexico seemed less objectionable than what Robert Owen proposed, a Utopia in England, a leveling—though the objections came from everybody but members of the royal family. George III, in his own opinion, had long since blown off the top.

The apex of the pyramid was that strange edifice of nothing, but George III, out of his mind, plowing a desolate wasteland—and his thirteen children, including card players, tailors' models, bankrupt gentlemen, the unhappy Queen of Württemberg, several spinsters, several bigamists, a shipwrecked sailor, fishermen, military governors, a suspected murderer or two, pale horsemen, a dynasty far from sensible. Oh, what divinity did ever hedge in this king, who talked with absent friends, mostly farmers like himself! Had he not been so wild, so uncontrolled in his sexual appetites, he would have been capable of much goodness. His family had a character of goodness mixed with much folly, a self-love and extravagance which led to the sacrifice of the most altruistic, the most noble aims, it was said.

Frederick, the Duke of York, had viewed the cubes of human populace without malice, no one being more aware of the empty top than he, occupied as he was with racing, whist, and improper stories. Such was his irresponsible life that, upon his demise, when it was proposed that a statue be erected in his honor and memory, *Punch* drew a caricature of sartorial elegance strung on wire, confronted by an edifice of unpaid tailors' bills. Even the tailors laughed. No one would have been more amused, however, than the Duke himself, who had appreciated his own insubstantiality, as if all his life he were a fish cast up out of water.

There was, however, even in that harum-scarum, exuberant royal family, so much at odds with the world and themselves, at least one supporter of Utopia, the Duke of Kent, a great pigeon fancier, a great designer of clocks, a great lover of humanity. With Robert Owen, he would have collaborated in the establishment of workers' paradises, and all rectangular, and all rational. Oh, consistency, thou art a jewel! The Duke had served as military governor of Gibraltar, but with such cruel discipline, with such little understanding of men, that innumerable complaints had been sent forth at every hour from that high fortress, by every imaginable carrier, even by pigeons. Shipwrecks, disasters, gaming debts, innumerable comic tragedies had checkered a career far from rational or admirable—though his speech was that of an advanced liberal, and the little hair he had was dyed, and he expected to live forever. This Hudibrastic, plaintive gentleman experienced a steady decline from bad to worse—yet embraced the philosophy of humanistic progress. He cared but little for money, that "imaginary" wealth, as he had no money—at a Canadian post, had entertained his guests with many lavish last suppers, which were never paid for, had gambled away a sum exceeding astronomical calculations. No one complained so much as the Duke did against the pollutions of an evil system—though a Spanish fortune-teller at Gibraltar had predicted that his only child, not yet born, was to be a great queen. He considered that he led the most regular life, and felt despised unjustly—though he was known, among his thoughtful sisters, as Joseph Surface, and though George III, plowing an imaginary landscape, retained enough hard-headed common sense to refuse him every request for an increase in his allowance. Burdened with towering debts, at the period of the Duchess's expectancy, he was unable to procure money so that the heiress presumptive to the throne of England might be born on English soil. The Duchess, with her lapdogs, her canaries, and her ambitions, came as close to England as she could—their ship lying off coast, during storm-tossed moments, as the dogs barked, the canaries fluttered, and the ocean itself heaved and sighed. Had it not been that a poor alderman under an umbrella advanced money, Victoria might have been born at sea, like coral-fluted Venus herself. After her safe delivery, on English soil, fortunately, then she must be exposed to the fine sea air, though swathed in protective flannels. The Duchess, a creature of habit, who had been quite poor in Germany, with hardly a cow, must perform her peregrinations from town house to country house, and vice versa, an endless migration, inevitable as the course of the stars or calendar of a Turkish sultan. The sick Duke suffered greatly. He was reduced, after a few abortive attempts in other directions, to the necessity of carrying in his pocket the plans for a rectangular paradise for mill workers—in lieu of any actual wealth. The poor Duke poured his heart out to Robert Owen, the New Lanark socialist, in a few long letters—how he was about to be forced to sell his house, was about to leave ungrateful England and make his way in Germany. He would have come to New Lanark if he could have—but was detained by circumstance, the Duchess, the anatomy of melancholy, clocks, etc., so sent his physician instead. The Duke was, however, a distinguished convert—the inconspicuous lover of all mankind, in an age of organized fantasy experiences, Robert Owen believed—and not merely, as some thought, the rival queen bee in the hive.

The Duke, a two-legged man, was as much a victim of circumstance, in his own view, as the worst thief dangling from a noose—for he had no freedom of will or of motion. Gifted, however, with vision, as the thief was not, he would destroy the existing order at one blow perhaps, cut off the ghostly top of the pyramid. Under his manipulation, a committee was organized for the establishment of a model community—the lords spiritual and temporal not to be included there, naturally. For they would be gone for a long weekend in a green country, as usual—away from the heap of fermenting brickwork, which exuded poisonous dew, away from the dark alleys, away to the Lord's cricket ground, the Lord's billiard table, the gentleman's game of fox hunting, the lady's game of dressing throughout mirrored eternity. Meanwhile, though absent, they would draw an interest of six per cent on workers' paradises, on which mythical corporations they were to be the entire stockholders and owners, in fact. Also, among their number, almost all diseased, almost all at the portals of the grave, almost all with one foot in the grave, there was a gentleman who would outlive them—"The crown will come to me and my children."

In return for this assistance, which he did not seem to recognize as an abortive movement or miscarriage of justice, or which he chose to ignore, Robert Owen helped the Duke to straighten out his personal difficulties, by advancing large sums of money on Utopia at strategic points between town house and country house—a sum which, though unacknowledged as a debt, Queen Victoria, flush in the midst of many wars, would repay to a bankrupt, threadbare Owen family.

The opposition, considering what human nature was and is, could not but be stronger than the Duke's support, especially as the Duke died, quite suddenly, in 1820, as a result of getting his feet wet. England, Robert Owen said, had lost its greatest friend. The Duke "had daily witnessed and hourly felt the hollowness of this existence, the shallowness of what most people call happiness."

With each year, Robert Owen turned more and more from New Lanark, a private philanthropy, to the world, a public philanthropy—for he saw not much hope that the ghostly top of the pyramid would dissolve of its own accord. Fragile reed though man might be, he was still a thinking reed, as even the negativists had admitted—and would create a better world than this, which was made up of the attribution of false values to false things. Certainly, the workers, such fragile reeds, could look for no salvation from the ghostly top—they must look to themselves.

There were rumblings from the top, as the Quaker partners became more and more alarmed, and Caroline prayed for the reunion of all her family, complete with silver dessert set, in heaven above. What viper had dreaming England nurtured at her bosom? Robert Owen, a mad cotton lord, would strip off the gilded clothing and show man to be a two-legged animal, which awful fact it had been civilization's chief mission to forget. He would attribute more value to a few pots and pans than to the Apollo Belvedere or salty spinsters. He would tear down the pillars of their ancestral houses. He would incite the workers to sow dragons' teeth which would spring up as men. Not one butler would there be in all of merrie England and not the possibility of another Shakespeare. Prospero, Ariel, Caliban—all would be unthinkable.

Lord Lascelles lamented that Robert Owen made "much noise in the public prints."

Paradise Was Lost

Indicative of the macrocosm was the microcosm, a reflection in the small of larger issues. Partner William Allen, although wearing a Quaker's gray, was fanatic in his conservatism. He had entered the partnership only reluctantly, at the express word of God—because of "the strength I might have in opposing any infidel plans of R. O."

Liberty, he believed to be neither in doing what we please, as if we were waves tossed by every wind, nor in being governed by laws of human conception and authorship. For him, the old order had its own peculiar virtue, which was the handwriting of God on every wall. He believed this world to be, by its very nature, adjusted to dissolve. It had been destroyed by water, and it would be destroyed by fire. This human life was not, from his point of view, the sty of Epicurus, a bedlam. Far from being merely sensual creatures, men were ever subject to the law of God, and free in proportion as they acknowledged it, enslaved in proportion as they ignored it. How foolhardy to build a village on any human frontier, when one could march directly to the great capital, the center which was God's. The flight of the alone to the alone! It would be well to recognize that man could not live ethically in accordance with nature, at least at this date. Animal man, wherever he was, must be overwhelmed and conquered by ethical man, an angel with streaming hair. A flame of fire! By this means only could the brother of the wolf be converted to serve as guardian of the flock. A free monarchy, like England, seemed the nearest approximation yet to that state where the wolf guards the golden pasture.

William Allen, far from rejecting the complicated machinery of civilization, considered that the division of society into governors and governed, rich and poor, learned and unlearned, single families, sects, and classes was God's plan, a good deal ahead of Robert Owen's. The simplest state, such as his junior partner had in mind, would be, inevitably, a state of tyranny. Without the power of traditions, customs, and rival interests, there would be, in fact, a despotism, inevitable as the worm in the wheat. The will of the Machiavellian prince would be the only, the absolute law. Such a prince is generally inclined toward exotic dreams. Wrapped in clouds of darkness, he transfers his power to a few smooth-cheeked agents, his eunuchs, who are as ruthless as he, but actively so, as they try to make real the delusional world their leader lives in. If murder is his dream, they kill for the abject pleasure of killing. In such a government, the sovereign is the heir of all his subjects. He seizes on their property, sometimes before their murder, sometimes after, as the impulse strikes him. He does not have to show even the thread of an excuse. There being no law but his own arrogant will, he may decide on any successor to the crown—good, bad, or indifferent, strong or feeble-minded. Dying, he is not dead. If there are, however, competitors for the crown, a civil war follows—and woe to the innocent bystander in the streets of that city. The victor removes his brothers and near relations, by various means—imprisonment, decapitation, putting out their eyes, or making them swallow drugs which will deprive them of their senses, so that they hiss like geese, so that they squeal like pigs. Nothing but fear could support such a state or could endure the reduction of existence to the relation of an all-encompassing despot and thoughtless slave population, suspended midway between life and death, like Mahomet's coffin, a thing said to be midway between heaven and earth. Far from abandoning the complicated machinery of English government, William Allen would die in the Slough of Despond to defend it. At least, if he had not been a Quaker. The subtle refinements of civilized life should not be thrown overboard for the sake of a blank page in the books of nature, he thought. Fortunately, the spirit of God dwelled among the tombs of old faiths, beyond the reaches of materialistic socialism forever—was not to be destroyed.

Robert Owen declared that he had opened the Book of Nature. William Allen was most surprised at what his junior partner read there. Social organization, for which Robert Owen would sacrifice the institutions of the past, was nothing worth striving for, William Allen believed—even wolves hunt in packs, and hornets are gregarious. As for the universe, of which his junior partner talked so much, it was a thing devoid of meaning, except for God's word. The fact of God Himself showed the universe to be unreasonable. Man, alone and lonely, must be ever on guard against cosmic processes, whose ends were not his ends, as might be gathered by anyone who had ever observed a dead sparrow falling. The wicked prosper, as Jesus Christ remarked, and the good die young, and the sins of the fathers are visited upon the children. Thousands must pay for the crime of one, who may be only their human nature aggrandized and made explicit, an unholy of unholies. Our only salvation, from William Allen's point of view, was to withdraw from the arena of conflict and to place our souls like sparrows in the hands of God. If then falling, they do not fall. A better book by far than nature, a crudity, was the Bible, wherein was written all that was necessary for a man to know—the moral law, the taxation system among the Levites,

the amount of the widow's tithes, the measurements employed
by the glorious architect Solomon, the multiplication of Jacob's
spotted kine. Other than these clarities, there was, there would
be an eternal mystery. Our globe might be, as some thought, on
the upward road to heaven, but when it reached the crest of the
hill and started to go down to hell, the stars following like a royal
funeral cortege, what rationalist could stop it? He might bark
at the stars, but what good? Far from supposing our intellects
supernatural, a power to extend beyond the stars, men must pray
simply for Gabriel's descent to the green hills of England—an
unmechanized being, with beard of gold like barley, who would
bring with him the one secret of happiness not posited on nine-
tenths vanity and illusion.

William Allen believed that, this side of paradise, there must
be all kinds of differences in warring nature—the dove, the serpent, the wheat, the worm, chaos. It was not for nothing that he
had visited in secluded Asiatic villages, untouched by progress or
industry, where the farmers, poor mystics, had treated all worms
as if they were in their place. What was the result but a paradise
of worms? For nature was ever the negation of human values.
It would be the same should the rich man treat all paupers as
if he were in their place. Besides, who could consider riches the
key of happiness? William Allen aspired after a bliss higher than
this earth affords. In a sense, he was poverty-stricken, like lep-
erous Mordecai, who sat with ashes of coal on his head and was
unimpressed by the dazzle of any earthly prince, even the proud
vizier of Ahaseurus, wearing a crown of diamonds. For had not
God promised more and brighter diamonds than these, the poor
result of coal? This present earth was an empty carriage, a parade
of mummers, as compared with the New Jerusalem, where seraphim and cherubim with their wings outspread would not hide
longer from the face of dusty man. For while we are at home
in the body, we are absent from the Lord, and why prolong the

period of our absence? What a joy it would be to come home again, like the prodigal son, for whom the fatted calf would be killed. The Lord would sweep, on that day, the first grain from the first threshing floor. Man should then eat of the prime bread, a sweetness as of dew. This expectation was William Allen's only goal in life.

His junior partner's attitude toward happiness as physical enjoyment only, his rearing of infants as "happy animals" less interested in their souls than the abdominal viscera, his attempt to release man from the fear of death or hope of heaven—these seemed to William Allen the work of the Devil himself. Paradise was forfeited long before the cotton trade arose. There had been a silk manufacturer, an evil Pharaoh, slaughterer of the first-born, dreamer of dreams, long before the rise of industrial England was so much as thought of.

All social changes must take place slowly, over a period of centuries, for fear they should throw the baby out with the bath. Had not God moved but slowly, since the seventh day when He rested?

William Allen was a mystic and a gentleman of the old school. In another environment, preferably Asiatic, he might have covered his head with ashes and fed his heart to ravens—instead, he went to dinner parties and would not ask for a second helping of roast beef. He had taken a vow that until the slave trade was abolished, with God's help he would not use sugar in his tea. God helped him for forty-three years. There was a precarious moment when the divinity hung in the balance, the Emperor of Russia having offered him a cup of tea with sugar in it. The spirit triumphing over the flesh, William Allen called for plain tea, with profuse apologies. He thanked God that, at another dinner party in Moscow, he was able to hand in a Russian princess of the blood without tragic embarrassment, such as might be caused by an ill-timed cough or stubbing his toe. He was always embarrassed. His spirit was caught between two advancing armies—although he was peace-loving, and would not have stepped on a fly. He knew his littleness. Being a self-made man, he would have liked to kick the ladder out from under him, to deny his relation with lions, tigers, and yawning cosmic forces. He knew the impossibility of this. He prayed God to accompany him from room to room, and point out the least conspicuous chair. Thus he had kept, with God's help, to the plain road of truth—though according to his junior partner's assumption, he was launched into the wilds of the imagination, was lost in a maze of obscurity. Rather, Robert Owen, a chaser after that will-o'-the-wisp, the science of society, was the lost soul. Perhaps the past history of mankind, as Robert Owen said, ought to be scratched out. Only God, however, could efface the writing on that page of nature—for this world, its human institutions, its furniture, even its nests of foxes, were God's signature on space. "It is a mystery of God to conceal a matter, but it is the nature of kings to search it out."

Pain and sorrow knocked at William Allen's doors more loudly than happiness. His diary records his constant searchings after the truth, his communion with "One who sitteth on a high throne." How could an honest man dangle an illusion of perfection as a bait before the eyes of that poor, mute fish, humanity? William Allen insisted that reading be introduced into the New Lanark schools, as from the sacred word alone the children might learn who their true Maker was. They must understand that the split in the universe had not been caused by the split between Tories and Whigs, but that there had been a quarrel among good and evil angels, long ago. Man was but a poor dog tied to a post, and barking at shadows, as all around him circled the transient union of flesh with spirit. Till flesh dropped away, there could be no harmony, no happiness. The children must understand their relation to a higher nature, or otherwise they should never be transported to a better world than this. Apart from God, there was no reality. Apart from God, human personality was the great lie, whether adhering to Pericles or the slave he threw to the dogs. The true religion was only this, therefore—to realize, as an inward light, though not the light of reason, man's nothingness, and that a poisonous dew can destroy him quite as effectively as the collapse of giant stars—no great catastrophe necessary. Did not an eagle drop a serpent on a king's head in a garden enclosed and protected—for there was always the sky's immensity? The children must walk with utter humility and eyes downcast. Yet would the tales of Miss Maria Edgeworth and the Shorter Catechism be able to withstand the awful powers of the infidel and infidelity, the aggregate of Democritean atoms, the concept of a universe devoid of angels sporting in fields of asphodel, somewhere in future time? Surely God, the supreme will, was ever the cause of sensation and would pluck out the eyes of the offender. Surely God, not Robert Owen, was everywhere. William Allen was staggered by the thought of his junior partner's inflated ego. Robert Owen would rue the day he set out to reform the world. God Himself had not promised so much. Robert Owen was a helmsman without a helm to steer by, a vessel lost in the wide gulf. A single nuisance, yet multiple as the sands of the sea, and never to evolve, in time or space, one perfect pearl, which is faith in the Almighty God. Had not God, speaking out of the whirlwind, taunted Job with his ignorance—that he had not seen the copulation of elephants and knew not the composition of hail? Robert Owen was less wise than Job, certainly. A poor optimist—as if nature itself did not preclude the fact of happiness, nature being the mistaken mother.

William Allen's "apostolic mother" refused to stay in the same room with Robert Owen, as he contaminated the furniture with his philosophy, she complained. Singing and dancing, moreover, were in direct opposition to William Allen's faith in his Creator, who had a sad, unhappy face, as He had witnessed, from His high vantage ground, the crystallization of Lot's wife, a plot against Wellington, and numerous other disasters. The bare legs of the mill children in their Greek tunics suggested a training for immorality in brothel houses. Military drill might well cultivate in the children a taste for the moribund pleasures of war, such as that of Hyder Ali, who erected, for his delight, a pyramid of human skulls. Every Tamerlane must have his army, his prisoners caged like featherless birds. The attention of so many distinguished visitors would make the mill children conscious of their importance, spoiled, unwilling to adjust to the harsh demands of adult life, when they should be no longer cherished by a mad millionaire, who simply preferred these pets to peacocks. The adjunct of his vanity. If so happy now, how would they be happy as saddlers, tillers of the soil, workers in wood and bronze, blacksmiths, butchers? How would the dancers ever turn to face reality, when their hands should be blistered at the plow? Or should every farmer wear a golden crown like that of George III? That would be a state of luxury, indeed—but doubtless would comprise no more happiness than present disorders, since even a king is made to plow the infinite, yea, yearn for heaven above.

William Allen carried credentials from above, stamped with the authentic seal of an ever-active God, whose rain falls alike on the rich and the poor. He came to New Lanark as minister of justice, ambassador of the deity, spokesman for a higher law than nature's, etc. He carried no golden book or sickle, but was simplicity itself, fawning under a black umbrella. A long, light, loose gentleman.

In the Owen household, it is true, he found no skeleton, everybody most kind. He could not help admiring the lady, whose devotion to a higher power was evident throughout Braxfield manor. There was even her open Bible on the drawing-room table, its pages marked with a crimson oak leaf, a stain of autumn upon the holy, pristine words, as if God were aware of her precarious

situation. Yet there was something sinister in the whole atmosphere—a feeling of lingering decay, a feeling that there ought
to be a murderous lord on these premises or at least a skeleton
playing a harp hung among barren trees. Surely, this materialistic socialism would cut away all faith of man in his Creator, if
it had its way! William Allen told the wide-eyed Owen children
that they would come to find God and the community of angels
no fiction, as they now believed, but the most potent, the most
fruitful truth. It was only God Who could lead the Owen children through the wilderness, William Allen said—God Who
could decoy the birds of heaven in one net, God Who could open
closed doors, God Who could restore a lost manhood, revive
Lazarus. God was not the product of a diseased imagination, as
Hamlet was, but the one true story, beginning, middle, and end.
All works of fiction ought to be burned simultaneously throughout the civilized world, in huge bonfires, and Shakespeare's son-
nets as well, though William Allen had rather enjoyed them, the
crying of a soul in distress. But how much better if Shakespeare
had cried out after, not a dark lady, but God! William Allen felt
that the needs of the body were few, as compared with the needs
of the soul—and that the absolute was absolute, a Jacob's ladder,
a rock of ages, a golden rose, a New Jerusalem, a crown of crowns.

He interviewed, with painstaking care, the workers of New
Lanark cotton mills. He went around in good weather with his
umbrella under his arm, always expecting a deluge to overwhelm
him and cast him, like Jonah, into the mouth of the whale. He
was Daniel, indeed, in the lions' den, helpless as the infant Moses
in a cradle of bulrushes, God's most humble servant, the child of
David, the child of Judah. The workers still believed in God, he
found, and the extremes of mortal destiny, and would not give
a straw for the things of this world. Yea, they said, a rich man
should no more enter the kingdom of heaven than a fly. Not a
few had witnessed wonderful deathbed scenes, when the corrupt

body had seemed phosphorescent as a fish. They had heard, in fact, the rustle of Gabriel's skirts, like a surf on a lonely shore, when blind Jamie breathed his last. It was beautiful. Many a man intended to wear thick-soled shoes in his coffin, in case he should walk the roads of burning hell. Many a woman planned to hold in her hand a small keepsake, such as a baby's curl. There was an ancient dame who thanked God for the mole on her face—for by it, she would remember earth when she became an angel, and every homely item, even the chicken scratching in the dooryard, and the smell of hot kidney. Some were keeping their hair combings in chimney corners, so that they would have all their hair in heaven. Others saved their old, ruined teeth. The familiar views persisted. Indeed, Robert Owen had never tried to undermine their faith in a higher power, the workers reported, and that his views had not made the slightest mark on man or stone. In spite of this failure, he was a very good man, an excellent employer. He even paid a preacher to curse him in Gaelic every Sunday morning, a show which was as good as a cock fight repeated on mirrors of the infinite. Everybody was happy, apparently, as Robert Owen was the loser.

William Allen came away from his visit in an almost cheerful state of mind, happy that New Lanark had not deteriorated under the effects of John Locke's view that the mind is born a blank page, where any writing can be traced. "I now feel very peaceful," he wrote in his diary. Yet rumors, year after year, besieged his fortress in the City of God. If he so much as stepped his foot out of the door, he heard of that man's doings at New Lanark, his public speeches in London. People were beginning to identify him with his junior partner, so that on two or three occasions, he had suffered an intense social mortification—as if it were he who fostered bare-legged dancing.

In 1822, William Allen wrote his final letter to the skeptic, deist, pantheist, positivist, sentimentalist, cold-blooded

machine, blind fool, harmonist, atomist, dictator, communist, worm, terrestrial Elysianist, Don Quixote of the cotton
mills, etc. He appreciated Robert Owen's benevolent intentions, but was sorry to say he felt their principles to be diamet-
rically opposed, like the road to heaven, the road to hell. He
was grieved by Robert Owen's lack of faith in a superior being,
Who had handed down, of old, a complete set of values, and
Who had hidden a Bible in the widow's dough at New Lanark.
He wished his correspondent, in spite of their intrinsic differences, the best of health, personally. ". . . And may that Great
and Holy Being, Who seeth not as man sees, so influence thy
heart, before the shades of evening close upon thee, that it may
become softened and receive those impressions which He alone
can give, and then thou wilt perceive that there is indeed something infinitely beyond human reason. . . . At present, however,
it is quite plain that we must part."

God, not human reason, had been a pillar of cloud by day,
a pillar of fire by night. God, not human reason, had multiplied the loaves. He reminded his correspondent, first, of these
forgotten truths, and second, of his failure to carry out the least
command of a financial superior at New Lanark. He had waited
patiently for a change of circumstance. He had desired that all
males from the age of six upwards wear trousers or drawers. His
agents informed him that the children were still dancing in their
nightshirts, to the tune of a Scottish flute, a heathen instrument.
He had desired that the children give up the study of moral
geography. His agents informed him that the children were still
examining the economy of nations which practice infanticide,
prostration before wooden gods, etc.—that, according to the
religions of such peoples, the children were taught, the soul of
man may be secreted, even during his lifetime, in a gourd or the
hairs of his head. Children, through such comparisons, come to
an awful doubt, the feeling that there is no everlasting truth, no

rock of ages, but only error, William Allen believed. He had not objected to the study of anatomy, but had despised, in his heart, some of the deductions drawn from it. He would have permitted an examination of human skulls, but only on condition that the conclusions drawn as to man's nature were God's conclusions.

John Walker, another of Robert Owen's Quaker partners, sympathized with the great work going on at New Lanark. He would have been an active supporter, had it not been for his sense of the unreality of all things, including himself. He was not sure that God upheld the continuity of moments, or made a difference between sweet and sour. There were blank spaces—and at such times, almost anything might happen.

John Walker pitied himself, with his whole heart—for he was a martyr to luxury, as he said, having been born with a gold spoon in his mouth, a crown of vipers on his head, a pair of crutches in his hands, the great cross of great wealth upon his back, a dim eyesight, an overactive sense of hearing, a skin like a drum, a dry palate, an unreliable apparatus for smelling. His hardship was that he had everything—wife, children, palaces, swans, servants, horses, saintly aunts, a pet zebra, and marble statues which had been fished up by fishermen in the Aegean Sea— and nothing, absolutely nothing could give him happiness. Due to his unfortunate sensory equipment, he was like an Aeolian harp, played upon by every nervous wind. He had once heard, while shut up in his closet, the clanging of buoys in a distant harbor. When an old peasant woman three miles down the road was dying, he had heard the rasping of her breath, like a wind at the shutter. So that in an atmosphere of utmost privacy, he could find no privacy whatever. He had been known to faint upon smelling a rose, as if a poison had been distilled throughout his system. If he so much as looked at a haystack, his eyes were fountains. He suffered from blinding headaches and felt, indeed, like an Atlas, with the entirety of earth on his head. His sympathies were so diffused, so unorganized, he could hardly put one foot in front of another. When he thought of the cotton children, then at that moment there would obtrude upon him, as equally sad, the lamentations of wild goats at their communal burial place. So that he was utterly helpless even to lift a hand. What was the enormity of his own personality, that he himself should become a majority—wild goats, cotton children, woodpeckers, the base of the pyramid? He felt that he had not been naturally endowed with a sense of reason, order, and correct standards. His nearest approach to happiness was his feeling of deprivation—that he was not limited to the things near at hand, but was amorphous and, being everywhere, was in no particular place, as if he were himself the very idea of all mankind.

During a prolonged visit to Rome, searching for mystic certitude, he had almost become a convert to the Catholic order. Almost overwhelmed by incense and ritual, he had felt like swooning in the paltry Vatican, among blue-veined, marble Madonnas, cousins-german to the poor remnants fished up from the Aegean Sea. At such times, though aware of a pig squealing on its way to slaughter, perhaps in England, he had felt an influence of heavenly beams lighting up what part of his mind was not absent, and had seen a cosmos evolving, with mighty grandeur, out of the human physiological chaos, and a figure encompassed by stars like golden pomegranates. He had heard, while the pig squealed under the butcher's knife, a swan singing for the last of earth, most melodiously. Oh, how he had yearned to throw himself at the feet of the Pope, who seemed at the center of harmony, so far distant from pigs squealing. Oh, how he had yearned to be a hair-shirted priest then, not merely a poor, sensual Quaker— but as he was already attached to his wife, good lady, and her children, there was no escape from skepticism and disorder. He had remained as the priest of his own soul, caught like a fly in the spider's web of his own weaving.

As a result of many confusions, John Walker believed that the highest good should be a ceiling placed upon desire, a limitation. Man should be taught little more than necessary for his body's perpetuation. Could John Walker have made his choice again, could he have lived his life over, he would have been a farmer in a turnip field. In such a life, had it been his misfortune to beget children, he would have raised them as ironmongers, blacksmiths, butchers, candlestick makers. That state would have been at least less puzzling than this, he believed.

ℑehovah and Rousseau

George III had dreamed of reclaiming the wastelands of the world. He had even thought of America, a project abandoned by him for many reasons, however, among these, a tax on tea. The tax had seemed, to the shaggy Colonists, not finite, as it was, but a subterfuge for the exertion of ghostly powers which, if unbridled, would relegate an independent people to what, from some points of view, was still their status, a corporation held by an absent Crown. It is doubtful that, his mind clouded, George III recalled what had been for him, even at the time, a detached problem, less real than his face in a mirror framed with golden birds. A great gulf swept between George III and the world. He was happily unaware, for the most part, of the War of 1812, although its issues were as nebulous and ill-defined as he. In fact, his malady, which was a split personality, seemed to increase with every year of his life. In 1814, it is true, at the time of the visit of the Allied sovereigns to England, he showed signs of returning reason, most remarkable, and was informed of interesting events and episodes, such as the Napoleonic wars, the Prince of Wales' attachment to rival ladies, the bombardment of the American coast, the Princess Sophia's delicate health, the Balkan problem, the eviction of the English farmers. Having plowed a field of wheat in dreams, he was at a loss to understand this world's disorders, and his reason departed as suddenly as it had arrived, like the first snow which is also the last. Although he suffered occasionally lucid intervals thereafter, and could then distinguish people by their footsteps, he was filled, for the most part, with the idea that he was dead—"I must have a suit of black, in memory of George III, for whom I know there is to be a general mourning." While a wedding went on in one of his palaces, he, scathed by the hand of heaven, was the lonely, suffering tenant in another. Fortunately, he no longer identified himself with the unfortunate king. On the whole, he was happy. He was, in his later years, both deaf and blind, almost a skeleton. Occupying a long corridor, in which there were rows of pianos and harpsichords, beautifully attuned, the deaf, blind king wandered up and down, striking first one instrument and then another, evolving, with slow motion, the fragments of Handel, who had been his favorite composer. "God is not the God of the dead, but of the living." Also, he carried on, with absent friends, all farmers like himself, many conversations on such subjects as the grafting of fruits from one tree to another and crop rotation. Not now George III, a thing unthinkable, he was Ralph Atkinson and Henry Trenchard, things thinkable, under which names he had once written articles for agricultural journals.

Who wanted to make a paradise of England, if that meant the destruction of the old world, the giving up of cherished institutions, for the sake of a theory untried, unproved, unknown, and dangerous? Surely, the world was wasteland enough. Robert Owen would drag the human race, it was complained, through sloughs of despond to a distant paradise, before the half of them were ready for the journey. What were, indeed, the facts and laws of human nature of which this cotton lord spoke with such sublime authority? He had lost sight already of the creature man, and of the relations in which man exists and acts—since man is not an abstraction, and life is far from being a fairy tale of Utopias or even of a New Jerusalem, quite another matter. A change in the thermometer, an attack of bilious fever, a cough—such slight details, time and again, had been known to change the course of history. Unless Robert Owen could apportion the elements of fire, air, earth, and water, he could not improve the human race. Nor could it be that all thought lies within the provinces of the physical sciences, as some of it must always escape our description. If man was the creature of his circumstance, how did it happen that Robert Owen, born an Episcopalian, had become a Unitarian—or that a clerk at McGuffog's should rise to be a cotton lord?

Who really wanted heaven, when it came right down to earth? Who wanted to turn England into a community of people like meticulous ants or bees, to have no souls of their own, those appurtenances to be colonized on the mountains of the dead moon, as if they were without extension and void? Perhaps an immutable principle within each bee accounted for its willing co-operation in the erection of the hive—bees being born as queens, workers, drones. Men, however, are born as individuals with the power of choice. Should the wise be leveled with the foolish? Even in the hive, terrible things happened. The bees kept pets, and these pets were sometimes allowed to eat their babies. Thus the argument went, always far afield.

Metaphorical language is not in itself bad, so long as no one expects a correspondence to words in actuality. Robert Owen's Malthusian opponents recognized, apparently, no difference between word and truth. They searched the Bible for living statistics with which to oppose his bloodless statistics as to the mortality rate in cotton mills. Biblical sentences showed, they said, the vast multiplication of human beings from our first parents in the Garden of Eden, six thousand years ago. If in spite of the murder of Abel, the slaughter of the Philistines, the great

flood, the burning of Sodom, the plague of grasshoppers, armored
Pharaohs on armored horses plunging into a purple sea, fightings
without and fears within—if in spite of these and other disasters,
the human race had increased to its present incalculable extent,
what would our number be should peace, health, and compe-
tence become the order of the day for another six thousand years?
The mind of man could not stretch so far. At the end of even
a thousand peaceful years, the human race would have multiplied beyond the means of its subsistence. There would not be a
half acre of land and water upon the face of the globe for every
human being who would then exist—many poor farmers, never
a deer park. There must be, therefore, a retardation in the growth
of population, by natural means, such as war and poverty, until
that point when God should lead the remnant of the saved to the
New Jerusalem, where the multiplication of human beings should
cease forever, and where beads of perspiration should stand out on
nobody's brow.

Robert Owen, cotton lord at large, denied the conclusion
of this emotional arithmetic and swan song for the industrial
masses. The fear of increase in population beyond the means of
support, he declared to be a phantom of the imagination, calculated to keep the world in unnecessary ignorance, vice, and
crime forever.

As Lord Bacon had said, "All our valuable knowledge of the
world has been gleaned from minute observation." What was
necessary was a study, not of the fantasy, the dead Philistines,
but of the facts of human experience, such as might be seen at
Holkham, a model community for evicted farmers. Robert Owen
pointed to Holkham, a wasteland which had been turned into a
very fine farm for the poor, through the efforts of themselves and
their patron, the benevolent Mr. Coke. Holkham, Robert Owen
said, was not merely a community of exalted paupers, as some
believed, but the picture of England as it would be when put

under a reasonable order. The British Empire, he said, was even at that moment the waste and wild that Holkham had been. To make of England a co-operative society, or second paradise, it was necessary only to follow, closely, the example of Mr. Coke, who had organized the farmers at Holkham, and of New Lanark, that vast machinery, where the mechanics were organized. England would then support a population many times its present number—and need have no more expectation of that happy day when hail mixed with human blood falls down from the sky, and the lion walks in the empty streets, and billowing angels come.

Similarly, Robert Owen, wishing to show the English people what might be achieved through co-operation on a larger scale than Holkham, for they were always challenging him to produce one working example, interested himself in the material success of the celibate religious communities which, thick as mushrooms in a field, had sprung up in the American wilderness—the Shakers, the Rappites, and others. He investigated these, but unfortunately from a distance. In a letter to *The Times*, he shows himself an apologist for the Rappite community. The good features could be retained without demagogy or the employment of superstition. He attributed less importance to their strangely suicidal theory of time than to their excellent vegetables. The morality of such a group, he inferred, had been a due regard for utility. They had not been avaricious. If their leader was corrupted, it was because the so-called saviors of society must sell out to the capitalists of physical force on whom they depend. The world was perhaps more mistaken than he. A unit of society had survived where the individual, unaided, left to his own resources, would have fallen to the roadside, the wren building its nest in the human skull, which eventuality was the one and only New Jerusalem, so far as could be observed by any living man. The Scriptural communist had at least suffered less than others. The only beauty of it was that it could have been worse.

To withdraw, however, the irrational, and to infuse throughout those veins a rational philosophy, would be possible—with the result of a greater happiness for a greater number. A step in the right direction had been made, and in a remote wilderness.

On the lookout for still other examples of co-operation, Robert Owen visited, over a number of years, communities far from ideal—like the West Riding of Yorkshire, where children of five years were sent into the clammy, poisonous pits at dawn—like Oldham, where in the collieries toward the hills, children of four years were brought to work in their nightshirts—many work-houses, factories, chimneys, underground passages, graveyards, warrens of the poor. How terrible to witness the degradation of the future world! How terrible to witness the creation of a dwarfed, beaten-down, sickly humanity! What freedom of will did these lit-tle children of the nineteenth century enjoy? Social disorganization crawled upon the tracks of social immorality, even as they crawled up the tracks of underground passages, whipped forward like blind goats. Robert Owen heard, before Elizabeth Barrett Browning, the crying of children. Could this reality be, as some had said, only a dream in the mind of God? Then what an evil dream!

At the prison of Newgate, Robert Owen found the one bright spot in England—Mrs. Elizabeth Fry, of Poultry, having effected the most admirable reforms. In the bitter winter of 1816, when the Thames was frozen over hard as stone, and a fire kindled on the ice roasted an ox whole, and many were homeless, Mrs. Fry had entered the prison of Newgate, alone and unprotected, like both Daniel and the angel who shut the lions' mouths, and had knelt to pray with the inmates—toothless, blear-eyed old infants with rheumatism, running sores, and other ailments. What the world had not accomplished in centuries of cynicism, Mrs. Fry accomplished in a month, through the employment of simple kindness. In a fortnight, through her efforts, these women became like the best-behaved children. This was not, as

so many thought, merely an isolated instance of reform, merely
a prison. The women's side, Robert Owen said, was the miniature of England as it would be when conducted under the correct principles—the men's side, where there were madness and
drunkenness, the condition of England at the present moment.
All could be changed. The worst prostitute, even Moll Flanders,
had often the soul of generosity—was a Mrs. Fry in a slightly
different circumstance from that of Mrs. Fry. Christ had said,
long ago, to the thief on the cross, "Thou shalt be with me this
day in paradise"—meaning that both were the victims of a social
circumstance. Shades of Daniel Defoe!

Was not the variety of existence its chief charm, both before
and after Waterloo? Everybody who was anybody said so. The
pleasures of the imagination, many believed, were greater than
those of truth, and science, the archfiend, the enemy of mankind.
Everybody who was anybody was suspicious of that pallid abstraction, the science of society. There were, it was generally agreed,
more beautiful enterprises than to establish logical connections,
as between cause and effect. Every man was his own sad law. Not
all could enjoy the same idea of happiness, this side of paradise.
There was, for example, a pale duchess who lived quietly in the
country, noted for her care of forty dogs, many monkeys, many
parrots, her ideal community—and rarely did she go to bed, for
she was suffering from a fatal illness. Many a sunburned widow,
renting a pigsty for sixpence a year, might think the duchess fortunate—but many a poor widow, with her apron full of chestnuts,
would survive her. No use making matters worse than they were,
by putting the duchess into a pigsty, and putting the widow into
a monkey cage. "Dust thou art, and to dust thou shalt return," the
Bible says. And a little knowledge is a dangerous thing.

So life progressed quite merrily, at least in the higher circles,
though the Habeas Corpus Act was suspended, and many cruel
laws were resurrected, and there were many shameful hangings.

There was no way to avert fate, no way to avoid poverty—"The poor ye have with ye always." There was much less a way to get rid of war—soldiers being killed, alas, like seals in pathos of Arctic distance. Still, in those circles where an opinion counted, this emptied the world of the unfit—and war had been ever the greatest customer, more properties acquired than lost. It was the rich who suffered as the poor could not. The poor rate took an unjust percentage of just profit, as a tax was placed on everything from soup to nuts, both before and after Waterloo—a tax on hair powder, swans, horses above the size of ponies, marble tombs, windows, corset stays, the ermine which covered the judge, the rope which hanged the thief, the burlap which was his winding sheet. Something ought to be done to change this evil tax. Still, it was better to be a ruler than a herd of smelly paupers. There were basic differences to be respected—impossible to make a silk purse out of a sow's ear, everybody, even the poor widow said. Jove and the gods, a corporate body, had felt no twinge of sorrow to witness the hanging of housemaids by one rope drawn around their necks, and the twittering of their feet like birds, but only for a little while. There was a stratum below the level deserving sympathy. Similarly, Catholics should be restricted from the higher walks of life. The subject of Catholic emancipation was evaded as much as possible, both before and after Waterloo, for fear of causing an increase in George III's insanity—as Ralph Atkinson, phantasmal farmer in an old straw bonnet, distrusted the Pope of Rome, distrusted ghostly powers, wanted to reclaim both England and Ireland. Meanwhile, the child mortality rate did not decrease—there was a constant influx of cherubim into heaven. And George III ordered his tomb.

Evading the real issues, everybody who was anybody accused Robert Owen of wishing to turn England into a prison, army barracks, beehive, dormitory for the poor, pigeon roost, pigsty, heaven on earth. He wanted to get rid of all the exotic elements, it was said, for he thought man to be as circumscribed by sense as a mole or a lobster. What a far cry from the truth of human nature—for a man, though blind, would yet see, and though deaf, would yet hear. Had they not the example of George III? If Robert Owen had his way, Jonathan Wooler, the "Black Dwarf," wrote—speaking perhaps for the liberal element—he would turn England into a "nursery for men, a kind of pauper barracks, where men, women, and children should be reduced to mere automata, their feelings, passions, and opinions measured out by rule, working in common, living in common, having all things in common except their wives—with abundance of food and clothing—but without liberty or hope of anything beyond." These were "pretty plans" Robert Owen had drawn up on paper—"and if he had to make the beings who are to inhabit his paradises, as well as to make the laws that should regulate them, there can be no doubt that he would manage very well." If he must fill his barracks, then let him choose bishops, pampered sinecurists, fat pensioners, Parliamentarians from pocket burroughs, and all those rich enough to suffer from the gout—but "let the poor alone—the working bee can always find a hive." Mr. Canning opposed the rational villages on the ground of their being inimical to individuality. Another wrote that if Robert Owen had his way, "it would make us a race of beings little removed from the brutes, only ranging the confines of the parallelogram instead of the mazes of the forest." Tiger, tiger, burning bright!

In the struggle for existence, the nation had learned to face its exterior enemy. But who was the interior enemy, and how identify him? At the time of the revenue tariff on raw cotton, Robert Owen had called a meeting of factory owners, to ask for its repeal, and to consider means for the improvement of the conditions under which workers were employed. The first motion had been carried with wild applause—but to the second, there had not been an assenting voice. Most were genuinely sorry to see that their brother cotton lord had flown off his perch.

Yet even during the Napoleonic wars and the period of oppression following, there were a few who saw Robert Owen as the angel of light struggling with the angel of darkness.

John Milton had written, in the seventeenth century, of Lucifer, or Cromwell, tall as a Norwegian pine tree, storming the crystal citadel of God, or Charles I—and had justified Cromwell, but never the ways of Charles I toward man. John Bunyan had preached, from his window at Bedford jail, a warning against the Mr. Badmen of England and this world, which they were leading, through their greed, to a terrible destruction at some future time. Both Milton and Bunyan, as poets, had fallen into the pit of beautiful language, had stumbled over the block of flowered verbiage. Both, therefore, paled in importance by the side of one unwept, unhonored, and unsung—John Bellers, no poet, who had proposed, in 1695, a community for English workers, and one which could be immediately realizable, as it did not take into account the war of angels, the apple tree, the serpent. Robert Owen, long years after he had reached his own conclusions, which were independent even of Plato, had found Bellers' pages tucked into an old Bible—where, but for him, they would have remained forever, doubtless.

Bellers described, in plain language for that day, a Utopia to be made up of members of the English working classes, the large body of the worthy poor. All the necessary steps were given. The future, he said, must lie in a safe beginning under God—"for not all acorns become oaks." With this reservation, he added that nothing could be left to chance. Utopia should be carefully situated. Utopia should never be near the idle, morose, fierce, wild, lashing sea. Utopia should exclude drunken fishermen, who had caused the downfall of the last one! As to the instrument for such a work—God would provide it, even as He had raised

Queen Hester from the dust to a shining crown. Not all rich
men were content to rest upon their private grounds, browsing like sleek cattle—"There is many have a touch of a more
universal love." God's care having been exerted in the selection
of the leader, greater care must be taken in the selection of the
people—nothing too much. Provisions must be made as to the
number and kinds of workers, including community bedmakers
and community cooks, for thus the women should be released
to factories, the number and kinds of industries. Utopia should
exclude from its borders the professions and middlemen, as beings
not necessary, as beings problematical. Such a community, once
in operation, would be like the example of primitive Christianity,
and not so easily undone as single men—"For if plundered, twelve
months' time will recruit again, labour bringing a supply as the
ground doth, and when together, they assist one another, but
when scattered, are useless, if not preying upon one another."
Bellers could not believe that any, having experienced such a way
of life, would prefer insecurity. Patience was required on the part
of the founders, however. If the old proved brittle at first, yet
children were a "soft clay," who would take the impression of the
molder, and who might be brought up with no memory of any
other way of life. The word "academy" might be more attractive
to the inmates than "workhouse" or appellations to suggest the
compulsion of their original poverty. Perhaps the inmates should
wear caps and gowns, for they would have access to schools and
libraries as well as to factories and fields. If not a costume, they
should be willing to wear such clothes as had suffered some defect
in manufacture. Gradually, such a community might spread to
include others—like an oak tree spreading its boughs.

"What!" said one observer of Robert Owen's paper Utopia.
"Shall each inherit six feet of earth, finally?" Still another would
prefer to be locked into his kennel with his dogs. Still another
would have faced a musket sooner than this regimented happiness.

For a godless cotton lord, it turned out that Robert Owen
knew the Bible all too well. It was impossible to arouse the attention of an audience merely by quoting, at that date, arid statistics. Gentlemen yawned, and ladies slept behind their fans. To
startle mummies from their languor, Robert Owen turned their
own ammunition against his Malthusian opponents at the top of
the pyramid—bombarded capital's citadels and swan boats with
Biblical metaphor. His speeches, on such occasions, "shocked
the civilized world." What was the amazement of everybody to
find that Robert Owen's was a Scriptural communism—though
devoid of religion—and that God—though there was no God—
had been the true author of the science of society. What was the
amazement of everybody to find that Robert Owen's proposed
community was the one promised of old! It was disrupting to the
superiority of those who had held, they believed, a monopoly on
the word of God—and whose success in business was the direct
result of their religious virtues. It was colossal. It was as if God
preached God's funeral sermon. It was as if God, though alive,
imagined Himself dead, and had gone into mourning for Himself
publicly. Nobody was deceived. From a day in the London Tavern
when Robert Owen first began to speak with the speech of angels,
close acquaintances cut him on the streets, and he was refused
admission to many drawing rooms where he had been welcome
before, as a kind of amusing eccentric, who believed man to be a
godly machine. After all, if he had his way, all the drawing rooms
would be darkened, and all the furniture would be shrouded, and
everybody would be nameless, like the workers in cotton mills,
who had had so little individuality to start with. Fox-hunting clerics, naturally excitable, turned purple at the mention of Robert
Owen's name—here was a fox who could not be caught, by means
natural or supernatural—here was a rival preacher!

Playing with language is a dangerous business. Perhaps, from a
later point of view, it will seem that Robert Owen drew the very

conclusions which he had denied as possible, and espoused the very dogmas which he despised in his heart. Certainly, when he abandoned Biblical language, his followers did not—and from about 1814 onward he was bound to be, in spite of himself, a figure almost legendary in proportions.

Robert Owen's, apparently, was a sermon to end all sermons, to empty all gardens of their peacocks, to empty all kennels of their fine dogs, to shove all people, high and low, into one awful compartment. No sooner would Napoleon be made to eat grass than up would crop this cotton lord, wanting to unite labor, wanting to unite mankind, preaching one world, even if at the cost of the British Empire and all its sacred institutions, its vested privileges, the Church, the home, the family, the aura of tradition. It was not funny. It was a mighty serious problem—for while the poor were largely inarticulate, as they should be, this man was not, and gave expression to what they had probably been thinking all along about their masters. That a few rare men should govern these had been a divinely appointed mission—till Robert Owen suggested another character of God as universal.

In the works of Isaiah, Robert Owen said, were shown the calamities of ignorance, the changes necessary for social improvement, the punishment upon the house of Jacob for their sins. He quoted all old prophets. Wherefore had they imagined that God had placed one man in a high station and another in a low? Wherefore had they imagined the vast majority to be brutish and incapable of thought? Wherefore had they imagined themselves exempt from leveling, when the workers were united? There was a new era at hand. The women with their girdles of satin and satin stomachers, their strings of pearls, their golden sandals, their tinkling bells, should come to dust and ashes. The cotton lords, the clerics on their payroll, the biased surgeons, the entirety of mercantile England should be blotted out, that a new and greater England might arise. England, whether she knew it or not, was

on the eve of a great political and economic revolution, when
the workers should storm the empty citadels, when the parasite should be evicted. The time was even now at hand when
the *status quo* should be dissolved in the science of society, with
its assurance of a rational public education and rational public
employment. Another and greater battle of the pyramids was at
hand—and the top already blown off, long ago. God was tired of
all their self-worship, tired of the difference between what they
said and what they did. God had joined the party of the humanitarian socialists, long ago. He would rather break bread with
Thomas Paine than the united bishops. He heard the prayers of
scattered children and not of the united cotton lords. Wherefore
had the lords spiritual and temporal imagined that they were a
chosen people? Wherefore had they imagined that they fasted,
and God had heard not? They had locked themselves into the curtained drawing room. They had eaten a great deal—and had fasted
for strife, contention, self-indulgence. Wherefore had they ever
imagined themselves under God's government? They had trusted
themselves under the feathers of an evil government which was
their own, not God's. They had suffered from vain imaginations,
selfish perturbations, superfluous cares, immoderate fears. They
had worshiped a return on their investment. Yet God saw that
they would be like gnats in a storm, like blasted boughs. It was
not an acceptable day to God, either before or after Waterloo.
For their hands were defiled with blood and their fingers with
iniquity. They had slain the children of England before Waterloo,
and they had slain them after. Many a poor widow in her pigsty
was worthier of the love of God than they were. Many a poor
drunk was worthier of God's love. They expressed themselves in
excesses. Their fingers were stained with blood and their hands
with iniquity. What were the fabulous sums spent each year
on diamond cutters' bills, hand-wrought silver services, egret
feathers, and such baubles, while the children of England were

consigned to pits of everlasting darkness? Yet in the pit of darkness, the coal mine, shone already that great diamond, the science
of society, a thing to flood the world with rational brightness.
For the workers, though beaten, though starved, could never
be destroyed—and would unite, inevitably as raindrops, at a
certain temperature, congeal into hail. God was on the side of
the farmers, the mechanics. The spirit of progress could not be
stopped by nay-sayers.

Yea, Britannia, a Lot's wife, was on the verge of a new order,
when reason should replace the dream of chaos. What was Lot's
wife looking back for? The future lay in front. She herself had
helped to build it. God, long ago, had listened to the still, small
voice of John Locke in the wilderness—long ago had effaced
many of His writings, on the advice of David Hume, and had
for some time past been in close association with the authors of
American liberty. God, long ago, had broken the covenant with
the Children of Israel in the wilderness. Moses, true, had put a
veil over his face, that the Children of Israel could not look stead-
fastly to the end of that which was abolished. The minds of men
had been blinded, and their hearts had been clouded—so that
they knew not what they did. But now the veil had been done
away with, and the laws had been abolished, due to the great
progress which had been made by scientists, especially Bacon,
especially Newton. God was tired of God's dualism. God was
tired of all the Malthusian agonizers, attributing to Him a suicidal theology, though He had been ever a principle of creation,
and the book in His hand was the green book of Rousseau. God
was tired of their standing armies, their wars. God was tired of
their attribution of guilt to all but themselves. God was tired
of their worship, a mixture of sensuality and boredom. Science
would be omnipotent, in short, over all people who walked in
gardens, who sacrificed in gardens, who sat among the graves,
and who considered that they were holier than others. God gave

not a straw for the smoke of their incense, and they had done nothing but blaspheme Him upon His hills. The old order must be done away with, and all its mistaken institutions. God would never shed a tear. Science, He saw, would regulate man's moral frame and nature, and all discord melt away into everlasting harmony, like snow in August. For the age of materialistic socialism was at hand—and very far from that transcendent altruism which may accompany the most brutal egoism in practice. The slave and the bondman would be free. God, in short, would bring forth a seed out of Jacob, and out of Judah an inheritor for His holy mountains—yea, the union of labor. The sky would open, and there would come a white horse, and the name of its rider would be Faithful and True—for the message in his mouth would be the science of society. "And when these things come to pass, then look up and lift up your heads, for your redemption from CRIME AND MISERY draweth nigh."

Oh, what a rational community would be God's, when God was no more! When the twin sisters Science and Practice ruled the earth, and the nations were united, there would be no more spirit of competition, no more crowns, no profit, no loss, no satin petticoats, no lords spiritual, no lords temporal, no mythical corporations, no parents, no nurses, no Greek, no Latin, nothing of our present political and domestic arrangements, no wars, no populating of vacuums, no money, no dance of bloodless categories, no snuff, no kid gloves, no extremes of rich and poor, no lawyers, no wigs, no assumption of superiority, no silver spoons, no nooses, no Jove, no Jehovah, no stocks, no bonds, no myth at all. "Then shall the wolf dwell with the lamb, and the leopard shall lie down with the kid, and the calf, and the young lion, and the fatling together, and a little child shall lead them." There would be playing of harps and flutes, a dancing of barefoot children on the green, the greatest happiness to the greatest number. There would be no model communities, all rectangular, with factories and fields adjoining, and the slaughterhouse at some distance removed. There would be public employment for public good. There would be public education as a public property. A man would reap the grain he sowed, would have something more than an illusory crop. And the bones would flourish like tender grass in that New Jerusalem, a thing of this creation after all. Then Sharon would be a fold for the flocks, and dew on the grass like pearls or God's tears. And the former things would not be remembered, would be as if they had never been.

Interviews with Emperors and Kings

On the old king's death, in January, 1820, George IV came to the throne of England. A selfish, mean, pompous gentleman, described by Dickens in the character of Mr. Turveydrop. He was profoundly opposed, like his father before him, to transubstantiation, the invocation of saints, and Catholic emancipation, but for the most personal reasons—alas, he was a bigamist, whose left hand knew not what his right hand did. This much can be said in George IV's favor, however—he was an unwilling king, a creature of circumstance, and he disliked signing death warrants before breakfast. The old rip led an extraordinary life, indeed—never getting up until six in the afternoon, and transacting the large part of his business in bed. Though there was a watch hanging on his bedpost, he would not so much as turn his head to look at it. Due to his irregular habits, not a few criminals escaped the gallows, temporarily—a cutthroat's doom was often lost among his voluminous bedcovers, satin and velvet. Perhaps a few escaped permanently. Quite often, he emerged from the royal chamber clad like a cattle thief, a gambler, a lady-killer, or a cutthroat. He complained that the glove he wore did not fit him. He was tired to death, he said, of all the stuffy people around him, and tired of all his jeweled mistresses. He yearned for his younger days when he had traveled with a fast set in London low-life taverns and was indistinguishable from other villains. A Falstaff, he yearned for Doll Tearsheet, cock fights in dirty lands, bumptious barmaids, mayhem, rough souls ill met. Most people believed that he had inherited just a touch of his father's madness, though perhaps more comic than cosmic.

George IV was not alone in his flare for the romantic outfit. In the face of many great realistic problems, great repressions, factions, angers, discontentments, in the face of the rise of English liberalism and the progressive spirit, there were hues and cries for a return to the institutions and ideals of the medieval past, when men were men, and wrongs were righted—no more popular writer, for many years, than Sir Walter Scott, authority on knights in armor and bosom friend, like Beau Brummel, to florid, absent-minded George IV. To Sir Walter Scott, Tory spokesman, the beggar, Alice Blue Gown, seemed picturesque, the repository of the nation's culture. As perhaps she was. A mysterious outlaw, Tom Swing, a kind of Robin Hood, went about the English countryside, setting fire to crops on farms where the threshing machine had supplanted the flail. When Robert Owen stood for Parliament in Lanark borough, the people for whom he had done so much sent up his opponent, whose eyes had turned toward heaven in a fine frenzy rolling. The only community was emotional.

Robert Owen had gone to the Continent, to attend the convention of the crowned heads of Europe at Aix-la-Chapelle. It was this experience which, at a trying period, most discouraged him as to the possibility of effecting the regeneration of society through monarchic governments. George IV was about to emerge on the scene, George III still engaged in the business of entertaining shadows. Europe, although supposedly at peace, was at war. The Holy Alliance, made up of Russia, France, Prussia, and Austria, was determined to stamp out every movement to promote liberty. England opposed this aggregation of unholy powers.

In Switzerland, far more wonderful than Mt. Blanc was that humble gray priest and schoolmaster, Father Oberlin, with whom Robert Owen, his wife, and her sisters, had the pleasure of drinking tea one Sunday afternoon, in a vegetable garden. Father Oberlin confessed that, although employed by Rome, he could hardly find enough money to keep his little school going from one month to another. Only with the greatest difficulty had he maintained what he had accomplished. To do so had cost him many sleepless nights, with no encouragement but the emanation of his dead wife. He believed that society is the abstraction, and the individual, reality—faith being the mustard seed which can move mountains, though not in Switzerland. He believed in divine interposition at every hand. He had always had a ballot box filled with "yes" and "no" slips which told him what to do—the voice of the Lord. Thus he had built a bridge between two mountains and had instituted a community kitchen. Thus he had saved a people whose diet had been grass cooked in milk. He had been polite to his would-be murderers and had escaped assault. The Lord, like the ballot box, was always with him. The institutions of the past, he believed, expressed, whatever their errors, the profoundest needs and aspirations of man's nature. Who questioned them questioned human nature, out of which they had grown. There could be no perfect happiness short of God. No sooner would man achieve one goal than he would look forward to another. Though his tongue lolled out like that of a tired dog, he would soon be ready to chase after happiness again. Nothing would satisfy him for long. Father Oberlin wished Robert Owen good success in his program to reorganize human nature, but warned that he would be opposed by all governments, religions, and industries in the world.

A pleasant afternoon was spent with Louis Philippe—formerly a schoolmaster and traveler in the American wilderness, where, at a remote outpost, the people had begged him to remain as their doctor, due to his excellent knowledge of bleeding. He was to become, however, the King of France. As "Citizen King" of France, Louis Philippe would use the tricolored flag of the Revolution instead of the white flag of the Bourbons, the cock of Gaul instead of the blue shield with gold fleur-de-lis. Under his administration, silk-weaving would become an important French industry, and Paris, the chief market for hats and dresses in the world. Also, by the way, French merchants would carry on a bloody war with the chieftains of perfumed Arabia. That pleasant afternoon, Louis Philippe was deeply sympathetic with a rational view of society, but tugged at by many strings, mostly irrational. "I live, therefore, very quietly," he told Robert Owen, "and take no active part in any of the movements of the day. But I observe all that takes place, and the day may come when I may have more liberty to act according to my own views of the necessities of the times." He wished Robert Owen success in his endeavors to disenthrone all ghostly powers, including himself, of course.

The French Prime Minister was very effusive, kissing Robert Owen, much to his embarrassment, on both cheeks. He expressed his admiration for the work at New Lanark, his interest in the public speeches at London. But was the age really like the ripe peach which falleth? Might not some other century be better for such world-shaking reforms? Some day all these theories would be universally practiced, certainly, and the workers dominate the world. Not, he feared, in his lifetime. He accompanied his guest through three reception rooms, as a mark of respect, and left him only at the outer door, with many apologies, both for the weather and human nature.

The journey through Europe was one disappointment after another. True, La Place and Humboldt, discoverers of continents on the moon, asked eager questions as to society, whether it could be isolated as in a glass jar, all the ingredients known, no mysterious fluctuation of events, and the experimenter looking down, as if he were not himself a dissolving vista. "They seemed to have lived to this period in worlds of their own," Robert Owen said.

Everybody in Geneva was reading his *New View of Society*—as if it were the season's most popular fantasy. Comparisons were made between this and an obscure, almost forgotten work—Robert Bage's *Hermsprong, or Man as He Is Not*. Hermsprong, who had drunk deeply of the heady principles of Rousseau, planned a semicircular community of congenial spirits, to be located in the American wilderness, within a half-mile circle, where they should enjoy association with superior Indians, such as would put most white men to shame. Hermsprong, however, abandoned his proposed community on the instant of learning that he was the inheritor of a large English estate, including rector and hunting dogs. Was not this the pattern of most revolutionists, that they were revolutionists only until they acquired property?

There was a grotesque incident in a Geneva drawing room. The renowned Captain Hall had just returned from a visit with Napoleon on the island of St. Helena. Far from considering Napoleon as the concentration of evil, Robert Owen had always looked on him as one who had carried to their extremes in practice the mistaken attitudes of most governments under the present system. Robert Owen inquired of Captain Hall as to Napoleon's reaction to the *New View*, which he had heard was one of the discrowned potentate's favorite readings. What a scene then took place! Captain Hall, imitating Napoleon, paraded up and down the drawing room, but not with the old aplomb, as when reviewing his armies—there was a look of living death in his eyes. So had Napoleon, much reduced, walked under the weeping-willow trees at St. Helena, within sight and sound of the surf beating on jagged rocks, and with greatest difficulty had been able to walk forward, as he suffered much from a cancer of the stomach. Captain Hall's shoulders drooped as under a great weight. Far from thinking in terms of a new moral world, from which all punishment would have been removed, Napoleon was thinking in terms of the old—and Captain Hall retired to a satin divan, as his fingers clutched the empty air. He complained of his keeper, Sir Hudson Lowe, a bigoted, empty-headed man, and of the invasion of space throughout his frame corporeal. He pointed out that the shortest way to British India lies through Afghanistan, where there are mountains of diamond-faceted light. Once more, Captain Hall resumed his stumbling walk. Captain Hall, if not Napoleon, seemed human nature at its lowest ebb on a barren shore. Robert Owen could not help thinking that a mind accustomed to detail comprehends but little of the mind accustomed to philosophic generalizations—communication between the two being sometimes difficult, if not impossible. Bogged in such incongruous aspects, being himself half in love with death, how could the captain comprehend those rational principles which never fail when put into operation?

In Frankfort, more disappointment, more power of corrupt illusion! All the kings of Europe were about to convene at Frankfort. Here, Robert Owen met a M. Gentz, Secretary to the Congress, who had arrived a few days in advance of the crowned heads, to smooth the thorny way for their coming. M. Gentz, although in the confidence of every European ruler, confessed that even he could not foresee the course of history. It was a game of chance, requiring the genius of a gambler for high stakes. He seemed quite happy about the whole thing. Through M. Gentz, Robert Owen met a M. Bethman, whose mother, a medium, advised the despots as to what should be their policies in Europe. She was in communication with the most opposed spirits. Some said that the universe was in its cradle and others, that it was in its grave. On more important matters, the lady was sufficiently discreet.

At a dinner party of the Germanic Diet, Robert Owen grew impatient with fickle hopes, false vistas, pretentious claims, the usual indifference to the good of mankind, and overeating. He rose, unannounced, and read a proclamation which he always carried with him, like a toothbrush. Now, through the progress of science, he said, the old idea of man born in sin had been displaced forever. The means existed, at this moment, for the foundation of a happy, united world order, omitting despots and partisan rivalries. Contrary to his expectations, no one was in the least dismayed by that bald statement. "Oh, yes," the Secretary agreed, and apparently speaking for all the despots, his friends, "we know that very well, but we do not want the mass to become wealthy and independent of us. How could we govern them if they were?" Robert Owen saw then the impracticability of the present system in Europe being maintained under a national education and employment of all the people in constructive work. According to the views of the tyrants, there must be subservient peoples, differences of class, or every husbandman and tiller of the fields would wear a golden crown. Result, competition. He left the dinner party early.

To Caroline, he confessed that to overcome in all classes in all countries prejudices of the most formidable character would require the wisdom of the serpent, the harmlessness of the dove, and the courage of the lion. Having lost faith in the redemption of despots, he lectured to her sisters, as he hoped that they might help to spread the light of communism—though never was there a less impressionable audience, for each had her mind on her future husband, a flaming cleric.

In due time, the kings of Europe descended on Frankfort. Every man on the street was a king. Frankfort seemed, indeed, almost a classless society, as if every farmer were wearing a golden crown. Robert Owen himself might have been mistaken for the ruler of an obscure country, perhaps Sardinia. He was merely, however, the salesman of an idea, which was the science of human society, for the benefit of the average man.

Accosting the Emperor of Russia on a side street, Robert Owen offered him a copy of his memorials. The Emperor refused, curtly, as his suit fitted tightly, and he had no pocket to receive such a ponderous scroll. Learning this strange salesman's name, however, he apologized for his rudeness. A man in his position had to be careful. The Emperor asked Robert Owen to come to his rooms at some later date, perhaps a Sunday night. They would then go into the problem of redemption, viewing it from every angle, as it was a subject of greatest concern to him personally, and one he would like to explore at his leisure. Similarly, he studied Bach in otherwise empty moments. He must warn, however, that he was hard pressed by visitations of spirits from the world which lies beyond beyond. Should spiritual beings be active on that evening, he must give himself up to them, without stint or measure, with utter generosity. Not only were they his political advisers, they were also his dearest friends—an old tutor who had died vacantly after a long period of sublime unconsciousness, Constantine of Byzantium, a dissolving lady of the Moscow ballet, a shoemaker, a horse doctor. These would cross like birds, the gulf between the immortal and the mortal frame. They had read the book of nature, from its beginning to its end, and had found no blank page, and nothing mysterious but themselves perhaps. They knew all the secrets of the ethereal gases. Robert Owen refused the Emperor's invitation, though he was sorry afterward—for this man, he said, was as kind-hearted as the surroundings of despotic powers would permit.

Uniformly, Robert Owen found that the ministers of despotic powers differed from their masters, in that they favored the new society. His stay at Geneva and Frankfort had only enlarged, however, his concept of the errors in the existing systems. More and more, from that visit, he would think of a Utopia in the

American wilderness, a community which would be not merely the building again of that which had been destroyed.

At Aix-la-Chapelle, Robert Owen completed two addresses in behalf of the working peoples to the governments of Europe and America. Lord Castlereagh, that great supporter of the *status quo*—and, ironically enough, even then suffering under the effects of depressing medicines, and a future suicide, for he was to cut his throat a short time later—was obliging enough to read both addresses to the Congress. He reported that they were considered the most important of all the papers which had come up. A polite, distant remark.

Members of the Swiss Society of Natural History were quite at home with one another and with Robert Owen's views. They saw that two lines of thought about men and the universe were converging—the positive utilization of human sciences and the importance of the unfailing common man. The new system, as they visualized it, would be unified and diversified, one and many, pervaded by rationality and individuated within rationality. Man's aspiration, in such a state, would be the quest for enrichment without loss of integrity. The finite would seem no longer the puppet of the infinite—as it would be recognized that the only strings were ever the political. Perfection of individual life would imply the similarity of modes of action. Human departures from the constellation of human statistics—poor wandering stars—would seem neither grand nor wonderful, but traceable to an unmysterious origin, such as a brain fever or weak eyesight. To recognize the origin of belief would be a great assistance in the control of belief, it was believed.

The past ages of the world, Robert Owen announced, shortly after his return from Europe, presented the history of human irrationality only. A great change was at hand, however, when that province, human nature, should be brought within the domain of the universal sciences—and when theology, with all its dolls and clerics, should be put away, as having belonged to the bleak childhood of the human race. "We are now advancing," Robert Owen said, "toward the dawn of reason, and to the period when man shall be born again." He was fully acquainted with the powers of darkness against which he had to contend, the monstrous nurses, clothed in the garb of all the religions and superstitions of the world.

He went to Ireland, to carry his message of enlightenment to the depressed Irish people, a nation of hollow-eyed beggars and dead babies. If only Ireland could see the light, perhaps the world would be persuaded by this one example! No country was ever more at odds with truth than this.

Through many ages, English landlords had displaced the cruel Irish kings who walked in mist, but not their cruelty. The English had grown as rich as Caesar, while the Irish continued poor, helpless, lice-ridden, a nation of tramps caught among brambles. With the sea all around their emerald island, the Irish were never great fishermen—doubtless because they believed the waters to be inhabited by their dead. The Irish bogs, also the abode of the dead, were hardly crossed by roads. Thus the whole of Ireland was a mystery. Fairy beings mixed with saints. All the women walking by the sea were the resurrected dead. Otherwise, the Irish nation argued on the nature of Christ's body, whether the body was made bread, the blood was made wine. Famine, alas, was always with them, like a clock ticking. No manna fell from the sky. Jonathan Swift, a century before, had publicized Ireland's starvation, both for the benefit of the English consciousness and the Irish, by circulating a recipe for the cooking of the young— what more delectable than a toasted baby, decked out with a few green bay leaves? That was the Dean's profound sense of tragedy, laughing its head off. His voice was taken as a hysterical laugh in the dark of an asylum. No improvements had been made. There was hardly an Irishman who could tell whether he was in his body or out of his body. There was hardly an Irishman who did not glory in his infirmities, and who did not believe that his weakness was his strength.

Yet Ireland, Robert Owen believed, could have been the happiest of nations, if released from its great love of extremes, such as Death's hoary visage scaring the pygmy realm, humanity— and overshadowing all of life. All that Ireland needed was a true understanding of the science of society. Happiness was easily attainable, within the reach of every man in his senses. Ireland, under the correct principles, could support all its people and many more than now existed.

Robert Owen, speaking before an audience of Catholic divines in Dublin, urged that they consider Ireland's earthly future as well as its unearthly. He repeated his views of the true destination of human life. The potato was—by the way, and speaking ex cathedra—worthier of study than chasubles and manna. The humble potato, Ireland's chief food product, edible only nine months of the year, would not increase because priests wore its flowers in their hats—but was worthier of study than the transmigration of souls. Should more potatoes be raised, there would be fewer souls migrating to another sphere. The potato was but one aspect of the science of society. There was the whole subject of rationalism as opposed to the geographical gods.

The united Catholic divines reported their unchanged position. They considered the ravens, who neither sowed nor reaped, who had neither storehouse nor barn, and God had fed them— yet how much better were men than fowls of the air? No system, they were convinced, could divest human nature of its frailties, this side of paradise where the laws of nature cease. Weariness, painfulness, hunger, thirst, fastings, cold, nakedness, stripes, imprisonments, persecutions, distresses, death by the sword, death by fire—these had been the lot of Christ's servants always. The greater the suffering, the greater the vision of good. Perhaps the lowliest housemaid had seen the most exalted vision, such as Raphael's sheet of light or Michael's scarf. Moreover, to suppose strength possible for all would be to go in opposition to the law of God and the doctrine of the remission of sins. The more there was to heal, the more compassionate the healing. All the rudiments of arts and sciences could be traced, not to the statistical constellation, but to the poor wandering star which is the abundance of a thatched saint's revelations. What man, merely by the employment of reason, could add to his stature one cubit—or take away an inch?

Returning to London, Robert Owen found that he had made an impression on Madame Tussaud, mistress of the museum of wax figures, who proposed to add him to her famed collection. She was persuaded by her Jesuit confessor not to do so, however—she might have as many murderers as she liked but no infidels.

There were more important issues at stake. Lord Sidmouth had two hundred copies of Robert Owen's *New View of Society* struck off, with blank interleaves, on which the governments of the world were to write their opinions. Some got lost in the mail, some were never returned.

In 1822, Robert Owen's bill for the establishment of a model community in England came before Parliament, sponsored by a committee headed by the archbishops of England and Ireland, a host of peers, scholars, and reformers. All saw some advantage in a form of labor within the gates of a rectangle. All, or almost all, rejected the science of society as deficient in reality. One of that number suggested that the population of the first rational village be made up entirely of cutthroats and felons. There were others who did not see how distress could be removed by feeding at certain hours as if they were horses or exercising them at stated times. Catholics were urged, by Protestants, not to sacrifice their Redeemer.

There was, however, an enterprising convert to Robert Owen's science of society—Abram Combe, who visited New Lanark one afternoon in 1820 and was changed, by that event, from an irrational to a rational way of life. At Orbiston, near Glasgow, he would found, in 1825, a "deistical compound," a huge, somber pile of rectangular stone buildings occupied by several hundred workers. Thus would Eden be restored. Combe agreed with Robert Owen that scientific discoveries had placed a boundless power of mechanism within man's grasp. At the same time, he was a convert to spade husbandry, which Robert Owen recommended as superior to the plow. Combe was to be, alas, a victim to his enthusiasm for spade husbandry—and with him would pass away that new heaven and new earth, Orbiston dissolving like a dream. He died of heart failure in August, 1827, for he had spaded too much in the sun—the "earliest confessor and martyr to the New Views" but one who deserves appreciation for the vaster experiment of community and brotherhood.

New Harmony, the Goal of Man

Undoubtedly, it is difficult to keep the rational from seeming the irrational, the most Utopian project in the annals of history. Robert Owen, like Pantagruel, was cast up on stranger islands than Cut-off. Islands where absurdities are recommended by the plausibility of an argument, where fact is disregarded, and where no standard of measurement is acknowledged—every man an archipelago, a little out of this world.

Buffeted by winds, the voyager on the wide seas of human nature comes to an island where the palm, the oak, and the fir tree grow in abundance, and where all people are birds multiplying without carnal copulation—clerichawks, monkhawks, bishop-hawks, popehawks. Here, at least, the law of diminishing returns is suspended, though moon and stars should fail.

On the neighboring shore of Whims arises the coral-roofed Palace of Quintessence, a bodiless, green-haired goddess who cures with a song, it has been said, the sick, tough, wrinkled, moldy pilgrims to her shrine. Common sense takes flight when assaulted by her logic, most illogical. At present, and throughout eternity, she is playing ball with her bodiless progeny or little sisters, Word, Shadow, Essence, Abstraction, etc. Only the ball, which symbolizes earth, is visible, tossed from one invisible player to another. Others are engaged in games of cosmic chess, billiards, poker, etc. A few monkhawks sit perched among the palm trees, taking down, in shorthand, everything that happens.

Meanwhile, a little beyond the range of their vision, a bright-eyed toad is hopping among pebbles polished by the waves of the sea. This toad has suffered detachment of one leg from his body, it will be seen on close examination. Were he to lose, by chance, another leg, he would have two—and another, one—and another, not even a shadow of his lost members to hop on. Should his head be cut open, and the forepart of his brain removed, he would still show an inclination to pursue his former habits—he would snap at flies, lick dewdrops from hairy-tongued lilies, tremble at the approach of his mate, yawn, sleep. Should the remainder of his brain be removed, he would evidence no interest whatever in his surroundings—flies might buzz. Should his body be pulverized and cast, like pollen, into the sea, he would still have, according to the Goddess of Quintessence, his body immaculate and complete in another sphere, with essence, substance, being beyond being, and other moral attributes. At the moment, he hops on three legs, naturally.

Alas, how many islands this world contains! So many are the degrees and varieties of human genius—a contradiction, likely as not, of both opinion and experience, caused by the shortness of life, the uncertainty of present things, and the insufficiency of the solar system. There are islands ruled by reasonable words, where words become things—and the centaur acquires its peach-colored entity in intellectual space. On such islands, headless men perplex themselves with metaphysical arguments and, having departed from their natural sense of things, assert to be true what they cannot reduce to practice—but on such islands, the theory suffices for reality. There are crystal islands, where the lost handkerchief may be found—and the lost eyeball. There are islands of stain, where trees and herbage never lose their flowers and leaves—for they, like the birds and beasts, are an embroidery on velvet, a tapestry work made by supernatural moths. There are islands, as yet unvisited by man, where trees bear tools, such as mattocks, spades, trowels, hatchets. Islands of miraculous productions, where three couples of foxes in one yoke are plowing a sandy shore, and where the white crow gathers grapes from thorns, figs from thistles, and much from nothingness. Often submerged, but visible on Sundays between the hours of three and five, is an island ruled by the Goddess of Co-operation, half woman, half fish, who sits combing lice as big as raspberries out of her long green hair, as she tells of the wonders of materialistic socialism, a thing unheard of. Not far distant from this island, which is noted for its slimy creatures and crawling things, is a bald rock ruled by a pack of philosophic, toothless bums, more out of their bodies than in them, who peruse blank volumes to prove the fallibility of human testimony, or hearsay, which they do not admit as a factor in any doctrine of mathematics, the one science uncolored by the human mind—all other knowledge being a series of false erections, whether the long-legged plover buffeted by vortices, or an angel with a thorn in his side, buffeted by Satan.

The father of modern socialism could not help seeing that, so long as his rational theories remained undemonstrated, they might be considered a fairy tale like the fairy tale proposed by capitalism, a thing for consumption by the gullible, a place for fallen sparrows.

In 1824, there appeared, in *The Times*, an advertisement of a town for sale in the American wilderness—nothing spectacular, perhaps, in an age of so many migrations and new frontiers. Father George Rapp, of Harmony in Indiana, on the banks of the Big Wabash, offered his property to any buyer with the requisite cash. The plain, unvarnished facts were stated, in as little space as necessary. There was no meaning between the lines, nothing to raise false hopes or cloud the heart of the reader. There were no implications as to metaphysical pearls, mankind centaurs, golden asses, everlasting youth, aberrations of human cogitations, moral labyrinths, loadstone of the soul, miraculous cure, harmony, carbuncle as big as an ostrich's egg, essence, mysterious bottle of ten thousand secrets, metempsychosis, asexual angel, absolute, manufacture of chalk from cheese, grasshoppers marching in battalia, superstition, invisible bells ringing, allegory, Parmenidean sphere, a region where the crowing of cocks is not heard, manna small as hoarfrost, nameless graves, Constantine of Byzantium, elephants accoutered with castles on their backs, underground passage, lizards musical, harpers harping, fox who will be the one survivor, Jezebel's white bones in a turnip field, or other miracles to make this town a paying proposition. Listed for sale, quite simply, was a town, with everything in it, and nothing mysterious—threshing machines, large sheep stables, pigstys, log dwellings, distilleries, a brewery, a granary, brick kilns, manufacturing establishments, twenty thousand acres under cultivation, orchards of bearing fruit, the peach, the cherry, the persimmon, three kinds of nut trees, good drainage system, excellent wharf. The Wabash was navigable for most parts of the year, broad highway through the virgin forest, a land likely to witness new developments.

For some time past, it had seemed to the world that Robert Owen might easily become a harmless recluse at New Lanark, studying innocuous paperbacked Utopias and watching the children dance in paltry Greek tunics. No such thing! He was like the mother eagle in her nest, hatching an egg which would be the New Moral World.

From the contamination through so many ages, of the errors of theoretical men without practice, such as Plato and Sir Thomas More, and those of practical men without any accurate or extensive knowledge of principle, he had felt that it would be difficult, except by practical demonstration, to convince these two classes that by a union of principles derived from extensive practice in accordance with these principles, an intelligent, united, wealthy, virtuous, and happy society could be formed and made permanent. Would the human race, with such a prospect at hand, any longer wish to maintain its present heterogeneous mass of folly and absurdity, and doom their offspring, through succeeding generations, to be inferior, irrational men and women, filled with every injurious notion, and governed by the most ignorant and misery-producing institutions?

Where Father Rapp had acted as a pioneer, Robert Owen felt that there might be established immediately the science of society. He tucked the Rappite advertisement into his brief case, along with his cubes of populace and statistics as to mortality rates in the British islands. In a few days, he wrote a letter to Father Rapp's agent in England, Richard Flower.

Richard Flower of Albion, Illinois, had come to England with his son Edward when, due to his opposition to the introduction of slavery in his state, threats of reprisal had been made against the younger man's life—and even a few attempts at assassination by prowlers in the wilderness. The elder Flower had been commissioned by Father Rapp to sell his property—his commission to be five thousand dollars. In England, the younger Flower's business was to sponsor a bill for the reform of the rein used on dray horses—a bill which was passed almost unanimously by weeping Parliament.

While acting for Father Rapp, the elder Flower had intended to sell real estate, however, and not heaven on earth. It is possible that his enthusiasm for American freedom ran away with him. He was profoundly embarrassed when Robert Owen expressed his desire to purchase the Rappite property, as a site for the creation of a new moral world, and was forced to retract many quotations from Pope's *Essay on Man* and Thomson's *Seasons*, from which he had drawn his portrait of the happy life in Indiana caves. What was good for himself, an experienced frontiersman, was not good for an established cotton lord.

America, Flower said, was young, crude, and undeveloped. The frontier settlements were an implicit maze, far from orderly, a scene "where flamed Ambition's wild desire," etc., etc. There were snares, thorns, bloody eyes, furious looks—and "Avarice, a fiend more fierce than they." There were few gentle knights pricking on the plain. There were, west of the Alleghenies, few evidences of Platonic philosophy, few lawns, fences, four-postered beds. Instead, there were many real ills of life, diversities of tongues.

The settlers could be divided into three types, all, like the wilderness around them, unshaven. First, there were the bushy hunters of small game, such as the much disparaged but beautiful skunk, which exuded an odor to keep off most of its enemies. These Ishmaels lived in earthen huts sodded with grass. They aped the Indians, whom they were determined to extinguish. They were always moving from place to place. Second, there were the farmers, industrious and God-fearing, apparently—but for that reason, the most disappointing group of all, as what seemed like gnarled stability was only another cloud, only another form of deception. Many of the farmers, having cleared a tract of land, were ready, like the hunters, to move on. The profit motive drove them, and a certain restlessness. The land of promise was always the land beyond. Third, there were the professional and mer-cantile class, out to get their neighbors' souls or their scalps, and puffed up by vain knowledge—preachers, lawyers, doctors, storekeepers, mechanics, barbers. Like the hunters and farm-ers, very few intended to stay where they settled. None of any group would endure confinement in a rectangular-shaped village. Utopia, from their point of view, would be a prison house, a house of shades—or very likely, a bedlam. All were "by the winds of autumn driven."

John Quincy Adams, former American ambassador to the
Court of St. James, was astonished to hear that Robert Owen
should attempt to create a communistic way of life in a land of
unlimited opportunities where, he foresaw, competitive individualism would be in the ascendancy for centuries to come. Utopia,
at the moment, seemed a bit superfluous. A communistic society, he warned, could only attract the worthless, the downtrod-
den, the lazy, the ne'er-do-well, the shiftless, the shifty-eyed, the
improvident, the out-at-the-elbows, the eye which imagined itself
to be the entire body, the scum of the earth. America was "the
land where the hunters after money most abound"—and many
an immortal chapter had been written by unscrupulous traders.

Robert Owen was more encouraged by these reports than discouraged. In a land of so many shifting arrangements, the science
of society might have a better opportunity than in one where
all the social relations were petrified and stratified. America was
already free. The human drama, however, unlike the meaningless
flailings of an idiot, must exhibit purpose and idea. A cerebral
government would be a golden mean between extremes—operating on the assumption not merely of a world of flux, not merely
of a world that is ended. Its realm would be that of human life.
Its aim would be not only the prolongation of human existence,
but also an increased quantity of that existence—at that level of
experience which is neither a bodiless angel nor an almost bodiless
oyster, both manufacturing pearls. Man as man would be the great
objective. If God was the author of a harmony which even God
could never quite realize—and most theologians had admitted
this—yet it was better to operate on the assumption of its possibility than its impossibility. Perhaps the whole concept of God was
diabolic—and for him should be substituted an unknown cause,
a power of powers. The popular version of God, like that of man,
was defective and sinister in its effects. Men who were only a degree
smarter than their subjects had depicted the greater potentate as a

system of absolutism, raining manna on the obedient, hailstones on the disobedient. Such a God was backward spiritually and in material resources. His was only an epic state of mind.

There were, according to Robert Owen's view, three distinct states of society. First, he said, was "the common one all over the world, in which human nature has been compelled to believe in or profess a belief in some district religion." The code of supernatural ethics had already been thrown aside, but the transition from despotism to the science of society must be carried out, even under catastrophic conditions. "We advance to a position where we can no longer believe those principles (the district religion); we become like vessels on the ocean without a helm, chart, or compass to steer by, and this is the worst state in which human nature can be placed. But this is a gulf through which we must pass, if the condition of society is to be improved." The third and superior state of existence would be that of the future, when religion should be no longer the deification of manufacturing interests "Everything that savors of irrationality will be withdrawn and cast into the sea." The ego must be absorbed by altruism—and the ear, though it is not the eye, recognize that both are members of the same body. "This change [from the irrational to the rational] is absolutely necessary if man is to be born again—the one regeneration which he and past generations have been looking for. . . . And this change can be wrought simply by acquiring a knowledge of the eternal and immutable facts, which are the laws of human nature, plain, simple, and unmysterious. . . ." Destiny would thus be fulfilled.

America, the Promised Land

Man wants but little here below,
Nor wants that little long.
'Tis not with me exactly so,
But 'tis so in the song.
My wants are many, and it told,
Would muster many a score;
And were each wish a mint of gold,
I still would long tor more.

        —JOHN QUINCY ADAMS, "THE WANTS OF MAN"

Like a bright star in an otherwise clouded heaven, Robert Owen saw, beyond the rolling seas, the promise of America, a place where there would be an end to the concocting of holy lies. Although as baffled an explorer as Christopher Columbus, he would at least recognize the importance of his discovery, that the ragged archipelagoes indicated a new continent, the science of society, not merely a path to the Orient and its dream of dissolving flesh.

There was a morning in the rose garden at Braxfield, a moment of decision, fatal and final, wherein the ship of state broke loose from its rotted moorings, and the course of the universe was somehow changed. Robert Owen turned to his son, Robert Dale, who had witnessed with him so many scenes of mutilation, and proposed, as casually as if he were ordering a fabric at the cotton mills, that they should manufacture a better human nature—"What say, shall it be New Lanark or New Harmony?" That young man replied, with fervor, "Oh, Father, let it be New Harmony." Thus simply was begun the work of creation.

The father could not guess, of course, the son's true motive, that his enthusiasm was engendered by no compassion for man in the abstract but a mill girl, Jessie, whose proximity was maddening—no theory of society but Jessie in a strawberry-colored muslin dress, and her radiance, like a fire banked down under ashes, her sulky underlip. Jessie, rescued from early death in the cotton mills, was an adopted "daughter" in the Owen household—the living image, visiting celebrities said, of her father, and the prettiest of all his children. Robert Dale had fallen in love, imperceptibly, with the perfume of her holiness, as he called it— but was forced to keep silence, in deference to his mother's wish. Not that Caroline made any class distinctions, really, but Jessie was transparent, from her point of view, a social climber, with her head already a little turned. In his autobiography, *Threading My Way*, written toward the evening of his life, when the fire in his loins had long since gone out, Robert Dale was still more concerned with Jessie than a lost Utopia or any other form of government. She was his belle vision in the American wilderness, the goal toward which he struggled—indeed, a Holy Grail, as it were.

Late in 1824, Robert Owen departed for old Harmony in America, to complete the purchase of real estate and properties from George Rapp and his associates. Much to his disappointment, Robert Dale was left at home—William, a hardier brother, being chosen to accompany their father on this initial voyage between the Old World and the New. So that, in the pressure of events, must be deferred that happy day when Jessie with her light brown hair would stand framed by honeysuckle at the door of a rude log cabin—though as it was, Robert Dale enjoyed a last long look at Jessie in the flesh, impressing upon his memory the rustle of her petticoats on the stairs, her little hands like doves, her little feet like mice. Oh, what social chasm could ever yawn between himself and Jessie, a finished pattern without fault, and with a bunch of violets between her breasts? Although it was planned that the entire Owen household be reproduced in Indiana, complete with Caroline's sewing basket, Robert Dale hoped that, in the wilderness, this old world, with all its unequal arrangements, would have dissolved—and Jessie would be his superior. There was no need of hurry, Caroline said—she would wait until New Harmony was put on a permanent basis, as she feared instability. What, she wondered, in the perfection of Utopia, would become of Our Lady Violence, all dressed up with no place to go? Caroline could have found her thimble in her dark. She knew exactly in what drawer, under what tissue, was her wedding dress, a filmy whiteness, which would also be her shroud. She was quietly amazed that only herself and perhaps the postman appreciated the disintegration of her family—that they contemplated the order of the universe, to the exclusion of everything else, such as the crow's-feet on her brow, and her hair which had already turned to gray. How could agnosticism redeem the godless world?

According to *The Times*, the curtain had dropped on Robert Owen's little drama, not soon to be lifted up again. The curtain rose in Washington, D. C., the early spring of 1825, in the presence of an Olympian assembly—an audience constituting perhaps more drama than the play. They were not mere dreamers projecting themselves on cold eternity. They shot their enemy first and asked him questions afterwards—but never shot at an invisible enemy, for the maxim was: "Don't shoot until you can

see the whites of his eyes." Theirs was, on the whole, a deep con-
viction of the necessity and of the holiness of violence.

In the national audience, however, was at least one philosopher, that hermit in the White House, John Quincy Adams,
recent successor to Monroe, and no one so remote and lonely
as he. Monroe had been a common man, who had climbed the
ladder of success by sheer fortitude. Monroe was not the author
of the Monroe Doctrine. John Quincy Adams' most important
work, to date, had been the formulation of the Monroe Doctrine,
by which the American continents should move in their own
orbit, uncrossed by wandering meteors and stars of lesser magnitude—"are henceforth not to be considered as subjects for colonization by any European power." An amorphous nation would
have been, at this era in history, a dead one. As Secretary of State,
Adams had stood for the acquisition of territory from neighboring powers. America could attain its historical perfection only
through conquest over the puny. Adams had backed, but from
a safe distance, the War of 1812, a confused issue. In 1819, he
had forced the Spanish crown to cede the Florida peninsula, with
flamingoes and roseate spoonbills comprising the large part of its
ambient population, to the United States government, which
could never bear to come into contiguity with Spanish vice and
easy living. Also, and this was probably not the determining factor, Florida had been a sanctuary for communities of unfriendly
Seminoles and runaway slaves, who had gone marauding in
Georgia. Aside from these endeavors to define the nation's natural
boundaries, Adams, as ambassador to the Court of St. James, had
shaken hands with George III, whose rolling periods and stately
pauses he had found most confusing—but had assured the king
that the power of language, race, and religion would comprise a
bond forever between their two peoples. In Washington, Adams'
position was precarious. He was not the people's choice. He felt
as uneasy as Daniel in the lions' den—for he was surrounded on

all sides by red-blooded Jacksonians, and there was not an angel
to shut their mouths! The national capital was split wide open
and full of busybodies, vain babblings, debates, envyings, wraths,
strifes, backbitings, whisperings, swellings, tumults. Never was
there so much dissension—or perhaps it is only the usual scene.
The greater issues seemed forgotten. The battle was, to quote
Adams, against "the skunks of party slander" who were "squirt-
ing around the House of Representatives, thence to issue and
perfume the atmosphere of the Union."

Adams had been hoisted into the supreme office as a result
of political bargaining with land-hungry Henry Clay—while the
true people's choice, Andrew Jackson, who had slain giants with
the jawbone of an ass, was placed out of reach of fortune and
men's eyes, seemingly. Adams had thought Jackson would be content with the office of Vice-Presidency, traditionally both empty
and harmless—but Jackson was rallying the forces of the nation
around him and about to descend on Washington. His primary
work, to date, had been to march at the head of various ragged
armies for the wrestling of territory from foreign Davids—for
he and his shaggy pony were themselves Goliath. He seldom
bothered to declare his wars. He had whipped the Indians and
Wellington's veterans—and now had his eye peeled to detect
Eastern bankers skulking among purely imaginary mulberry
bushes on the White House lawn. He was opposed to the ways
of strangers. He had never read a book through in his life but
The Vicar of Wakefield. He did not waste words. He had invaded
Spanish Florida and had hanged two rotten Englishmen as casually as if they were sneak-thief Indians—and now had his eye on
several corrupt lawyers, whose ways were not his ways. True, as
governor of Florida he had been a despot outrivaling the Spanish!
This was not the important aspect. Crude, persevering, tactless,
an enemy to feather beds and higher philosophies, Jackson was,
in the mind of the vast unwashed, their symbol—the acme of all

the Indian chieftains he had chased to happier hunting grounds than any of this creation. Unlike Adams, who had no legend, Jackson was, even in his own lifetime, a walking legend. He got away with murder.

In 1828, the Jacksonians would sweep Adams and his party out of the White House, like so much dirty chaff. Western Democrats, their hair unshorn, wolves in wolves' clothing, would move into Washington—common men, speculators, gamblers, horse thieves, etc., stampeding educated fools, bankers, etc. Under the regime of Andrew Jackson, capitalistic despiser of capitalists, the nation would progress as if, contrary to Thomas Jefferson's belief, God will give the battle to the strongest. By 1840, the reality of power would have become the myth of power—nothing so wonderful as the old days when men were men and there were natural elements to combat with, west of the Alleghenies. William Henry Harrison, in order to attain the supreme office, would be forced to campaign as a rude, simple pioneer, unacquainted with bathtubs and luxury, bagging wild geese and his enemies with equal alacrity, in perils in the wilderness, in perils in the city, in perils everywhere. His several thousand western acres deep in clover, turreted house, atmosphere of tradition, numerous rents, fees, mortgages, would be, like his four-postered bedstead with sprigged taffeta curtains, somewhat beyond the range of public omnipotence.

In the spring of 1825, however, as Robert Owen addressed the ferment of ruling powers, relaxed Joves and Jehovahs, perhaps not even they could guess the course of future history—from their point of view, a series of fragments comprising a loud noise, but never the music of the spheres.

There could be no harm, at least, in a snooze between gladiatorial sessions, as they witnessed the land of words made real, the communistic colonization of America! When all the trees in the American wilderness were cut down, and all the rivers were

dried up, and all the hills were leveled—when there was nothing else to do, then they might put their heads together most
co-operatively, to achieve that greatest of all miracles, a rational
government emanating from the nation's capital. As if, by a mere
decision handed down from Washington, the Great Shepherd
might lead the heavenly flock out of the storms of life, and the
groans of nature in this nether world be put to an effective end.
As if, by a decision at Washington, all orchards would bear, for
the good of the public, which was ever so hard to please, stones
of rubies, emeralds, diamonds, chunks of coal, and bigger nuts
than before. As if the golden apples of the Hesperides might be
gathered on the banks of the Wabash far away—and Andrew
Jackson had not been a frontier lawyer and trader in Negro
slaves. The manufacture of words could be, if no other opportunity presented itself, a very good business, not bound up with
mortal conditions and circumstance—and Gideon's fleece be
caught, like Absalom's hair, among the cherry boughs. Right
now, it provided a pleasant diversion away from dirty, perfuming skunks—and a fool's calendar in the hoary registers of time
and circumstance.

The gentlemen of the Supreme Court, already in alliance with
conservative interests, listened as if wrapped in an enchanted slum-
ber. America, which was made up of so many caverns, taverns, and
undiscovered pockets, was to be covered with rectangular-shaped
villages, they learned, and in the near future. Such villages would
include natural mankind, happiness, gas lights, shade trees, schools,
bathtubs—but would exclude themselves, the hangman, money,
four-postered bedsteads, lions, tragic consequences, lawyers, bankers, decayed gentlemen, dead horses, etc., etc. Each man would feel
himself already in the kingdom of God, beyond which there was,
as everybody knew, nothing to aspire for. Such a kingdom would
be its own miracle, its own blindness. A woman would hold her
tongue. What was the cash value?

New Harmony would be the name of this first town, Robert Owen said, exhibiting his toy model—the old Harmony to be torn down, as the Rappite arrangement did not present such a combination as required for the creation and perpetuation of a virtuous mankind. The old Harmony would serve only as a temporary quarters, while they were building the new. The New Harmony would be erected from two to four miles from the river and its islands, of which the inhabitants would have a beautiful and extensive view, there being several thousand acres of culti-vated land on the rich second bottom—corn, wheat, hop, barley. In his many travels, he had seen no place so naturally suited for the emancipation of mankind from its old masters, who had urged, in others, a belief in the cessation of instinctive life. "And here it is, in the heart of the United States, and almost in the center of its unequaled internal navigation, that Power which governs and directs the universe and every action of man, has arranged circumstances which were far beyond my control, and permits me to commence a new empire of peace and good-will to men, founded on other principles and leading to other prac-tices than those of present or past, and which principles in due season, and in the allotted time, will lead to that state of virtue, intelligence, enjoyment, and happiness which it has been fore-told by the sages of the past would at some time become the lot of the human race." He was anxious that governments should become masters of this subject, thereby to retain the direction of the public mind for the public benefit. New Harmony should meanwhile be considered as the Theater of the World, for it would present, on a small scale, arrangements to be induced among nations—"and these new proceedings will begin in April of this year."

There were objections from the floor. Was not the Ohio known for its snags, curves, hidden islands, and unnavigability in certain seasons? Was not the Wabash even less reliable as a highway? Was not the proposed district already infested with the germs of malaria from the breaking up of the river bottoms? Would not other traders resent communism? What were the New Harmonists going to do for money? How would they be able to obey their own laws and those of the surrounding United States, a thing not conducted by reason? How would they deal effectively with rival Salvationists and political skunks within their borders, perfuming Utopia?

Robert Owen denied the unhealthfulness of New Harmony, through citation of statistics, to show a steady decline in the Rappite mortality rate. The glad tidings of communism, he was convinced, would spread throughout the nation. If every gnat were allowed to seem an elephant in one's path, there could be no social progress whatever.

His manifesto, announcing that "a new society is to be formed at Harmony in Indiana," appeared in every newspaper throughout the nation, and was endorsed by many prominent leaders, both American and European. The invitation to partake in this great experiment was extended, moreover, to the "industrious and well disposed of all nations"—no references required.

The eternal war with nature was soon to be over, it seemed to say to those who read between the lines. Poverty, disease, storm, avarice, sleet, hunger, the battle of pygmies with long-billed herons, all discord would melt into everlasting harmony.

Before the print was dry, out of their caverns in the rock crept the children of Rousseau, to say nothing of Lot and his daughters. Many a footsore soldier, tired of fighting on both sides of every war, turned toward Utopia. Many a hermit, tired of skinning rabbits, determined to become socialized and tread the paths of science, though sweet were the primeval groves. From all directions came men and women with nothing but the bags upon their backs, discontentment, and the character of the well disposed. Poor farmers without farms, barefoot shoemakers, disfrocked priests, frontiersmen staring on infinity, a whisky trader or two, rabid schoolteachers, shepherds without sheep, naked tailors, representatives of every state and almost all nations, even Russia. It seemed impossible that the truth which they had not experienced could be fictitious—that what lies beyond this shifting world must be shifting, too. "Nature at last her ruins might repair," as rocks fell to dust. New Harmony was the El Dorado of communistic Hope, the Garden of Eden, the lost Atlantis, the Fountain of Youth, flowering Siberia, rock of ages, Elysian field, immortal frame, many slogans. New Harmony was the land of satins, the land of words made real, the land of free housing. New Harmony was many things to many people—the lion who eats hay with the lamb, evergreen tree of life, community kitchen, an angel with a white cock in his hand, new garments, dance of goats, seven years of plenty, free hospital, our faith equated with pearls, streets of gold, universal suffrage, Arabian phoenix, hop, corn, barley, four-hour working day, trees bearing spades and tools, the mind's leisure, a New Jerusalem, new shoes for baby, silver spoon, human solidarity, a chicken in every pot, happiness. "Fate leads the willing and the unwilling draws." There were some who might have preferred Philadelphia and a bank account. There were many who could have been diverted from their course by the mere spectacle of a setting hen—doubtless, just this happened, in innumerable instances.

On April 27, 1825, Robert Owen addressed the new community of hopeful graybeards, tired striplings, moldy enthusiasts, nursing mothers, inarticulate philosophers, poor widows, discrowned potentates, would-be carpenters, and others. Also, there were many from the surrounding country who had stopped by to witness the birth pangs of a rational world order while their horses champed impatiently in the streets. He entertained no hope that New Harmony could spring full-grown, like Minerva from the head of Jove—or like old Harmony which, although

formed in 1805, had been the result of a thousand years' gesta-
tion in the tragic wombs of Europe. He expected no miracle.
"New Harmony, the future name of this place," he said, "is the
best halfway house I could procure for those who are going to
travel this extraordinary journey with me—and although it is not
intended to be our permanent residence, I hope it will be found
not a bad traveler's tavern, in which we shall remain only until
we can change our old garments, and fully prepare ourselves for
the new state of existence, into which we hope to enter."

Ironically enough, the meeting place was the Rappite cruciform-shaped church, the "problematical" building for which
the plans had been handed down, it may be remembered, from
heaven, along with the date of the world's end, and Aaron's rod
that budded. Robert Owen, speaking from Father Rapp's pulpit,
threw down an ace which was mistaken humanity—and Father
Rapp's little game seemed lost. With great skill, he shot the billiard ball of God in a new direction—as, in the streets outside, a
drover shouted to another. Aloofly, without a flicker of the eyelid,
he passed the Tree of Life and Knowledge, under which were a
man, a woman, and a cow, the very sty of Epicurus. Thus simply,
the handwriting of an old ordinance was blotted out. The worship
of the hermaphrodite butterfly, exaggerated to the status of angel
or other nonexistent being, was happily over. No longer would
men, while wallowing in gutters, be deceived to think themselves
translated upward among stars. The old errors of conduct were
here abandoned. The old man was put off, and the new man
was put on. Man, as evidenced by this community here gathered
together—though "all were by the winds of autumn driven"—
sought to improve his environment and, in consequence, his
character. Man sought to get out of the war of all against all.
Leviathan, a government in which private vices are viewed as
public virtues, was here abandoned, in favor of Newton's law of
gravity, Rousseau's natural man, Shaftesbury's reasonable man,

and other aspects of humane progress. Materialistic socialism, the product of the science of society, rejected, in fact, the degradation of man's nature, walking on water, sexual abstinence, clouded hearts, dominions of death, economic chaos, etc. This community, as now organized, would differ vastly from that state in which men who are naturally antisocial bind themselves by contract, in order to assure self-preservation, though the power of the leader who preserves them is unlimited—his throne may be set above the stars, and he may order them to engage in suicidal wars.

Shortly after the first meeting, Robert Owen presented the Constitution of the Preliminary Society for the approval of the group. First, this Preliminary Society was instituted generally to promote the happiness of the world. Wild applause. Its objective, more specifically, was to prepare the way for other communities throughout the United States. Applause. The aim of such communities would be to procure for their members the greatest amount of happiness, to assure it to them, and to transmit it to their children to the latest posterity. Applause. Persons of all ages and descriptions, exclusive of persons of color, were to be admitted freely. Silence. Persons of color might be received as helpers, if necessary—or it might be found useful to prepare and enable them to become associates in Africa, or in some other country, or in some other part of this country. Applause.

Their exclusion, while lamentable, was a temporary defect— an acknowledgment that the world was not yet perfect. Silence. It was hoped that, in two or three years, the Negro representative might sit at New Harmony's council table—there being no racial inequalities. Silence. While pecuniary inequalities, like racial inequalities, were not intended, there must be, for two or three years, during the period of this society's incubation, a staff of scientists, whose feathers would give warmth to the altruistic egg. Such scientists, as they would be independent of the community, would wish to be paid in the coin of the realm. Silence.

During the first two or three years, or until the Preliminary Society should have attained the status of a Permanent Society, Robert Owen would assume leadership, in virtue of his previous experience at New Lanark. He was to enjoy, however, no special privilege or exemption from the common lot. A Committee, though appointed by Robert Owen, was to be augmented, twice a year, by popular elections. This Committee was placed in charge of community life, but only for the time being—it was expected that, in two or three years, even a nominal supervision of affairs would be unnecessary, as every man would be operating according to the rational principles.

Practical provisions were made to insure the success of New Harmony. Members were to occupy such houses or dwellings as the Committee provided for them. All members were to provide, if possible, their own small tools, such as spades and axes. Livestock possessed by members would be taken and placed to their credit in the community books—all cows and horses to be shared in common. Labor notes would be received in lieu of money at the community stores, where goods would be provided at cost. The children of members would be located in schools, but would board and sleep in their parents' houses, for the time being. Many promises were made. It was hoped that, in a few years, money would have become obsolete, like the banker who manufactured it. Members might travel at their pleasure, provided the Committee could conveniently supply their places during their absence. It was hoped that, in a few years, they might draw, for the expense of travel, a sum not to exceed one hundred dollars in any year, unless the distance they had to transact was more than six hundred miles. Provisions were made for a dispensary. Provisions were made for a community newspaper, to keep the people informed on what was happening, and lectures on community happiness, to keep them happy.

At the end of three years, the Preliminary Community would have emerged from its chrysalis as a full-fledged moral butterfly—the evils of the individual system having been put off, like old garments, forever. At present, every man had a new beginning, as no inquiry had been made into his antecedents and past history. It was hoped that his frailties would drop from him, like the leaves from a tree in autumn, and that the next spring of this society would see a burgeoning of the human spirit, beautiful as that of the wild cherry or peach. The banks of the Wabash would be furnished with bees, and the hills would be whitened over with sheep. Man, a machine, would know and understand all his parts.

The future, that spring, was very bright, almost dazzling. There was not the slightest suspicion, evidently, of the fact that happiness may not be a valid aim of mankind, and that moral duty is never moral joy—nor of subjectivity, that the only object may be the person, whose life begins where the state ends, like the butterfly confronted by a glacier. Some said that Robert Owen was the leader whom God had chosen to bring them out of the wilderness into New Harmony. Only a leader chosen by God could hope to build, as he did, a new society, without first destroying the old.

It was unfortunate, of course, that scarcely a month after the formation of the Preliminary Society, their leader should depart from among them. The *Gazette*, in perhaps its first issue, lamented the absence of their "Founding Father," who must "wind up his trans-Atlantic affairs" before making his permanent residence in New Harmony, which was the foundation of socialism, the very rock of ages. On his return journey, it was understood, he would be accompanied by his wife and other members of his family, as well as numerous scientists and educators, wise men from the East. All looked forward to the second Coming of One, which should be, barring accidents, the autumn of the year. Meanwhile, it was good to have an Owen face among them, as a reminder of their high task in history, which they were to divert from its former course.

William Owen, alas, was not his father. He was something of a realist and destined to become a far from transcendent brewer in Cincinnati. A farmers' and mechanics' paradise seemed to him less likely than a paradise of middlemen and pompous lawyers. His first and perhaps final philosophic attitude was that all things tend to their end.

William was impressed by the number who had got salvation and interior radiance intuitively or by surreptitious whisky drinking—certainly not as a result of correlated mental operations. How could these rude, crude creatures, like bulls in a china shop, suppose themselves to be "natural men," the children of Rousseau? They discoursed glibly of universalism, yet did not know how to handle a dinner fork. Some could not spell their names, yet felt that they had solved the mysteries of nature. Much of what William called "experience" had been and would continue to be inaccessible to them. William was afraid that El Dorado had attracted nothing but drones. He was puzzled to know what to do with those who professed to do anything and everything. He was trying to eliminate the worst at the beginning—else how could this community not fail before its second spring? Oh, what a sorry situation was his, thus to find himself the head of Utopia, where there were so few heads to depend on. The errors of the past, William felt, had already suppressed the idea of humanity as a whole. Awakening at night, in a cold sweat, he felt that this community was a Nebuchadnezzar victimized by an impossible dream—and might yet come to eat grass. Who should interpret the dream? Only himself. New Harmony seemed doomed to witness the death of all that was good in the old world, the birth of nothing new. It was like a revivalist meeting or reptilian-headed comet, purely temporary—the mere ghost of a heavenly body, and all too transparent, too thin a veil to hide the hoary stars.

They were fooling themselves. Or if analogous to those homogeneous glowing gaseous nebulae from which planetary systems are said to evolve, how many aeons must transpire before the animal man became ethical man, a bodiless angel? William would not be around, certainly.

Troubles multiplied like dragons' teeth. There was already, in the first few months, as perhaps from the first day, a serious housing shortage. Obviously, because of their belief in the temporary status of humanity and its institutions—a belief which William was prone to share—the Rappites had not intended their buildings to be occupied by families with children. It was either a monastic cell or a barracks they had built. Already, the Rappite buildings showed signs of deterioration—they would not withstand the winds and rains another year or two. In order to provide housing for the large influx of Owenite population, it was necessary to allocate a few small families to hog houses and sheep shelters. Utopia was exactly what had been predicted, the sty of Epicurus.

William was glad that his mother had elected to remain in New Lanark. He found himself thinking, as time went on, almost as much of the Rappites as of the Owenites. Being comfortable had meant nothing but that the whole existence of the Rappites should be harnessed to the idea of death. It was difficult to get the Owenites in harness to the idea of life. As a result, William withdrew himself into a shell of distant politeness. He determined to tie himself to no scheme in which the one is sacrificed for the many. Why, in the land of opportunity, choose oblivion? The only truth, William was inclined to believe, was embalmed in religious doctrine—where, for all he cared, it could stay. Indeed, the ideal of progress might be only a substitute for the lost belief in an eternal life. The age encouraged business enterprise, such as forbidden in this great artifice, Utopia, a body without hands, feet, eyes, ears, or other parts. William decided to go into business as soon as he could escape from a house of shades.

There were more intangible than tangible results. That old Adam who ought to be resisted was a shiftless, amorphous fellow, with holes in his shoes, his hat, and his mind, no backbone, no ambition. Development diverged, branched off, was lost in cloud and mist. At the Rappite tavern, which had formerly been so well conducted, for outsiders only, the Owenites sat drooling over their beer, and all the while imagined themselves reborn. A rational happiness would be, for such people, forever beyond Hyperborean, like cold starlight—a thing not to be attained in the flesh. The elements of decomposition were surely accumulating. The mistaken individual had not renounced himself. Warped images, persisting from childhood, had weighted down this symbolic Noah's Ark. All gravitated toward misery.

To build new houses was out of the question, William reported. There were no new materials to be procured in the whole country, no rocks ready blasted, no brick, no timber. They had no hands to spare, else the branches in the society must stop—and in that case, the society itself would be like a still-born infant or a profundity which has no right to come into existence. The sugar was gone, quite gone—and the river being low, they could get none until it rose, at which time there would be an inundation of the lowlands. For an aphorism, they were sacrificing the potato crop. William was alarmed to hear of his father's public speeches, in which all mankind was invited to settle in New Harmony—where already the wolf snarled at the door. New Harmony was not in need of mystic ecstasy, nor any tendency to dismiss reality, a wolf at the door. New Harmony, far from needing mankind, which could always be dispensed with, needed skilled workers and, more than all else besides, a good black cook from Louisville. Communism could wait until some other century, and with it, the domain of high abstraction, rationalism. For during a night bombardment, one hardly sits in his house considering the ineffable music of the spheres—that is, unless one is already dead, happily.

The *Gazette*, spokesman for the communistic colonization of America, expressed none of William's confused, disquieting views. The *Gazette*, a pioneer of good journalism, preceding *Godey's Lady's Book* by five years, was dedicated, as the latter was not, to simplified costume and existence, woman suffrage, destruction of the aristocratic spirit, united labor, removal of excess baggage from the ship of state, extended democracy, the view of man as a two-legged animal whose needs are few, common sense, plain living, and other laudable aims. Its first issue, in the autumn of 1825, bore the motto, "If we cannot reconcile all opinions, let us endeavor to unite all hearts." The prospectus announced— "In our *Gazette*, we purpose developing more fully the principles of the social system, that the world, with ourselves, may, by contrast, be convinced that individuality detracts largely from the sum of human happiness." The *Gazette* displayed, instead of small-town gossip, essays on such deep subjects as The Facts and Laws of Human Nature, The Harmony of the Universe, The Breeding of a New Humanity, The Habits of the Whale as a Type of Grandeur, The Remarkable Advances Which Have Been Made by Science, The Death Rattle of Myth, The Geological Ages of the Earth, The Creation of a Superior Circumstance. At least, that is the gist of it.

The *Gazette* columns, moreover, welcomed the free expression of criticism from all and sundry. Lo, a neighboring Illinois farmer objected to the unusual proceedings at New Harmony. Looking up from his furrow, he had seen bacchanalian revels, a goat-headed Greek where there had been an angel. This Athens of the wilderness was an outrage to the local inhabitants. The Owenites had denied God, and they had made the sexes equal, and they burned candles at evening dances. They should have saved their candles for a rainy day. No society founded on Robert Owen's principles could last—"They will at the outset commit suicide on themselves, if steadily adhered to." The Owenites were doomed from the beginning. The light was already gone out of their body, and their throat was an open sepulcher, and the poison of asps was under their tongue. The Illinois farmer had seen not so much as one nail driven into a wall. The *Gazette* replied without rancor, as its business was to unite all hearts, that after the fatigue of the day, when they could not see to handle a plow, they considered themselves at perfect liberty to devote their evenings to intellectual improvement or any rational enjoyment.

Piece by piece, in spite of the most hopeful of all editorial policies, there emerges a discouraging picture of Utopia in its beginnings. The Rappite city was a disappointment. True, there had been some changes, some improvements over the celibate order. The smaller Rappite church, the slender spire of which was furnished with heavy bells, so that the whole edifice seemed likely to topple, was being used as a kindergarten and a school for graybeards. The wholesale transformation of men was still considered possible. Now, where there had been celibacy, there was free love. The cruciform church was become a dance hall, where the Owenites danced in the rectangular pattern, feeling the confluence of beauty with truth, and perfect harmony. Lord Byron's stanzas, written after his separation from his wife, were recited in the "celestial" rooms. Yet there was something strangely missing, as if humanity were not enough for human happiness. Women were made the equals of men, both conspiring together to be the immortal body of creation—the polarity of the sexes seemed unreal, but so did the body of creation. It was all hollowness, all emptiness. Words could not provide the correct reality. Problem, persisting like the Rappite graveyard—how to avoid the extinction of this community on earth?

The Owenites felt haunted by their Rappite predecessors. Perhaps time's arrow had really fallen short of such a people, though they were suicidal as lemmings. Here, the rude log cabin marked their first humble efforts—there, a neat frame house bespoke their improvement in taste and workmanship. The cruciform church showed evidence of great skill in building. The Rappites had left behind them respectable evidence of their devotion to the branches of industry. Yet to what good end had they devoted themselves? And was all mankind ephemeral as those who had nailed the beams together?

The Owenites were aware of their deficiencies in practical arts, as compared with their forlorn predecessors. Even in a world governed by the Owenite theory, a spade remained a spade. There were too many vagrant deities floating around. There were too many idlers in the streets, like uprooted Indians, possessed of nothing but pride and melancholy, too many who did not know what time of day it was. The hands were horny with age but not skilled. To some, older circumstances adhered, like dung to birds' feet. The message of immortality came from throats which were open sepulchers. Many were toothless. A little goat cried and cried with his fleece caught in the thorn bush. Windflowers grew where there had been wheat before. It was most discouraging. There were a number of people ready to move on, although the majority were willing to wait for the second coming of one, Robert Owen, who would put things right.

The *Gazette* reviewed their situation. They were eight hundred people who, in the short space of three weeks, had been drawn together from the four points of the compass, necessarily without much deliberation, or any reference to their professional usefulness. No satisfactory division of labor could be effected, considering that there had been no selection of laborers to begin with. There were twelve seamstresses and mantua-makers, but not a saddler, and two watchmakers, but not a coppersmith, a number of professions which would be extraneous in Utopia, and many missing which were needed most badly. There were only thirty-six farmers and field-laborers to feed their large population, still swelling like a tide. The industries established by the Rappites were going to waste. The Rappite mill stood idle—for want of weavers. The brewery stood idle—for want of brewers. The flour mill on Cut-off stood idle—for want of millers. The dye house, with its great vats of shining bronze, imperial as an instrument of Jacob, was unused, for the reason that Esau did not know how to operate it. There were, of course, redeeming features. The hat and shoe manufactories had more orders than they could fill. The manufacture of candles, soap, and glue had exceeded their most sanguine expectations. There was an excellent apothecary shop, where pills were given out free. As many as three hundred and nine wild pigeons had been felled in a single day. The river abounded in fish of every kind. Setting of hills and sky was marvelous beyond belief, a location which had exceeded every description of it. Deer might be seen bounding over their fields and browsing in their corn. The crow flew into the face of the scarecrow the Rappites had put up to guard their hop and corn fields. Nature was freed from the oppressor, at least.

The Pears Family

What was the soul of the wheelwright or carpenter in New Harmony? The feeling for superiority, apparently, had been eradicated by one blow, and the abstraction of enlightened mankind erected in the place of a flamboyant Asiatic or European despot. Yet how discover union among so many fragments like ice floes, so many subjective sovereigns afloat in Arctic nothingness? Every man experienced a kind of grandeur—imagining the invulnerable principles of perfection to be within his own breast, and "mankind" to be himself exaggerated, however ungrammatical, however at odds with human nature and the science of society. The neurosis of the individual, released from certain of the conventions of the past, and encouraged by the theory that man is not responsible for his sensations and opinions, assumed, in New Harmony, the status of the universal, with the result that there was what there had always been, a kind of chaos. What is man but a series of competing mythologies, most fearful and wonderful, and what would man be if these were taken away from him? Is there, indeed, any statement as to universality which can be made with certainty—that all men are, by their nature, rational, or even that all men are, by their nature, mortal? To arrive at either conclusion as final, it would be necessary to check all the instances in past, present, and future time—an example to the contrary being sufficient to declare its invalidity as anything short of the usual wan generality. One black swan upset the hypothesis, faithfully believed in for so many generations, that all swans were white. In New Harmony, every man seemed an instance to the contrary of the universal, an irrationalist, an immortal, a black swan. Mankind as a unity was by no means an established organization, even within a half-mile square—and the New Harmonists, to the world outside, seemed an unsecularized minority, a community of deviates, a mistake.

There may not have been, as in old Harmony, such wild social contrasts—coolies on one side of the fence and a mandarin, their enhancement in eternity, on the other, like a somewhat bewildered mule. There was, however, a feeling for the supernatural importance of every man over every other—as if this were a community of mandarins, each perfuming the universe with his own idea of happiness, with the result of a stench almost too great to bear.

The Pearses, husband and wife, wrote voluminous letters, describing their astonishment to be citizens of the New Moral World in a place where there had been, they believed, a tentative New Jerusalem. It was only a month, Thomas Pears wrote, since the last of the Harmonists, or Rappites, had departed, with nothing but the bags upon their backs, and their strong delusion, that they should believe a lie—but the deserted village was now filled up by the Owenites, some of whom had not the bags upon their backs. Hundreds were still on the roads leading into New Harmony, where, it was hoped, kind nature would save the embryo blossoms of rationalism from the cruel blasts of capital. They were fitting up the houses which the Rappites had deserted so hastily and for such evasive reasons. They were grateful to find an old coat hanging on a nail. In spite of some despair, such as might be expected at the beginning of so great an enterprise as theirs, which was to overthrow evil in every guise, there was much enthusiasm, much excitement, a sense of lonely grandeur. "And all this," Thomas Pears wrote, "has been the accomplishment of one man, who has drawn together people from all points of the compass, various in habits and disposition, to mix together like brethren and sisters."

Thomas Pears was a cultivated gentleman, of much experience and much skepticism as to its reality and value. Man seemed to him a poor, deluded bubble, wandering in a mist of lies. The future world, however, was at hand, as that which had decayed and waxed old was ready to pass away, with all its vexations, its ambitions, its monsters wearing sullied crowns, its travesty on reality. Thomas Pears, in spite of his expectations, was scrupulous, for, whatever the future might be, he was still in the past and present, and did not wish to deceive, by false claims, his correspondent, who probably could have seen through him anyhow. Mrs. Pears' uncle, Benjamin Bakewell, to whom he addressed his letters, intended to found, should New Harmony prove successful, a community of glass blowers, all blowing glass, all equal. Uncle Bakewell was acquainted with the principles, it seems— "Hold the fleet angel fast until he bless thee!" What he wanted to know was their operation in actuality, how to make two grains grow where there was one before—and if life's taper was at the close, how keep the flame from wasting?

Mr. Pears, in spite of his leanings toward rational communism, could not see the forest for the trees. He complained that, as bookkeeper of the new order, his head was so full of "Debits and Credits," he felt lost—result, his situation was just about what it had always been, in Pittsburgh and London. His mind was what it had seemed, alas—a maze of terrible arithmetic, having many bypaths and no center but perdition. He had crawled, like a poor baboon, out on the proverbial limb of the wrong sum total, time and again, until he hardly knew whether he was going or coming, was likely to swing out in space. Try as he would, he found it almost impossible to relieve himself of false associations of ideas. Every time he subtracted these from his mind, it seemed to him that he had nothing left but zero, an impossibility. That was to say, himself. There were, although they had departed from a mistaken order, many mistakes, from Mr. Pears' point of view—a fly's buzz at his nose, the distant bleating of sheep on a hill, and ghosts of Pharaohs lifting up their heads in this Newtonian sphere, as full of holes as any other. Mr. Pears was not yet a complete New Harmonist, he confessed, although sure that he would "catch" some of Robert Owen's spirit—sure of the ultimate success of the human family, if somewhat worried about his own. "But whatever may be the fate of this establishment," he wrote, in one of his early letters, "its principles will never be lost; and if not suddenly, they will gradually bring about that change in society so ardently desired by its founder." He hoped that New Harmony would act as if the eyes of the world were upon it—for was not this the chief wonder of the world, a society of Socrateses on the river Wabash, a gadfly to the dead horse of capital? "For my part, I rejoice that I am among those who have so devoted themselves, and I feel confident that the laurels of Owen of Lanark will be green, when those of the destroyers of mankind shall be no more remembered."

Mrs. Pears was less inclined toward ecstasy as she contemplated the potentialities of the human race—her youngest was teething. To her aunt, Mrs. Bakewell, she confided some doubts, very early, as to the wisdom of their having joined the New Harmony movement. Almost from the first day, she had begun to "cast many a long and lingering look toward Pittsburgh and its kind inhabitants." The journey from Mt. Vernon to New Harmony, a distance of only twenty miles, had seemed an infinity. Her skirts had dragged in mud all the way. There were cold stones and leafless brambles. Such a cold, wet, dirty spring of the year was this, with hardly a blossom. Even then, Mrs. Pears had wondered if the prospect of paradise on earth was not a treachery played by the male imagination? Arriving in this Eden, what had they found but a welcoming committee? They, with their seven children, had been placed with another family, the Pearsons, in three miserable, rain-sodden rooms and a kitchen no bigger than the dark closet under Aunt Bakewell's stair. Mrs. Pears could not shed a tear, as there was no privacy, the Pearsons looking on. To relieve the congestion, their two elder boys had been taken from them and put into a house across the way, with a Mrs. Hectorina Grant, whom Aunt Bakewell would remember had been someone in the past. Hectorina enjoyed the sweetest baby girl, like a rosebud, untainted as yet by that great canker, human sorrow. Yes, there were agreeable people in New Harmony, if only one had the time to visit and talk of old Sabbath bells, conscience, memory, Pittsburgh, London, the golden past, the soul of man.

Mrs. Pears' life was more difficult in New Harmony than it had ever been. No, she had not put off her old garments—and was far from doing so. She was worn to a thread. Poor Mr. Pears, far from being free to help her, must bear the burden of community finance on his narrow shoulders—and yet to escape from money, he had left Pittsburgh! Money, Mrs. Pears had heard, was to become obsolete in just a few years—and well it might, for it was scarce as hen's teeth already. There was no rest for the weary. Maria, her eldest daughter, had been very poorly for a few days past—"I believe her illness chiefly proceeds from fatigue and a bad cold caught while washing." Poor Maria! Yet for Maria's sake, Mrs. Pears had come to New Harmony, so far from Pittsburgh, its dear associates, its crown of life inwoven with purple and gold, its feather beds, its churches, its good people. She had so hoped that Maria might be relieved from some of the heavy work. It could not be. Poor Maria had hardly ever scrubbed or washed recently without complaining of a pain in her chest. Although there was supposed to be a universal education, and that was why Mr. Pears had left Pittsburgh, her Palmer had been put into a den of carpenters, and her younger girls were braiding straw hats half of every day. What schooling they got was ineffectual. Baby Clinton seemed, except for his teething, the only happy one, for he had discovered his toes, and lay with his feet above his head. A man on his way out of New Harmony, a student of lost Utopias, Morris Birbeck of Albion, had drowned in Fox River, upholding a son. Oh, what greater love had man than this, Mrs. Pears wondered.

No, she had not found happiness, nor even a decent store.

Benjamin Bakewell, Father of American Glass Blowers, was less interested in the Pears family than in the experiment to regenerate mankind. All around him, he saw fallen glass blowers who, if united, might erect a city of glass, such as the world had never seen before, even in works of fiction. News from New Harmony, Uncle Bakewell wrote, was received with as much eagerness "as if a mail coach had arrived from Jupiter or Saturn. It must appear a new world to its inhabitants, though perhaps not quite so cold as in the planets just mentioned." Could they, from where they were, see the Elysian flowers by amber streams? Could they bind its odor to the lily? Aunt Bakewell, limited by feminity, was more concerned with the Pears family than with regenerated mankind—she sent a few yards of flannel for the coming winter. "Keep yourselves armed by faith," she recommended. She wondered that Robert Owen could have so far departed from the religion of Moses as to hand down laws of human nature, exactly as if they had been written in God's handwriting! God, a good Presbyterian like Aunt Bakewell, had never changed His mind as to man's original sin and depravity.

It was a difficult summer—let alone the thought of winter, which Mr. Pears had heard was very severe in this region. Writing in September, when the first yellow leaves were falling, he described the discord to which he had been eye witness in New Harmony, not a place out of this world by any means. From the commencement of harvest, there had appeared to be no harmony at New Harmony. Everybody had tried to see who could do the least work. To this pleasant state of competition had succeeded the wonderful "Reign of Reports." While the branches of business withered and fell away, vice was gilded. Mr. Pears could not imagine what they were going to do for winter beer, unless they got busy and harvested the hop field, a radiance of uncreated essences, a confluence of bright beams, and all going to waste, for no known reason. The "Master Spirit," Robert Owen, being absent from their midst, they should progress but slowly until his return, for they had just about exhausted the resources of correct thinking. "Expectation hangs on him, and should he be delayed till Spring, the spirit of Harmony will be severely tried in many."

Winter clothing would be most wanted, as usual, by those who had the least to get it with, Mr. Pears reported a little later. Bearded men, with their feet wrapped in rags, their clothing ragged, their pockets empty, found it difficult to feel the effects of resurrection they ought to feel, or that the spirit of Harmony had covered them with a shining mantle, or that the voyager here had outreached the farthest flight of birds. An old man stood on the streets with the fly of his breeches unbuttoned. An old dog howled all night. Arithmetic was, as usual, precarious. Mr. Pears was not worried about future profit, knowing that there would be none this year. There were no supplies laid up for the coming winter—"The hogs have been our Lords and Masters this year in field and garden." Poor farmers, booted with wisps of hay, had to buy their chief food products at neighboring markets. In answer to Uncle Bakewell's inquiry, made a few weeks ago—yes, tea and coffee were provided, though it had not been intended, originally, that the boardinghouse rates should include such luxuries.

An excellent embalmer was now in the community's services.

Mr. Pears apologized for what seemed his gloomy, pessimistic attitude. "Most of those who come to look at us seem highly pleased," he wrote, "but they see only the outside, and we have not forgotten the 'fair side of London.'" How different that life was from this! Did Robert Owen's heart run away with his head here? The Belle Vision had captured the imagination of the people, but happily they had not seen the rugged passage which they had to travel—"The Promised Land is farther off than most of us anticipated."

Mrs. Pears felt that nothing in this new life could compensate for the loss of her old life in Pittsburgh. Her eyes were so bad, from much sewing—she could hardly see to lift her hand before her face. At times, she felt like an animated mummy. How much brighter her eyes had been in Pittsburgh, where she had looked at the things which were not seen. How often she rejoiced that her dear friends did not share such misfortunes as hers. True, not everybody suffered as Mrs. Pears did. Some were chameleons, quite unprincipled, taking on every color. There were balls almost every night. The dancers, walking through muddy streets, were soon black from head to foot. Maria had wept, but to no avail. Mrs. Pears had put her foot down. New Harmony was a miserable place for a Christian soul to be in, a Slough of Despond. Doltish people, bridled like geese, must be deceived by such a false show of happiness. Although she might be in the minority here, Mrs. Pears felt that she was in the majority elsewhere. As she constantly reminded Maria, the world included Pittsburgh still, and London. Poor Hectorina Grant had lost her lovely child, a few days back, and a number of babies were perishing of whooping cough, and the germs of malaria had infested many of the older inhabitants, and Maria was still poorly. To be carnally minded, Mrs. Pears felt, was death.

After two more weeks of hope betrayed, Mr. Pears wrote: "We ought to be in a new world, but most of its inhabitants have yet to put off the old man and become new creatures before it will be the world its founder anticipated." Mr. Pears, try as he would, had been unable to put off the old man or get himself into a new world of motion. Jefferson had written, as Mr. Pears recalled: "The tough sides of our Argosie have been thoroughly tried. We shall put her on her republican tack, and she will now show by the beauty of her motion the skill of her builders." New Harmony was an excellent ship, but dry-docked in a ruined hop field—no motion but the invisible processes of disintegration and decay, so far as Mr. Pears could see. He had humbled himself to the level of his brother, and what had happened? He had lost his job. He had been dismissed from his post as bookkeeper, and only because, in his and the community's confusion, he had debited and credited the same sum twice. True, he had drunk a little on the side now and then, but not enough to cause the dancing of arithmetic. The real reason for his dismissal was that the Committee, that great God on wheels, had objected to his soul, and to his idea of the pursuit of happiness. Having lost out as bookkeeper, Mr. Pears had been at loose ends, indeed, until put to work as a sorter and picker of wool, like a slave in the South. He had almost taken, after a few days, to singing shanty songs, as if he were black. He had been almost happy. When he had thought of a way to cut corners, lo, he was out of a job again, and walking the streets like a tramp. He might have commenced the pottery, but there were no implements—the Rappites having taken away all but the oven. He was now engaged in a sorry effort to get into the schools. Every day seemed a year. Nothing ever happened.

Truly, philosophy is no innocent thing.

Mrs. Pears thought, by way of postscript, nothing so bad as a despotism which pretends to be a democracy. They were living under the aristocracy of a Committee, the very Dogs of Hell. "It makes my blood boil within me," she wrote, "to think that the citizens of a free and independent nation should be collected here to be made slaves of." A letter from Pittsburgh was become her only consolation. When she thought of herself almost a thousand miles from Pittsburgh, it was almost more than she could bear. Like the poet Cowper, all she could say was, "I am out of humanity's reach." Indeed, she felt like a bird in a cage shut up forever. Oh, what a little island was this life of man, and girt around by eternity! If only Aunt Bakewell, by some miracle, could descend on New Harmony, how she would pity the Pears family.

The Pears letters show, if nothing else, the gradual waning of their hope for improvement at New Harmony. Perhaps, indeed, theirs was an ambiguous situation, a dawn of reason which seemed reason's twilight, a sunrise which seemed the sunset. Benjamin Franklin, observing the half sun on the back of Washington's chair, noted the extreme difficulty of distinguishing between a rising and a setting sun. "I have often and often, in the course of the session, and the vicissitudes of my hopes and fears as to its issue," he said, "looked at that sun behind the President, without being able to tell whether it was rising or setting; but now, at length, I have the happiness to know that it is a rising, and not a setting sun."

These unheroic, often mistaken street-corner idlers, some of whom could not have told the difference between beginning and end, a mare and a stallion, did, however, contribute to the march of liberal progress. Humanitarianism, by the fact of their organization, puny and forceless as it was, advanced to meet the great enemy, nationalism, the irrational entity. If humanitarianism, wandering like a moth in the wilderness, could never come, at that period, face to face with the flaming angel of nationalism, yet the first advances had been made. Mr. Pears, with his feet above his head in the back office, and his head filled with whirling Debits and Credits, was at war with heaven's matchless kings, at war with injustice, whether he knew it or not.

The Fool of Nature

During the lamentations of the Pears family, where was Robert Owen, and what was the cause of his delay? He had reached New Lanark, had said good-by to Caroline, had wound up his trans-Atlantic affairs, domestic and financial. While Mr. Pears sat with his feet above his head in New Harmony, Robert Owen was far out at sea, pacing the deck like Christopher Columbus, and more convinced than ever of the probability of a New Moral World.

He was accompanied, on his return voyage, by two disciples, Captain Macdonald of the Engineers, who had made with him a walking tour of Scottish cotton mills, and Robert Dale, who wished to discover natural man and bring him to the light of day. There may have been, although historians are divided on this subject, a shadowy third—Stedman Whitwell, rhapsodic London architect, whose chief delight was to erect community palaces on paper, and author of a rational nomenclature to replace the names of all the cities, towns, and villages on earth.

The voyage, although long and perilous, was happy, except that the ship's passengers included a cruel Spanish overseer and his company of dwarfs. These dwarfs were forced, at his command, in cloud and mist above the vast sea rolling, to walk like wingless cherubim a tightrope between mastheads, in training for their jobs as acrobats in America. During an abusive scene, seeing that dwarfs are human and can never fly like blackbirds, Robert Owen rose up as if, at last, he had been admitted to the presence of the British Parliament, that body before which he had yearned to speak. His words were simple and few, almost casual. If this master spirit should once more maltreat his children, he would pitch him into the sea and let the vast sea roll over him. Fortunately, a warning sufficed—murder was not, at this point, necessary.

There were otherwise the usual storms, starless nights, dolphins at play, the chimney of the glider whale on far horizons. The ship's captain sat up, night after night, to hear Robert Owen's theory of the rational aspects of nature and the science of society. He was inclined to agree that happiness is the instinct of the universe. By that statement, however, might be meant a terrible thing—that the ship goes down, and the sailor is carried away of the flood. Such a great misfortune inspires a certain awe. A secret pleasure accompanies this grief. It extends over the whole of life. And though the stars hold to their courses, and though a rational nomenclature might be made to apply, so that all cities would show their position in space, as on a mariner's chart of this watery world, what compass or system could direct him to the lost constellation, a woman with gray hair, a lilac bush, a dusty well in the interior of Ohio? The lost constellation is the important one. Surely, the ship's captain was inclined to believe, he who sits in the cloud thrusts his sickle in the earth, and the earth is reaped. Man feels, in the knowledge of this fact, a certain loosening of his bonds.

On November 7, 1825, the important part of their journey seemed over. When Robert Dale saw the distant line of the Jersey shore and New York harbor, its waters dotted with ships and barges, its wharves piled up with bales of cotton, and everywhere an atmosphere of peaceful, busy prosperity, he wrote, "It is the Canaan land of all my hopes."

Unfortunately, human nature does not always second the philosopher. New York was already a mixture of corruption and chaos, and its stone mansions were as full of angles and gables as an old cocked hat. Tammany had been organized for a number of years. There were taverns, banks, gallows, ancient dynasties, undertakers, numerous patriarchs, fortresses, churches, bridewells, preachers who read the Bible upside down, slave ships from Guinea, meaningless rebellions, whores of Babylon, vultures, manias for land speculation, gambling tables, lithographic maps in which cabbage plots were laid out as New Jerusalem, cock fights, silver crucifixes on mantelpieces in shady houses, drunken whalers, subtleties enough to puzzle a Chinaman, cutthroats, perfume and stink factories, clouds of glory, hammocks slung to the walls instead of bedsteads, burlesques, temporary arrangements of all kinds, mystic spinsters, high finance, fat burghers driving in parasoled pony carts, piratical adventures, nameless graves, much ingenuity, men who skulked about the docks like cats prowling among dead fish, diamond-studded gamblers, fortune-tellers in glass beads and trailing petticoats, Samsons, barbers, fallen sisters, much ambition, contracts cosigned by God and the Devil, an almost overwhelming happiness in the very idea of peril.

Jessie, Robert Dale thought, need not be a lady in America, but could spin and card her own wool—oh, charming thought! While his father and the problematical Mr. Whitwell lectured on New Harmony, Robert Dale sat in his room at the Howard House on noisy Broadway, conjuring up Jessie, without whom all happiness would be as nothing, an emptiness. His letters to Scotland were like poems. Although he was oppressed, at the moment, by purple velvet curtains and other interior decorations, for everything in this room was something else, and the andirons were a pair of Turks, and the arms of the chair he sat on were a pair of lions, America, he wrote, was a romantic forest, a green thought in a green shade. In this distant wilderness, man might come to the realization that a thought has its existence, even when put out of mind. He sat thinking. What whirlwind could ever lay the beauties of Jessie in the dust? He had no doubt of that moment of holy realization, when out of the mist of time a white woman rides on a white horse—the Spirit of Propagation, without whom there could be no happiness whatever. Ethics must recognize what had been recognized by unethical thought, that the self precedes society, as spring, when there are waxen buds, precedes autumn, a desolate season, when the barren stalk rattles in the wind. In America, he hoped, might be witnessed the wedding of egoism with altruism—to say nothing of his own projected ceremony, when Jessie should stand like a Hebrew woman at the well, and he should come to her, the prince of space.

While Robert Dale sat wrapped in such happy thoughts, a waiter entered, most unobtrusively, to present him with a visiting card—a piece of green pasteboard, with the single word "Page" written large thereon. A green calling card was unusual—perhaps a sign of American naïveté. Robert Dale asked that his visitor, the human appurtenance to this strange cardboard, be admitted, though little suspecting what truly national personage he was about to behold—no man, but a vision, and yet a parody of his own symbolism, as if he were both an aggrieved God and the colossal joke which God had played, to wit, human nature, most unnatural, a tumult to prove the edifice of every system unsound.

Lo, into the room came a tall, bent man, walking in a solemn and high-stepping way, somewhere between the floor and the ceiling. This fretful character was as thin as a beanstalk but widening out, most miraculously, at the bottom—when he stood still, his legs described a triangle turned on its apex. What was strangest, as if he were a hyperbole in the place of reality, or the exemplification of a thought, he was clad in green from head to foot. He wore, in fact, a suit of light green broadcloth, very elegant, a coat cut with a broad Quaker collar, also green broadcloth, reaching to his ankles like a drapery. His hat, gloves, shoes, all were pea green. There was a string of onions around his neck. He carried a green satchel and a rusty fowling piece. His long hair, a faded yellow, was divided at the center and drooped, slightly curled, to his shoulders. His face was a little green at the edges.

Obviously, the man was mad. He had a look of unnatural brilliance in his eye, as if he might suddenly exhibit a smattering of the most profound knowledge—an inflated period, a windy doctrine. Obviously, there was a moisture on his brain. He suffered from unscientific vagaries, mechanized religions, slogan-making, illiberality, the fear of slander, and a fiery zeal to champion lost causes. His nose quivered like a rabbit's. Though a sage might bind the rules of nature, he would be a phenomenon to unbind them, for no reason but that he was basically illogical, disorganized, and ever about to fall to pieces, literally. Yet if the man was mad, his was a calculated madness, a method of getting on, an eternal misleading and misdirecting, a belief in those things which pass knowledge. He licked his lips. He seemed an apocryphal figure, who would carry every hog into captivity and depopulate every hen roost on earth, while protesting his innocence. A compound of marvelous accidents, an apparition from another sphere, a thing to endure when every island flees away, and when the mountains are depressed as valleys.

He opened his mouth, betraying no teeth, but before he could speak, he must bow profoundly, from hip to toe, as if he were performing exercises for his health's sake. After several minutes, he opened his mouth again. "Gentlemen," he said, addressing Robert Dale and Captain Macdonald, who had followed him into the room, and looking about as if he faced a much larger audience, "greetings from mankind made real to dwell among us! Greetings from the world of the dead to the world of the living! I have come, in my public capacity, to welcome a brother philanthropist. But you do not know who I am." He paused significantly, then continued, with a deep nasal intonation, "My name is Page. I am the Page of Nature. She has enlisted me in her service. I wear her livery, as you see, in reminder of the official duty I owe her, on both sides the vast Atlantic. For lo, I have walked in cotton towns and cotton fields. I have pitched my tent in the high places and the low. Nature, wherever I am, talks to me, instructs me in the way I should go, and tells me how I can best benefit my fellow creatures. Her standard is the Roman eagle and five pumpkins, five hundred bushels of onions, fifty cartloads of oysters, two hogsheads of molasses, and a good shotgun. She wears a cattle thief's breeches in Windsor and a whore's petticoat in Manhatta. Wherever she is, she howls like an old dog. Withal, she is mysterious and beautiful, working in secret ways, as I, her truest servant, know—for I have seen her whirlwinds, tornadoes, and greasy multitudes."

Yea, this Page was a prey to illusion, like a tree where mimic moths cling in semblance of bark, yet recognized his own insubstantiality, like an old tree falling. "There is a dry rot at the heart of nature," he whined, "and an iron rod in the hands of governments. The rocks melt into tears. No sooner has a man proven his predecessors fools than he becomes the greatest fool of all. Such is our progress, from fool to fool, from page to page. A fable weighs more than its demonstration—better to have been the writings of a fool than the fool himself." He bowed, like a priest in a cathedral, addressing the unseen God, and seemed to be lighting many candles. "Language has been more often torn by brambles than Moses was," he said. At this point, he seemed carried away by his emotions. "In the olden times," he chanted, wiping his brow with a green handkerchief, "I was King David's page, and I was a great comfort to him, as he had been to his master Saul, when the evil spirit from the Lord was upon him, and when David's playing on the harp refreshed Saul and caused the evil spirit to depart. David had his dark hours also, when his sins weighed upon his spirit, and on such occasions I was able to console and encourage him. Thus have I talked to dying kings, including the late George III, whom I taught, under clouds of woe, still to be basking in sunlight, and, though deaf, to hear, and, though blind, to see. But nature's service is better than that of any king. Lo, she has many skunks in the American wilderness, many addled eggs, and much of a muchness. Lo, she is prodigal."

With that, he drew from his green satchel a thick roll of man-uscripts, of green paper. On these, he said, nature's secrets were written in black ink, although by right it, too, should have been green, even if to the merely human eye the words might have been unapparent. Robert Owen could certainly have read a green writing on green paper, since his was the mind immortal, placed high above this brute creation, and he was never buffeted about by a thorn in his side, being a man more out of his body than in his body, and caught up to paradise in the twinkling of an eye, and exalted above measure through the abundance of his revelations and the glory of his visions. Alas, what fools we lesser mortals be! Nature was made up, this poor page in her service knew, of many puzzling things—necessities, soldiers with wooden legs, persecutions, bushbeaters, reproaches, pot-bellied squires, fornications, schoolmasters with birchen rods, exaggerations, stub-born rocks, deadly salts, boa constrictors, Samsons, Herculeses, geraniums, barnacles, scrofulous saints. "I am become a fool in glorying," Page said, "but ye have compelled me, though I be nothing, alas, but the apostle of nature's marvels and wonders." Rivers were not formed to feed canals, Page said. Man's reason, Page said, is inadequate to comprehend the entirety of nature. There is nothing to connect these things in nature—a comet, the growth of pearls, and an old man with a broken back. Only the soul of man, a thing most unreasonable, can connect these three, a trinity like any other trinity, such as the horse, the rider, and the crown. All things are not three, and all things are not one. There is nothing beyond beyond but beyond. Not even the law of gravity can be relied on, Page said—for though there are many fallen sparrows, lo, Christ was caught up in the cloud, like the glider albatross, a fatty bird, and did not come down again. Yet what happened once may not happen twice, since nature never repeats herself, not even in one green leaf. There is always a deviation. Whatever else may be said, Page said, there are no nouns but verbs, no fixations but processes, no honor but dishonor, should man omit that which the eye hath not seen, the ear hath not heard. As yet, though men had tried for centuries, none had succeeded in formulating a law to describe, with mathematical accuracy, the rise of waters on all shores. What a poor water is mankind, tossed to and fro by every wind, and many tides on many unknown shores, Page said, and many pale horses, many pale riders, many chief captains, many lambs, many stars falling, many stars unshaken, many dogs, many mushrooms, many peoples, many nations, many scrolls, many avengers, many beasts full of eyes within and blindness without, many blasphemies, many false apostles, many clouds, moons, Alphas, Omegas, beginnings, ends, thoughts, intents, confusions, glories, empires, sick adventurers, adventures, blackbirds.

"Yea, black ink cannot be inappropriate," Page said. "For in the summer holiday, indeed, Nature's vestment is green, but she has also her seasons when all is black—the starless midnight hour, the wintry storm of blackness, the ill-timed regret, the ill-timed tranquillity." Then must the heart of mankind be black, too. Then must be realized no harmony but a system of discrepancies, beautiful as the rotted peach. Then must be realized the lie of communism, a thing opposed to nature, yet believing itself natural. An old man with his cane as high as his chin will seem, even in Utopia, as unreliable as dust and ashes. He will cry out for the God of his fathers, a thing dwelling apart, and for old apron strings to cling to, and old nurses.

Seeing the look of utter astonishment on the young men's faces, Page apologized. People of their years could not be expected to be concerned, he realized, with the revelation of divine truth. He hoped that he might be forgiven for his flight of fancy, as he was ever the creature of circumstance, and his sensations were his master. He was about to go out to prowl on the Battery, to observe a well-conditioned cock fight. Perhaps he would take in a gambling table or two. He asked that his green manuscripts, the secret of nature, be handed to Robert Owen, who might study such spidery hieroglyphs at his leisure, even as mummies in their tombs are said to be the most ardent students of eternity. He left an obscure address in Brooklyn or that neighborhood, with directions as to how he might be reached, up three flights of broken stairs, past a decayed landlady or two. "And the heaven departed as a scroll when it is rolled together," he concluded. And might God have pity on Robert Owen's soul, and God the Unitarian fiend expell!

After Page had gone, Captain Macdonald sat looking intently at the fire. He had always been impressed by the simplicity of nature and man. God, from Captain Macdonald's point of view, was no engineer like himself, but a good, old-fashioned, red-cheeked farmer. The world of truth, far from being something to strive for, or a competitive system, was a daily habit of life, a serene, resistless wisdom, an elegy in a country churchyard. "Are we crazy, too?" he asked at last. "Have we been poking into the great subjects and thinking of the world's reform until our brains are addled and we are fit inmates for a lunatic asylum?"

Their visitor had given them quite a shock—a feeling of diffusion where there had been concentration, a feeling of hopelessness where there had been hope. Perhaps, as Page had suggested, reality belonged to the sensibly perceived but not to the logically thought. The predicates "true" and "false" might, after all, apply to a very small area. Perhaps even "green" was not "green," and there were no apron strings whatever to attach the poor, wandering soul of man to, no certitude of truth. Perhaps the old lies were best, as having served their purposes, however precariously. They sat thinking. Like bright stars of lesser magnitude, they saw the eyes of the Page of Nature, twinkling in the hazy firmament of his face—as if he represented, as he had said, the supreme governor of an unpredictable order, a lashing, a beating, a mighty storm, many tides, and harnessed ever to a dead, indifferent moon.

They were on their way to an estate in the interior off any main line of travel, actual or projected. God knew when they should see England again! They had cast their bread upon the waters, so to speak. As travelers in a social bark, they must go forth over the wide seas of human nature, and find no footing anywhere. Man might reach maturity, Robert Dale felt—and man might reach infancy, Captain Macdonald dreamed. Both agreed that man could never be a machine. Who would expect to find a grass blade in a world of cold abstractions? Rationalism seemed, from Captain Macdonald's point of view, less wonderful than those who walked before the lamb in white—from Robert Dale's point of view, less wonderful than the island of Atlantis, where the sons of gods had intermarried with the daughters of men. Only through such union could be achieved the composition of the future world.

Noah's Ark, the Maid of Mist, the Boatload of Knowledge

Land of the West, we come to thee,
Far o'er the desert of the sea;
Under thy white-winged canopy,
Land of the West, we fly to thee!
Sick of the Old World's sophistry,
Haste then across the dark, blue sea.
Land of the West, we rush to thee!
Home of the brave: soil of the free—
Hurrah! She rises o'er the sea.

—SUNG BY THE OWENITE PARTY

ON THE BOATLOAD OF KNOWLEDGE

Life itself was to be the masterpiece of art, a rich fountain of unsullied happiness, untainted by personal desires—in a universe of which man may be only an insignificant atom, but an atom loving the whole of which he forms the part. While the Pears family were lamenting in New Harmony, and had all but lost faith, Robert Owen and a party of scientists waited in Pittsburgh for the waters to rise.

The boat, when it was embarked upon the Ohio flood, was dubbed, by bystanders, Noah's Ark, the Maid of Mist, the Boatload of Knowledge. Rarely had the Ohio borne such passengers as these—opposers to slave-holding oligarchies, hostile laws, white supremacy, suspension of natural rights, Oriental dream, whisky trade, nonexistent township, nonexistent centaur, the Four Horsemen of the Apocalypse, irrationalism, capitalism, marriage, monasteries, money, deception in every form. No wonder the people who watched Noah's Ark set sail were as amazed as if all God's messengers were gathered aboard. Some said this group might establish a great new American commerce, with the virtue that the goods it dealt in would be intangible.

Nothing can be conceived which can be called good without qualification, except a good will. About eight miles from the new Rappite location in Pennsylvania, the ice closed in, arresting Noah's Ark for a month which seemed eternity. An unexpected factor had disturbed the best of plans. The human will, not being free, was victimized, alas, by circumstance, in this case a transient thing. The world had vanished without any violent transition. Everybody was happy, naturally. By strange chance of shipwreck, disease, poverty, fortune hunting, restlessness, and other disasters, they had come to comprise, on Noah's Ark or the Boatload of Knowledge, a harmonious order, such as one day might be the lot of man.

Thomas Say, naturalist, lay on a makeshift bed, imagining conch shells and other harmonies. His grandfather, a Quaker physician, had been transported from Philadelphia upward to heaven by choirs of angels, and, having passed beyond the seventh crystal wall, had beheld the face of an old black cook, bearded with lichen. Even in heaven, he had been outside neither time nor space. Thomas Say looked not for such supernatural revelations, one's self objectified—but only for the Spirit of Nature, a woman who binds together heaven, earth, and hell, and who is the invisible sum total of delicate nuances and shades, the rock goose, the sleep of flowers, a wilderness unprofaned by the pruner's ax. Charles Lesueur, fellow naturalist, looked for white animals in a blinding snowstorm, but nothing human, as human nature was not his province. The action of brutes expressed merely the character of the species, not of the individual—unlike that of man, Lesueur believed. The problematical Mr. Whitwell discoursed on the papery edifices of Byzantium, with many citations from Gibbon to prove the decline of the Roman Empire—while he erected, to take the place of Rome, a community palace on paper—our characters to be regarded as the temporal unfolding of the extra-temporal. William Maclure, mountain climber, who was aware of no veil drawn over the face of nature, and could therefore not wish to penetrate beyond the veil, and who had invested a large sum in Thomas Say and Lesueur, utilized this opportunity to balance his financial records—liabilities in one column, assets in another. Liability, six pairs of paper-soled shoes, one empty convent—asset, Thomas Say, a hundred preserved butterflies. Robert Owen, embellishing Mr. Whitwell's papery palaces with the science of society, considered that perhaps underneath space and time, all beings were identical, multiplicity and individuality being the quality of illusion only. To be man was a certain way of being an animal—to be happy, the satisfaction of natural wants. Excessive joy and excessive sorrow were both unnecessary.

Robert Dale recalled the enforced delay of the Boatload of Knowledge as the happiest period of his life—when, if ever, the chaff was swept out, and harmony realized. The frozen water was like a mirror of glass hemmed in by pale, glutinous sunlight. Tears froze on the cheek. Every man was armored in ice. It was as if the earth had returned to its first condition, a Parmenidean quietude, all crystal, stainless, and perfect, without wind, without motion. There were no human beings except philosophers, and no contradictions in the laws of nature. Man was satisfied with a gratification of his most simple wants—there was no flaw, with the possible exception that Jessie, sweet Jessie, was absent from this paradise. The social phenomenon presented, however, no longer a double face, a series of cruel paradoxes. All problems seemed to bear their own solution, even if remote. Robert Dale picked up the fallen branches for firewood, grateful to the forethought of Providence, which had made possible the least exertion on his part. Oh, how perfect this static earth was, how ineffable, a counter-earth to compensate for every loss but Jessie. He almost enjoyed, however, the loss.

Before leaving Scotland, Robert Dale had read Cooper's *Pioneers*, as an introduction to the American way of life and that man who, being without a state, is something more than man, either a god or a beast. Some of the primitive scenes in Cooper's works, he now saw with his own eyes. There were white animals other than those Lesueur looked for, in fact, a few rare human beings, great in their boldness and faith. Robert Dale soon discovered, in the deep silence of the forest primeval, a smoking chimney and a frostbitten democrat. This democrat, one Leatherstocking, was a man who might be worshiped as a god when he was dead, for such was his self-reliance that he had always triumphed over the elements. He had an immense will to live. His wife, who was the third, for the other two were out under the snowy spruce trees in their graves, wore cowhide boots under her skirts, handled an ax or a needle with equal grace, and seemed unaware of her hard lot. His children, the productions of three wives, were of every possible age and description. Most were healthy, but there was one the color of cornmeal, and there were some, Robert Dale was told, who had gone to the kingdom of Jesus, out beyond the snowy hill.

Leatherstocking was a man of stoical equanimity. He distrusted education, as if it were a grinder who dies of choking dust, or a flat-chested bookkeeper, neither of whom he had met up with. His children would go to school over his dead body. Leatherstocking was, however, a source of marvelous information, a walking school himself. He taught his guest how to recognize buckeye, horse-chestnut, birch cherry, and ash, individualized under ubiquitous snow. He taught his guest the habits and haunts of wild game, to detect the white ptarmigan which looked like a snow-shrouded bush until it moved, and families of deer where there had seemed an emptiness. Leatherstocking, the child of nature, had very little feeling for nature, however. He considered it more or less his enemy. He could not have told the difference between Rousseau and the fleas on an old dog. He was surprised to hear of nature's kindness or that snow was spiritual. He had all but lost his ears in a hard winter. He had never guessed that nature would heal nature's wounds. Certain ills were necessary. He had thought somewhat of heaven, in cold winter evenings, he admitted, and though he hoped for resurrection, had thought how embarrassed he would be, out there beyond the snowy hill, with as many wives as pigeons in his brace. Or happily, perhaps the things of this earth would be forgotten. As for politics, Leatherstocking valued his horse more than the governing gentlemen at Washington, who were just so many names without bodies attached. Democracy and rifle shooting went together—and that was the end of it. He could not receive with meekness any word engrafted on him. He was a man, not a fruit tree. He was his own hard master.

Robert Dale was pleased by Leatherstocking and his rugged, unspoiled individualism. America, he found, was a land of equality, a land of power and might, where no one need hunger or thirst, a land of many blessings, many opportunities—the dumb ass speaking with man's voice forbade the madness of any dream but this. In return for lessons in trap shooting, Robert Dale entertained the pioneer family with descriptions of the old country—its Lethean lakes, its sickly aristocrats, not worth a coonskin hat, not worth Leatherstocking's little finger.

William Maclure proposed the reorganization of society "so as to drown the self in an ocean of sociality." Leatherstocking was doing all right as an anchorite with a large family. William Maclure had crossed the Alleghenies by foot more than fifty times, studying rocks. Leatherstocking broke rocks. William Maclure was, all in all, a greater Leatherstocking, with greater limitations.

William Maclure was, in fact, a man of such great common sense as to seem almost senseless. Having decided that the mind is the source of most of the evils the flesh is heir to, he wanted to stamp out most of the mind. He attributed the world's downfall to the flowers of rhetoric. On the altar of his society, therefore, he was willing to sacrifice the peacock with its crown feathers of the trinity, the word of God, and other ornaments. William Maclure condemned, most wildly, imagination, which, he said, "has been so beaten up, mixed, and compounded with the wisdom of our senses that it is difficult to draw the line of separation between them." He drew the line between ornamental and useful studies, rejecting all assumptions as to the universe's being a project of the mind, whether rational or irrational, good or bad, white or black. Man was but a raindrop. The study of natural sciences, he believed, might be pursued, in all countries and all climates, at the least expense to money or morals. As to his idea of the science of society, it was largely important for what it excluded—fishing, shooting, horse racing, bull baiting, corporal punishment, capital punishment, Jehovah, Rousseau, the histories of ancient nations, luxurious living, the universe, and such excesses. William Maclure urged, quite simply, the revival of Spartan character— every child to learn shoemaking—for though every child should not turn out to be a shoemaker, still he might be, in time's necessity, grateful for a knowledge of this art.

The old geographer knew what he knew. He had studied rocks and had picked up, in the course of his travels, quite a fortune,

was richer than any Spanish grandee in the realm of the imagination, or Mohammedan prince lugging the tomb of a scrofulous
saint over the high Himalayas. By sheer republican simplicity,
he had acquired enough territory to make a diamond-studded,
emblazoned Austrian potentate in a glass-paneled carriage look
rather sick. He, the true American spirit, could have bought and
sold the Duke of Ciudad Rodrigo, laurel-crowned monasteries
of the Jesuits in Ireland, the Persian mob, the Australian bush,
and half of Texas. He owned, in fact and not in fancy, Spanish
castles among dusty olive groves, the Valley of Murada, the estate
of Carman de Croix, an Irish convent occupied by nuns and
doves, a Mexican monastery occupied by priests and buzzards,
Virginia Big Lick plantations shaggy with grapevines, Texas ran-
chos limitless as the horizon's blue, Indian villages occupied by
flea-bitten dogs, many gold, silver, and copper mines, an island
off the coast of Florida, various speckled birds' eggs in various
nests. To say nothing of a million reals in Spanish securities,
forty-one thousand francs in French securities, and other intangibles. He had seen snowflakes falling in an abyss between two
terrible mountains. This, and not man's interior, was immensity.
His brass watch had ticked in so many altitudes, its accuracy
could be explained only by the accuracy of its owner, who might
have been stung by a flea-bitten Indian, but had not yet lost his
purse, his footing, or his head. He was not, however, in the least
smug. In the world to come, he knew, there would be no such
mistaken men as he. There would be, however, an arduous reality.
The roots of inharmonious growth went back into prehistory,
like the mountains.

What was he doing on his way to Utopia in the pocket country? Among his many travels and adventures, this was, for the
great student of material rocks, nothing final, but only another
attempt in the right direction. At Alicante, Spain, he had financed
a communal farm but, a revolution uprising in that country, had

been fortunate to escape with the amount of his investment. This same sum he was willing to sink over and over again in Utopia or perhaps his own division of it, the shoemaking department, which he considered had most important implications as to the whole of man's welfare. His investment at New Harmony was $100,000, but his liability was limited to $10,000, the price of an empty monastery. There were, obviously, many aspects of existence on which he parted company with Robert Owen—among these, the idea that happiness could easily be attained and made permanent on earth. This, he considered merely a revived idea of antiquity, like the religion of the Great Mogul at Delhi. A community brain, moreover, like the idea of happiness, he believed to be an aspect of rhetoric.

William Maclure has come down in history as the Father of American Geology. Sad to relate, Say was only the Father of American Zoology, and caterpillars, though future butterflies, were not so lucrative as rocks. For Say, however, every land was a land of promise. In Florida, during the great controversy as to ownership, he had been the unmolested surveyor of natural creatures. He was an authority on luminescence, putrefaction, glowworms, union of unlike pairs, sexual scent, suspenseful shadow drama, the wild pig who eats cocoons, the glacial color, tempests of pollen, lethargy, water beetles with fringed legs, birds' dung and the implications thereof in mortal history, hawk moths, snails, related subjects. Through all his researches, he had a vital sense of the Spirit of Nature beside the untrodden ways—sometimes a veiled nun with a rabbit's purple eyes, sometimes an Indian princess with Greek antecedents, more often merely the effusion of ecstasy. Nature, however inconsistent, was consistent with herself and had, at no time, experienced a violent break with the continuity of her life. Nature had always worked in co-operation with the finest thinkers, begetting no impossibilities and, of necessity, no improbabilities. At Lilliput, Missouri, where it was reported that there was a graveyard of pygmies, of whom the chief enemies had been woodpeckers, Say had been dubious and, applying his shovel, had exhumed, much to his delight, the bones of average-sized men. Once more, he announced, hyperbole had cast a veil over the features of nature, which was ever admirably adjusted in proportions, both inner and outer. Never was there so rich a catalogue as Say's, listing hymenoptera, hemiptera, diptera, coleoptera, birds, all natural, and all acting in accordance with reality as a whole.

Charles Lesueur, hatchet-faced soldier of fortune, who looked like Julius Caesar but whose chief triumphs were in the world of water, has come down as the Father of American Fishes, a position about as substantial, financially speaking, as Say's. Lesueur had been attached to the biological expedition of La Pérouse, and had been left on the coast of Australia to examine and describe the remarkable marine animals of that region. Otherwise, he would have been lost, as the rest of his party were, in a storm at sea. Happily counting marine animals, he was hardly aware of his companions' protracted absence, and was perhaps even grateful for this opportunity to pursue his studies of nature unmolested by human nature. Weeks, months, half a year, ages passed, and Lesueur had hardly touched at the edges of nature, so to speak, though he imagined no gulf between himself and reality, for he was his own world. Alas, he was so unfortunate, in the midst of his great fortune, as to be sighted by an English sea captain, who believed that he saw, in the far distance, none other than the original Sinbad of the Rock, or at least Robinson Crusoe, or at least a poor shipwrecked mariner who would be grateful for rescue. He was mistaken as to Lesueur's gratitude. Lesueur, gasping like a fish brought up out of water, flailing, fighting, was carried aboard the English ship—raving mad, the captain thought, and treated him with consideration, with the hope that he might thus be wooed away from his concern with crabs. What a blow

to Lesueur, who wished nothing but the world of water, thus
to find himself shaved, dressed, fed, started on his way back to
civilization. When he thought of so many marine animals yet to
classify, he could have cried like a baby. Betrayed by his Gallic
sense of politeness, however, he was soon at ease with his jailers,
most of whom were as out of this world as he. The English sea
captain deposited Lesueur at their next port of call, an island
in the West Indies where, unfortunately, a hotel made natural
studies impossible, as there were more human sharks and fishes
than nonhuman. Maclure, coming along just in time, rescued
the impecunious Frenchman from a bad hotel and a threatening
landlord. Here was a gold mine, indeed, a man whose notebooks
described the marine animals of Australia, without so much as a
poor, withered flower of rhetoric, without so much as a funeral
wreath. Thus it had happened that, betrayed once more by his
Gallic sense of politeness, which would never fail him, Lesueur,
great lover of octopuses and all creatures evolving out of water,
was now a passenger in Noah's Ark on the Ohio River, on his way
to Utopia, the science of human society. It was enough to make
his blood run cold. Oh, how he yearned for the community of
fishes! His only consolation, considering Utopia, was the prospect
of fishes in the interior waters of America.

New Harmony, the Golden Rose

Now Vice and Crime no more shall stalk
    Unseen in open day,
To cross our silent, peaceful walk
    Through life's enchanting way.
      Old Ignorance with hoary head
      Must seek his everlasting bed.

Each warrier now may sheath his blade
    And toil in vain no more
To seek fair Virtue's genial shade,
    For now all wars are o'er.
      The battle's done, the day is won,
      The victory's gained by Truth alone.
                —OWENITE SONG IN NEW HARMONY

Presumably, the ice broke, and the struggle of love with hate began again. Noah's Ark pursued its course on the Ohio, carrying many philosophers, many notebooks, and the supplies which William Owen had asked for—all but what he had most wanted, a black cook.

There was great rejoicing at New Harmony, as the communicants awaited a solution, now imminent, of their many difficulties. A voice had once shaken the earth, but now it was to shake heaven, that those things which could not be shaken might remain. All old drunks were to put on new garments at last, it seems. Their faith was to make them whole. A Russian wheelwright declared that he saw, stemming out from New Harmony, a tree which would shadow the world.

Even Robert Dale was deceived, at first, by the idyllic vision. It was a pleasant life at New Harmony, with little suspicion that the beginning must be so near the end. There was a great charm in the good-fellowship and freedom from class distinctions. He was delighted by the solidarity of the human race, particularly as it expressed itself at evening balls and concerts. The young people, if not especially cultivated, were at least genial, as passionately fond of dancing as he was. He had not expected sophistication on the American frontier, so could not be disappointed with the simplest fare, the rudest accommodations. He "cared no more for the absence of luxury than young folks usually care who desert pleasant homes to spend a summer month or two under canvas—their tents on the beach, perhaps, with boats and fishing tackle at command, or pitched in some sylvan retreat, where youth and maiden roam the forest all day, returning at nightfall to merry talk, improvised music, or an impromptu dance on the greensward." New Harmony was a place for the sporting of virtues in the shade, a moral holiday, a release from narrow horizons.

"For here we have no continuing city, but we seek one to come"—the city rectangular, however, and not the New Jerusalem. Robert Dale, at this point, was chary of miraculous occurrences—would not have believed an ear witness to invisible bells ringing, would have measured the almost materialized angel with a yardstick. He accepted, in fact, no more value than he saw—and soon ascertained, to his everlasting satisfaction, that footprints of said angel adhered to one of the painted rocks on the Mississippi, and that George Rapp had purchased said pretense of grandeur for two dollars from an Indian runner on the St. Louis waterfront. It was the old, old pattern of deception, the utilization of a symbol as a substitute for human goodness. That he himself would become the prey of prostituted angels, he could not foresee, of course.

At that time, he was interested in the possibilities of Jessie. Should she be subtracted from the solar system, there would not be any possibility of community. His one object was to prepare a log cabin for her. He shrank, therefore, from no hard task which was assigned to him. He helped to pull down the dilapidated Rappite cabins, although considering that one of these would have been better than no shelter, and that Jessie would not have minded if the roof leaked a little or the swallows of death nested in the chimney. He took turn at sowing wheat by hand, although at the end of forty-eight hours, he found that his right arm was useless. He even tried to make biscuits, but gave up when it was suggested that, by a little manipulation, such as apothecaries employ in making pills, he might use his dough for bullets when he went rifle shooting. It was a great sport to bring down wild pigeons—their number seemed inexhaustible—they were not, like Jessie, unique in the nature of things. There would always be wild pigeons. He found that most of his efforts at common labor comprised a clog in the machinery—others accomplishing more in a day than he in a week. He accepted an invitation to teach in the school and edit the weekly newspaper—most gratefully, as in these capacities, his mistakes could be concealed—if the roof fell, it would have been a moral roof, and nobody the wiser.

What a wonderful scene of spontaneous existence was this, so far from the supernatural! Every season was a mating season. Boys and girls would stroll in the moonlight in groups, sometimes in pairs. Naturally, there were a few ill-timed marriages—a few who mistook the transient love for permanence, which is the most difficult thing in the world. His own heart, Robert Dale said, was occupied by Jessie, placed far above price, a pearl. Otherwise, he might have fallen victim to the proximity of a charming partner at ball or picnic—one, in particular, a lusty creature, who afterwards married the chief of Cincinnati's fire department, but no rival to the ghostly beauty at his side. By comparison with some of these buxom creatures of the frontier, Jessie seemed very refined, almost a creature of snow and light.

Robert Dale was glad to be in New Harmony, where the old walls between classes had been torn down. Or had they? Gradually, in spite of his tendency to ignore reality whenever he could, he was forced to the realization that evil persisted undiminished, even in this wilderness, so far removed from the whir of Scottish cotton mills. For there were cotton fields in Georgia.

It was a great shock, on a path outside New Harmony, one fine autumn evening, to come upon two horsemen and an octoroon, almost white, bound to a white horse between them. They were pleasant, oiled gentlemen, who asked the hour and best road. When Robert Dale inquired what was their business, they glowered darkly. They were, they said, honorable men, retrievers of runaway slaves for a harsh mistress. This wench, when she got home, would pay for the trouble she had caused them—tracking through marshes, fording rivers, sleeping in prairy grass with no roof but the stars above them. Everywhere they went, she had gone just a little way before them. And when they caught up with her, what was she doing, the silly fool? She was asleep with her face in the grass. She was not worth the horse she rode on. She was like the horse, an animal, but the horse was a prince of his kind, and she was the dregs, the scum—smoke-colored, with watery eyes, an underlip shelving out big enough for a bee to land on, stung with pride, untrustworthy, ready to bite the hand that fed her. Born black, she was. She would have the spirit taken out of her when she got home. It was impossible to handle her kind with kid gloves. They would take advantage of you. She must have the whip employed on her rump, and how she would whinny then, and submit to be fastened to the plow, and have the bit screwed into her insolent mouth, and walk a narrow furrow. For was it not written that nothing can rob the zebra of its stripes or the African of his black color? Yes, they had heard of New Harmony, a place where all people were to be made their equal. They spat at the idea. Not for the earth with a fence around it would they sell her to be made their equal. Without her kind to beat down, they could have neither jobs nor superiority. Tracking slaves was better than nothing. What was needed in America was a politics of force, dilated and at large, to suppress forever, among slaves, their consciousness of their existence as human beings.

After that, Robert Dale lost faith in Utopia, more or less, if not in mankind. He saw that the wolf depredated on calves running in the retired forest. Everywhere, among the brown leaves falling, he saw the Fool of Nature, a vacuity and a heart which, broken, never heals again. How find refuge from nature in any natural thing, unless it was Jessie, with the unfaded violets at her throat?

Yet it was a Pentecost of politics, this New Harmony—a grand hallelujah, every man being a sword of angelic flame and every man a chariot, whose winged horses were courage and desire. The extreme of skepticism was the extreme of mysticism.

In the Rappite cruciform church, for which the plans had been handed down, it may be remembered, from heaven, the problematical Mr. Whitwell, airy builder of nothingness perhaps, proposed his papery palaces to replace present cities, his rational nomenclature to replace the present names of present cities. He had noted, we are told, the incongruities of American names, such as a Banquo and a Bean Blossom to describe twin cities in this wilderness, though there was neither a ghost in the first nor a

bean in the second, but vice versa. According to this plan, which
seems to have been most seriously presented and accepted, each
city was to have a distinctive name, a compound word expressing latitude and longitude, so that its location in space would be
self-evident—cities which have no location in space not to carry
such names, and thus would be shown the impossibility of ever
going there. Letters were to be employed as substitutes for the
numerals used in expressing latitude and longitude. The first part
of the town name was to express the latitude, the second, the
longitude. The letter "S" inserted in the latitude would indicate
that it was south latitude, its absence, that it was north—the letter "V," west longitude, its absence, east. This system, though it
might present difficulties at first, especially to the uninitiated, had
the great virtue that it would make obsolete such monstrosities
and confusions as the name of a neighboring Indian chief, a poor
fellow without a tribe, one Occoneocoglecococachecodungo,
familiarly known, at least among squatters, as Dungo or Dusty.

A committee was appointed to consider the entire problem.
New Harmony, 38.11 N., 87.55 W., received, accordingly, its
rational name—Ipba Veinul. New York emerged as Otke Notive,
Pittsburgh as Otfu Veitoup, Washington as Feili Neivul, London
as Lafa Vovutu. Nor was it imagined that before this nomenclature could be effectively established as a general practice, the
Owenite community, as such, would have passed away, like the
dews from Jehovah, like the hoarfrost on summer grass.

Rational nomenclature was not the only diversion away from
the job at hand. An intoxicated engineer—but not, it may be
hoped, Captain Macdonald, who dreamed of a return to pastoral
sanctuaries—suggested that by the improvement of the steam
engine, it would be possible to reduce the distance between one
place and another, London to be not much farther from Berlin
than a stone's throw, figuratively speaking, and all cities to be
joined in everlasting harmony.

During such lectures, tatterdemalions sat up close to the platform or draped themselves at Robert Owen's feet, as if they loved him—the better-educated members keeping to themselves, as if they had their private pews. Meetings were generally closed by the recitation of an Ode to Co-operation, a goddess with long green hair, who would shed her radiance over the earth when the workers were united and all cities rectangular. Meetings were closed only to be assembled again—smaller units taking up the discussion where it had been left off. An Irishman at the Tavern, a great dancer of the jig, proposed to his following that they should build their rectangular city outside the narrow lanes and laws of sense—for otherwise, how be rational? And how escape fleas? The living sapphire of some other star might be a vast improvement over the Wabash pocket country—who knew? A Scotch coffinmaker, who had no following, decided to remain in New Harmony—he could keep busier here, outside of latitude and longitude, he said, than any place he knew of on earth. There seemed to be numerous Biblical patriarchs lurking about. There seemed to be numerous drunks. There were many sciences of society, in fact, and even a few plans to scrap the rectangle entirely, in favor of a semicircle or a hollow tree or a fox's hole—each science in the guise of a ragged, though perhaps rugged, individualist, alight with heaven's flame, who might stagger a little, but who had his own sweet version of reality, and his own quirks and fancies, often at odds with harmony, considered rationally.

Our focus, however, can be only on a few revealing characters—complicated, adventuresome, temporary, at large.

Constantine Raffinesque, Athenian nomad, a gentleman of Greek, Turkish, Hebrew, and French extraction, a walking league of nations, came to New Harmony late and left early. The period of his visit was a little before Utopia or a little after. According to Audubon's report, Raffinesque was "extremely remarkable" in appearance. He wore a long, loose coat of yellow nankeen, a

waistcoat of the same, with enormous pockets and buttoned up
to the chin, a pair of tight pantaloons, the lower part buttoned
over his ankles, and his beard long, where birds might nest, and
his long hair hanging loosely, like an ancient prophet's, over his
shoulders. Ordinarily, he was stooped like a burro under a bundle
of herbs. Nothing made him so angry, however, as to be mistaken
for one of the numerous herb doctors who then plied their trade
in the wilderness, with grasses for every disease, both real and
imaginary—prescriptions to guarantee longevity, a sound chest,
evolvement of new legs, or whatever else was necessary. He was a
picaresque scientist, a walking museum. He had gathered shells,
plants, and fishes on every shore from the Hellespont to the
Wabash and, carried away by his imagination, had made up for
the deficiencies of nature by describing nonexistent species as if
they were existent. Nature abhorred, however, as much as he did,
a vacuum—years later, what everybody had scoffed at turned
up as big as life. Raffinesque was publisher, editor, and sole sub-
scriber to a number of magazines devoted to nature's wonders.
None was so wonderful as he. He carried upon his person, not
only nature in futurity, but also his own version of the science
of society, a kind of exaggerated old-age insurance plan. As he
believed the social order to be merely a human fabrication or
invention, he had had his plan patented in Washington. There
was a fine for imitating it. Even the best of all possible sciences
of society, his own, he intended for all men but himself, conspiring with nature to fill her blank spaces with erroneous bodies, of great exactitude. There could be no blank spaces, so long
as he was abroad, and no necessity of paradise. While in New
Harmony, he advised that drinking water, as it was full of invisible bodies, should be sterilized—and soon, under his burden
of grass, had slipped into the wilderness from whence he came.

Audubon, lost dauphin in a kingdom of birds, and friend,
most inconsistently, of Daniel Boone, the unconscious builder

of mechanized highways, came to New Harmony before or after Utopia. America was already, from his point of view, a vanishing Utopia—for where men came, birds and winged creatures departed—thousands of pigeons falling each evening from the sky, thousands of pigeons in their country beaten by great clubs in the hands of mighty hunters. He predicted that the pigeon would one day be rarer than phoenix or angel.

Frances Wright, a link between the Rappites and the Owenites, a friend of both Frederick Rapp and Robert Dale, wished to combine the virtues of these two orders at Nashoba, for the freeing of Negro slaves. Bentham's ward, the friend of Shelley, the friend of Lafayette, Frances had been educated a rebel, who fit into no domestic map or moral sphere—her only goal, an infinite progress. Fortunately, she was rich, and able to arise above even that circumstance, and the circumstance of being a lady by birth. "She had," Robert Dale recalled, years after their estrangement over financial matters, "various personal advantages—a tall, commanding figure, somewhat slender and graceful, though the shoulders were a little bit too high; a face the outline of which in profile, though delicately chiseled, was masculine rather than feminine, like that of an Antinous, or perhaps more nearly typifying a Mercury; the forehead broad, but not high; the short chestnut hair curling naturally all over a classic head; the large blue eyes not soft, but clear and earnest." At the time of her coming to New Harmony, he could not have guessed her later development, those peculiarities of character which caused her downfall—"the courage untempered by prudence, the philanthropy untempered by common sense, the enthusiasm untempered by sound judgment, the inordinate estimate of her own mental powers, the obstinate adherence to opinions once adopted." She was known largely as the author of a small book entitled *A Few Days in Athens* and of a diary recording her travels in the American wilderness—though she was already what she would always be, a fighter. Mercury was restless—a spirit which could never be bound. Burned almost as black as a Negro from having ridden horseback under the burning sun, and suffering from ague as a result of sleeping on the cold ground with no roof but the stars above her, Mercury, like a slave pursued, carried everywhere the glad tidings of freedom and racial, sexual, political, economic equality. Frances or Mercury was lonely. At New Harmony, she hoped to find, if possible, a "few kindred spirits," who should join her at Nashoba, where each was to occupy a small brick house with a piazza, and each was to write poems and essays for the advancement of the human race. The Negroes, meanwhile, would render such services to themselves and to the few kindred spirits as would pay Frances a return on her investment, with which she would then buy other slaves at the auction block, these to be run in turn through the sieve at Nashoba, until such time when all members of the black race should have attained their freedom. Slaves, once freed, and the amount of their passage having been included in the price of their freedom, would be transported to another country. It was a long-time program. Frances hoped, however, that Southern planters, inspired by her example, would set up other Nashobas far and wide, so that the Negro might remain in America as the equal of his white brother. If not, there was always what she had in mind, Haiti—where, but a few years previous to Nashoba, a shipload of seven hundred starved dogs had been disembarked, for the express purpose of devouring Negroes, who had multiplied beyond the means of their subsistence. Frances was never to reach her ultimate goal—though as Madame D'Arusmont, she was to establish, at regal Haiti, a community of sleek Negroes, wafting purple fans above her by a purple sea. For her idea of Utopia would always be the "few kindred spirits" at the top, the masses at the bottom—a Greek city-state. At New Harmony, Frances blazed the trail, not only for Negro freedom, but also for that of woman. The Minerva Society, made up of many wingless creatures, met in a Rappite celibate dormitory, where Frances, determined to break up the time-hardened soil of conservatism in this field, urged, as woman's life was then so short in comparison with man's, the practice of birth control, that an ounce of prevention is worth a pound of regret.

Josiah Warren was a gentleman just full of Yankee ingenuity, wit, optimism, and golden ages. He was one person who, retiring from New Harmony, would never do so as a pessimist. Utopias would drop from him forever after, like cards from a magician's sleeve. "Grow old along with me!" Paradises would flourish in his head, like rabbits under a magician's hat. He was to produce, in fact, more and better societies than all the other society builders combined could think of—his preparation for these, a few years in New Harmony as a student of human nature and a self-taught education in the building of carriage wheels. He had sold his lamp factory at Cincinnati in order to join the New Harmony movement for the dissemination of light. As a manufacturer, he had designed a lamp using lard instead of oil, the former giving off both the cheaper and brighter light. Now in New Harmony he watched, casually, the operation of Robert Owen's many-headed schemes—his conclusion being that the oil of altruism should be withdrawn, and the lard of egoism should be injected—as simple a change as that—with the result that the great wick, the science of society, would then light up the entire world. It was simply a question of substituting his own principles, based on egoism, for Robert Owen's principles, based on altruism—and what an Aladdin's lamp there would then be in this wilderness, what a flame!

Other ambiguous characters on the streets of New Harmony. A long-bearded Irishman who believed himself a thing not seen and eternal, a philosophic nonresistant who slept with a revolver under his pillow, a woman in a black silk dress with a Greek cross around her neck and a pair of inglorious diamond earrings, a skeptic wrapped in the cocoon of mysticism, a whisky merchant or two, a terrestrial Elysianist, a necessarian circumstantialist. Alas, among so many discrepant visionaries, was not materialistic socialism doomed to an apparent failure—unless, by some miracle, all these could be caught up together in the clouds, to meet the Lord in the air?

Joseph Neef, ex-priest, ex-lieutenant under Napoleon, ex-schoolmaster, grappled with problems as great as the science of society. Neef, to put it broadly and boldly, without shame, without disguise, was New Harmony's nursemaid. Question—how to throw the bath out without throwing out the baby. Question— how to fold a diaper in such a way as to insure the greatest happiness to the greatest number. Question—how to spare the rod and not spoil the child. Wherever he went, Neef was surrounded by children—as if he were priest of another congregation, lieutenant of another army. There was neither the threat of hell nor a firing squad—but plenty of excitement otherwise, a little community within the community, a little republic within the republic. What protection had Neef against nature? He admitted to the children that his government was that of the worst despot, reflecting his will, though disguised as a democracy—but only because the members had not yet discovered the eternal laws of reason within their frames corporeal. Rather, how many noses had to be wiped, and how many knees had to be bandaged! Life was a never-ending struggle of good with evil. Neef's constitution, written while the sweat poured from his brow, provided merely that his little republic should be apprised of what was coming next—regulations as to crime, punishment, police, laws, courts of justice, and other traditional matters. He urged that the children should not imitate him and especially that they should not imitate his language. He had a most distressing habit which, try as he would, he could never cure himself of—to burst into a wild volley of oaths,

as if he were still Napoleon's lieutenant, to call on the Lord, as if
he were still a priest at the altar. When the little army retired from
a weed patch, scarred, torn, and defeated, unwilling to progress
the battle farther, he swore vociferously. When the little congregation seemed about ready to stray from the beaten path, he
prayed to God, whose high arm could reach where Neef's could
not. As Neef was rarely seen without a squalling brat under each
arm, and half a dozen others in his wake, perhaps his excesses
were understandable, even the children agreed. Could the teacher
of babes be a babe himself?

The Duke of Saxe-Weimar, who, after the failure of the Greek
struggle for freedom, had rejected the crown of Greece, was one
of the great travelers in the American forest. He had passed many
nights discoursing with friendly Indians in smoke-filled huts. He
had associated, on friendliest terms, with men from every walk
of life and not a few walks of death—lawyers, cutthroats. A man
determined to leave no stone unturned, he came, in the course
of his journeys, to New Harmony, this so-called Athens in the
American wilderness. While most appreciative of Indians, traders,
and other floating specimens, the Duke viewed New Harmony
as something less permanent than these. From the Duke's diary
may be gathered several valuable tips on old New Harmony, if
one uses his imagination to fill up the empty spaces.

First of all, the Owenite city was a something intangible, a
merely proposed rectangular shape, and not in evidence like the
Rappite city. The cruciform-shaped church, far from being God's
plan, had been Father Rapp's make-work plan, as idle hands
might get into mischief, naturally. Rumor persisted—Father
Rapp had castrated a son. Yet how not admire, however unwill-
ingly, a man who had had the ability to impose his will on a large
population, even to the extent of contravening an important law
of man's nature? Two lightning rods were on the house of the
man of God—Father Rapp had taken good care of himself. It

grieved the Duke that such a good man as Robert Owen should expect to change the course of all governments, all nations, and all peoples—a larger project than Father Rapp's had ever been, and doomed to failure.

Father Rapp's house, the only luxurious private dwelling, was now occupied, the Duke understood, by Mr. Maclure, who had not lowered his standards of living through the simple fact of being in New Harmony, as Robert Owen had, living at six cents a day at the Tavern. Mr. Maclure's windows looked out on a back garden which contained a curious slab, indeed—down among the chicken coops, in the midst of chicken feathers, broken glass, ashes, and bird dung, the footprints of an angel. What a contrast between realities—or were they one and the same? And when would the beams of common sense light up this sky?

The Duke gives hardly a portrait of Mr. Maclure. That great mountain climber and enemy to the flowers of rhetoric sat placidly at the back window, wrapped, throughout the entire history of Utopia, in thoughts as to the meaning of a single Greek word, *oida,* "I know," the perfect tense of the root *id,* "I see." The Greeks, after all, had a word for the science of society, to be based on nothing beyond the apprehension of our senses. Mr. Maclure had eyes, evidently, for little but the book in his hand—Condillac's fiction of a marble statue to which the senses were added, one by one, and which sensuous perception comprises the entirety of the soul, and from which evolveth the idea of an objective world. There could be, accordingly, no possibility of a soul from which the senses are always absent. Maclure accepted, evidently, this concept of being, rejecting the idea that a phantom, though it does not exist, is real because it is thought of, like freedom of will or a realm of purposes. Imagination, like the wolf at the door, Maclure believed, should be kept outside in the winter wind. An imaginary rectangle was as bad, in its way, as an imaginary New Jerusalem—since leading people to see what they did not see.

Mr. Say, his hands covered with blisters by his work in the potato field south of the back garden, was ridiculous-looking but at least contributed his share of labor, according to the Duke. A correct thinker was bound to be incorrect, the Duke observed.

All in all, New Harmony, due to its circumstance in a melancholy land already denuded of many trees, and scarred by the effects of Rappite industries, was not a place for paradise—unless considered as a place for those human beings who, losing their senses one by one, become marble statues.

High up on Indian Mound, the Duke discovered, there had lived an ancient hermit, a man with an obdurate capacity to resist two Utopias. Only the death of his horse had driven him to town. He had fought for Greek freedom and, that battle lost, had lived for many years in a cave on Indian Mound, with no company but a horse, the noblest animal, with whom he had shared his bed, his board, and his Athenian visions. The farther he got from mankind, the better he felt. He seemed to be suffering, the Duke concluded, from some kind of religious madness.

This ancient hermit was not the only crazy one. New Harmony seemed about to scatter to the four winds, in fact. "I can hardly believe that this society will have a long duration. Enthusiasm, which soon abandons its subjects, as well as the itch for novelty, contributed much to its formation, as to its dissolution." Some of the most turbulent, with an Irishman who wore a long beard, sat under the Rappite sundial, planning a community for alcoholics to be located in the cold mountains of Mexico—where, however, they would be unable to procure even the ghost of a living, the Duke believed. Mr. Jennings, of Philadelphia, a disfrocked clergyman, yearned for nothing so much as to wear his collar backward once again and represent the Lord, in whom all things move. The elegant Madame Fratageot, of Moscow, had been married for three days when her husband perished, most mysteriously, and for this reason had come to attach herself, like a bride, to Robert

Owen's science of society, but still mourned the loss of her first love, and confessed that she had been "egregiously deceived" in her expectations, as the community was too low, and the table so bad as to be beyond criticism. "The good lady appeared to be about to run from one extreme to another, for she added that in the summer she would go to a Shaker establishment in Vincennes." A charming young girl, Miss Virginia, had been interrupted in the midst of her piano playing by a brute laborer, who had demanded that she go take her turn at milking the community cows—music being no work, according to present standards of values, but a mere diversion. Miss Virginia, weeping, had retired from the room—poor darling, who deserved protection! Madame F., perhaps because of just such occurrences, had gathered the young girls of the better class around her, and there they were sheltered, like chicks under the wings of an old hen. Indeed, more seemed to have been lowered than raised by this community. A German patriot named Schmidt, who had been a first lieutenant in the Prussian artillery at Erfurt, and who had deserted to escape execution, confessed that, in this fatal community, his fine vision of freedom was very much lowered, indeed. He had expected to serve as Robert Owen's butler, which position would have been honorable, but had been placed, immediately upon his arrival in New Harmony, in charge of cattle stalls, as butler to cattle, which position he felt to be most dishonorable. What a Caliban was he to this Prospero. The smell of manure, he complained, was always in his clothes.

Was Robert Owen so infatuated with the idea of mankind, the Duke wondered, that he had forgotten sleeping workmen, deceived aristocrats, and other disgruntled specimens who comprised it? Evidently not. "Know thyself" was ever the first rule of this community.

The plates of human character, the Duke saw, were intended to facilitate the business of self-knowledge, as by these each person could be shown, from day to day, his capacities and their development, with the least possible waste of time. The plates bore the superscription, "Scale of Human Faculties and Qualities of Birth." They were marked with ten scales, labeled Self-attachment, Affections, Judgment, Imagination, Memory, Reflection, Perception, Excitability, Courage, and Strength. Each scale was divided into a hundred parts, marked from five to five, with a slide that could be moved up and down to show the measure of the qualities, therein specified, which the measurer possessed or believed himself to possess.

What a clever machine, of which all the parts could be known and studied! Alas, but the sleeping workman might find that he was not deficient in Courage and Strength—though woefully lacking in Imagination and Memory. One such fellow, with his hat drawn over his eyes, and an empty bottle at his side, seemed, so far as the Duke could judge, never to have moved from his position in the grass in front of an unfinished building during the entire length of his stay in New Harmony. Or Madame F., the egregiously deceived, might find that she was free from Self-attachment and Excitability. Or Miss Virginia might need Strength, which fact should have been evident to anyone in his senses.

The old French vinedresser complained to the Duke that the Germans had been makers of bitter wine, to judge by the sample they had left behind them. The Duke, far from being convinced of the inferiority of their manufactures, determined to visit, on his way out of America, Rappite Economy, where, he felt sure, the fare would be better than Owenite wild turkey and bread like bullets. Without regret, he said good-by forever to rationalism and its romantic visions of life in a green forest. No great good, he was convinced, could come from Robert Owen's science of society so long as it tended to surrender reality for the sake of a few cloudy aphorisms, a few wild theories.

There was, last but not least among New Harmony's citizens, old Greenwood, a seeker after happiness, who might have been, however, more at home among the Rappite candidates for heaven than among the Owenites. New Harmony experienced, during its second summer, almost a deluge, such as would inspire the imagination to believe that the world might be destroyed by flood again. The Wabash champed like a lion in its cage. During one of frequent thunderstorms, when the whole sky was illuminated by a green light, Robert Dale looked out of the window, expecting nothing but a scene of desolation and the usual Fool of Nature. What did he behold but a vision, most strange, most mysterious? Old Greenwood, thoroughly drenched, was parading up and down, up and down, like a sentinel upon the rain-veiled streets, and obviously going nowhere in particular. He carried upright, as a soldier carries a musket, a slender iron rod, ten or twelve feet long—but where was the war? Over his head, the lightning scrawled zigzags on the sky, and, all around him, trees fell—yet he was perfectly calm, perfectly self-possessed, at ease with nature. Robert Dale was puzzled by this display of exaggerated eccentricities. Perhaps old Greenwood had lost his power of reason, and that was why he did not have enough sense to come in out of the rain? Yet there was something even more compelling than the lack of sense—as if old Greenwood had determined on this strange course of action for some perfectly good reason.

Later, Robert Dale questioned old Greenwood—why had he not stayed indoors, why had he walked in the awful floods? Old Greenwood was by this time as dry as dust in a chimney corner, and as melancholy as a bat under the eaves. "Ah, well, young friend," he said, "I am very old. I am not well. I suffer much, and I thought it might be a chance to slip off, and be laid quietly in the corner of the orchard." He had simply not wished to take the responsibility of destroying himself, so had prayed that God would strike him dead. God, who had struck the Rappite house and the young colt and the trees of the green orchard, might also have spared a final blow for him. "If God had only seen fit to do it," he concluded, "I'd have been at rest this very minute, all my pains gone, no more trouble to anyone, and no more burden to myself." Only death could now translate him to a better state than New Harmony, a city whose gates are of pearls as big as goose eggs, and where the old do not grow older, and where the lion lies down to sleep with the lamb.

n Adult View

The following poem in opposition to the Owen community, first published in Philadelphia, was widely circulated, and of that order which despised a real millennium.

> *The Devil at length scrambled out of the hole*
> *Discovered by Symes at the freezing North Pole;*
>   *He mounted an iceberg, spread wings for a sail*
>   *And started for earth with his long, barbed tail.*
>
> *He heard that a number of people were going*
> *To live on the Wabash with great Mr. Owen;*
>   *He said to himself, "I must now have a care,*
>   *Circumstances require that myself should be there.*
>
> *"I know that these persons think they are impelled*
> *And by power of circumstance all men are held,*
>   *And owe no allegiance to heaven or me:*
>   *What a place this for work for the Devil will be.*

"Since Adam first fell by my powerful hand,
I have wandered for victims through every known land
But in all my migrations ne'er hit on a plan
That would give me the rule so completely o'er man.

"I have set sects to fighting and shedding of blood
And have whispered to bigots they're all doing good,
Inquisitions I've founded, made kings my lies swallow,
But this plan of free living beats all my schemes hollow.

"I have tempted poor Job, and have smote him with sores,
I have tried all good men and caught preachers by scores,
But never on earth, through my whole course of evil
Until now could I say, 'Here's a plan beats the Devil.'

"I am satisfied now this will make the coast clear,
For men to all preaching will turn a deaf ear;
Since it's plain that religion is changed to opinions
I must hasten back home, and enlarge my dominions."

The Devil then mounted again on the ice
And dashed through the waves, and got home in a trice,
And told his fell imps whom he kept at the pole
Circumstances required they should widen the hole!

The Book of Nature was written on leaves of sandstone and limestone, no everlasting material. For thousands of years, what is now the state of Indiana was a vast plain of granite rock covered by a deep, salt, tideless sea. Not only was there no human landscape—there was neither bird nor angel, which is a later development than bird or man, a combination of both. Gradually, transparent fishes began to appear in the Indiana sea—their fins are marked upon the sultry prairie rock. Without benefit of Noah, through endless ages, the waters withdrew. Then out of the mists of time rose pterodactyls, birds with human hands, but without Dresden lavalieres around their necks, as they were free from all ornamentation, even the pale flowers of rhetoric. In the later formations of rock appear impressions of leaves, lizards, bird tracks, convolvulus—but not one human footprint, for man was the inconceivable possibility, something which, apparently, no direction pointed to—and had he continued missing, the earth would still have seemed complete. Came the sea again, glassy as death, and an age of sea burial—but time after time, that Lazarus of birds and flowers was risen to new, incorruptible life. Then vast glaciers like crystal rivers inched down from the Arctic north. What could not move was destroyed. When the cape of the glacier was withdrawn, lo, appeared a rich soil, with many rivers, many streams. Soon this green area was populated by swans, cranes, geese, white heron, wild duck, the kingfisher, swallows, horny-tongued woodpeckers, a variety of birds, but no religious experiences. There were communities of lion-headed hornets, most co-operative, enemies to all creatures but themselves. It was an Adamless Eden where ants performed their marriage flight and lost their wings. Immense elephants browsed on the Wabash hills, lifting their trumpet trunks among the topmost branches of the maple and oak trees. As yet, their ivory was intended not for the keys of the harpsichord. The puma devoured the deer. Parrots mingled their cries with the cries of monkeys in Posey County. Where New Harmony is, there was a crocodile whose mouth served as a dormitory for plover. But that was not paradise. Or was it?

When man arose, he was already old and corrupt, like the earth before him—a creature with a history. There was never a first dawn. There was never a pale geometer impelled to create in the abstract, with golden compass, a harmonious likeness of himself. As Descartes said, years later, "I may have invented the 'rational animal' which passes in Aristotelian circles as man, and having ideas of myself and God I may, by way of imaginative patchwork or compromise, have pieced together the idea of an angel." As Thomas Paine said, surrounded by vulturous sectarians when he lay dying on Grove Street, Manhatta, "Nor is it possible to suppose that every world in the boundless creation had an Eve, an apple, a serpent, and a Redeemer." Man was his own shadow play, whether his soul existed with or without his body being a problem which he alone must solve, even as he converged on to nonexistence and the dismemberment of creation—for his supremacy to the brute facts could be established only in the interval between his life and his death.

Time passed, as time passes. In the early eighteenth century, when M. Voltaire was writing *Candide*, to refute Leibnitz's thesis that this is the best of all possible worlds, and Dr. Johnson was writing *Rasselas* with two allied purposes in mind—to discredit the possibility of the attainment of happiness in this world, and to pay for the burial of his mother's corpse laid out in a stuffy living room—the Wabash was still a stream described by inarticulate Indians. Soon the river was ascertained to be the river. While Jonathan Swift complained wryly that, like the tree which withers from the top, he should die from his head downward, Jesuit missionaries pushed through dense foliage, conveying the glad tidings of immortality to the Indians of Indiana. Traders followed. There were both masses and massacres innumerable, wildest orgies carried on under the shadow of the cross at Ft. Wayne, the cross at Terre Haute. The more Indians slaughtered, the greater the business. As is often true when a superior race goes out to conquer an inferior, the supposed inferior conquered, though subtly. White men wore the scalps of red men around their waists—though never forgetting, at the same time, to acquire furniture, livestock, and poultry. Indian progress to civilization was rarer, though there were a few glorious chieftains who employed their spare moments to learn of human nature from the bluestocking comedies of Molière, and to learn of themselves from the works of puny Rousseau. One or two of these children of nature appeared disdainfully in London drawing rooms and were the sensations of the social season, as ladies fluttered and beaus grew dumb in admiration. Everywhere, there was the cult of nature. Everywhere, the Indian was idealized, at the same time that he was being destroyed.

In an impolite world of things as they are, in the early nineteenth century, an Indian prophet arose—even on the banks of the Wabash—Lolawawchicka, the Indian Patrick Henry. If they did not hang together, they would all hang separately, Lolawawchicka said, a little belatedly. He proposed to establish a community of Indians in the Wabash valley, where the problem should be the Indian as an end in himself, rationally considered. Alas, but to achieve this plan, he must employ the most irrational means, the most forceful—must destroy the invading white race, by the use of painted arrows and propaganda. Lolawawchicka, or Loud Voice, was a most convincing orator, and capable, by much beating of his breast and much dancing, of arousing his audience to frenzied rage. He was, he said, spokesman of the Great Spirit, the Indian of Indians, who flies higher than an eagle and whose dwelling place is in the sun. In Lolawawchicka's father's house were many mansions, to include themselves and little foxes, themselves and green corn. Neither arrow nor bullet could destroy Lolawawchicka until he had achieved his mission, which was to save his people from their white saviors. They should be established in a happy hunting ground, where there would be no Christian traders, but many papooses, much feeling, no thinking, he promised.

Lolawawchicka, or Loud Voice, was, as he said, the spokesman of a greater spirit—his brother Tecumseh, a subtle philosopher who lacked nothing but the gift of speech. Tecumseh would have been at home, however, with the best thinkers of his day. With the great empiricists, he would have held to the idea of Occam's razor, that all false ideas should be scalped away—with the followers of Locke, that the mind is born a blank page— with the followers of Rousseau, that no writing should be placed on it—with the followers of Hume, that there is no rosary of thought but only so many detached beads without a string— with all those who saw the absolute dissolving. Tecumseh was very far from being, however, the romantic Indian as described by Pope—though proud science had never taught him to stroll to the solar walk. It might be a disappointment to idealists who dreamed of the green forest, but once he had rid the wilderness of white invaders, he intended to adopt their ways, in so far as rational—their methods of house building, crop rotation, wool spinning—all Indians, in his Utopia, to be dressed in linsey-wool- sey pantaloons and cocked hats. Thus would all Indians become the thing they fought against. Unfortunately, Tecumseh was a man bound by mortal circumstance. Unfortunately, Lolawawchicka, or Loud Voice, was Tecumseh's trumpet, daily newspaper, flam- ing sword of justice, popular opinion. Thousands of white set- tlers, always the innocent, were slain—any night might be the night of great maraudings, immense conflagrations lighting the skies, shriekings, scalpings, riderless horses. Tecumseh seemed invulnerable. Tecumseh, the Indian Napoleon, had at last his Waterloo, however, his just retribution. Not only he perished, but many of his people. Indian women and children were cut to pieces. Blackbirds feasted. On such an occasion, Andrew Jackson rescued an Indian baby from the arms of a dead woman in the field—and raised it as his own. The remnant Indian people, dis- organized and beaten down, scattered to the four winds. They insisted that Tecumseh's spirit rode on wind, perhaps so far as to the milky way, the solar walk. There would be, they said, a second coming of one among them, Tecumseh, riding a white horse wreathed with white men's scalps—and his realm would last forever. Meanwhile, by various means, the Indian faded, like the dews from Jehovah, like the hoarfrost on summer grass.

After the Jesuit and the whisky merchants had come the Protestant preacher—the Baptists conspiring with Daniel Boone in his struggle to possess the "dark and bloody ground," inferno of the Wabash valley. The preacher, equipped with both Bible and bullets, rode on his lean nag through the Indiana wilderness, singing a loud, loud hallelujah—and his song drove the last Indian away. When the wolves howled, down on his knees fell that astute preacher, with his gun cocked in his hand, reciting the Lord's prayer, that the Lord was his shepherd, yea, and had led him beside the still waters, yea, and through the valley which is the shadow of death. Even the wolves got religion then. Not infrequently, that preacher was a married man and bedded down each night with his wife and children in the sour, mosquito-ridden grass. Bullfrogs and Baptists flourished, we are told, in buttonwood swamps, until along came the Methodists, bringing ills of every sort, for Methodists and milkweed sickness always entered a neighborhood together.

There were many villains in those days. The Hoosier, before he answered a knock at his cabin door, cocked his rifle, yelling "Who's yer?"—from whence comes his illuminating name, the Hoosier being, the world over, a suspicious fellow. There were many unconscious heroes in those days, many Joads. Merely by the act of walking back and forth, there were many who made wonderful contributions to the idea of human progress. Their feet did the work, while their heads rested. There was, for example, a lice-ridden family which crossed by foot from Indiana to Tennessee twenty-five times in the space of a few years—so many times, in fact, that they lost all track of themselves, and hardly knew whether they were going or coming. One thing sure, they were always on their way. As soon as they got to Injianny, they yearned for Tennessee. As soon as they got to Tennessee, they yearned for Injianny. The place where they were not was always the better place, the greener pasture. Their feet traced a road through the wilderness. Pappy and man and mule, they all died on the road, and mammy lived to talk about it, and the cloudy number of times she had squatted and picked up her new baby in her arms—and Little Bro, no bigger than her hand, she buried in a holler stump filled with old cocoons and autumn leaves, and how when she come back that spring, Little Bro, the old cocoons, the autumn leaves, they all was gone.

There was also the devious history of Frances Slocum, like a green writing on a green page in the books of nature. Its beginning was elsewhere, but its end was Indiana. During an Indian raid, when war whoops sounded around her father's cabin, Frances, aged three, was fast asleep under her bed, where she had crawled to retrieve a corncob doll. In the great excitement of the moment forgetting Frances, her family fled. The Indian chieftain, seeing a pair of little feet which stuck out from under a bed, deduced a little body. With hardly the rustle of an ash leaf in the wind, he gathered Frances up into his arms. War was his business and perhaps his pleasure, but his heart fluttered when he put his cheek to hers. In the great evil of the white man's world, he had found this papoose, this bag of wild bee's honey, this sweetness and light. Farther than to the stellar walk—yea, infinities farther—he carried sleeping Frances. Her anguished parents searched for her. When her parents died, her brothers continued to advertise, begging that anyone who had heard tell of a white woman among the Indians, or any Indian woman who suspected that she was white-skinned, should come direct to them. Theirs was a great compassion, and theirs, a Biblical lament—"And other sheep I have, which are not of this fold: them also I must bring, and they shall hear my voice; and there shall be one fold, and one shepherd." Sixty years in the wilderness, Frances lived unknown. Sixty years, the summer turned toward autumn. When all hope seemed gone, for many winds had blown, and many rains had fallen, and the brothers had moved to another town, there came to that town one day, upright on a frisking pony, an ancient Indian woman, tobacco-colored, with long braided hair and a crown of wild goose feathers, and nothing in her look or manner to suggest that she was the lost child, Frances Slocum. "My name is Frances Slocum," she said. Yes, she had remembered, like a faint, glimmering star beyond clouds, her name, and a corncob doll, and had been aware, all her life, of a mistake which had been made by destiny—and happier they, whom stars unite in one dream. The Indian chieftain had been kind to her, and she enjoyed much happiness, much nature. Being an Indian princess, who might have been a sun-bonneted singer in a church choir, she said, "I am the old tree which cannot be planted again." It was an announcement communicating her pride and her felicity.

Not far from the old Wabash, there was, in the early years of the nineteenth century, a family of squatters who crossed over from Kentucky—shiftless, down-at-the-heel, daydreaming, ragged, honey-tongued—among these, a boy prematurely old, Abe Lincoln, the expression of all that was good in the weak and lonely.

The wilderness was doomed, though few could have guessed it, to become a network of roads—in the future, a loud honking, not of wild geese but of automobiles. An observer wrote, in 1824, of the already congested traffic—hundreds of families migrating to the West with ease and comfort, drovers from the West with their cattle of almost every description turning eastward toward a market. "Indeed, this great thoroughfare may be compared to a street through some populous city—travelers on foot, on horseback, and in carriages are seen mingling on its paved surface." Almost alone among the many migrants to and fro, the Owenites had dedicated themselves to the mental conquest and to many liberalizing theses, propositions, preambles, paragraphs, a universal suffrage. The irony is the contrast between all their portentous articles, sections, and items, and the bleak reality these hid. They were dedicated, for example, to the love of nature, when fewer and fewer would find tongues on the trees, books in the running brooks, sermons in stones, and good in everything. On the other hand, they seemed to have altogether the mentality and psychology of the old ascetic, for whom nature is always a defective material. The mass could not resist that mental contagion, that great dream of nonentity. Thus it will be seen that while Robert Owen preached one sermon, his people heard another.

Shortly after Noah's Ark dry-docked, the Preliminary Community assumed the status of a Permanent Community, as had been promised. This was a sudden revolution. Its political doctrine was based on an appeal to man's inherent goodness and magnanimity. It ignored the fact of a humanity guided by atavistic instincts and waves of unreasoning emotion. It ignored the fact of a great inertia. It placed great faith in the potence of theories and ideas. Nothing, evidently, was to be as it had been. Thomas Pears, former bookkeeper and great lover of transience, was thus appointed to act as Secretary to a Committee for the drawing up of the Permanent Constitution for the Permanent Community. There followed two weeks of heated debates and headaches—though there was some agreement that the killers of men should not be called the real, the strong, the masters of men. The document shows the luxurious blossoming of liberal ideas, like weeds in a cornpatch. All the evils, however, seemed removed. It bore the interesting preface—"When a number of the human family associate in principles which do not yet influence the rest of the world, a due regard to the opinions of others requires a public declaration of the object of their association, of their principles, and their intentions." There could be no mystery, no angel, no weeds. The Permanent Constitution reiterated, like a trumpet cry, the earlier promise of happiness to all sentient beings.

The Permanent Constitution provided, by clause and sub-clause, for the following, uninfluenced by sex or condition, in all adults: equality of duties, modified by physical or mental conformation; co-operative union, in all the business and amusements of life; community of property; freedom of speech and action; sincerity, kindness, courtesy, order, health, knowledge.

The Owenites held the following to be self-evident: that all men are uniformly actuated by a desire for happiness; that no member of the human family is born with rights either of possession or exemption superior to those of his fellows; that freedom cannot justly be limited except by a man's own consent; that the preservation of life, in its most perfect state, is the first of all practical considerations. Experience had taught to the Owenites the great lesson that man's character is the result of his formation, his location, and the circumstances within which he exists; that man, at birth, is formed unconsciously to himself, is located without his consent, and circumstanced without his control. Simple reason showed that to a being of such a nature, artificial rewards and punishments were equally inapplicable. Kindness must be the one consistent mode of treatment, and courtesy the only rational species of deportment. The Owenites had found, in practice, that an increase of intelligence is equally an increase in happiness—they sought intelligence, therefore, as they sought happiness. Their first and most important knowledge would be the knowledge of themselves, as beings to whom a complete good is always accessible. They had seen misery produced by the great leading principles which prevailed throughout the world— therefore, they had not adopted them. They believed that man has a capacity for social sympathy, that the strings of each human instrument are similarly attuned, and that the vibration of one harp can easily transmit itself to another, without supernatural means or endowment. The gospel of an unmysterious truth must now be spread abroad, freely.

Resolved, that science is creating, with golden compass and pencil, a new world on the banks of the Wabash—where education, like real estate, shall be a public property. Resolved, that the only mystery within these gates is the Order of Free Masons, they who wear skirts. Resolved, that man is an intricate machine. Resolved, that the exaltation of one power over another promotes the downfall of the human race. Resolved, that man is man, a creation of circumstance. Resolved, that violence has disappeared. Resolved, that there is no principle of right conduct applying out of relationship with human life and experience. Resolved, that the unused faculties have hindered survival in posterity. Resolved, that woman is man's equal and may wear trousers. Resolved, that there is not only astronomical, there is also biological uniformitarianism. Resolved, that as an arm implies a body, and the moon's movements take into consideration the entire solar system, so also must society be considered as a whole, to which all parts are related. Resolved, that there is, in such a system, no place for a swan-necked deity reflecting himself in the glassy mirror of an unreal, purely fugitive universe. Resolved, that the negative aspects of life must be dispensed with.

The mistaken writings of the past are herewith blotted out, on the recommendation of Thomas Pears and others—suffering to have no more its perennial source in man's own heart.

Serpents in the Garden

Robert Owen had gained, the Gazette reported, complete ascendancy over the minds of others. He was such a man as the world had never seen before, it was generally believed. "I bear witness to the sayings of Christ, 'I, if I be lifted up from the earth, will draw all things unto me.'" The furnaces, the dye houses, the shoemaking establishment in a corner of the cruciform church, all were to be put, at an early date, under altruistic management, when the ego should be harnessed like a tide to the moon of a rational social order. There were other glorious prospects. Some denied their will to live. An angel, it seems, was on the verge of descending to the hop fields, carrying a great key in his hands. All other knowledge seemed a vanity. Men yearned for paradise.

The first person to desert the ranks was Captain Macdonald of the Engineers. The Constitution, he said, was complicated, unintelligible, and unnecessary. He had simply wished for this community to revert, through the recognition of certain unwritten laws, to sweet Auburn in the vale, a place where might be heard the evening bells, the lowing cows, the gabble of geese, the water dog's voice, the milkmaid's song, the "loud laugh that spoke the vacant mind," and other sounds. Then every rood of ground would have maintained its man, as now its tree. All the works would be those of grace, Captain Macdonald's goal being only a rural society. There were other complainants. The new bookkeeper discovered that the burden of bankrupt capitalism in a communistic society was too great to bear. He wondered that he had been a critic of Mr. Pears backstairs with his little brown jug, under the Rappite handwriting—"May God have pity on our souls," or words to that effect, for he could not translate German.

Mr. Pears, as Secretary to the Permanent Community, felt worse than ever before—like a dissolving star. Mrs. Pears could hardly contain her furies. The Pearsons felt better, because they had been raised in their station, but the Pearses had been lowered, step by step. They had hoped against hope that Robert Owen's return would effect a miracle. Nothing had been produced but a pretentious Constitution. In fact, with Robert Owen's return, all hope had taken flight forever.

The pit of hell seemed open under Mrs. Pears' feet. To Uncle Bakewell, she wrote that she came away from each lecture on happiness more unhappy than she went—not that she was perverse, but that she represented an important part of human nature. The third part of the moon was already dark—yea, she was going down a very dark sky, so blind she could hardly see, and dogs barking all the way. She felt enslaved, enchained, pursued. There were so many troubles. She would never be able to do the work which Robert Owen expected of the women—never be able to stand her turn, six weeks in the community kitchen, cooking for multitudes! The idea of equality made her sick to the bone. Oh, that she could live in a house upheld by those twin pillars, praise and blame! There was much of her which was reducible to no system. Neither was she a machine, nor was she a string in the community harp. She must be the whole harp or nothing. As for the males, they were not concerned about the fate of Christianity, caring for nothing more than this world affords.

Mrs. Pears, however, considered the sacrifice she had made so blindly, foolishly—leaving Pittsburgh—her place to be empty in the choir of heaven, for all she knew. What good had come of it? Not even a feather bed. Mrs. Pears was convinced that a Christian soul could not be an Owenite. They were poles apart.

Mr. Pears did not agree with his wife at this point, however. His correspondent, Uncle Bakewell, should have good cheer, as the true Christianity and the Owen system were the same, like the evening star and morning star which, being deceived by the report made to their senses, men had for so many ages considered as separate celestial bodies, and still persisted in naming as such. There was always a lagging of time. Mr. Pears was sure that if Robert Owen's principles could be put into practice, they were not far from being the most perfect Christians of their day. Never had he heard less of deism than in this community of deists. They had used all their sugar.

In spite of the Permanent Constitution, with its guarantee of happiness, there was much unhappiness—and nature convulsed by a storm, and threatening thunderclouds. No one had found in life what could never be found there. Two weeks after the adoption of the Permanent Constitution, the English farmers, soft-spoken men with thistles under their tongues, declared that they were homesick for God, the presence of that stupendous might, and could not endure proximity to so many foreigners. Their one craving was for the sublime, the old assurance of a meaning in their sufferings. Very shortly, they withdrew to form, two or three miles beyond New Harmony, a separate community which, though it should be at variance with its fate, would have at least the hope of an Almighty God. They named it Macluria, in honor of William Maclure, that great friend to farmers everywhere. Macluria kept some of the features of New Harmony, discarded others, especially self-knowledge. Its legislative body, called "The Council of Fathers," was made up of the five oldest male members under the age of sixty-five years. Women were given no voice in community affairs. A system of blackballing was instituted, whereby undesirable applicants could be turned away. A listless member could be expelled by vote. Three days, and Macluria was a strange, mysterious people, dwelling apart—and what was very sad, New Harmony was deprived not only of communists, but also of future cabbages, for these seceders had been the chief providers of foodstuffs. Macluria was but the beginning of the movement toward divinity. Hardly was Macluria established when a second group of farmers, inspired by their example, announced their intention to withdraw—reason, same, homesickness for God and the old way of life when men were men, too many foreigners with abstruse ideals. They called their community Feiba Peveli, a name denoting latitude and longitude, whereby they could be located between the last of the hop fields and the old Rappite bull pasture. Their plan of government was almost identical with that of Macluria—God, fathers, blackballing, no voice for women, and all men to labor by the sweat of their brows. Three days, and Feiba Peveli was a strange, mysterious people—and what was very sad, New Harmony was left almost without food producers at all. There seemed a general movement toward dismemberment.

The *Gazette*, however, taking a most cheerful view, announced that by this new exodus the congestion of population at New Harmony had been greatly relieved. Macluria and Feiba Peveli were but the branches of this great tree of life. "All minds seem now to comprehend the true grounds of future co-operation, and all hearts have united in claiming the benefit of Robert Owen's experience and knowledge in reducing to practice the principles which form the basis of our association. General satisfaction and individual contentment have taken the place of suspense and uncertainty."

So at the time of depression, there was a feeling of expansion. The *Gazette*, two weeks after the exit of the last farmer, admitted that their reason had been often at variance with their common sense. While they had been discussing the abstract ideas, while they had in vain tried to reconcile clashing opinions, they had neglected the practical means within their reach which alone could bind man to his fellow man. In short, they had wasted their energies in fruitless endeavors, like men more imbued with heaven than earth. This situation, however, had changed, as they had seen that it would be impossible to have a movement of any body without a center of force. Already, New Harmony was a center of force around which many communities were revolving—Macluria, Feiba Peveli, and various others throughout the United States—hardly a day in which news did not arrive of some new star in this planetary system, the science of society. The *Gazette*, for the moment forgetful of latitude and longitude, listed names which might be applicable to such communities—Lovedale, Peace Glen, Everblest, New Duty, Philosophy, Lovely, Voltaire, Elysium, Platonea, Socrates, Utopia, Confucia, Powhatan. The growth of their ideal, they realized, had been incommensurable with even their wildest expectations.

For the benefit of branches of this parent order, the *Gazette* listed a number of helpful hints—from which may be gathered what had been the former experience at New Harmony—though its streets no longer presented groups of idle talkers, and there was now an order very different from that of desolation. There must be, if such a community endures the gale—for we are all at sea on a wide ocean—no abuse, growling, carping, murmuring against the work of others. No anger ought to be felt against the female members upon their aversion to the work of cooperation, or when they indulge in brawling, loud talk, hair pulling, or other forms of excitement. The lazy and the intemperate must be treated with the utmost consideration, not as objects of scorn. There must be no distinctions in eating and drinking among the members. Adult members should not stalk about in the dining hall during meals. Children should not be allowed to run wild in the dining hall and should be encouraged to be careful of their language.

Evidently, where there had been the reign of reports before, peace now reigned in New Harmony. Alas! No sooner were the *Gazette* pages dry than cropped up a great battle between Goliath and David, Esau and Jacob, right in the heart of New Harmony. The mechanics, greaseless illiterates, who were lucky to be alive, for they knew not the secret of any machinery, complained that the educators were trying to make "hewers of wood and drawers of water" out of them. They had expected equality of all classes in New Harmony, and what had they found but the old injustice, themselves like poor babes delivered up to Herod? How did the educators justify their existence, since the mechanics had experienced, as yet, no enlightenment on any subject, but were as puzzled as ever they were, if not more puzzled? Where were the manufactures, the free goods, the stout shoes? The pale, lily-livered educators complained that they were being stamped down to the lowest level, as by an almighty foot, and that they could not willingly suffer their minds to be destroyed by a communistic society, which must come to recognize, for its own salvation, that the productions of the brain, while invisible, are as important as any other. The mechanics were legion, and the educators were few. It looked as if New Harmony was about to lose all those few minds which did the correct thinking—the educators with their strange mania for golden birds. They chose Robert Dale to lead them to "some happier island in the watery waste," a sanctuary for the pleasures of the intellect. Robert Owen offered no objection. With that great remnant, the mechanics, he might still be able to build a better world. He pointed to Cut-off, a rich soil, which might be submerged in another season. "Lo, it is yours," he said. Theoretically, the educators might have enjoyed living like the wild goats on the island of Calypso—actually, this was another story, Cut-off, where there were many wild pigs. The educators were forced to remain in New Harmony, at least for the time being. When the mechanics urged that Robert Owen assume unchallenged leadership—thus to guide them out of this wilderness—the educators accused him of despotism. There could be no agreement. Many strains and tensions were splitting the social rock. There were drunks in the cruciform church, and sacrilege in the graveyard. The preachers who camped at the gate saw ample fulfillment of their prophecies.

Complaints, both serious and facetious, began to pour in from all sides. Why were the Wise Men of the East paid for their services, while the mechanics were not? Why was it that the people of New Harmony were not permitted to see the model of the proposed rectangular village, although it had been shown to the President of the United States? Had Robert Owen revealed, to the people of New Harmony, the entirety of his scheme, and what were the threatening, concealed elements? Why a rectangle? What was the superiority of the hollow square over parallel sides at a convenient distance apart, or over a hollow triangle, pentagon, or hexagon? How, in the erection of the new building, should the unevenness of the ground be avoided? How level the hills? How keep the aspen leaves from quivering? Why had they never seen the golden book of nature, the mechanics wanted to know. How could nature's pages be blank, the educators wanted to know.

It was the spring of the year, almost the end of spring—and Mrs. Pears reported to Uncle Bakewell that her condition was unimproved. Her health had received a shock in this place from which she would never recover. Even Mr. Pears was beginning to be homesick for Pittsburgh, though he had left it so willingly.

Uncle Bakewell replied that he was not in the least surprised at the course the new moral planet had taken—it was nothing unusual, alas, but old as the hills. Not suddenly could a change be brought about in the minds of ill-doers, Uncle Bakewell feared. If the mass should divest itself of old humors and habits, he would become a convert to sudden conversions, too—but was convinced, by this experience, that the past must be our safest guide to the future world. He had longed "to see by experiment whether man is altogether the creature of habit, and that he may be formed into an angel or devil, according to the circumstance with which you surround him." He had hoped that man might be illuminated. Yea, he too had wished to build a world of glass, employing the talent of glass blowers, and all beautiful devices of air and light, the last decision of character, the rose that fades not, a luster of the present hour. His hot blood had grown cold at the very thought. In consequence of mental isolation, he had imagined a vacuum, a mythological Elysium, an abode of shadows less real and more real than earth, an abstract heaven over the naked rock. He now realized, as never before, that God is the greatest glass blower of all, beside whom other efforts shatter, and that a man's self is more than its ingredients.

Mrs. Pears' letters continued in a sad vein. She was a dry thorn burning, etc. What a misfortune to have been born twice! She suffered from a variety of religious experiences. Cruelty seemed to her, as much as kindness, a characteristic of man. She felt a kind of oblivion engulfing her, and found it difficult to remember Aunt Bakewell's face, so wise, so old, so placid, so unadventuresome, so secure.

New Harmony became increasingly regimented, Mrs. Pears reported. Maria was to be taken from her and placed in a large boarding school. Robert Owen had been remonstrated with as to the propriety of housing young males and females in the same building, but had said that in six months' time they would be so used to it, they would not mind. How Mrs. Pears was going to get through the cooking, washing, and scrubbing, she really did not know. In Maria's place, she must accept a family with an infant under two years. It made no difference that Clinton could take care of himself—there would always be another baby to look out for, another voice crying in the middle of the night, more wet diapers, more teething, more troubles. If Mrs. Pears was sick, she would have to go to a hospital—no sweet Maria to pat the pillow, but leering strangers. How cruel to divide families in order to unite them! If this was logic, it was unhuman, the beating of tides on a barren shore. Its prevalence, Mrs. Pears felt, would put the human type in danger. And that was not the worst of it. If one was sick, it would be necessary to have the doctor's permission to stay at home from work.

Mrs. Pears looked forward to nothing now but a New Jerusalem—Pittsburgh being out of the question. Where was the infinite variety, the integration of all riches which had been promised at New Harmony? There was nothing but coldness, a desertion of the spirit. One was made as tame as barnyard poultry, finally. "I absolutely begin to feel myself a complete slave." Even Mr. Pears had come to the point of admitting a complete failure—"that when men abandon practice for theory, they lose themselves in the wilderness." The grand forces had originated in the nature of things—not in systems of bookkeeping, not in Constitution writing.

The Pearses continued their letter writing. Mrs. Pears knew that Aunt Bakewell would be as outraged as she was by the new fashions in clothes. The women's costume was a pair of undertrousers tied around the ankles, with an exceedingly full slip reaching to the knees. The men's was a pair of wide pantaloons, a top garment very full, bound around the waist with a broad belt. A fat person dressed in this elegant garment might be compared with a Russian or a feather bed tied in the middle. It was difficult to distinguish the sexes from a distance. The men with their bare necks looked as if they were equipped for the executioner. Mrs. Pears had been eye witness to a macabre wedding—the parties with their bridesmaids and groomsmen in striped burlap, black and white like prisoners. The bride wore the uniform in which she had done a week's scrubbing out of rat-holes, so it could not be very nice. She had first dressed herself in stainless white and a veil, but was persuaded by Robert Owen and the bridegroom to lay aside these trappings of the old, immoral world. The change had cost her many bitter tears. Robert Owen had performed the wedding ceremony, with no more feeling than a butcher. Both Mrs. Pears and the bride had been sick at heart. A marriage beginning so inauspiciously was bound to end in disaster.

Even Sunday was not a day of rest, as Mrs. Pears had to catch up on her sewing. She was turning a few old skirts. She felt that far from attaining, she had lost her inner equilibrium. She had begun to take cognizance of things only when they were presented to her in succession, moment by moment, and was terrified to realize that the past seemed faded like a dream. Where was the Mrs. Pears within Mrs. Pears—where was her soul?

Who, finally, was happy in New Harmony, a scene of conflict between individuals and a still-born collectivism? Many years later, an old woman recalled her childhood in the Owenite schools. The republic within the republic, headed by Neef, was not happy. Old Neef, the creature of habit, had continued the strategies of war. Old Neef, gloomy as Napoleon after Waterloo, would send a "detail" to milk cows, or blow his whistle when an "attack" was to be made on a weed plot. The children were a regiment, but they could not see their enemy. They were never allowed to fall out of line. They were given exactly fifteen minutes for each meal—old Neef standing guard with his perpetual whistle. It was an everlasting mush they ate, with a rhythm of heads bobbing up and down, every spoon at the same level with every other. That was the only harmony. Old Neef, escorting the children to bed at sundown, faced something worse than Wellington. He was all thumbs. In bed, the children thought that if they ever got out of the army, they would kill themselves eating sugar and cake. They had visions of houses made of raisin muffins and trees bearing taffy apples. They wanted their parents, too. It happened that their bunks were suspended by chains from the ceiling. One child would swing back, and set the whole row bumping together, as all would sing, softly, not to disturb old Neef's slumbers at his post—

> *Number 2 pigs locked up in a pen,*
> *When they get out—it's now and then,*
> *When they get out they smell about*
> *For fear old Neef will find them out!*

The Declaration of Mental Independence

New Harmony continued a Babel-like confusion—democracy, communism, dictatorship, a combination of all. Few could tell, from one day to the next, which was which circumstance they were living under.

More and more, the present became unbearable, a nightmarish myth, a community of sleepwalkers—for by omitting all which did not come within the domain of reason, it seemed that they had omitted reason itself, and lived in a world in which the operations of law were either totally suspended or very fickle. More and more, people began to exhibit openly what they had concealed, for the most part, before—a preference for the soul as it had existed outside community—a looking back toward Colchos' golden fleece, in fact, the past, which would have been their future, too, had it not happened that they were sidetracked by false promises and false goals.

They stood on street corners in little knots, talking about the wonderful jobs they had enjoyed, and the great opportunities they had abandoned, for the mere chasing of a will-o'-the-wisp, this science of society. They sat all day at the Tavern, talking about the large cabbages they had grown at Knoxville, which was no Utopia, and the wagonloads of onions they had sold in St. Louis, which was a jumping-off place, and the five hundred pumpkins they had had for the picking near Springfield, and freedom at Chicago, where no one had ever tried to get rid of life's incongruities. It seemed that many who had come to New Harmony with only the bags upon their backs had slept in mahogany bedsteads in Pittsburgh and elsewhere, though there had been no such thing as absolute right or absolute justice. It was wonderful how many had been rich who were now poor.

The discussion of New Harmony's failure was now almost the only great activity. Men took a perverse pleasure in it. What fool imagined that he could establish harmony where God had not, where even an angel had fallen in the hop field? Could anyone in the world direct the forces of the world? The only possible harmony would be the acceptance of the world as it was, with all its makeshift arrangements, its hawks eating swallows—good as an aspect of evil, evil as an aspect of good, this side millennium. If thousands perished at sea, for example, that was lamentable, but had a direct bearing on the prosperity of conditions elsewhere—to say nothing of the happiness of fishes in the deep. Or if the whale swallowed Jonah, that fact might account for the instability of markets—impossible to change the latter unless one could progress backward to the former, to prevent what was, in the first place, unpreventable. There were few in New Harmony who could accept this world as nothing but a pure unity of relations—few who did not believe themselves to be the most important nonrelations. There was a vast suspicion that world-wide separation and division were basic to existence, and that the economic war, far from resulting from human institutions, had come down as a result of a war between the angels of heaven, long, long before the discovery of America. Human reason, whatever efforts it had made, had always left something exterior to itself, an element beyond reason, and whose depths could not be plumbed by thought. Thus did the bad live in happiness and leave the world unpunished for their crimes. Thus was Utopia a place merely of no birth, no age, no sickness, and no death.

Only Robert Owen maintained that earlier vision which had led him to the wilderness. In his speech on May 9, 1826, he declared that his expectations had been realized and surpassed. Within one year, the mass of confusion, and in many cases of bad and irregular habits, had been formed into a community of mutual co-operation and equality. At Macluria, the members had built temporary but comfortable shelters, and the young people were weaving more cloth than would be necessary to clothe them. Feiba Peveli likewise prospered, with well-fenced gardens and excellent fields. Great oaks grew from little acorns. No system of equal magnitude, involving such extensive changes in the conduct of human affairs, had ever made progress in any degree approaching to this in so short a time. Hereafter, no one who came and visited Macluria or Feiba Peveli would doubt the practicability of this scheme. The battle was not lost. New Harmony would go on—to ascertain whether a large, heterogeneous mass of persons, collected by chance, could be amalgamated into one community—assured that deliverance from poverty, ignorance, and the oppression of riches was at hand.

So, though the spirit of New Harmony was, in the minds of most people, dead, it was beautifully alive in the mind of Robert Owen. Even as this community disintegrated, he continued to formulate his plans. On July 4, speaking from Father Rapp's old pulpit, where he in the peak-shaped hat had urged mental dependence, Robert Owen presented, for the benefit of all mankind, his Declaration of Mental Independence, a document which he considered of more importance than that composed by the original founding fathers of the United States. "I now declare to you and to the world," Robert Owen said, "that man up to this hour has been in all parts of the earth a slave to a trinity of the most monstrous evils that could be combined to inflict mental and physical evil upon the whole race. I refer to private or individual property, absurd and irrational systems of religion, and marriage founded upon individual property, combined with some of these irrational systems of religion." From the hour of this statement, he expected a great change in the affairs of nations. The principles of a new harmony, or freedom from the unholy trinity of property, religion, and marriage, would spread from community to community, state to state, continent to continent, until this system and these principles should "overshadow the whole earth, shedding fragrance, intelligence, and happiness upon all the sons of men." The science of society, Robert Owen saw, could be contained within no small laboratory, as an isolated phenomenon—could never be preserved like dwarfed oaks under a glass jar. It must be everywhere or nowhere. "From present appearances," he concluded, "in twelve months we will be able to contend against the world."

From the date of the Declaration of Mental Independence, a new calendar was adopted, the *Gazette* carrying under its dateline the statement, "First Year, A.M.I." For surely, this was the infancy of the science of society.

Unfortunately, the word "ought" is a different thing from the word "is"—people of fifty summers could hardly reduce themselves to one or imagine themselves as bald sucklings. A rational communism, they felt, was heartless, ignoring the details which it could not comprehend. In this vast sea of rational human nature, every man was as a drowned sailor, and the differences between one man and another were too quickly dismissed. As fishes care not whether they feast on mechanics or educators, so rationalism cared not which was Matthew, which was Mark, which was Luke, which was John.

Paul Brown, who has no other importance in mortal history, would rather have witnessed the death rattle of the universe than carry his own shirts to the laundry. He took great delight in reporting New Harmony's failures and imperfections. "From the first time I set my foot within this little town of one-half mile square, I think there is not one within the range of my observations during my traveling in other parts of the United States, where the same number of persons, living together within such a compass for so many months, and daily and hourly passing and repassing each other, have been so perfectly strangers, and void of all personal intimacy with each other's feelings, views, situations, and very generally, names." Everything was at sixes and sevens. The mechanics, discouraged by the intricacies of the Permanent Constitution, had created in its stead, Paul Brown reported, a Trinity of Dictators—God the Father, God the Son, and God the Holy Ghost. While people were wrangling with one another, a large patch of cabbages went to ruin from neglect. There were holes in the fences made by "brutes and boys." These openings had grown ever wider, to admit pigs, cows, and horses, who ranged at pleasure through once fruitful fields. There was a congregation of crows in every corn field. Potatoes rotted. It was a worms' paradise. There was a pilfering spirit abroad, so that Paul Brown was afraid to step out of his boots for fear they would not be there when he returned. Sorrow seemed to inhabit the whole landscape. "Two dames of House Number Four, where abide the pastorals and shepherds, had a battle with their fists last evening." There were no hierarchies, no degrees, no recognition of the fact that a hair's breadth may change the entire destiny of man. When Paul Brown went to get his laundry at the community washhouse—and he saw no reason why it could not have been delivered to him—he came away with such shirts as he had never dreamed of. It seemed to Paul Brown that this people had worshiped the Moloch of abstraction, a shirt which fits no one. There were none of the ordinary comforts to make life endurable. Washwomen, instead of attending to their business, were far too busy dancing a rectangular pattern. Tongues were always wagging. Not only did Paul Brown predict New Harmony's ruin, before that year was out, before ever the cherry trees should blossom again—he would have been genuinely disappointed if, by some trick of fate, communism should supersede capitalism, a system in which he was at least sure of the shirt on his back.

The *Gazette*, like Robert Owen, was not ready to admit the failure of the great scheme to enlighten the world, could not admit a reversion to chaos in doctrine and chaos in practice. It offered a mild rebuke to those who, from a neglect of principles, indulged in "an unhappy state of mind." Surely, there was no invisible canker at the heart of this golden rose, community. Surely, great improvements had been made over the mistaken orders of the past. Already, in a few short months, drunkenness had become a thing unknown—a drunk was now almost a rarity. At the beginning, there had been some few persons intemperate, thievish, aristocratic, violent, ill-advised. These characters had departed and had perhaps taken away some good from their experience, some few seeds to scatter elsewhere. The *Gazette* admitted, however, that a few families, though they still remained in New Harmony, were engaged in a system of trading speculation and betting on horses, largely apocalyptic. Education, a public property, would show the meaninglessness, however, of such diversions away from the real goal. The Declaration of Mental Independence had laid the foundations of the new science of society "on a rock immovable through future ages." Progress in the right direction was inevitable.

New Harmony, like the waning Indian, was facing, however, its darkest hour—in spite of the *Gazette* editorial policy. Many people were leaving, many had already left—among these, the Pears family, bag and baggage, scrip and scrippage.

Safely arrived in Pittsburgh, which was, after all, not irretrievable, Mr. Pears wrote a letter to the *Gazette* and the press of the nation, while Mrs. Pears, much improved, looked over his shoulder, and poor Maria coughed her heart out, as usual, inevitably. Mr. Pears' purpose was to warn others who might be so foolhardy as to expect a great change in human nature and society.

Decay and retrogression, he had found at New Harmony, were more important factors than development and progress. He realized, as the result of his experience at New Harmony, that the march from imperfection to perfection was not to be achieved in a single day, nor could man, if once past his zenith, ever reach it again. Rationalism was a mythology, like any other—though without such bodies as Jove and Jehovah—for it had no character but the homogeneity of dew, no principles but those which were lost in cloud and mist.

New Harmony, Mr. Pears believed, was not a place for freedom-loving men or men who had enjoyed the material goods of life, in past existences—only paupers should have been invited there. Where were the square palaces built which were to supersede all other buildings—had one even been begun, at this late date in history? Where were the gardens, conveniences, improvements, great machines, which were to provide for all those willing to work and unable to find a remuneration for their labors? Who had been eye witness to one promise kept in old New Harmony?

"Many a time and oft' have I seen him—Robert Owen—and others ride out to pitch upon the spot on which the palaces were to be built. . . . The school children paraded, as did most of the men and boys armed with hoes and axes and shovels, prepared for war with the forest. The provision wagons and all arrived in safety at the Happy Spot. Some trees fell beneath the strokes of the woodmen, many a sapling felt its roots assailed by the hoe, and it was said that fifteen acres were cleared that day. The train returned in triumph and some wag who was with them is said to have made the following couplets on this exploit:

Yea, we shall see the happy day,
It's e'en beginning now,
One Tree this day was cut away
Where Harmony shall grow.

. . . Where are the gardens? In Athens, for aught I know. In Harmony there was none. Generally, the first comers of the Owenites attempted to make gardens—but these, and what the Germans left, were demolished as if by magic—altho' the fences were not very good. But unluckily the hogs escaping from their confinement, after destroying the sweet potatoes, destroyed the gardens, also—for it could not be worthwhile to repair old fences when we were promised new ones. So in 1825 we bought our vegetables. . . .

"The cotton and woolen establishment and dye houses and steam grist mill erected by the Germans, still existed when I left New Harmony. So did the Cut-off mill and tan yard. 'Improvement, what moral evils are destroyed?'"

New Harmony, even in the summer of that first year A.M.I., was the laughingstock of the American nation, alas. There were many sermons, many satires. There was hardly a day which did not see some new objection raised to New Harmony, both by the fundamentalist preachers who camped at its gates, shouting hell-fire, and by drunks in distant taverns, singing nursery rhymes. Beelzebub had fallen. Robert Owen's community, like Humpty Dumpty, had fallen—all the king's horses and all the king's men could never put it back together again.

The best-seller in the American nation, that first year A.M.I., was a little book entitled *The Three Wise Men of Gotham*. It was embellished with a picture of the feeble trinity who put out to sea in a bowl, with the inscription, "If the bowl had been stronger, my tale had been longer." This book, distorting the Owenite community in the concave and convex mirrors of ridicule, was the rage of Pittsburgh, Philadelphia, Cincinnati, Knoxville, and many a hog wallow, many a cave, many a sheep shelter, many a hollow tree. It was censored nowhere. Judges passed it on to cutthroats, and cutthroats passed it on to lawyers. Every copy was worn to tatters. Every page was interlined with comments. There were chapters relating the autobiography of a man-made machine, a Frankenstein monster, assembled part by part, with no part missing but his mind—chapters criticizing the Owenite attitude toward education as a public property, to be poured into the head of a fool through a funnel, though his head was a sieve, and he was already happy—chapters criticizing Owenite idealism, Owenite depravity, Owenite frivolity, and the Owenite book of life, a series of blank pages. Not a few pages were devoted to the exhumation of Robert Owen's gruesome past, every bone. Robert Owen, it seemed, had shown cupidity in his relation with the child workers at New Lanark. He was the greatest of cotton lords, who had climbed up to the empty top of the pyramid, which he now occupied.

Where Father Rapp had preached the world's downfall, Robert Owen read *The Three Wise Men of Gotham* to the assembled Owenites, one Sunday morning in August when not a breath of wind disturbed the air. There could be nothing hidden—"but the members," he urged, "should not heed in the slightest what the world has said or may say relative to our discussions here." All that was necessary to do was to destroy the suspicious spirit of sectarianism loose among themselves. If they should meet as a body in the cruciform church three times a week during the coming autumn and winter, they would still come to understand the principles of human solidarity.

Restlessness increased, all that autumn. Difficulties multiplied as the leaves fell. Unfortunately, it was found that there were no facilities for heating the great hall—and thus no possibility of community meetings, and no possibility of playing on that great harp, community spirit, of which every string was out of tune with every other, anyhow.

William Taylor, cardsharper and forger, saw the opportunity he had been waiting for in a land of opportunity—to pick clean the dead body of this society, to be himself a whole congregation of crows. There had been no one apparently more inbued with the Owenite principles than he, and no one more alert to co-op-erate with every plan for organization and reorganization. As New Harmony seemed ready to split wide open, he offered to buy from Robert Owen, hard pressed for funds, fifteen hundred acres of land, "with all thereon"—presumably, rough furze, the withered stalks of Indian corn, a few leafless trees. The contract having been signed in the presence of witnesses, Taylor caused, during the night before it was to go into effect, the transportation to his land of movable properties located on other parts of the New Harmony estates. When morning came, lo, he was the surprised owner of "all thereon"—not only trees, but mules tethered under trees, cows, sheep, goats, cattle shelters, chicken coops, looms, plows, axes, spades. Most alarming of all thereon, lo, there was the Rappite whisky distillery, which had stood like a Roman ruin among the hills. Never was there a scene so ambiguous, in fact— exemplifying capitalism, as well as the happiness which is the instinct of the universe—and all on a cold, wet, windy morning.

Taylor's first step was to repair the Rappite distillery. Within a few days, perhaps three, he had opened a saloon in a cow shelter, a rival Utopia—not a stone's throw from New Harmony, just across the old hop meadow, which served ineffectually as either a geographical or a moral barrier between the rational and irratio-nal orders. Money being obsolete, Taylor announced that, as in the New Harmony store, he would accept labor instead of cash— hours to be exchanged for half pints, minutes for sniffs. Soon, irrationalism flourished where there had been rationalism, and wags where there had been philosophers. It was possible now to manufacture whisky openly—and the more drunk, the happier.

Never was there a more innocent-appearing gentleman than William Taylor, the devil's own partner, moon-faced, beardless, unwrinkled, childish, with a missing front tooth, dimples, an almost benign look in his eyes which could see farther than a buzzard's, unsuspected diamonds, a metaphysical speech, and, most important of all, a cloudy system of bookkeeping, by which it seemed that everybody owed him for forgotten half pints imbibed, long ago, back behind the gooseberry bush, a little distance from the footprints of an angel. What was most embarrassing to the laws of reason, William Taylor continued to wear striped burlap, the community costume—insisting, at every turn of the corner, that he still co-operated with Robert Owen, yea, to his utmost, for he too wished to see the old world dissolve, go out like a light.

The chaos of Hesiod, William Taylor swore to have existed everywhere, especially in his own head, which was as confused and beset by dreams as Robert Owen's was. Whatever new harmony there was, it was only what he had imagined. He felt there to be no resemblance between objects, our ideas and sensations. A horse, far from being simple, was in truth complicated, a most profound machinery—a horse being not only a thing, but an idea of it, and therefore evasive to reason, since the horse may change when the idea of it does not, and vice versa. The same was ever true of mankind—nay, worse, mankind being a thing which had no properties whatever, since it might be both tall and short, fat and lean, light and dark, male and female. What man needed most was a sense of space and the irrational, a sense of his emptiness, the realization that his will power was formed in consequence of ideas manufactured solely in his brain, and that such ideas were the direct result of erroneous reports of erroneous sensations—the realization that he would be forever like the fox chasing its own tail, which tail he may believe to be paradise. To wit, from William Taylor's point of view, a thousand qualities of a thing cannot communicate the intimate nature of a thing, which may possess a hundred thousand other qualities, passing beyond the domain of our sight or our reason. Accordingly, a chunk of coal may be more beautiful by far than diamonds, and an oyster worthier than pearls. William Taylor was unacquainted, in fact, with the inward recesses of any being whatever, other than himself, who was also a wide sea and many undiscovered shores, many undiscovered pockets. To a being so constituted, how could there be a science of society? Having immersed himself with Thales in water, having burned with Empedocles in fire, having listened to the music of the spheres with Pythagoras and eaten of Anaximenes' air—William Taylor's conclusion was that life is merely life, for which no formulae can be made. He knew not whether the eyes were made to see with, the ears to hear with. He knew not whether the first chicken preceded the first egg, or vice versa. He knew not, and he cared not. It was no business of his to go poking into mysteries and raising the dust in old chimney corners. Could one man's view of reality be truer than another's? Indeed, as to the laws of nature, William Taylor had often questioned their existence, since these were relative to the beholder, changing whenever a man's mind changed—so that what went up would never come down, if Elijah thought so, though Newton might argue his head off. This community had been, in its own sad way, an Elijah, supposedly, had taken off into the blue. The greater the rationalist, the greater the irrationalist. "Eat, drink, and be merry," William Taylor said, "for tomorrow you may die." Better to feast than be the feast of worms.

William Taylor, in view of his belief in the relativism and subjectivism of happiness, and his distrust of any value but pleasure, proposed that the Owenites gathered around him should hold a funeral for the science of society, all merry drunks to be the mourners. The drunks, under his direction, got busy with hammer and nails. To build a coffin for the idea of all mankind, a featureless body, they worked as never before in the whole history of Utopia. What they planned was an Irish wake, with plenty of maudlin happiness. The body of mankind, though featureless, was to wear white cotton hair and striped burlap trousers, William Taylor's. The coffin was to be equipped with the aforesaid body of mankind, an Indian cigar, a copy of the statistics as to mortality in the British islands and immortality in America, a bundle of wild oats, and a cube of populace, showing the ghostly top blown off. There were to be many ceremonies, such as befitted the entombment of so important a corpse, the science of society. The pallbearers, wearing lopsided wreaths, and followed by a brigade carrying shovels, were to parade through the streets of New Harmony—the corpse to be set upright in its coffin, under a high silk hat, visible to everybody. The funeral sermon, composed by a great wag, was to be a sentence from the works of Robert Owen—"Civilization! How the term has been misapplied." The body of mankind, while Mary Magdalene in a resurrected Rappite bonnet beat on her breasts, was to be lowered into a grave in the midst of the hop field, and was to be marked by a small stone, to show that here lies the sage of the ages, dead at the age of two. What happiness! As a reward for their labors, the mourners would then adjourn to further mourning, each provided with a half pint into which to shed his tears.

Alas, for the best of plans! Before the proposed funeral of the science of society could take place, a drunk broke into the Rappite fortress, where the coffin had been concealed, and stole it. Whatever became of the drunk or the coffin, neither was seen again. Enthusiasm, even for the funeral of the science of society, waned. The drunks had not the energy to build another coffin, and William Taylor had not the generosity. They had had at least the fun of making plans, William Taylor said—if not realized in this lifetime, then in another. The funeral for the science of society was thus most whimsically delayed—though William Taylor, Paul Brown reported, had at least swept away "the last cobweb of fairy dreams of a common stock and community."

Hard autumn, hard winter! That winter, the Wabash was like a road of iron, the wagon wheels emitting sparks as teamsters with their loads passed from one shore to another. Most people sat at home, hugging cold stoves, as Descartes did when he arrived at the conclusion that there was nothing in the world but himself and God. Every man was in a state of coma, imagining nothing but himself. Every man was like a mariner who sees the pole-star continually changing its place, yet always where he is. There was no way to escape self. There was not even a revelation. To take a bath, it was necessary to break the ice in a wooden tub. Most people were cold, dirty, and miserable. It seemed that the greatest happiness would be for a man to dip his hands in the feeling of spring. Most people saw their senses gradually departing from them one by one. It was so long a winter that migrant bluebirds, arriving in April, were glassily frozen in whirling snowstorms. When spring came, finally, the very idea of New Harmony seemed to disappear, like the ice melting from ice-shrouded cherry and persimmon trees. The state of torpor was over.

A large group departed to form a community near Cincinnati. Now the public eating house was closed, and no one so much as thought of opening it again. Each must fend for himself. The failure of a united human family was acknowledged casually, as something less important than a barrel of flour. It was hardly discussed at all. Until the winds could be trained always to blow from one direction, further talk seemed useless, if not extravagant. The communal property was resolved into real estate lots. Signboards appeared almost overnight, as if by magic. There was a spurt of nervous activity, like the tail of a comet. Having granted that human happiness was an ever receding goal, the manufacture more and more of less and less, New Harmony's citizens seemed to have come to their senses and were at least reasonably happy. At one of the Rappite houses, a wax figure and puppet show was set up, and all went forward merrily, as in the old, mistaken order. None so merry as William Taylor, pointing to man as the puppet who, having abandoned his internal sense, had danced on Robert Owen's strings. Only a lean dog whined, as if he had lost the bone of Utopia. He kept smelling around on the ground, looking for it. Oddly enough, there were now a number of people who said that they intended to stay in New Harmony, after all. It was not so bad. One place was as good as another, New Harmony no worse than Pittsburgh or Cincinnati, just as much chance for a future here as elsewhere, same troubles always cropping up, one man like another, death like a thief in the night, might as well make the best of a bad bargain, might as well not cry over spilled milk, might as well put their shoulders to the wheel, still a free country.

Perhaps the New Harmony experiment had been a premature one, the *Gazette* admitted—like an oriole lost in a snowstorm. Yet the editors could not but chastise those who liked to think that no square palaces had been built, and who pointed to the German architecture as if the merits of systems could be decided on a merely superficial demonstration. Perhaps they had chopped down no trees, but they had been at least pioneers in an idea to overwhelm the future world, the science of human nature and society. It was possible, the *Gazette* admitted, that Robert Owen had ascribed too little importance to the early antisocial circumstance which had been the individual experience in a world of dog eat dog. Perhaps he had minimized the tenacity of habit, custom, memory—and had overlooked the profound fact that man often feels in his heart a doubt which prevents him from accepting what has been proven to him. Perhaps man is, by his nature, not only a two-legged but also a two-headed biped—the one head humiliated by meanness, the other dazzled by imaginary greatness, even a city of glass. Then, too, the size of the communities had made their management difficult and cumbersome. The circle was so large, so inconclusive, a periphery lost in space beyond perception of the brightest eye. The circle having been too large for present habits and experience, smaller circles had been described within it, as by Plato's divine geometer. Hence had come about, in their green fields, Macluria, Feiba Peveli, and farther-scattered communities throughout the United States. New Harmony, strictly speaking, could no longer be considered a community, but a central village, after the old order, the one place where the true social state was not, though it was hoped that many would remember this lost Atlantis, this golden fleece. Not now in New Harmony, but on the lands outside, at Feiba Peveli and Macluria, could be found the science of society in operation. True, too true, the original founders of Macluria had already scattered, and their barns stood empty. Their place was to be taken, however, by a party of German religionists, a Scriptural community, who would arrive in time for the planting of corn. Little was known of this people other than that they were of an order similar to the Rappite, and given up entirely to self-effacement. True, too true, Feiba Peveli was already a field usurped by jimson weed and orange trumpet flowers. What had been its exact location could be calculated by a fence and a clump of beech trees—though should these fail in time, there would always be a name indicative of latitude and longitude—and there would always be a name, Feiba Peveli.

Exodus from New Harmony

Life and its negation seemed inexorably bound together, an essential condition of existence—as if happiness delivers us only from one want to another, an empty longing. The science of society, even though unrealized, had seemed more oppressive than God's order, the ebb and flow of the human heart, the secret life, the longing, the suffering. In God's order, there were problems which could not be solved by the application of human reason—and God's order had persisted, even in rational New Harmony, where there were many cries unheard, many questions unanswered, many differences between experience and the logic of an argument. The Owenites had shipped too many pages in the book of nature, it was generally felt. In autumn, the leaves fell. The soul was tired of machineries, tired of false promises. Re-enacted in human nature forever, it was felt, would be the war of bodiless angels, a pathology more beautiful than fact. God was ever a greater reality than man. God, the great father, bound self to self, assured a continuity of events from the beginning to the end, made the future to include the past, made it impossible that anything be lost or forgotten. He respected the individual. He led him not to the chill periphery of things, where color loses its color. Thus, though a man might reach the age of eighty years, and had shed his skin many times, so that there was nothing of him which was, he was still an identity indestructible. For the sake of Utopia, that cold abstraction, who would destroy the mind, the self, the soul, and memory? Perhaps even the drunken consciousness was as valid an expression of the cosmos as blind reason—so much happening without reason, as when the fairest were cut off in the flower of their youth, and the good died young. Without God to bind together the lost fragments—each mind like an ice floe, each with its burning phoenix—what meaning had life at all? It was a phantasmagoria. Not science but God could bridge the gulf between this world and the next.

Meanwhile, as emotion seemed about to take the place of reason, a quarrel, long brooding, arose between Robert Owen and William Maclure. The great communistic venture was doomed to close ignominiously, with a dispute over private property between the two directors of a movement which would have abolished private-property ownership forever.

William Maclure, it may be remembered, had limited his investment in Utopia to ten thousand dollars, the price of an empty convent or an Indian village. William Maclure was no savior of society. Convinced that Robert Owen's extravagance and disparagement of money had led him to ignore these boundaries on high finance, he put up bulletins at the Tavern and other public places to announce his divorce from Robert Owen and the science of society. Accordingly, said William Maclure would not pay off any debts contracted by said Robert Owen, or in any way be responsible for any transaction said Robert Owen might do or attempt to do in said William Maclure's name. The language was legalistic—with not even so much as a swan song for the cubes of human populace, the scales of character and virtue, the truth which had faded at the moment of its realization, the premature closing of accounts with a higher reality than finance. All William Maclure was looking out for was his own ample pocketbook. Robert Owen replied, by means of other bulletins, to what he termed this "extraordinary advertisement," that the partnership between himself and William Maclure was in full force, that he would pay all debts contracted by William Maclure in his name. He hoped to come to a reconciliation of their differences, so vast had been their agreement on a program to rehabilitate the human race. William Maclure could not say that who stole his pocketbook stole trash. He was not to be deceived by the withered flowers of an arid rhetoric. He called Posey County's hard-riding sheriff. Either Robert Owen must produce that greatest of all miracles, cash, or be thrown into the Mt. Vernon jail. William Maclure was sick and tired of the whole fantasy he had seen in operation. If Robert Owen imagined that his nose was made of glass, that was his business, not William Maclure's. A rational society, at this date, was as realizable as centaurs and the lake of Charon. Though they had denied revealed religion, they had promised the impossible, such as a three-hour working day, such as that saints shall run after their heads when they are decapitated. William Maclure did not propose to lose his head. He objected to the whole prodigious constellation under his ex-partner's hat—no greater opium-eater than Robert Owen, imagining that he could drag the whole of humanity up Jacob's ladder. The sheriff was inclined, of course, to favor William Maclure's views. Oh, how he would enjoy clapping this rabble-rouser into a rectangular-shaped jail, as cellmate to horse thieves, chicken thieves, and wife-beaters—and there let him organize such scattered chimeras into a science of society, if he could, and let them all dangle by one noose from a sour-apple tree. Unfortunately, however, William Maclure, even the sheriff had to admit, was the one in default—the owner of many an empty convent owed to the ex-cotton lord and bankrupt Utopist the sum of five thousand dollars.

Oh, the pity of it all! The creator of a new society cannot create *ex nihilo*, out of the empty air. Yet to many this quarrel over finance had seemed like a post-mortem dissection performed on the body of the new social order, and not an experiment to resurrect Lazarus. "Let the dead bury the dead," was William Taylor's merry comment, as he handed out free drinks to everybody.

Poor, disparaged human nature! As the curtain was about to go down on his little drama, Robert Owen declared that man was not the subject of praise or blame. What he had held to be true in the beginning, he held to be true in the end. Still, in spite of all that had happened, there must be disentangled from this great mesh of particulars certain fundamental threads or principles by which man could best be guided to the attainment of a meaningful happiness. That happiness would be neither an eternal space nor whisky. Still, in spite of all that had happened, he believed man's true goal to be not lonely grandeur, but co-operation, an order excluding the incomprehensible part of self, that bee which is thought to hum after its existence has terminated. Else Hamlet himself were the character of all mankind, and every man suffering more than he deserved. For too long, obscurities had been allowed to distort or blot out man's true nature. Wars had been fought, whole nations emasculated, merely for the sake of a ghost in clanking armor, a hallucination. Away with fantastic prophecies extracted from the flight of birds, wands, words from which every hope could be derived, superstitions, miraculous cure, spectacle of Trojan horse, expansion at any cost, the old wranglings among gods and despots—for if once these were dispelled, then man would emerge as a being to whom all things are possible. Away with the clap-trap, and up with the flag of a united labor! How many, through wounded pride, love of personal power, thwarted ambition, and other unworthy emotions, would combine to blow athwart, if they could, the course of a rational labor! Passivity under such a mastery would lead to total death, both of the individual and society. To avoid that disaster to the world, this community had been organized. It was dire necessity that now, before the coming struggle of powers in mighty deadlock, a science of human nature should be evolved out of man's reasoning nature; that people, the great mass of mankind, should no longer expect a higher power to bend the lightning or translate them upward to a golden sphere beyond the region of air, while the real problems persisted, as old as the hills. What happened to this world would never be the result of disembodied spiritual beings acting upon it from afar—but the consequence of the composition of human nature and its institutions. Even the red-blooded pioneer was become, as a result of nothing mysterious, a mystic albino with bleached silk hair, the eyes of a partridge, the wings of a heron—a progress exactly negative, the attainment of purveyors in illusion and whisky. Time and again, man had been brought to the brink of nothingness, with a Bible in one hand and a whisky bottle in the other. Time and again, the workers had been deceived by pure fictions, the wild dreams of the conservatives posing as the apostles of a future world. They had expounded doctrines repellent to common sense in order to keep the people both baffled and enslaved. Even on the sacred heights of speculation, the exploiting landowners and manufacturers had been true to their own interests. They had spoken in strange tongues. "Though I speak with the tongues of men and of angels, and have not charity, I am become as sounding brass, or a tinkling cymbal. And though I have the gift of prophecy, and understand all mysteries, and all knowledge; and though I have all faith, so that I could remove mountains, and have not charity, I am as nothing." The despotic governments must bear responsibility for the debacles in which they come to end.

On a comparatively peaceful Sunday in May, 1827, when all the hedges were whitened by a snow of flowers, Robert Owen stood once more in Father Rapp's old pulpit, to deliver his farewell address to the assembled citizens of New Harmony. It was a farewell which promised, however, his coming again.

A second year of community enterprise had just expired. This singularly constituted mass had contained materials out of which he had hoped that a united community might be founded and made permanent on earth. Throughout all the universe, among the many permutations through which matter had passed, only man had attained to the power of reason, so far as was known. The educators in the New Harmony schools had fallen short. They had withdrawn their pupils into separate cliques, had educated them in different habits, dispositions, and feelings. They had allowed themselves to be guided by the old peacock motivations, pride and vanity. They had objected to equality, as they had objected to reason. Thus that great object of New Harmony, the science of society, had not been attained. The obstacle, the stumbling stone in the way of the mechanic was the educator.

Robert Owen had observed the most subtle processes of man's repression. He would employ, in the world, what he had learned in the world's theater. There, where nations betrayed each other, he would remember the betrayals among individuals in New Harmony. A complete reorganization of the world was necessary, in order to lay the numerous ghosts of civil and holy wars. There was a man in New Harmony who refused to carry his own shirts to the laundry. Thus he was become himself the symbol of exploitation, the despotic power, the unholy aspiration for supremacy. Seraph and snake had dominated, side by side with a shirt, the working classes of the world. For the sake of a shirt, seraph and snake were first erected. Such powers were the true enemy of life. They sprang from the same low mental level, the conspiracy of priest, politician, and businessman to present a united front against those poor washwomen, who had not the shirts on their backs, the workers of the world. Capitalism had generated its protective religion, the values to uphold a high finance. Such heaven as priest, politician, and cotton lord prescribed was always a circle drawn away from the real circle of mankind—a community of gilded dragonflies, a community of gravedigger spiders.

The most trying period in New Harmony, Robert Owen said, was now past. It had been, at its best, no nonrational operation, no ghostly promenade between two stars—not an intrinsic incoherence, but an attempt at social reconstruction on the principles of an eternal truth. They had witnessed many steps for the improvement of man's condition. Those who had elected to remain in New Harmony might accomplish much for the advancement of the human race. New Harmony, although not itself a community in the strict sense, was surrounded by communities. Applications were being received every day from people far and wide who had heard of this golden rose, the science of society. There was a great difference between New Harmony in its beginning and New Harmony now. In the beginning, they had been strangers to each other's characters, habits, sentiments, and, very generally, names. Now, however, as the science of society had got its foothold, they had acquired similar views and similar wants. Since those persons had removed from New Harmony who had been disposed to do so, the remainder of the population were gradually taking the situations best suited to their inclinations and former habits. The saddler was become a saddler, and the wheelwright was become a wheelwright. The baker was become a baker, and the carpenter was become a carpenter. The lands around New Harmony had been put into a good state of cultivation and were well fenced. This territory exceeded anything Robert Owen had ever seen in Europe and America, both in its natural situation and the immense variety of its productions—"the rich land, intermixed with islands, woods, rivers, and hills in a beautiful proportion to each other, presents, from our high ground, a prospect which highly gratifies every intelligent stranger." The bad reports which had gone out might serve to keep New Harmony from being overwhelmed by numbers.

It was, in fact, a beautiful season, this month of May, when the butterfly creeps out of its oval cell, like the spirit of man from its dark wrappings. Far from being discouraged, Robert Owen saw, in New Harmony, what he had always seen, the sure foundations laid of independence for these people and for their children's children through many generations. "From the new order of influences arising around them they must become a superior race—intelligent, virtuous, and happy; beings whose chief occupation, after a few years of temperance and industry, will be to distribute to others the means of becoming as independent, prudent, happy, and useful as themselves." He had no doubts as to New Harmony's positive future, when man's real welfare should be substituted for vainglorious physics and whirlwinds. From his dwindling resources, he had paid every debt incurred by this community, and had given a sum of money to be used in the education of New Harmony's children. "With the right understanding of the principles upon which your change from the old state to the new has been made, you will attain your object. . . . Industry, economy, beauty, order, and good feelings are silently and gradually growing up around you, and the right spirit of the great system, not derived from enthusiasm or imagination, but from a real knowledge of your own nature and of your true interest, is gaining ground among you, and cannot fail soon to be general. . . . New Harmony cannot be numbered among the colonies of the social system, but there is progress, and the day is not far distant when it will join the ranks of the faithful. . . ."

From a distance, he would watch New Harmony's progress, with great interest. In no sense was his absence to be construed as indifference. These narrow streets shaded with locust trees would be a part of him forever. New Harmony had been the cradle of the world's future order, the science of society—and as such would never be forgotten. Where there had been one community before, there were now ten, including two groups of Germans, from Pennsylvania and Germany, who believed with them in man's perfectibility. "When I return," he said, "I hope to find you progressing in harmony together."

Shortly after this speech, Robert Owen departed once again for England—lecturing in the East before he sailed, but as if he were the Wellington, not the Napoleon, of that Waterloo.

"All agreed that a battle was fought," said one commentator, looking back on this period to which he had been eye witness, "that there was some gain, and some loss, but though many years have now passed away, it still remains for time to prove whether the battle was for the good or evil of mankind." It was not the fault of the people, according to Paul Brown—not the fact of an unwilling mentality, but so many shifting arrangements had deadened their sympathies and created a vast inertia. "The internal affinities of Robert Owen's Commune," said another, "were too weak to resist the attractions of the outer world." There were no religious ties, all critics agreed. A man named Smith said that the communistic order might have succeeded, even so, had there been sufficient police and deputies. According to another, Robert Owen made the great mistake of looking upon society as a manufactured product and not as an organism endowed with imperishable vitality and growth, not as an organization of individuals whose inner beings were constantly striving without end and without rest. He had seen personality merely as the existence of a superstition. He had known nothing of man's unquenchable thirst. According to another, "While requiring other people to think, Robert Owen was himself unreceptive as a thinker." He had not understood that the vast majority of mankind endure the battle of life not so much through the love of life as the fear of an external death. Self-love, many said, was a spirit which could not be exorcised. How often one man will destroy the whole life

of another, for the sake of some inconsequential addition to his
own life or happiness! Self-love, the supreme ego, had caused
the emasculation of individuals and of societies. There were, all
critics agreed, too many cranks in New Harmony. Robert Owen
had had to use the defective material of humanity—and what he
needed was a society of angels to begin with. Everywhere, he had
wanted the opposite of what he found—he had wanted desire for
knowledge, but he got apathy; he had wanted equality, but he
got rivalry; he had wanted temperance, but he got intemperance.

Josiah Warren, ex-lamp manufacturer, believed that with the
exception of financial difficulties, all had gone forward quite
delightfully, in accordance with their fundamental inclinations.
But it was to escape financial difficulties that the community
had been started. It had had, from the beginning, a negative
goal. Retiring from New Harmony, and only at its close—he was
almost the last leaf on that great tree of life, a rational society—
Josiah Warren did so as no bitter critic of Utopian idealism. He
did not consider it, as so many did, the result of a disease of the
intellect. The law of happiness remained, though Josiah Warren
would have no covenants but proximities. His many Utopias,
diverging widely from New Harmony, had as their chief principle the sovereignty of the individual over society, and complete
freedom to dispose of one's person, property, time, and reputation as one pleased. The aboriginal self was the only thing on
which society could be grounded—and it escaped analysis, was
a science-baffling star. The only feature in common with New
Harmony was the exchange of labor instead of money, which
had been Josiah Warren's contribution in the first place. New
Harmony may thus be considered as the embarrassed forefather
of a number of extravagant sons, each with its nonconformist
individualism and self-reliance. The most famed of these, the
Village of Modern Times, Long Island, was destroyed only by its
popularity, when a New York reporter discovered and advertised

this gem of gems, this place for the vagabond intellect—and the metropolitan area, from which it soon became indistinguishable, moved out to meet it. How filled with nostalgia is he who contemplates the golden ages, according to Josiah Warren, lamp manufacturer at large! There was a principle of non-intervention. There were no crimes, no punishments, no jails, no churches—just as in New Harmony. Everybody did exactly as he pleased. Each had the secret of happiness. One man advocated a plurality of wives and was, like Modern Times, swamped by applicants. Another rejected clothing, for both himself and his children, and started almost the first nudists' colony in the United States, or at least the first to receive much publicity. A cultivated woman ate nothing but beans and salt for a year, at the end of which period, a living skeleton, she died, most happily. Modern Times was a fools' paradise—and the most expansive of American communities.

Robert Dale, writing many years after the failure of New Harmony, attributed its difficulties to the lack of belief in a higher power. There was no unity of action, as there was no unity of belief. These differences of opinion were "the rocks on which the social hulk struck and was wrecked." The community had promoted its own downfall, as the services of the valuable members were reaped by the indigent, and no system of reward and punishment was employed. "Robert Owen distinguished the great principle, but, like so many other devisers, missed the working details of the scheme. If these, when stated, seem to be so near the surface that common sagacity ought to have detected them, let us bear in mind how wise men stumbled over the simple puzzle of Columbus; failing to balance the egg on one end till a touch from the great navigator's hand solved the petty mystery."

He had been surprised at the swiftness with which his father had changed the Preliminary Community to a Permanent Community—though still in "the state of mind in which, more than thirty years before, Southey and Coleridge may have been when they resolved to found amid the wilds of the Susquehanna, a Pantisocracy free from worldy evils and turmoils and cares, from which individual property and selfishness were to be excluded. . . ." Besides, he was looking for a fit habitat for Jessie in this wilderness. In such a mood, he was easily persuaded by Frances Wright to accompany her to Nashoba, a place for the freeing of black and white slaves, the blacks from serfdom, the whites from marriage. "The marriage law existing without the pale of the institution is of no force within that pale," Frances said. Arriving at Nashoba, however, Robert Dale was disappointed, even at the first glance. He found a second-rate land, with scarcely a hundred acres cleared, and only three or four squared log houses for Frances' "few kindred spirits" who should enjoy free love and poetry. The slaves were working but indolently under the management of a lazy, good-natured Shaker. Occasionally, all might stop their work to dance together. A girl named Sukey had hidden a tip in a sugar bowl—and was going to whitewash herself if she could. Southern neighbors, far from being tempted to imitate the example of redemption at Nashoba, accused Frances and her sister of cohabiting with blacks. They threatened to burn Nashoba to the ground. There were other disorders. Frances had been suffering, for some time past, from brain fever, caused by her riding in the hot sun, and was already burned black as a coal, and had had to be transported to Nashoba in a hammock swung inside a covered wagon. At Nashoba, her condition became worse, as there was no excitement, no audience, only a few acres of dusty sunflowers and smooth-domed mushrooms. She encouraged Robert Dale to hope that in New York and European capitals, they might be able to find the outlet they desired.

In after years, Robert Dale would look back on Frances as an evil spirit, the very soul of restless enthusiasm, without whom there might have been a truly balmy age in New Harmony and in the wintry world. As an Indiana Senator, he would regret that, under her influence, he had written articles on contraceptive devices and the nonexistence of his Maker. Had he had the gentle, self-abnegating author of *Frankenstein* at his side, how different Utopia might have been, and how different his whole life might have been, too! Now, however, he was hurried away by the violence of his sensations and victimized by Frances to walk in many bypaths. He espoused every unpopular cause she could think of and not a few of his own creation. Never were these two so happy as when, appearing on the stage together, to urge the emancipation of the Negro, birth control as a method of reducing white slavery, woman suffrage, the organization of study clubs for women, prohibition of whisky, etc., etc., they were so successful in arousing the emotions of their hearers as to find themselves bespattered by mud, rotten eggs, and obscenities. None in the audience could have guessed that where they saw Frances, that marvel of a woman who wanted to wear a man's pants, her partner saw a ghostly beauty, Jessie, in a strawberry-colored muslin gown. Frances, striding back and forth with her hands clenched, as she urged that the women of the world arise, seemed much more in evidence than Jessie, a girl like a white cloud caught among branches of an Alpine tree. It was a period in which Robert Dale sowed his wild oats, politically.

laucas, 1940

Glaucas, 1940. Comes Glaucas, itinerant sewer cleaner, with his long hair hanging in his eyes. He is as shy as a groundhog and as strong as a black bear, though he knows of neither being for he is no student of nature.

Glaucas is a child of nature in New Harmony. His name is not in any record of birth, nor was he counted in the last census, nor will he pay taxes, nor will he be inducted by any army. He is mysterious, being himself, Glaucas. He is like the little goat which cries with its fleece caught in the bramble, cries throughout the entire history of Utopias, past, present, and future—of such great unimportance as to be of great importance. The whole county depends on him, for no particular reason. Everybody says so. He is the word not spoken, the thought not thought. In other words, though he is not in the census, his opinion would carry more weight than the Gallup poll. For in New Harmony, Glaucas, barefoot stroller, is the wonder of wonders, as if he wore twelve stars in a crown on his head, as if his footstool were the earth itself—is the very idea of "all mankind," made flesh to dwell among us. If only Glaucas would say something more than "Horse feathers," which is all he ever says when it comes to politics and women, then people would know what to expect in Posey County—Mussolini, a black angel on a black horse, Hitler, a brown angel on a brown horse, Stalin, a red angel on a red horse, Roosevelt, a white angel on a white horse. Glaucas cares nothing for none of these.

An old sailor, who is become a farmer of a gooseberry bush, says that Glaucas came up out of the sea, encrusted with weeds and shells, a long time ago. Now he goes down under the earth to clean out sewers. Ever, from the beginning, he entered into the flux of events and was himself a fluctuation. Somebody said that his mother used to sing in a church choir and got him by a preacher over the river. Somebody said that his great-grandfather planted a golden rain tree in New Harmony. Nobody knows, not even Glaucas. Nobody cares.

The Third Age of New Harmony

To be regenerated is an experience engendered by emotion, elation, enthusiasm, intuition—but rarely by reason or the perpetual vivisection of reality. The soul, when it retires within itself, is its own master of events. Only he who feels deeply can tell how the woodpecker becomes the unadulterated angel, how the sewer cleaner becomes a god—though such transitions, like that from all to nothingness, are always going on. After the departure of the Owenite, New Harmony settled down to normal. Rationalism, like an embryo in a bottle, was a form which perished before its realization. Rationalism, William Maclure believed, had contained too many elements of fantasy to insure its birth into this world. It was not only the unrealized embryo, it was also the bogus angel. This section of the earth was, however, no more accursed than any other, and likely to suffer few permanent ills from its having been the scene of two Utopias.

Life, in spite of excessive attempts to alter it, had witnessed few alterations. A change in the orientation of human life was not held impossible, but rather that it must come about over a period of centuries. Lesueur painted a drop curtain which showed the Falls of Niagara and a rattlesnake as the two features "most characteristically American." Old Neef, freed from baby tending, was persuaded to exercise his lungs in a community orchestra. Madame F. was, if anything, even more high-minded, for though she had fallen in Utopia, she was now restored to her former position of supremacy. Thomas Say was, if anything, even more wrapped up in his conchology, as now he did not have to dig potatoes in the hot sun. Nobody was prostrated by the light of an angel on his way through the corn fields—or if he was, that was not William Maclure's business or subject of inquiry. Nor were there many evidences of pure reason, which had mixed the truth in with too much imagination, too many cherubim who were birds. There were no such things, officially, as metempirical diamonds—no diamonds in this community but the empirical ones worn by Madame F., dear soul. A genuine action would explain itself.

William Maclure could not see that existence as a whole has a purpose or universal meaning—how man's mind could ever know it, or what purpose it would have to him if he did. All knowledge was but partial. William Maclure attributed the fall of man to the useless manufacture of words, the supposition that for every noun there is a shape in reality. Hence, if one uses the word "unicorn," it follows that there must be a unicorn in time and space. Even the most beautiful language or attempt to populate vacuums, he believed a poor substitute for a shoemaker's last and a strip of rawhide. One pair of shoes was better than droves of primrose-colored unicorns harnessed to diamond-studded plows, better than that which passes human understanding. It would be useless to worry about death, considering that men are torn from themselves while still living, and dwindle at last into nothing, though their hearts continue to beat as in their unthinking youth.

William Maclure dropped, in fact, existential determinism, either religious or rational, questions as to beginning and end, questions as to whether the universe is made up of one or many

MARGUERITE YOUNG

truths or is all a pack of lies, questions as to whether man can bring into his own frame the principles of cosmic organization, or whether such principles are already mysteriously in operation like the canker at the heart of the rose. The fact remained, a rose and a cabbage would be two different things, with separate sensations upon the smeller of the smell, whether in a religious or a rationalistic state of mind. There was an external reality. To trade a loaf for a lily was so much foolishness. When men realized their propensity to trade something for nothing, they would be better off than now. The word of a celestial butterfly would never change the course of any mortal butterfly. It would be useless to attempt to engraft man's reason upon the tree of life, since man had no special organ of reason and such a tree was never seen on earth—plenty of apple, plenty of hemlock, but no tree of life that William Maclure knew of. Similarly, what was mankind? William Maclure had seen no such animal—many Toms, Dicks, Harrys, but no mankind. A shoemaker without a philosophy was better than a philosopher without shoes. Music of the spheres, not worth his old shoe, William Maclure thought. Happiness of the universe, not worth his old straw bonnet. Innate goodness or innate evil of man, not worth an empty convent. Life was life.

The old *Gazette* gave up the ghost, and the *Disseminator* took its place—without so much as a change in the course of earth through space, evidently, without so much as a blackbird falling. The Owenite motto, "Ignorance is the fruitful cause of human misery," was abandoned, and with it, an inquiry into outlandish subjects, such as a marvelous millennialism. "We ought not like the spider, to spin a web from our own reasons, but like the bee, visit every store, and choose the most useful and best," the *Disseminator* stated.

Now where there had been two Utopias, there was a community of self-dependent workers—not one of whom looked forward to a three-hour working day, an old-age pension plan, or heaven on earth. At William Maclure's seminary, neither a city as measured by the burnished reed nor rectangular, students worked for room, board, and clothing, in exchange for education in the practice of manual labor, such as house building, farming, and sewing. In the four corners of the cruciform church, shoe-making, cabinetmaking, carpentry, tool, and tin-plate departments were consistently enlarged. Everything went forward most harmoniously, though there was no public discussion as to harmony—whether society might be considered as a mass of matter, maintaining its balance so long as each molecule, or man, performed its movements in correct relation with every other, in such a way that no slight disturbance caused a crack in the whole, was not asked. The "philosophic apparatus" was confined to a chemical laboratory—the only demonstrable evidence, it was considered, being that uncolored by memory and imagination, and which could be placed in isolation under a glass jar. Science being detached from the particular quality of happiness, many waste materials were found to have a positive use, and gases were manufactured from corrupt fats, and valuable chemicals were reclaimed from manure. In fact, New Harmony, where there were two dead Utopias, was now noted throughout the nation as the citadel of a dead science. Wholesome cabbages grew along back fences, and there was no ghastly ludicrousness in this, nor in the watermelons sweetening. Doubtless there were a few formulae to describe what was happening when nothing was happening. It was believed, however, that science, removed as much as possible from the emotions of men, would reclaim the world.

The drawing school was turned into a museum of the natural products of the region—skulls, bones, rocks, conch shells, a few petrified fishes. Gradually, to this collection, so paltry to begin with, were added many riches—grandmothers' nightcaps, baby shoes, dolls with battered heads, the skeleton of a horse, a horseshoe, an Indian peace pipe, a Rappite shawl, and a harpsichord which had belonged to Shelley or Shelley's wife. In fact, if anybody had anything he wanted preserved, he sent it to the museum, where it was sure to be tagged and put under glass forever, whether it was a tooth-marked spoon or a pair of old galluses. Along with such relics, there was added a large oil painting of Robert Owen, a little green at the edges, in the act of purchasing property from George Rapp, a little gray at the edges, while wooden-faced Indians witnessed this strangest transaction in history, which they had never witnessed at all.

So in a few years, most men had forgotten their position in latitude and longitude, if they had ever known it at all. Some enjoyed freedom of will, and some enjoyed being enslaved by their wives or circumstance. Some were going to heaven, some were going to hell, and some were going to Vincennes to buy up dead horses. Nature took its course, on the whole.

William Maclure was a good-humored philanthropist. Although he promised to leave his property to New Harmony, he intended to hold the reins so long as he was in his flesh corporeal. Unlike King Lear or Robert Owen, he did not propose to wander in the storm with a couple of cosmic fools, while daughter states argued over a premature inheritance. As he had promised no miracles, his absence from New Harmony—or from the world, for that matter—could make little difference in the affairs of men. He was not a messiah. He suffered from various ailments, increasing in severity each year. When, after a few years, William Maclure, his health seeming about to fail completely, sought the more equable climate of Mexico City, he promised not to return, but left Madame F. as his agent in New Harmony so that none should suffer. He enjoyed, in Mexico City, many vistas, both old and new—the immensity of mountains, his own immensity. He was amused at the spectacle of himself, propped among satin pillows, in a gilded carriage drawn by winged cherubim, presumably, and six long-tailed, cream-colored horses replete with plumes and bells. What a climax to his long life spent in austere mountain climbing! His head lolled, but the old republican had not lost his common sense, which had been unmixed with imagination and falsehood, or as nearly so as it was possible to come. Though none lived now so luxuriously as he, this carriage was, as he knew, not the rich parasite's equipage it seemed, but only the deathbed of a two-legged animal whose legs could no longer move beneath him. He still believed that every child should be a shoemaker. He was aware as ever of those who "labor in the sweat of their brows"—and have not a roof above their heads. Such a situation, he believed, could not go on forever. He hoped that the workers would become independent of any master, even he who sits in an emblazoned chair above the world of gases, even the pioneer of the infinite. Great blobs of fat were almost blotting out his eyes, as water drooled from his nostrils, and he could swallow not more than a drop of water, due to the excessive growth of his head and his throat—but he would not give a straw in the wind for all your winged Madonnas, your doves of peace, your heavenly mansions, and such nonentities. What he yearned for was Madame F., really, her hand in its thread glove, her utter reliability, the mole on her chin. Nor, at this date, would he give a straw in the wind for all the riches of all the sultans of Turkey, or thousand black umbrellas upheld by soldiers of the Chinese emperor to protect his sacred personage from the drizzle of rain. William Maclure, fattening as he died, associated with Aztec runners and, listening mildly to that proverb by which they announced their dinner hour, agreed—"It is time for the big ones to eat the little ones." This was the last law of life. He would have crossed the High Sierras on foot himself, if he could have, or died on some lonely mountaintop, as a student of vultures. Natural history had always interested him—a subject to be studied at the least expense to morals. But the lumbering frame would not move, would not be operated by a cosmic principle of harmony, even

for one more rugged climb of climbs. Both the head and the feet
had faltered, exaggerated beyond their normal size, and there was
a sore which would not heal again, and an invasion of vacancy,
and a dark star. William Maclure hoped only that Madame F.
could get to Mexico City before death did, to cheer him with
gossip and scold him for his inattention. William Maclure, having no other company, was the slightly humorous eye witness to
his own decay, on which he would have liked to have written a
series of footnotes, as sense by sense departed from him.

As has been said, nobody expected William Maclure's coming
again. Madame F., during his absence, was an astute manager,
who knew every sparrow that falleth, and scolded endlessly, as
she considered the highness of flour, the lowness of sugar, and
various crisscrossing lines of the many policies she pursued from
dawn to dusk. Her keys rattled like authority. Her tortoiseshell
comb was the object of her veneration. Her amethyst brooch
was her reward for subtle Homeric fighting, to balance all her
accounts on the banks of the Wabash. Her diamond earrings were
the memory of her lost love. Her high heels were her aristocracy.
With her black satin petticoats somewhat awry but a symbol of
her aloofness, many keys, and an air of slight disdain as if, in spite
of her present glory, she was somewhat fallen, she appeared alike
in the ballroom, which was a den of carpenters, and the poultry
sheds—having once managed, by similar underhand tactics, a
thousand souls in Russia, it was believed. She was always poking
and prying around and kicking up the dust. She would never let
well enough alone. She would always look the gift horse in the
mouth. She was not above spying on a man in his most private
moments. Weeks after a man thought he had got by with murder—smoking his pipe behind the fence during working hours—
it seemed that Madame F. had seen him, though how she could
be among the bushes and in the bookkeeper's office at the same
time was just another of life's little mysteries. It was impossible to

tell what she was going to do next. No sooner had a man arrived at one conclusion than Madame F. had arrived at another. While no man could see through Madame F., every man was as transparent as glass to her. There were no mysteries that she knew of. She could even tell what he was going to say to excuse himself before he so much as opened his mouth. Human nature repeated itself with a remarkable monotony, she said. Woe to the man who had the smell of liquor on his breath or a bottle under his bed! He would be ferried over the Wabash, sent packing. While most men utterly despised the old woman, most men utterly admired her. She gave them, in some inscrutable way, a sense of comfort, and though proud as Lucifer, bore the weight of labor on her shoulders, so it was no wonder if she lost her temper now and then, for she had a right to. After all, Madame F., dear soul, was getting up in years, and would not always be among them. They might as well humor her.

Say, shut in his island universe, tried his best to ignore Madame F.'s endless rustlings at the boundary line between his domain and hers. If only he could shoo that old marsh hen away! In that case, his happiness would have been complete, if not perfect. As it was, he was harassed beyond measure. The moment he seemed to be getting somewhere with his natural researches, there stood Madame F. at the doorway, with some new story to tell, some new lament about the littleness of eggs this season, the flatness of a sick hen's eggs, or perhaps only another account of her husband, who had perished after three days of wedded life, and Say did not blame him. Madame F., with her self-attachment, her perpetual widowhood and its enjoyment, and her endless connivings to make both ends meet though they were meeting very well, gave Say a pain in the head—a throbbing pain. She was a worse threat upon the sanctity of nature, in his opinion, than any European despot or apocryphal horse. She was a continual intrusion upon his and nature's privacy. What he wanted was a wilderness, and what she wanted was a weedless garden. Fortunately, the yogi butterfly of night, suspended by an invisible thread, was something not comprehended by Madame F.'s economy. There were motions too subtle for her vision to detect, seemingly, and some virtues which lay beyond the capacity of her understanding.

Say, painting butterflies at every stage of their development, winged or wingless, young or senile, found an ethereal flame implicit in all aspects of being, the great in the small, the world above in the world below repeated in microcosm. The macrocosm was problem enough, but think of the swarms of little worlds, each reflecting the whole—the infinitely large, the infinitely small, as if this world were limitless. Say was enraptured to behold this world as the one true fable, having no rim and no exterior star—for everywhere was everywhere. Even Madame F., whom he would have excluded, he found repeated among certain anthills and marauding beetles. Himself, he felt to be only another gossamer wafting in the infinite, only another fungus translated upward into sap. He was astonished each year to see how a butterfly could survive extreme coldness, be frozen to a rod of translucent glass, be hung like an icicle on the bleak December bush—yet revive to the fullness of its being in spring, if it had not miscalculated, poor aerial navigator, on its position as to the direction of the onslaught of winds. True, some butterflies fell in the spring of the year like immense, ragged snowflakes, their wings having been hacked away by greedy birds. There were accidents, anomalies, losses. Yet how beautiful was nature, a musical chord which could never be covetous or jealous-hearted—since the whole was always the whole. Say found that it would be impossible to assign morality to one world, nature to another.

William Maclure, answering Say's complaints, had said that he trusted Madame to run his little world. "She has a great share of ambition and wish to rule, which is perfectly gratified by her present situation, having the command of half a town, thirty pupils, and others, with eight thousand acres of land, settling fast with farmers from all countries." So that though the beauty in one object is the same as the beauty in another, and nature is ever kind, there seemed to be Madame F., a separate sphere, intrusive, scolding, always out of order—always contingent on to this.

Madame F., when she was in New Harmony, was irritating because, in spite of all her mistakes, she was terrifyingly efficient. Madame F., when she was absent from New Harmony, seemed as precious as the Spirit of Nature herself. Say found it difficult if not impossible to understand Madame's peculiar bookkeeping system, written in crisscrossing lines on unnumbered slips of paper, in wild disarray in a desk drawer, like Shakespeare's manuscripts when he left London for the last time, with little care for his reputation or his immortality. Seemingly, Madame F.'s bookkeeping, unlike Shakespeare's writings, had no rhyme or reason which anyone but herself could comprehend—"three ducks owing" on one slip, "eight pounds lard" on another, though everything was "perfectly clear" to her, and how she had worried about "hog sickness" was evident. To Madame F., enjoying herself in Paris, Say wrote that he missed her sadly, sadly, and appreciated her in her absence as never before. Here he was, caught in the delectable condition of "a toad under the harrow," with no hope but of her coming in the spring, which would be the "era of his deliverance from New Harmony." Then he, too, might be free to visit the great museums of Paris, in search of further aspects of nature and conchology. Now, at this moment, he was palled by the wilderness.

Alas! Madame F., in spite of good intentions, for she had loved New Harmony, was infinitely delayed. She sailed from France to Vera Cruz. By arduous carriage journey, she traversed the road built by Montezuma over treacherous mountains. She reached Mexico City in time to say good-by to William Maclure, whose hand she held at the last. When he could no longer hear her, she did not speak. A few days later, she was herself stricken by a fatal illness. New Harmony, the *Disseminator* reported, had lost its most distinguished citizens, as if by one blow. New Harmony would never be the same again. That was spring, which should have been the era of his deliverance—and Say felt a strange coldness enclosing him, and little hoped for resurrection now, little imagined that he might not be hacked away by giant birds. His days ahead were few. In autumn, Say succumbed as a result of infection by the germs of malaria from the river bottoms—and New Harmony, the *Disseminator* reported, had lost its great lover of the Spirit of Nature in the Trackless Wild.

When, many years later, Say's grave was opened, he was found—the story goes, although it cannot be verified—to have occupied it with a strange woman, whose hair cast a shining light around her. Nobody had seen a redheaded woman such as this in old New Harmony—all the other redheaded women could be accounted for, one by one. Perhaps this was the Spirit of Nature, whom Say had ever sought—there was a little book which fell to dust and ashes as it was lifted from the clawlike, delicate bones of her hands.

Not Condillac's *Logic*, of which Mr. Maclure had left the extant edition, along with an empty convent, to New Harmony and the workers of the world.

Robert Owen's Ideal
Made Real to Dwell Among Us

Robert Owen, after the debacle at New Harmony, when others disparaged human nature, did not disparage human nature and the science of society. Infinitude of choices hung upon his choice—whether we will choose man or a drifting kinghood sheeted in fire, man or vials of poisonous gases. Robert Owen was assured, in spite of life's phantasmagoria, that the new moral world would not break like a bubble around him. To establish social harmony, he had proposed as his ground plan a harmonious universe—for if the universe was breaking into uncorrelated fragments, how could governments not fail to do so? He was assured that the world of eternal objects was not separate from the flux of events, that the inherent plan could never be a nightmarish destruction, the babblings of a tyrant. Although he would have been the last person to suspect it, his was an aesthetic view of life, a great musician's. The most intricate theme in music may consist of twelve notes, but to throw these together haphazardly is to achieve nothing whole and beautiful, nothing innate. A rational order, having reduced human nature to those twelve laws which Robert Owen held to be eternal, would comprehend the theme in each phrase, developing a music as absolute, as impregnable as that of the spheres. No mere Wall Street bubbles.

He found, upon his return to England, no great change, nothing improved, not even the death spasm of a passing order, the empty formulae, the injunctions against the dispossessed poor, the old limitations of patriotism in the traditional sense, and those sporadic helps which were not helps at all, but hindrances. There were conditions to encourage mass immigration, either to another continent or another sphere. While the poor suffered chaos, like autumn leaves caught in a whirlwind, the upper classes were hardening into patterns of an even stricter order. There was a profound gulf between the rich and the poor. Thackeray was popular. Thackeray, "the Son of Imlah," came before the "throned kings of Judah and Israel," as a prophet and scolder of the vain among all classes. He did not seek to change the world, but rather to show a series of static objects occupying space—static, although each might desire to be other than he was. There would always be an England, he said, and many mistaken eccentricities, as beautiful as the withered apple—among these, dyspeptic lords glorying in their apoplexy, their illiteracy, and their dogs, tyrannous, rouged Jezebels with private vicars and public vices in their wake, old tumblers in country barrooms, runaway kings dressed like cattle thieves, bewigged parasites in great houses, long-haired French artists, poor relations arrayed in cast-off satin, pot-bellied Anglo-Indian merchants, composite clubmen playing at chess while Rome crackled above their heads, sentimental widows with parasols and simulated virtues.

Although the Reform Bill had occasioned the greatest expectations, its enactment, in 1832, was to bring little improvement in the material circumstance of the dispossessed workingman. The Reform Bill, according to a commentator at that period, gave more power to the already despised tradesman, lowered the importance of the cultivated classes, and did nothing, or less than nothing, for the laboring population, for whose welfare it had been proposed, and in the face of every obstacle. The true aristocrat was brought to the brink of pauperdom, or thought he was, and thus could not father the lower classes, as in former times, in that grand old feudal order when each had felt responsible for his village. The new mercantile class was both atavistic and unreflective—a machine. None so oblivious to the lower class as they, who had escaped it—"for there is never any love lost between small capitalists and the poor." Many a rotten borough was dissolved, and many a rotten borough was evolved, almost in the twinkling of an eye. A member for the borough of Lugershall arose in the House of Commons and said, as unctuously as a bishop on parade—"I am the proprietor of Lugershall. I am the member for Lugershall. I am the constituency of Lugershall, and in all these capacities I consent to the disfranchisement of Lugershall." What difference, finally? The Tories, imbued as they were with the dream of a future which should be like the past, grinned from ear to ear. They believed, and rightly, that they had not lost their places at the top of the social pyramid, from where they had sowed so many anonymous benefits upon the world. Life went on, a thing far from exact or scientific—even like the compass which does not indicate the true North but only that strange evasion of truth, the magnetic North.

The ornate George IV having disappeared from the scene, there was now a different king, whose head has been described as very like a pineapple. His father and brother having taken so long dying, William IV had waited for the throne fifty-six years—and, once elevated to that position, was almost crazy with a vast, jovial excitement. He made most extraordinary speeches, empty and vain, to express his hatred of the French, who had nursed despotism, and his fear of Russia, that she was about to invade England and float the czar's standard over Windsor Castle. Aside from such delusions of international grandeur, the remote, confused, bawdy gentleman acted as if he were a sailor lost in a storm far out at sea. He was always getting his bearings, always being blown athwart or ripped asunder. He employed, in fact, the most picturesque naval slang, to depict both his distrust of Russian ambition and his fear of the widowed Duchess of York, a rival sailor, for she was always accompanied on her afternoon voyages by flotillas and the guns sounding in the harbor. More, he employed naval slang to depict his most private engagements. According to one report, "His eccentricity seemed almost to have amounted to insanity"—he had little sense of the dignity which adheres to the wearer of the crown. Quite suddenly, in the middle of an evening party at Windsor, in the presence of his assembled guests, who were as rigorous as mummies, he would exclaim to his lady, as if the salt spray blew against his cheek, "Come, my Queen! We are shoving off to bed, windward!" It was scandalous and a subject of more importance, at least in restricted quarters, than the problems of the workingman or the science of society, dead subjects.

We see Robert Owen as one who stands between two tidal movements—the withdrawing French Revolution, the rise of dialectic materialism. A nineteenth-century man, his roots are in the eighteenth century, his branches in the twentieth. He is a figure between imagination and the death of imagination— Shelley, Coleridge, the cloudy idealists behind him—unflowery technicians before him. He is not so much himself an individual as a symbol of the progressive spirit. Urged by such men as Robert Owen, the nineteenth century would be a gradual withdrawal from the heights of romance to the plains of common experience. Yet there was romance in the very movement of reform, since not all the supernatural elements could be expelled, and not all mistaken goals. The lure of the past, the distant, the mysterious, is very hard to get rid of—in the act of getting rid of it, many a man acquires it. The process is best exemplified by the nineteenth-century reformers themselves, a prey to fantasy no less than the nineteenth-century empire builders. What wild, restricted empires were often theirs! Carlyle, influenced by German absolutism and his own supremacy of ego, believed men to be a rabble to whom could come no salvation except through hero worship. The desire for fixed points of reference sought out such ancient and tribal gods. Whom did Carlyle admire but the leaders of hordes? A few great mystics, by a sheer combination of horse sense and angelic stature, managed to impose their will, which was the will of the universe, on others. The ideal society was thus a monastic order under the rule of a clouded but practical superman. All men should renounce self, all should hear the "everlasting nay" of the universe—all should become, as by an almighty edict, obedient shoemakers, wheelwrights, brewers, aye, for the shake of clouds. For the questions posed by the human spirit were never to be answered. The result of this philosophy in practice being only that the Negro rebellions in distant islands should be stamped down as by an almighty foot. Not all reformers were so extreme as Carlyle, but many were mistaken in their expectations as to possibilities. Ruskin cried out at the invasion of the widow's strawberry beds by iron rails—and would have turned time back to where time had never been, aye, to a golden age when there was neither bedlam nor traffic jams, and when a taste for marble statues was a moral quality, the taste of angels. Man had separated, he felt, his religion from his life. Oh, the tedium of that life, as Ruskin portrays it! "You don't know what to do with yourselves for a sensation: fox-hunting and cricketing will not carry you through the whole of this unendurably long mortal life; you liked pop-guns when you were schoolboys, and rifles and Armstrongs are only the same things better made; but then the worst of it is, that what was play to you when boys, was not play to the sparrows; and what is play to you now, is not play to the small birds of State neither; and for the black eagles, you are somewhat shy of taking shots at them, if I mistake not." Were men, therefore, to give up bird shooting? William Morris, designer of the Morris chair, planned Utopias in vacuums, all going forward most successfully. Perhaps Robert Owen seems less the dreamer than any of these. Beyond the cloud and mist wherein he walked, there was the science of society, when it should be devoid of old enchantments and promises of an unrealizable heaven on earth.

As the British Empire expanded its boundaries, Robert Owen expanded his activities to unite the world in one family. New Harmony's success in operation would have proved nothing, should the world continue as what it was, a prison house, a bedlam. One might as well believe all stars were good but the earth was accursed. Robert Owen, great monist, had to cope more and more with the problem of grandiosity. The socialists compared his journeyings by sea and land to those of Moses, the Apostle Paul and an angel winging between two hemispheres, though doubtless winging in opposition to the Monroe Doctrine.

New Harmony was a mere raindrop in the great ocean of sociality. Shortly after the New Harmony experiment and its rather dubious end, Robert Owen projected a plan for the communistic colonization of a large tract of land in Mexico in the provinces of Texas and Coahuila, to be made up of people from all quarters of the globe, who might mingle as one nation. The prophet in England and New Harmony, who had promised a bunch of golden grapes to the tired fox, mankind, promised more golden grapes to more golden foxes in Mexico, it was said. He had overlooked the fact that his Utopia might well serve only as a buffer state between Mexico and the United States, who were ever quarreling about boundaries. Never had there been, outside of Ireland and Indiana, a theater so naturally suited to man's redemption as Mexico, Robert Owen said. Appearing before the government of Mexico, which had not been reluctant to pursue the experiment of social regeneration, he urged only that within the borders of his borderline Utopia the Catholic Church should be permitted no citadel and no authority—for it would be impossible to work for the good of mankind in co-operation with ancient miseries and mysteries. The united clergy of the Catholic Church protested to the government of Mexico, which could not but recognize their claims in Utopia as elsewhere, even purgatory, hell, heaven. Robert Owen had omitted from his calculations, they believed, the proper knowledge as to what must be designated by the word "humanity." For them, humanity was the flotsam of lost souls. Thus, Utopia could not be founded, at this date, in any part of that already insolvent order, Mexico.

There was already a brooding feeling of restlessness in Mexico—the acrid moans of little goats, the alternation of light and shadow, a tragedy unredeemable, a prospect without future. Yet a renegade within the ranks of the Catholic Church—a half-Spanish, half-Indian bishop in the High Sierras, surrounded by one-eyed men and two-eyed dogs—agreed with Robert Owen as to his laws of human nature and the questionable morality of all the institutions of the past, the decay inherent in their view of time. Were not the Sierras abysses enough, without the necessity to imagine others? Man's soul must be cut free from its attachment to the birth strings of death, the monstrous mother. Mexico must be released from all its Spanish, its Catholic oppressors, and the Indian be given back his land. The science of society was the one salvation possible. Thus had Saint Christopher carried the infant Jesus over a dark river, the arroyo of death, and all the while that body grew to be a man. Through the science of society, the Indian bishop hoped that it would be possible to overthrow all principalities, all powers founded on man's weakness. Throughout these tragic mountains, where now the vulture hovered, there would be established rectangular villages white and gleaming, schools, colleges, hospitals, and model farms. Similarly, a one-legged, one-armed, one-eyed captain of a poor handful of marauding peons, a perhaps professional soldier, agreed with Robert Owen upon the probability of a whole man and a united mankind, when all bishops should be overthrown, when the mountains of Mexico should be swept clean of mental cobwebs, human spiders, corruptions, illusions of all kinds. The mountains should be washed with human blood, and an entire purgation was necessary, an entire release—a thesis of violence, however, with which Robert Owen could not agree.

During the agitation which preceded and followed the Chartist movement in England, Robert Owen had been similarly skeptical of any abiding result. "Equality best chance," Robert Owen said. "Without equality, nothing done." He lifted his banner above all other banners, yea, even the Chartist movement—and his army of followers increased as if by magic. It was as if an ancient seer of Chaldea or Syria had come to lead the workers of England out of the industrial wilderness—"presaging," his followers reported, "the ruin of wicked cities, singing the splendors of the New Jerusalem." Few pinioned creatures soared away into distance, and the ground gave way under no one, and it did not appear that the earth itself would dissolve like dew. There would be, instead, through mutual agreement, a vast change in the affairs of men—and accomplished without violence or bloodshed. Owen societies, from the 1830s onward, sprang up in every shire in England. A member of this early movement toward socialism recalled, "We were a society united for the most unbounded confidence—nay, by many of us, Robert Owen was worshiped almost as a god." His principles, said another, "breathe universal love of our fellow beings, industry among all classes, equality of privilege for all the human race, peace and good will to all mankind, the equal distribution of labor and wealth, and universal knowledge and happiness." He had always, said another, "the glittering vision of this planet with rectangular paradises before his eyes." He was the hero whom they worshiped.

His language was as glittering as his vision—alas, as if all mankind would wear a crown of rubies and inhabit a city of glass, those very concepts of value he wished to destroy. Time and again, he announced that the Rubicon between the old immoral world of capitalism and the new moral world of a scientific society was at last crossed. "For Truth, Knowledge, Union, Industry, and Moral Good now take the field, and open by advance against the united powers of Falsehood, Ignorance, Dis-Union, and Moral Evil. . . ." The First Coming of Christ, he explained, was a partial development of Truth to the few, conveyed, of necessity, in dark sayings, parables, and mysteries, as man was not then in a position to understand plain, simple language. The Second Coming of Christ, however, would make Truth known to the many, and enable all to enjoy endlessly the benefits in practice which it would assure to mankind. So great would be men's joy, as partakers in the light of reason, they would then speak plainly, and be beguiled by no vain babblings, no enticing words—care not for fables, endless genealogies, the substitution of embroidery for truth. "The time is therefore arrived when the foretold Millennium is about to commence, when the slave and prisoner, the bondsman and the bondswoman, the child and the servant, shall be set free forever, and the oppression of mind and body shall be known no more." In the millennium, there would be neither Greek nor Jew, circumcision nor uncircumcision, cotton lord nor cotton slave, no region but the world, no nation but all peoples, no forms, no ceremonies, no crown of crowns, no falsehoods, no embitterment, no hard tasks done by man for the glory of God or an absentee landlord system, no imaginary wealth. There would be, instead of tenements, many rectangular villages, and instead of separations, a most cordial union of the human race, and instead of wars, an everlasting peace, and instead of boundaries, free trade—kings, clowns, and corpses having been removed from seats of power. The fall of man from innocency and from the plain road to intelligence and happiness was caused by the priesthoods of the world having induced some of our ignorant ancestors to feel ashamed of part of their nature. Oppressed by needless fears and remorses, they had wandered in a maze and had been led to sacrifice the very good they looked for. "Priesthood is the chief of the Satanic institutions. Celibacy is a virtue only according to the unnatural imaginations of a most degraded order of men called the Priesthood. Man is a geographical animal, and the religions of the world are so many geographical insanities."

"Six times, after he was fifty years old, and twice after he was seventy, Robert Owen crossed the Atlantic, in the services of communism," wrote an early biographer. "Let us not say that all this wonderful activity was useless. Let us not call this man a driveler and a monomaniac. Let us rather acknowledge that he was receiving and distributing an inspiration, unknown even to himself, that had a sure aim, and that is at this moment conquering the world. His hallucination was not in his expectations, but in his ideas of time and methods."

Robert Owen retraced his footsteps in the European maze, visiting Paris, Geneva, Berchtesgaden, where he urged his program of a rational society, a union of workers and of nations. He returned to Ireland, visiting many centers of starvation. He traveled the length and breadth of England, omitting no cotton town and no potter's wheel from his itinerary. He flooded the so-called civilized world with books, lectures, tracts, newspaper articles, letters, speeches—urging that the present situation was not the permanent situation of the human race.

In October, 1831, the working classes rebelled as one body in Bristol, driving the bishop's servants out of the bishop's palace, demolishing both ecclesiastical and business houses, with the result of a loss of many pounds sterling. Lords spiritual and lords temporal believed that Robert Owen's incendiary propaganda had aroused the antagonism of the masses. There were other agitations, other violences. Robert Owen was considered, throughout the 1830s, a spokesman for meteors and comets and conflagrations. He was held responsible for an unknown young man's swallowing of prussic acid. Henry Phillpotts, Bishop of Exeter, cited most solemnly, and as a matter of irrefutable fact, suicides, murders, and sudden deaths which had been caused by Robert Owen's literature. A copy of one of Robert Owen's books, the Bishop said, had burned like a coal in his hands. Robert Owen could not explain, the Bishop accused, how out of the rubbish of the old, irrational world, he had sprung up so beautifully rational, like Minerva out of the head of Jove—or how by destroying the world, he should build the world. The many bishops had as their cohorts many sextons. A sexton at Warrington refused to finish a grave upon learning that it was to contain the corpse of a socialist. The extremists among both Whigs and Tories believed that Robert Owen should be silenced. Others, less cautious, argued that his blowing off steam was good for him and would do no harm to the English way of life, its ancient privileges. Saints flourish in an atmosphere of martyrdom, like fairies in an Irish bog—so why not ignore this fabulosity of "all mankind" as if he were happily nonexistent? Lord Lansdowne thought that Robert Owen's system would lead to its own dissolution, so needed no help from the government—that there must always be, in spite of unitary enthusiasm, a diversity of judgments respecting happiness and social good. For the bird of paradise does not have the same perspective as a hog. And Robert Owen was a bird of paradise, very far from the average which he believed himself to represent.

The Owenite movement continued to grow, as if the social millennium were at hand, at last, in accordance with the promise made of old by saints and sages—as if the Lion of the Tribe of Judah had been prevailed upon to open the book of life. The Owenite membership ran into the fifty thousands—it was a kingdom within the kingdom and not, many bishops complained, a remote, dwindling order. Owenite lecture halls, dedicated to rational thinking and social amelioration, were established at every large center of population and many villages. Owenite missionaries were travelers throughout all England—and though considered, by many bishops, as strolling vagabonds, Satans whose only occupation was that of treason and blasphemy, made many converts under the hedges and along the highways. Owenite missionaries, in the near future, were to be sent to carry the light of reason into the most remote wildernesses, in America, Africa, Australia, India, wherever there were men. Owenite converts sang their songs at every tavern and under the shadow of every church—"A heavenly city when science rules the earth." The faces of even the oldest men and women were illuminated with this hope of hopes. It was beautiful. They heard the cocks crowing in dark lanes and alleys, to herald the dawn of socialism, when all men should be free. All the people in the world now might have passed away, like the dews from Jehovah—but there would be new people—and this expectation had taken the place of that for an eternal life.

The dream of at least one model village had never quite died out, though Robert Owen had lost all faith in the efficacy of such a village to cause a great change in human proceedings. A group of his followers withdrew to Harmony Hall, a community named in memory of New Harmony. It was a humble enterprise, like that of the community bull at Woolwich which had not outlasted the victory at Waterloo. Critics came from far and wide to see the secret horrors of Harmony Hall, the many skeletons. What they saw was a railroad track that transported dishes from the community dining room to the community kitchen without help of human hands. They had to admit that the "socialist cabbages" were no smaller than any others. They had to admit that the socialists seemed reasonably happy. When Harmony Hall failed—becoming, in rapid succession, a Quaker meeting house, a poultry concern, and, as a result of a great fire, a heap of ruined bricks—no Owenite saw in this instance the death of socialism. The Owenite movement went on, with renewed vigor, having put away forever such childish things as a toy village. It was working hand in hand with "the great, the unknown Cause, unchangeable as Fate"—and could not fail. When the Owenite time stores failed, it was "only because of woman's immortal indisposition to do all her shopping at one center"—and the cooperative labor movement would still go on.

A skeleton was used in the Owenite initiation rituals—though Robert Owen did not countenance this practice. This bony edifice, it was said, was all there was of man.

Two movements advanced, in fact, throughout the nineteenth century—nationalism and humanitarianism, the empire of darkness, the empire of light.

In 1835, Robert Owen consented to act as "Preliminary Father to the Human Race" to lead it to a "Land of Promise," where charity should reign, and where there should be no morbidity of imagination.

Three years later, in June, 1838, the young Victoria, prodigal of monstrous nurses, was crowned Queen in Westminster Abbey. As a select public wandered among marble tombs and statues, Queen Elizabeth, complete with red hair, ruff, white satin petticoats, and a crimson stomacher, stepped out of her niche in a wall and fainted—the wax figure seeming, for the moment, the great majesty herself or her shade returning among them. This, however, was merely a backstage incident, soon hushed up, and probably of no significance whatever. Miss Charlotte Yonge reported the real proceedings, pertaining to Victoria. When the Queen

rose from her knees on first entering the Abbey in her robes of
state, the Archbishop turned her round to each of the four sides
of the Abbey, saying, in a voice so clear it was heard in the inmost
recesses, "Sires, I here present unto you the undoubted Queen
of this realm. Will ye all swear to do her homage?" Most of the
ladies cried, and the Queen turned very red, as if she longed to
creep under the Archbishop's protective wing. It was the most
exalted of ceremonies. The music was impressive, both flutes
and harps, a sound to make the walls of flesh dissolve. When
the Queen came in, they sang, "I was glad when they said unto
me, Let us go into the House of the Lord." As she was being
crowned, they sang, "Zadok the Priest, and Nathan the Prophet,
anointed Solomon King." Oh, glory of glories! The Queen shook
like a leaf. Miss Harriet Martineau described, with great gusto,
the scene, the immensity. "The throne was an arm chair, with a
round back, and beneath its seat was a ledge, on which lay the
Stone of Scone. It was covered, as was its footstool, with cloth of
gold, and it stood on an elevation of five steps in the center of the
area. . . . The acclamation when the crown was put on the Queen's
head was very animating, and in the midst of it, in an instant of
time, the Peeresses were all coroneted." The young Queen complained of the heavy ruby which the Archbishop forced on her
hand. "The great merit of this coronation," according to a male
commentator, "is that so much has been done for the people. To
amuse and interest them seems to have been the principal object."

Time passed. In February, 1840, the Queen, very proud, very
sure of herself, appeared in white satin, orange blossoms, diamond earrings and diamond necklaces, as the bride of a German
Protestant prince, very shy, very unsure of himself. Everything
went according to schedule. When the Archbishop had effected
holy matrimony, both on earth and in heaven above, the guns
from the Tower thundered the announcement, exactly as on the
occasion of many a man's losing his head. The English public

was self-congratulatory, enjoying a vicarious pleasure. Soon the favored two had settled down to domestic life at Windsor. Etching, singing, playing the piano, reading the Bible aloud, they were apparently a model couple, very sensible, very sane, exactly what those should be at the acme of existence. Impossible to imagine that this same castle had once been a private mad-house. The English public was gratified by numerous births in the royal household and an enlargement of the royal nursery. When Prince Albert's pet dog died and was buried on Windsor's Grand Terrace, the House of Lords sent many wreaths and ele-gies, and from both pulpits and newspapers came expressions of sympathy, and there was hardly a dry eye in England, as almost the entire English public, high and low, went into mourning. In fact, there was a very great despair—in view of the circumstance, very unreasonable.

Meanwhile, in contrast with the exalted family scene at Windsor, and all its respectable peacefulness, there was external chaos, war following war—nobody understanding that fact better than Queen Victoria herself, padding around the royal nursery in her long nightgown and bedroom slippers, to see that none of her babies had the sniffles. "You cannot make war without soiling white kid gloves," she said—though doubtless referring to other gloves than her own.

In a narrow defile between two mighty mountains, hemmed in by walls of everlasting ice and snow, a multitude of English soldiers, poor cotton weavers on a holiday, were slain by the long guns, English manufacture, of the Afghan raiders, safe on the clouded precipice above them. For the sake of carbuncles as big as Jews' heads cut off at the nape, and for the sake of many other considerations, largely mundane, many Christian soldiers, with nothing but the bags upon their backs, were sent to certain death in India, and many horrors were perpetuated. There were wars throughout India and the Orient, in far-off mountain regions, jungles, deserts, at Jalalabad, Bokhara, Lahore, Rangoon, and all those places which, as names, evoked romance and deathless dreams in the England of that day. Oh, Xanadu of the soul, and caverns measureless to man! In retribution for the spoliation by nameless Moslems of the bodies of two otherwise nameless Presbyterians, Macnaghten and Burnes, the beautiful bazaar of Kabul, a city which had been dedicated to holy thought, a city of gleaming temples, clusters of bells, bearded patriarchs, and many doves of peace, was burned to the ground before evacuation by Her Majesty's forces. Unfortunate but necessary to the march of progress. Throughout all of India thereafter, there were head-hunters, both Christian and non-Christian, acute mental sufferings, dysentery, destruction, festering sores, confusions as inevitable as the march of progress, according to some points of view.

Nor was India the only theater. Just as France conquered Algeria because its ruler flicked a fly-swatter in the face of the French consul, and as other wars for the expansion of empire have been fought on the pretext of other and less important matters, England fought a long, protracted war with China, and for no realistic reason, apparently. The Chinese "Sons of Heaven," as they were called, refused, in 1839, to allow opium to be imported for Chinese consumption from India, where the British held a monopoly on langorous poppy fields and fäerie lands forlorn. Here was the English merchants' opportunity—a poetic pretext for invasion. As a result of this war opium factories were opened at Hong Kong; China became a place of gossamer waftings, and the Chinese "Sons of Heaven" lost some of their old arrogance in their dealings with Windsor. "As children say the snow brings more snow, so did this war with China bring on others." Throughout the entirety of Queen Victoria's reign, there was always a war going on, though England grew stuffier and stuffier, more and more respectable, more and more serene—perhaps as the result of that great opiate, Matthew Arnold's "sweetness and light," and easy virtues in the drawing rooms at Windsor.

How different the world outside! The New Poor Law, passed in 1834, as it placed husband and wife, parents and children in separate pauper barracks, had virtually the effect of destroying the family, an institution so admired by Queen Victoria and the Victorians. Dickens describes the unholy situation, the seamy side of life which everybody who was anybody wanted to ignore—but nothing so ludicrous, finally, as Mr. Micawber in a debtors' prison, addressing his plea for the reorganization of society to the absent British crown. There were few who could endure the barren truth of statistics, in the nineteenth century— it had to be presented with great good humor and crocodile tears, and seem the romance of distance, like the adventures of conquest and war. So admirable and tragic-minded a lady as Miss Charlotte Brontë averted her eyes from the "gruesome details" of industrial suffering, as she believed these should be something more than the subject of popular fiction—perhaps in the same spirit with which, when her sister Anne, fully dressed, her bonnet tied beneath her chin, sat dead in a cheap hotel by a window overlooking the wild, wild ocean, she merely informed a servant that the lady was indisposed and would not have her tea that afternoon, thank you. It was not an age for frankness. The more one suffered, the more likely one was to keep his mouth shut.

As a result of lack of sentiment where sentiment was most needed, many people were left to the one certitude of starvation. Not only was the situation in England the extreme of tragedy, a mass burial. Ireland, too, faced starvation. A sunless wet and cold had destroyed the entire potato crop in Ireland.

The potato, upon first being introduced into Ireland, had been viewed with abject suspicion, as cousin to the deadly nightshade. The potato, for many ages Ireland's staff of life and not of death, was become sacred, the very gift of the saints. Now, during the great, sunless cold, priests went around in Irish barren fields, sprinkling holy water on tubers which, in spite of all their abject blessings, refused to grow—for such was the mystery of life. In some districts, it was quite impossible to build enough coffins to house the Irish dead, so that their bodies were wrapped in canvas and carried out to the opalescent sea, as if this were God's will.

Oh, the poetry of it, the beauty of it! By the end of 1846, Ireland had lost, as a result of famine, immigration, fever, sea burial, and the misuse of the imagination, two millions of her people—and was aroused now from a philosophy of fairy fatalism, but all too late, of course. Sir Robert Peel's motion, that year, repealed the tyrannical Corn Law, a man-made thing, but effected no visible improvement in the lot of the cadaverous living, nor could resurrect the watery dead who wore, by now, pearls in their hair. Macaulay regretted that he had opposed repeal— but too late, of course. Others were not so generous, even in retrospect. The ruling classes were "God's Chosen Peoples" and their first duty, the subjugation of the world, for the purpose of showering blessings upon it.

In line with this thinking, the expansion of Empire continued. Queen Victoria's footsore, ragged Methodists, Baptists, Presbyterians, at home at war with each other and with the Episcopalians, pushed through burning deserts to the fortress of the Baluchi, a thousand miles from nowhere, only to find nobody at home, and the water poisoned in the well. English and Irish soldiers, greatly outnumbered, fought valiantly but hopelessly against the hordes of the Moslems, who drove their sword hilts, studded with diamonds, straight into the mouths of the Christian fallen. Was this the city of diamonds which had been promised of old? Evidently not.

As the Irish continued to die like flies at home, the United States and Quaker missions sent several vessels loaded with corn meal to Ireland—as a thing more valuable than prayers or holy water. When the vessels moored in Galway Bay, church bells tolled throughout all of Ireland, in joyful thanksgiving—but there is many a slip 'twixt the cup and the lip. As no recipe had accompanied this corn meal, it was made into an inedible cake. Nothing was improved.

In 1848, the French Revolution reasserting itself, there was a shout of joy among English and Irish workers alike, as they saw now the possibility of a real improvement for the landless and propertyless. Feargus O'Connor, an Irishman with a lion's mane, attempted to form a people's army, to march on Parliament with demands for the rights which they felt to be theirs—the rights of food, shelter, clothing, and employment of an honorable nature. That suave traffic officer, the Duke of Wellington, the very symbol of international empire, had only to lift his hand as the procession turned toward Parliament—and grumbling, the crowd dispersed in all directions, like autumn leaves falling in the halls of Valhalla. This was practically the death rattle of the Chartist movement. It was heard from less thereafter. Feargus O'Connor, a lion in a cage, died raving insane.

Where but from France could come the real enlightenment? Any system of values is hollow and empty unless it fits the needs of collective human beings. When, in 1848, Louis Philippe, disguised under the name of William Smith, fled from France to England for sanctuary, Robert Owen fled from England to France, with the old message of man's capacity to control society for the best interests of all. In Paris, while Red Republicans and Bonapartists rioted in the streets, each party shouting the watchwords "Liberty, Fraternity and Equality," so that it was difficult to tell which was which, Robert Owen wrote a serene, calculated letter to the world. His letter, appearing in every newspaper and on every wall in Paris, was a plea addressed to both parties, a *Dialogue entre la France, le Monde, et Robert Owen.* Both parties, he informed them, were mistaken. "I come to your country in this important crisis to the history of all nations, to explain in the spirit of kindness and love for you and the entire family of man, in what manner you may render useless all the implements of destruction, give happiness to France, and, through its example, insure the permanent progressive happiness of the world." The good Archbishop of Paris, preaching a similar message, was shot through the back, quite by mistake. It was only by chance that Robert Owen himself was not shot down. For there was everywhere a vast confusion of purposes and identities. Not only in France, but also in Italy, where the Pope fled from Rome disguised as the Pope's valet, a pale horseman on a pale horse behind the episcopal carriage—and the valet, wearing a peak-shaped hat and a number on his forehead, indulged in what giddy sensations when he considered himself God's truest representative on earth. Normalcy, however, was restored. When things got back to normal, finally, Napoleon's nephew, first president of the French Republic in 1842, then Emperor of France in 1852, instituted a most important change. The old paving stones were torn up, so that they could not be used as barricades in another people's war. Asphalt pavements were laid down instead.

Moral, sentimental, and strategic ideas combined to build the British Empire. For a bottle of whisky and a strip of cloth, many an African chieftain turned over the whole of his land and people—hence to be under the absolute ownership of a musty office in London. The sacrifice of the many for the few!

Prince Albert, along about 1848, as time hung heavy in his hands, conceived the idea of a Crystal Palace to exhibit the fabulosities of Empire. Such an edifice, he believed, would improve the condition of the working classes, and would make visible to them the love and interest of the royal family, things which, as they had been invisible before, might have been doubted.

Prince Albert slaved many hours to bring this Crystal Palace, this heavenly city, into visible existence, for he believed it would express the spirit of progressive science as well as of conquest. He was opposed by everybody, liberals and illiberals, scientists and theologians. A most unprogressive Colonel Sibthorp prayed for a great storm of hail and lightning to shatter the Crystal Palace into atoms. An anonymous gentleman complained that the glass roof was porous, that droppings of fifty thousand sparrows would bury the people inside.

The Crystal Palace, though transient, was like that thing of beauty which is a joy forever. It was an Aladdin's palace. There were, within these walls of dulcet glass, all the riches of Asia and Africa and far-flung places—cotton balls, cotton bolts, corn, wheat, orange trees, stuffed kangaroos, stuffed birds, live peacocks, lotus flowers, tapestries, the masterpieces of the armorer's art, diamond-studded sword hilts, turbans, gold, copper, silk. A paradise of marble statues! Queen Victoria was a frequent visitor as the building went up. "We remained there two hours and a half"—before the opening—"and I came back quite beaten, and my head bewildered from the myriads of beautiful and wonderful things which would quite dazzle one's eye. . . . All owing to the Great Exhibition and Albert—*all to him!*" So many oranges in winter! The presence of God seemed to bless and pervade the entire edifice.

"The shock of delighted surprise which everyone felt on first entering the great Transept of Sir Joseph Paxton's building was as novel as it was deep," Sir Theodore Martin wrote. "Its vastness was measured by the two great elms, two of the giants of the Park, which rose far into the air, with all their wealth of foliage, as free and unconfined as if there were nothing between them and the open sky. The plash of fountains, the luxuriance of the tropical foliage, the play of colors, from the choicest flowers, carried on into the vistas of the nave by the rich dyes of carpets and stuffs from the costliest looms, were enough to fill eye and mind with a pleasure never to be forgotten, even without a vague sense of

what lay far beyond in the accumulated results of human ingenuity and cultivated art. One general effect of beauty had been
produced by the infinitely varied work of the thousands who had
separately co-operated toward this wonderful display; and the
structure in which it was set, by its graceful lines, and the free
play of light which it admitted, seemed to fulfill every condition
that could be desired for setting off the treasures thus brought
together. . . . Beautiful at all times, the sight which the Transept
presented on the opening day, with its eager crowds raised row
upon row, with the toilets of the women, and the sprinkling of
court costumes and uniforms, was one which men grew eloquent
in describing."

At the festival held here, while a densely crowded mass of
human beings stood in the slight drizzle of rain outside, and
myriads of aristocrats filled the galleries and seats around, and
trumpets flourished, and thousands of hallelujahs rent the air,
a Chinese "Son of Heaven" came forward to prostrate himself
before Queen Victoria, who was quite squat, having lost her
girlish figure, even as he had lost his pride. Never, as she said,
not even on the occasion of her coronation, had she felt so much
glory as in this House of Peace, for never before had been combined such peculiarity and such beauty on earth.

The greatest triumph of the day, however, all commentators
agreed, was the perfect behavior of the English people—thirty
thousand within and seven hundred and fifty thousand without. "There were no demonstrations of Red Republicans, of
hostile Chartists, or of Irish agitators," according to one report.
According to another, "The crowd at the Crystal Palace vanished
quietly away." According to Thackeray, how "frail and weak" was
the hand that swayed the scepter, how transient the scene, as
if a wizard had erected "a blazing arch of lucid glass." Difficult
to visualize the distant mutinies, the process without harmony.
Perhaps the Chinese "Son of Heaven" had the last laugh after

all—for though he had fallen on his face, he had saved his face, being no son of heaven but a rank impostor who had rented a costume for the occasion. And was laughing up his sleeve.

Yes, this Crystal Palace, this House of Peace, was a colossal joke, built during the progress of many wars in India and Africa, and on the eve of the Crimean War. Horror followed upon horror, war upon war, and there was never a moment of peace, as bit by bit the exhibition of Empire grew beyond all bounds.

During the great progress of a mistaken history, Robert Owen kept longer hours than a mill worker ever did. He was unable to contain within himself the flame of his love for all mankind—English, Irish, Ameer, Russian, Turkish, the many nations which must be united. Clergymen and politicians, alarmed by the vastly increasing number and enthusiasm of his followers, furnished free whisky to the workers in the towns where he was to appear with his message of a united labor. Hence, wherever he arrived, bedlam had been prepared in advance. There were riots, stonings, and conflagrations, as clergymen and police stood by, watching the grand show, the expulsion of Lucifer. In city after city, the Owenite cathedrals were mutilated or destroyed. Owenite workers were dismissed by their employers and refused employment elsewhere. The unorganized mass were betrayed by the values they had accepted. The purveyors of a capitalistic myth were thus held to be infallible. In the amphitheater at Bristol, on January 5, 6, and 7, 1841, occurred a debate between Robert Owen and John Brindley—subject, that old question, the nature of mankind, whether only the defective suffer privation. Brindley spoke first and occupied both his and the time allotted to Robert Owen—his argument, that God and communism were everlastingly opposed. Whenever Robert Owen arose to speak, the sands in the hourglass were already filled. In the few moments he had, his speech was interrupted by the loud boos of Brindley's hirelings. He predicted, though his voice could hardly be heard above so many boos and catcalls, the ruin of Bristol, Leeds, Manchester, and Birmingham, when the spirit of aristocracy should pour hail and brimstone from the sky upon the warrens of the poor. Brindley had accused Robert Owen of being the author of Shelley's *Queen Mab* from which he had read, in the course of his argument, numerous passages to show the ex-cotton lord's espousal of sensuality and atheism. Robert Owen denied that he had written Shelley's poem, although he had been Shelley's bosom friend, he admitted. His denial, like his prophecy, was unheard, so loud were the boos of old boozes in the audience. Nor could they hear him when he said that he had not separated from his wife on unfriendly terms, but on the friendliest, and his wife was dead. Perhaps, in the midst of even this confusion, he drove home to the heart of the world a shaft of profound truth—that the workers of the world must unite to overthrow all those who deceived them. Perhaps not. At Burslem, the workers turned out to greet him with sticks and stones, for they were as drunk as Indians, and knew not that this was their Tecumseh returning among them. Poor, exploited human nature! It was not the subject of Robert Owen's praise or blame. Perhaps some old drunk, reeling home, or coming to after a long period of unconsciousness, would realize the rational truth within his frame corporeal.

Lloyd Jones, socialist leader, was twice attacked by the clergy-inspired mob, but managed to give his speech on the characters of Moses, Jesus Christ, Martin Luther, and Robert Owen as the four truly great leaders born to mankind. He was far from alone in his opinion. He recorded, for posterity, a letter written to Robert Owen at this period of his great, though seemingly hopeless activity—"Every man who has a soul to comprehend his honor and his duty must respect you for being the friend of the working classes—to the white slaves who are born in the most Christian country, commonly called the Paradise of Clouds, or England—these homeless people brought home to England honor and freedom, and the English capitalists repay them with naked distress."

Ralph Waldo Emerson, on the occasion of one of Robert Owen's visits to America, in the 1840s, asked him who was his disciple and who would be left to carry on his work when he was gone. He answered, "No one." "He was the better Christian in his controversies with Christians," Emerson said, preaching his doctrine of "labor and reward" with the "fidelity and devotion of a saint to the slow ears of his generation." Emerson, however, as the spokesman for transcendent individualism, held the whole communistic project an impossibility. Robert Owen had skipped "no faculty but one, namely, life"—for such men had treated man as a plastic thing, or as something that might be put up or down, or manufactured into gases, or "a vegetable from which, though now a very poor crab, a very good peach can by manure and exposure be in time produced. . . ." Life was, he continued, rather a thing which "spawns and spurns systems and system makers, which eludes all conditions, which makes or supplants a thousand Phalanxes and New Harmonies with each pulsation." All men should become themselves lovers and servants of that which is just—then "straightway we live under the laws of Plato and Christ"—no system required. "All men plume themselves on the improvement of society and no man improves."

Time had taken its toll, even from the best of men. As Robert had grown old, he had suffered from the not unusual malady of an increasing deafness. That fact, and the influence of his eldest son, Robert Dale, were held to account for his annexation, finally, to this world of yet another, the empire of spiritual beings as they exist detached from flesh.

Cut off to a large degree, in his later years, from communication with the living, whose words he could not hear, Robert Owen relied more and more upon messages from the so-called dead, whose words, like the music of the conch shell, were a

repetition of the universal. The invisible and inaudible powers, purporting to be from the spirit world, were a company of
materialistic socialists and rationalists—Thomas Paine, Thomas
Jefferson, Benjamin Franklin, the Duke of Kent, Elijah, old
James Buchanan, and a certain nameless washwoman on Glasgow
Green, among others. They were not transcendent individuals
but focal points for the correct social relations. They were, like
Robert Owen, deeply concerned with the progress of the British
labor movement, a federation of world nations, the knowledge
that there is neither great nor small. Their manifesto, delivered
from the cloud, was a cry against the enslavement of the masses,
a cry against deception in every form. If, during their wanderings
through the ethereal vault, they had ever come upon a crystal
palace filled with disembodied diamond cutters, they mentioned
no such encounter as even possible. Nor had they ever assembled
before Jehovah's throne upheld by hunchbacks and cherubim, in
piercing cold above the seventh sphere, though they had been
everywhere. Nor had they seen good pasture land and apple trees
on any star but this. They had been all around the universe, to the
utmost corners, and their experience was such as to induce them
to believe in no decaying glory, no casket of illusion and memory, no new Jerusalem, no crown of crowns. Benjamin Franklin,
from his position in the cloud, presented an outline of his new
discoveries concerning the positive utilization of electricity and
the harnessing of cosmic elements. The Duke of Kent was as
punctual in keeping his appointments in the cloud as he had
been when he walked on earth. He said that there were no lords
spiritual or temporal, no dynasties, no royal families in the world
beyond—that all were equal.

In 1854, in a speech entitled "Address to the Human Race,"
Robert Owen made known his vast discoveries. A great moral
revolution was soon to be effected, by an apparent miracle.
He was compelled to believe, contrary to his previous strong

convictions, that there is a future conscious state of life, a state existing in a refined material, like the dance of golden atoms in the void, yet even more subtle. From the natural progress of creation, departed spirits had attained the power to communicate, by various means, none supernatural, their feelings and knowledge to us living upon the earth. These beings were not, as Robert Owen had once believed, the product of the diseased imagination. They showed, by irresistible evidence, that the potentialities of man's development are limitless, and that there is no boundary line, moral or geographic, which cannot be crossed by the progressive human spirit. Through the aid of reliable American and English mediums on both sides the Atlantic, Robert Owen had heard the voices of innumerable spiritual beings, like a surf beating on the shore of heaven. Thousands of nameless men and women had spoken to him, clearly and lucidly. Their revelations were made for the express purpose of changing the present false, disunited, and miserable state of human existence to that which it was intended to be in the nature of things, a rational order. This state would arise, they said, from a new universal education, or formation of human character, when the science of society should be practiced. This was their mission in the air. Enjoying an immaculate perception in all things, they were preparing mankind for an everlasting new harmony. They would infuse in all peoples the luminosity of their knowledge of charity, forbearance, and brotherly love. They would release mankind from poignant doubts about reality and from the dream of death. Already, having circumnavigated the universe, they had shown that there was no figure encompassed by stars like golden pomegranates, no power of powers. "Were it not for these new and most extraordinary manifestations," Robert Owen concluded, "there would arise a conflict between the evil spirits of democracy and aristocracy, which would deluge the world with blood and would create universal violence and slaughter among all nations."

Some felt, hearing this declamation and others of a similar nature, that the "Father of Socialism" had gone astray and was out on the proverbial limb. Others considered, more charitably, that one of his advanced years and deafness might well become the prey of fantasy or ruthless mediums. Indeed, from a strictly finite point of view, Saint John the Baptist was a colossal failure, because he was beheaded—but in the larger environment of spiritual history, he remains as a preacher with his head upon his shoulders. The unsubstantiality of Robert Owen's last hour, discoursing with bastard mediums at two dollars an hour, could not rob him of the substantiality of a lifetime engaged in activities for the real advancement of the human race. His spiritualism was, after all, only a restatement of his socialistic teachings—to unite all hearts, in the words of the old New Harmony *Gazette*. If he had retired into a realm of phantasmal unreality, he had still done so as a socialist, and never to aggrandize the concept of heaven and hell, crime and punishment. Dearest Caroline had now no use for any but the united family. Her charity was infinite, a perfume in the universe. She was become an associate of Mrs. Fletcher, Queen of the Unitarians. The elder Owen inquired, had Wales put off its old garments, and believed that man is incorruptible, and had embraced the cubes of human populace, the science of society. Old James Buchanan, lover of children and butterflies, was become, in the cloud, an associate of Bacon, Newton, Locke, Hume, and many other excellent philosophers. "Erect no unnecessary hypothesis whatever," he advised Robert Owen and the human race. "Happiness is the instinct of the universe," he added, somewhat extraneously. Daniel Defoe recalled that, had the circumstance been reversed, Benjamin Franklin might have stood in a pillory, and he might have been an author of American freedom, and presented at Windsor in a coonskin hat. Napoleon was rational.

The spirits were never inactive, never somnolent. Theirs was the highest flight ever attained by charity. They crossed the skies over Europe, shedding the radiance of their being on France, Germany, Russia, Poland, Italy, all nations. They were enflamed with an everlasting passion to liberate the suppressed masses, and to allow the buildings of rectangular villages where there had been dark factories and warrens of the poor, vast centers of mechanized starvation, yea, in the very shadow of the Gothic cathedral, the Gothic castle, the spire.

Alas, they buzzed like bees in a medium's capacious bonnet! At a séance in a boardinghouse of shady reputation, where there were both velvet curtains and mechanized mysteries, to say nothing of the twitterings of a few hysterical girls in the upper rooms, the spirits presented to Robert Owen their plans for villages which were to take the place of mercantile ruins, both present and future. These plans, drawn by visible pencils on blank sheets of paper mid-air, showed the ideal city to be not rectangular after all. The curved line, such as governs bodies, trees, and planets in their courses, was the truest one—all things moving by indirection. The new New Harmony, the spirits dictated, was to be circles within circles throughout eternity. The lines were a kind of spider's web, or like the honeycombs made by certain kinds of undeveloped bees, or perhaps like the ancient mazes. They were accompanied by designs such as those on Greek tombs in Thessaly. The spirits, Robert Owen said, had obeyed a greater logic than his. The Duke of Kent, always obliging, gave instructions regarding the proposed circular villages in the new harmony of earth with heaven, and names of members of Parliament who might be most sympathetic to a program for their immediate construction in England.

The end, needless to say, was near at hand.

In 1856, the British government annexed Oudh in India and gave to its tyrant a magnificent pension. "The part called the modern city is both curious and splendid, and altogether unlike the other great towns of India, whether Hindu or Mohammedan," wrote its English governor. "There is a strange dash of European architecture among its Oriental buildings." Gilded domes surmounted by the crescent, tall pillars, lofty colonnades, houses that looked as if they had been transported from Regent Street, cages of wild beasts and birds, gilt letters on butcher shops, English barouches—Oudh was a compromise effected between the new and the oldest order of things.

In 1857, in his eighty-sixth year, Robert Owen, deaf and almost blind, read a paper before the Social Science Association of Birmingham, entitled, "The Human Race Governed without Punishment." Attempting to read a paper before that organization the following year, at Liverpool, he fainted in the midst of his speech and was carried from the platform. This was almost his last public appearance.

For a fortnight, he lay as one in a coma, unable to lift his hand—a poor old man, in a broken-down hotel, a flophouse for improvident salesmen like himself. He had been rich, and now he was poor. He had been one of the few common men ever allowed to be seated in the presence of Queen Victoria, and now he was dying.

He saw his whole life pass before him, a shadow play on the wall of this Plato's cave. Everything came back to him. It was all as fugitive as a dream, yet clear and hard. Nothing had been diminished by time. He saw, as if they were still happening, the events which were past and gone, the thousand, thousand evils, the great suffering, the great disasters—saw, as if they were one, the laughing House of Lords, the weeping bishops of Ireland, a man named George Rapp, a man named Ralph Atkinson, bewildered educators, Tamerlane in petticoats, the exaltation of a lemon tree above mankind, the King of Delhi who had considered himself the king of kings, yea, and a certain Quaker martyr to luxury, and many pyramids. These were his anniversaries, his evening balls and engagements, his migrations from town to country house, his many errands. In a strait between two worlds, had he not always desired the better? He saw that each moment was eternity. He saw that there was nothing beyond beyond. He saw the poverty of heaven. He saw hundreds, thousands of little children chained like castrated dogs in coal mines and iron foundries, beatings, imprisonments, wounds of the spear, the stunted adult, the dwarfish mind, the soul without body, the body without soul. He saw, he hoped he saw the crumbling pyramids, when the workers of the world should be united. These were his Episcopalian communions, his Unitarian church membership, his marriage bed, his human family, his self-love, and his essential loneliness. For as long as one sentient being suffered, he would suffer, too. Were they English? So was he. Were they Russian? So was he. Were they German? So was he. Were they French, Polish, or Negro? So was he. Were they Jews, Indians, or Irish? So was he. Yea, and he was nothing of himself, he knew, with his life hanging on a single thread. Poor Maria Pears, a featureless stuffed doll in a wooden coffin, the huge parody. These were his peacock gardens, his crystal palaces. These were his long weekend in a green country, where he had seen the Pope of Rome in an old henhouse, the House of Lords in the Rappite maze. How cast off that withered garment, the spell of the past? Charity was still the goal. "And even things without life giving sound, whether pipe or harp, except they give a distinction in the sounds, how shall it be known what is piped or harped?" The world's confusion was still the world's confusion. "So likewise ye, except ye utter by the tongue words easy to be understood, how shall it be known what is spoken? for ye shall speak into the air."

Robert Owen rose from his bed, tottering, hardly able to put on his clothes and wind his watch. A little man, humped, almost transparent, the color of winter's gray thistle, a head which he had always believed to be too big for his body. He was going back to Wales, at last—and the seeds which he planted would

bear their fruits in the new moral world to come. Spirits perch-
ing upon his bedposts, innumerable voices of the light and air,
innumerable carpenters, mechanics, saddlers, tillers of the soil,
had said that in Wales he would find the cradle for the science
of society, never the grave. In Wales, they said, he would begin
his life's work over again—its end would be but its beginning.
So sick he could scarcely walk, he traveled by train third class to
Shrewsbury, with ancient, clucking dames around him, and by
carriage the last thirty miles, a second-class passenger, as Shelley's
bright hair streamed in the wind like autumn leaves. All the way,
huddled under his greatcoat, with hardly the strength to see him
to the end of his journey, Robert Owen drew up plans for the
reorganization of the parish at Newtown in Wales. All that was
necessary for the true science of society, he believed, he carried
in his bag—a few cubes of human populace, a copy of the laws
of human nature, a few old mortality rates, a map of the world,
a map of the stream of time, the theory of happiness, a blue
ribbon which had been Caroline's, a circular city marked on
paper, the design for a Greek tomb, a letter to mankind. When
his carriage turned toward Newtown, he shouted for pure joy.
He had come home, at last, accompanied by an old doctor
of Wales, toothlessly smiling, who had allowed him to read a
medical treatise, and Thomas Jefferson, in whom the worm had
created no vacuities.

In 1902, the people of Wales erected a monument in memory of Robert Owen. A sentence from his works was inscribed
on a slab of stone: "It is to the great and universal interest of the
human race to be cordially united, and to aid each other to the
full extent of their capacities." Attached to the front of the rail-
ings is a bronze bas-relief, depicting the father of modern socialism, with the veiled figure of justice behind him, holding out his
hand to a long procession of the workers of the world—a weaver
stooping beneath the bag on his shoulders, a potter carrying a

large jar, a farmer with his scythes, a carpenter with a bundle of tools, a woman bent down to a field.

Friedrich Engels, collaborator with Karl Marx, said: "Every social movement, every real advance in England on behalf of the workers, links itself to the name of Robert Owen." A man of "almost sublime and childlike simplicity," he was "at the same time one of the few born leaders of men." "His specific plans as a social reformer," Robert Dale wrote, more conservatively, "proved on the whole, and for the time, a failure . . . yet with such earnestness, such indomitable perseverance, and such devotion and love for his race, did he press, through half a century, his plans upon the public, and so much truth was there mixed with visionary expectation, that his name became known, and the influence of his teachings has been attended by sterling incidental successes, and toward the great idea of cooperation—quite impracticable as he conceived it—there has been, ever since his death, very considerable advance made, and generally recognized by earnest men and eminently useful and important."

Builder of Old Harmony

"Only the broad-fruited rain trees are in bloom." So wrote, in 1847, a traveler who had ridden three days and nights on horseback, hastening toward New Harmony, as he was not aware that Robert Owen's communism had failed. He found, in New Harmony, no subject so unpopular as communism, a sound lead, it was agreed, which had never reached to the depths of man's soul. A fat-jowled salesman, with a mercenary gleam in his eye, told how he had fooled "Old Bob" Owen, time and again—how he had kept his whisky bottle right under the footprints of an angel. Yet there were still a few citizens who confessed that the Owen period, with all its uncertainties, was by far the happiest of their lives—they were younger then than now, and filled to the brim with hopefulness. There had been a morning hour upon all sublunary things.

New Harmony seems, throughout the remainder of the nineteenth century, a compound of the sublime, the ridiculous, and the childish, a type of spiritual decadence, perhaps because it must be viewed in contrast always with what might have been. New Harmony deteriorated, turned toward the evening of the soul. There were, outside the chemical laboratory with its Gothic spire, no evidences whatever of a positive progress. The finger of the Rappite had written on every wall. And in Father Rapp's old garden, Robert Dale had entertained a not diluted Gabriel, time and again, and had heard footfalls on the boundary of another world.

No part of Robert Dale's Tennessee dream, it may be remembered, had been realized. Delayed by the "Fanny Wright" party in America, Robert Dale had returned to Scotland all too late for mortal happiness. His mother had died in a Glasgow boarding-house, facing no destiny but lurid wallpaper, in reminder of her poverty. Jessie had climbed the social ladder and was become a rich, bejeweled, befurred, rather too corpulent matron, the wife of a Glasgow cotton lord. Robert Dale, by comparison with Jessie, was almost a pauper, their situation almost the reverse of what it had been. Yet Jessie assured him, and the ghost of a girl seemed to look out of her eyes, that had he spoken his love, she would have followed him into the wilderness.

The one career left open to Robert Dale seemed, finally, to return to New Harmony—where, through industry and frugality, he might reclaim the thistle and wild goat pastures allotted to him as his share of remnant estates, and might create a little world of his own. He became, as a matter of course, New Harmony's most distinguished citizen. New Harmony was proud of Robert Dale, this perfect picture of an English country gentleman, riding his good horse Marmaluke through the streets under the golden rain trees and, like his father before him, possessed of a large nose and much good will, but unlike his father, a man who would never let his enthusiasm run away with him. New Harmony was proud of Rosebanks, a piece out of old Scotland, most elegantly furnished with a canopied bed, a harpsichord, pictures of pigs, pictures of the spirits of planets, many candlesticks, many items of luxury. Robert Dale was not only a home builder but an excellent estates manager, reclaiming his many acres from jimson weeds and ruin. Under his administration, the scene of two Utopias seemed about to become a third, but an improvement over the past, for the objectives he had were at least within the sphere of possibilities—not the end of the world but a better sewage system, the connection of Brewery Street with the ferry landing by a road to be flanked by a canal, perhaps the attraction of a few kindred spirits to this deserted village. From morning until evening, he was busy, out going over his property inch by inch, cutting down dead trees and other aspects of a melancholy nature, building sheep shelters, building hog houses and fences—or, more accurately speaking, he supervised the work. If he. never got around to the sewage system and the canal, they were at least his great dream and one which still persists in New Harmony.

Each evening, the light at Robert Dale's window showed that he sat with his head bent over a desk and his pen moving. The result of his labors was *Pocahontas*, a poetic drama. Its theme, though expressed nobly, in sonorous blank verse, was that most men are fools—"For all will follow, like silly sheep, the first bellwether, betrayed by the tinkling ornament on their leader's neck"—whether they be low-browed Laplanders or South Sea islanders.

The poet and visionary of better drainage was about to become a politician, wearing an old sheep's bell whether he would or not. When it was rumored that the state planned improvements in the pocket country, Robert Dale purchased land in larger quantities than he could afford. Improved at the cost of the state, they would bring in enough perhaps to make up for his father's losses on the idea of Utopia. When, however, in 1836, after long dickering, the plans for internal improvement became law, what was the carelessness of the Whigs? New Harmony, which had been the theater of the world, was forgotten—the one place where no improvements were to be made ever in time or space. At that moment, Robert Dale entered politics—convinced that by this method only would it be possible to gather grapes from thorns, figs from thistles, and much from nothingness. As his father had remarked that of the two parties, the Democrat was the lesser evil, he ran for Senator on what was, even then, a precarious ticket, almost certain to lose. A suicidal gesture, that! The Whigs now had something to talk about. Here was the worst Democrat imaginable—a man who had advocated birth control, the unreality of God, a liberation from the fear of death, woman suffrage, a thousand impossibilities. Robert Dale, faced with the record of his past, was forced to declare that he had changed his mind on some of the ideas he had entertained. On the whole, however, he was courageous—and, mindful of Leatherstocking, went around the county to talk to farmers at their own doorsteps, as man to man. He had always a kind word to say about the dead baby or the newborn calf. He knew what it was to have his crops cut down by a blizzard. How hailstones big as apples fell. As a result of such tactics, he was elected state Senator by an overwhelming majority—though his opponents attributed his success to his English accent and his poetry, neither of which they considered to be the American way of life. They suspected that he had buried his radicalism but for the time being.

As Senator, Robert Dale served brilliantly. He was still very much in love with many causes. His speeches gushed forth like fountains. He lent the services of his rhetoric to many excellent movements. The founding of free schools, the property and social rights of women. "The Temple of Freedom," he said, in opposition to that vast majority which believed that education would rob the mind of its freedom, "is no polished marble, no massive pillars curiously carved, none of the ornaments of architecture or luxuries of taste. It is but a humble schoolhouse." In general, he was less extreme than his father, more extreme than his opponents. He knew when to draw in his horns. He was merely human.

In 1842, Robert Dale was sent as Indiana's Representative to Congress—the Whigs insisting again that Indiana's pride in poetry was greater than Indiana's pride in common sense. He arrived in Washington during a great fever of national expansion—when new frontiers were opening, and the questions of housing, unemployment, old-age pension, such tired matters, had not yet presented themselves at the White House. John Bidwell, with a party of eighty men, women, and children, had traversed, in 1841, the immeasurable distance to Oregon, had achieved the impossible goal, had found "the land of promise." Now others were following. Here was a grandiose subject for a poet turned politician. "When you can whistle back the mountain eagle in his upward flight to the sun," Robert Dale said, "when you can arrest, by a word, the wild horse of the prairy in his mad career, when you can quench, in the bird of passage, that instinct which bids her be up and away to the regions nature designed for her—then, then only, expect to set up mete or bound short of the broad Pacific, a barrier to the restless enterprise of the West. Oregon is our land of promise. Oregon is our land of destination."

Never were there so many glorious speeches in Washington, so many bouquets of dead rhetoric. The beauty of it was that here the word was equal to the deed. To traverse a path to Oregon in the imagination is much easier than to traverse it in actuality. To fight a battle with the pen is much easier than to fight it with the sword.

Following an epic line of national thought, Robert Dale stood for the annexation of Texas, a wrestling of the Southwest from the puny powers of Spanish Mexico—in opposition to those who opposed this movement of aggression, on the somewhat lame plea that Texas belonged to Mexico and that its acquisition would mean the extension of Negro slavery. When, in a few years, the Mexican War broke out, more or less according to schedule, Robert Dale adopted the view of most apologists for that predatory act—America had been invaded by foreign powers, and the Mexicans deserved great punishment for their great crime. Reformers on both sides of the Atlantic were disappointed with this son of a liberal father—he had drifted very far from the philosophy of social amelioration, very far from Utopia.

As a result, however, of a war to which his rhetoric was midwife and nurse, though there was much evil, there was greater good, from some points of view—the United States being the richer by 918,000 square miles of virgin territory. California, as everybody knows, turned out to be a gold mine. The rivers and mountains were veined with gold. It was there for the picking, just like peaches. Monastic Spanish towns, where there had been priests, eucalyptus trees, physiological mysticism, and expansion unto eternity were blotted out by gamblers, traders, thieves, and ladies with checkered careers. Dirt was precious, and life was cheap. At least one early millionaire sent his shirts to China to be laundered, there being at that date no Chinese launderers in California. A strange denouement of the Oriental dream.

To the victor go the spoils. In 1853, Robert Dale received his reward for his many valuable services to the United States government. The great Western Democrat, as he was called, was appointed to wear his broad-rimmed hat as chargé d'affaires, then minister to the court of Frederick II in Naples. It was a post unfortunately isolated, an atmosphere unfortunately stultified, no expansion but the charm of a tired eternity.

The Western Democrat, deprived of Oregon and Texas, became an easy convert to indoor spiritualism which, transcending the finite individual, opened a door between the waking and sleeping life, and brought to light many things which had seemed lost forever. Upright in a high-backed chair, the Western Democrat witnessed calm where there had been a storm or crossed the gap, a very small one, between this world and the next. There were many miracles. The very walls of flesh dissolved. Such manifestations showed how every event was no longer

determined by a preceding event. Such manifestations, though
cognizant of past, future, and many intimate details of present
existence, were usually of a strictly personal nature. They could
assert the exact location of a dovecote in New Harmony, the
exact location of a picket fence, but were out of all relation with
the deserts of Mexico, where American soldiers had drunk urine
to satisfy their thirst. They attached the greatest importance to
some slight, insignificant detail, such as a letter lost in the mails
or a pair of garden shears dropped in the bottom of a well or the
exact shading of perfume worn by a dead lady. They showed the
ever abiding existence of the true subjects in phenomena. All else
was doubtless excess.

In sixteen months, the Western Democrat engaged in two
hundred sittings, each very much like the one before, and each
very marvelous. It was a series of dead seasons in Naples. He
beheld spirits whose detached hands moved like the flight of
swallows, spirits whose heads were upheld on shafts of light,
spirits emerging from dank velvet curtains. Winged children
passed above him, fading only when they reached the frescoed
ceiling upheld by jaundiced cupids. There were many returnings
from Elysium. The Western Democrat, though he was by nature
inclined toward skepticism, could not deny the evidence of his
senses. He heard the buzzings of thousands of buzzless bees. All
the buried and hidden islands of life, he saw, were densely populated. There was no such thing as perfect emptiness. This life
failing, there was always the expectation of the next. There would
be, the spirits told him, a reunion of the Owen family in the
mansions which had been lonely, to include Jessie, at the tender
age of seventeen, whom age could not wither nor custom stale.
Lo, he beheld an apparition of his mother in her wedding dress
which was her shroud.

The Western Democrat, during his nearly six years as chargé
and minister at the court of Naples, made hay while the sun

shines, so to speak. Republicans, had they been apprised of his activities, might have complained that, like most Democrats, he was off on another tangent, shooting at clay pigeons. The Western Democrat considered himself, even at this distance from reality, to be just what he had always been, his people's servant, the servant of Leatherstocking. Perhaps he was not far wrong. America was itself, at this time, swept by a rapping mania. There were many pioneers of the soul in the American wilderness. What was the nature of man, a thing resolvable never into twelve platitudinous, paltry laws which would contain him in a rectangle, a coffin? Could the Western Democrat but discover the key to life's mysteries, yea, the great key in the hands of an Italian angel, American taxpayers would not have spent their money in vain. The Western Democrat, being public-spirited and a universalist besides, devoted himself to a series of opaque studies for the benefit of all peoples everywhere, in whatever walk of life. Did the visions of crystal-gazers follow optical laws? The Western Democrat filled many sheets of paper with notes on crystal-gazing, disembodiment, immutability, nightmares, resurrections, subconscious attitude, alternations of personality, the strange appearance of the present world, the strange texture, and two-headed men whose ideas could be comprehended only through an examination of clouds and raindrops. The case of an unreal carriage, the case of an insane woman whose right arm was sane, protesting against the rest of her body.

Sorry to relate, there were no other events worthy of mention in Naples, and little gossip but that which concerned spiritual beings or esoteric departures from the normal. The Neapolitan despot and the American minister carried on, nevertheless, a lively business—many secrets, much intrigue. A courier ran always between the despot and minister, with his bag filled with the most remarkable dispatches which have ever passed between two powers. Exchange of notes between the despot and minister, as to why Saint Augustine, though ordinarily faithful, did not show up during a harsh rainstorm, whether the electrical phenomena could be said to have any relation with his failure to keep his Saturday night engagement, which he had not missed during many years; as to why Saint Theresa could not be lured from her hiding place for any reason whatever and why, in her stead, there had come, night after night, an old beast of burden, a voice without words; as to why a certain little Irish housemaid was running loose in Naples, kicking over furniture.

When not interviewing spirits, and there were thousands and thousands of them, more dead souls than living, Robert Dale turned to the writing of a book which, he was convinced, would effect a world-wide revolution in the affairs of men, as it would divert them away from their all-absorbing concern with the things of the putrid flesh. As a result of his researches into the misty occult, it would be shown conclusively, and beyond the shadow of a doubt, that there are footprints on the boundary of a better world than this—yea, even the footprints of an undoubtedly polygamous angel.

To say nothing of its wide success in Europe, there were ten million war-weary American readers of *Footfalls on the Boundary of Another World*, that great opus. Millions more, illiterate or too busy to read, would have accepted its Cartesian doctrine that the soul never sleeps. Hardly an old Kentucky mountaineer who would not have agreed to its long citation of witnessed marvels. The sinner might be caught, like the body, in a dark valley, convinced of the limitations of the flesh—but the saint, like the soul, would stand on topless mountains, seeing detached faces and the flight of homing birds. Hardly an old Kentucky mountaineer who had not ridden home accompanied by neighing spirits, yea, and dead bodies wet with heaven's dew. Whatever our reason might tell us as to the course of events, God had the power at any moment to steer the earth upon some unknown road in darkened skies—just as the teamster turned his mules in a different way toward home. Should one speck of dust act in an unprincipled way, it would show that the universe was not entirely a machine. And many specks of dust were acting in unprincipled ways! Hardly a man who would not have agreed.

Robert Dale urged perhaps only the conventional views. Accordingly, the soul must prepare itself for the great Day of Judgment, when the scrolls of the heavens are unfurled. Many will be missing from the census taken in heaven—for man is the architect of his own destiny, either heaven or hell. Man has the power to choose, and his choice assumes the role of an inexorable judge upon him throughout futurity. Death will deprive him of neither the old vices nor the old virtues. "That dark vestment of sin with which, in man's progress through life, he may have become gradually endued, will cling to him . . . ." Yea, though from sphere to crystal sphere he goes. And that is why dogs howl in the long nights. Heaven, hell, rewards, punishments, praise, blame—all must be considered as having their place in the mystical economy of things. Without these, reality would be featureless.

British and American freethinkers were disappointed to observe this latest aberration of one who was the son of such a father. Had the ghost of Hamlet's father seventeen noses, they asked, and was God's a writing of black ink on a green scroll? The younger Owen talked very fluently of God—"as if he had but recently been favored with a personal interview," as if he held a monopoly on truth. Some believed that his steps toward divinity had been taken for political purposes, perhaps to confound Republicans, who were now deprived of the chief arrow in their sling.

Serenely good-humored, like his father before him, the Western Democrat continued his researches as to luminous eyes in clouds and the whole problem of human behavior. His scrolls to show the undiscovered dimensions of the Old Moral World were as ponderous as his father's scrolls on the New Moral World. He made as many journeys as his father before him—or almost as many. He traveled throughout Europe, interviewing people who had felt clammy hands laid against them in darkness, people who had felt invisible birds pecking at their cheeks. And many who had experienced, though they were still alive and walking, a total cessation of natural events. There was hardly a European despot with whom he did not spend much time, enlarging his notebooks on evidences of interventions from another sphere. If a whole population concurred in believing hallucination to be reality, how should they prove themselves deceived?

At home, the annexation of new territory in the American Southwest had caused much anger among the opponents to Negro slavery. The nation was about to split into two pieces—the industrial North which worshiped the progress of big business, the agrarian South which justified slavery on the ground that it was saving the Negroes' souls. There was capitalism above the Mason-Dixon line, and there was feudalism beneath it. Yet for perhaps the great mass of men, the question of Negro liberation was the only one. When Stephen Douglas, defender of the conversion of new states into slave territory, visited Chicago to speak in behalf of his views, flags in the harbor were lowered to half mast, and church bells tolled, in mournful elegy for the Negro race. Everywhere Stephen Douglas went, he found himself hanged in effigy.

The Western Democrat, in the midst of his spiritual researches, was called home from Naples, to aid in the progress of material events—though his brief case was filled with papers to prove the unreality of materialism, and the identification of his subconscious mind with eternity. Never, in fact, was any ship so heavily laden with spiritual beings as that which carried the Western Democrat homeward—never were there so many unlisted passengers, so many kings, clowns, corpses, so many eyes imagining themselves ears. While Abraham Lincoln faced the cheering multitudes at Cooper Institute, the lately returned minister sat in the darkened parlor of a Broadway boardinghouse, demanding peace at any price—and saw spirit flowers plucked out of the air by spirit hands. Oh, fields of asphodel! Only the men whose limbs have been blown into space know what war is, they said—and therefore they advocated the ideal of an everlasting peace, even though this should mean the continuation of Negro slavery.

Abraham Lincoln had spent his boyhood at dusty Pigeon Creek, a lonesome hollow. None of the factors in his life could quite account for him. As a hawk-eyed, dreamy boy and young man, however, navigating the Wabash River, he doubtless touched on the shore of two Utopias—the Rappite, the Owenite, and both so distant. Abraham Lincoln and Robert Dale were "two great immigrants from the pocket country," who had left it at about the same time, as one biographer of the Western Democrat remarked—though Abe had been raised up among bean-growing squatters and had seen much violence. "When the awful form of disunion darkened the national threshold, both were willing to submit to slavery, if need be, in order to preserve our national existence intact. With both the paramount object then became 'to save the Union and neither to save nor destroy slavery.' 'If they could have saved the Union without freeing any slaves, they would have done so. If they could have saved it by freeing some and leaving others, also they would have done that.' It was not that they hated slavery the less but that they loved the Union more." Robert Dale lent his rhetoric to the service of conciliation. "For myself, while the sword remains undrawn, while kindred blood remains unshed, never shall I despair of the Republic. While there is Peace there is hope, for Peace is the life of the Union."

War broke out, in spite of all the reasons which could be brought against it, and in spite of all the spirits communicating with Robert Dale. Two years after the execution of John Brown,

Northern soldiers were inspired by his martyrdom to march to
their own graves, however reluctantly, in rotted uniforms and
paper shoes provided by Chicago mercantile interests, a merchandise probably intended to last just about as long as the wearer.
Ships loaded with Northern farm boys who had never seen the
ocean before went down in the ocean, before a single cannon
could be fired—doubtless because they were built for the greatest
happiness of the smallest number, that is, the usual Wall Street
vultures. They were the ones who wanted to blow Baltimore and
the South off the map. The irony of fate was such that Robert
Dale, spiritualist and pacifist, found himself appointed munitions
agent for the state of Indiana, to purchase gunpowder and material arms from Germany. For the big boys in Berlin were already
active. Republicans, seeing this plum fall into the hands of a
Democrat, were dismayed. Republicans felt that the misty, mystic
Democrat might be more concerned with the inflation of spirits than with ammunition to blow up Atlanta, more concerned
with disembodiment than with forcing the fortified entrance at
Mobile Bay. As so often happens, they were mistaken. The spirits,
though disembodied, were most co-operative, presenting a united
front. As a result of Robert Dale's enforced activities, many a
Confederate soldier progressed to another sphere, a better world
than this—and many a Yankee soldier found that his old clothes
adhered to him, like sin itself. Rank upon rank, proud regiments
of both the South and North, were thinned—having at least this
much in common, after all. How justify the sacrifice of multiple
consciousness and memories, the huge carnage of war, the human
beauty resolved to chaos? "Without slavery," Abraham Lincoln
declared, "the rebellion never would have existed; without slavery
it could not continue." Yet he feared that a premature emancipation of the Negro might alienate the border states and "give fifty
thousand bayonets" from them "over to the rebels." For a while,
emancipation seemed to hang in the balance.

Robert Dale wrote to Abraham Lincoln, probably at the dictation of spiritual beings in an abolitionist boardinghouse—but also because he remembered Utopia—"Shall the North have sacrificed a hundred thousand lives and two thousand millions of treasure to come to that at last? Not even a guarantee of peace purchased at so enormous a cost? After voluntary exertions on the part of our people to which the history of the world furnishes no parallel, is the old root of bitterness still to remain in the ground, to sprout and bear fruit in the future as it has borne fruit in the past?"

Not only was there the just cause of freeing the Negro, but also the great fame which Abraham Lincoln might reap in the eyes of the world, the great praise. "If you are tempted by an imperishable name, it is within your reach. . . . Such an offer comes to no human being twice." Abraham Lincoln said of this letter, "Its perusal thrilled me like a trumpet call." Five days later, in the midst of the tragic elements, the wild inclemencies, that war which is also anarchy, the Preliminary Proclamation was announced with the utter quietude of God when He created the world. But the world was still uncreated.

Certain gentlemen in high places were trying desperately to revive a scheme for compromise with slavery. A number of political figures were quite willing to reorganize the Union, omitting the New England states—though New England had been the greatest opponent to Negro slavery to begin with, and also its forefather. So that in the midst of the war, as so often happens, it seemed that the goal was changing. Robert Dale opposed with all the might of his oratory this diversion. Spiritual beings, which had previously been the apologists for slavery, now warned him of the impossibility of a compromise with slavery. A voice speaking out of the cloud, a certain ex-tobacco salesman with bleeding hands, cried out his warning. All should be free, or all were slaves. Robert Dale wrote, ". . . let Indiana, selling Freedom's birthright for less than Esau's price, resolve to purchase Southern favor by

Northern dismemberment and the world-wide contempt that would follow it—but let her know, before she enters that path of destruction, that her road will lie over the bodies of her murdered sons, past prostrate cabins, past ruined farms, through all the desolation that fire and sword can work. Let her know that before she can link her fate to a system that is as surely doomed to ultimate extinction as the human body is finally destined to death, there will be a war within her own borders to which all we have yet endured will be as but the summer's gale, that scatters a few branches over the highway, compared to the hurricane that plows its broad path of ruin, mile after mile, leaving behind in its track a prostrated forest, harvest crops uprooted and human habitations overthrown."

After the Civil War was over, what happened? Peace was handed down from heaven. Many an old oak tree had stood the gale of time. There were numerous cripples. Walt Whitman saw the face of Jesus Christ everywhere. Otherwise, there was disunion. It was also a problem, what to do with the Negro, how to dispose of him. Robert Dale, who had fought to free the Negro, opposed his immediate suffrage, political or economic. The Negro, before he could use the ballot, must be taught to read and write—though Andrew Jackson was no great scholar. The Negro must be suspended, as it were, between slavery and freedom, until he could learn to stand on his own two feet, as a person fully responsible for the formation of his own character and destiny. For many years to come, alas, many a Negro in the South would be suspended by a rope, with his feet somewhat above the ground—but that is another story. The overwhelming fact is that the Civil War ended with civil war.

Robert Dale was haunted by his conscience. He regretted the part he had played in the Mexican War. Perhaps the spirits had shown him his vast mistake. In Washington, the Western Democrat and former minister to the gilded drawing rooms of gilded despots wore a Mexican sombrero to advertise his change of heart. He was known among Republicans as "that Mexican." He urged that the United States support the struggling Juarez Republic in Mexico. He tried to float a bond for the relief of Mexico, to be subscribed to by public-spirited American taxpayers. Democracy, the spirits said, must exist everywhere or nowhere. The murder of Maximilian was unfortunate but necessary to the march of progress. It was sad that Carlotta should be locked up in an empty room. There must be, however, in the Western hemisphere, not even the ghost of a crown. No one was more vocal on this subject than the Emperor Constantine, ferried over the gulf fixed between the dead and the living by faceless slaves with lustrous pinions and American flags.

To some, the Western Democrat's constant quotations of the Bible at every turn of the corner in Washington seemed, like his sombrero, evidence of a diseased intellect. He was becoming, with each step, more and more devoted to the Catholic Church and its many vulnerable sepulchers, out of which the soul arises to wing its way joyfully toward the throne of heaven. The spirits differed from the saints, he said, only in that they were more catholic, being confined to no particular denomination or sphere. Quite often the simplest character, such as a certain fugitive slave with a thorn in his foot, would accompany the noblest, also in flight, such as Gabriel. When opposed as to his views on the existence of nonexistent beings, such as tobacco-spitting peddlers and lovelorn housemaids, who somehow had attained to the status of saints, he replied, with utmost serenity, "Time, the great teacher, will decide between us. Ten years—probably less—will see the question determined."

For a time, Robert Dale dropped out of the national picture. During the Civil War reconstruction, when carpetbaggers rifled the South, that scene of fire-burned earth and desolation, Robert Dale, retired in the pocket country, devoted himself to the building

of New Harmony a little nearer to the heart's desire. It was, however, though a better New Harmony than this, merely a fiction, an
aggregate of sonorous words—*Beyond the Breakers*, the story of a
town and all the people in it. Chicksauga, a better New Harmony,
was made up of at least one palatial household. The characters, at
least the good ones, enjoyed the serenity of those figures depicted
on Grecian urns—their hounds never moved, their buckets were
not broken at the well. Franklin Sydenham, or Robert Dale, a
cosmopolitan intellectual, a little world-weary, had returned from
European capitals to become the chief benefactor of Chicksauga,
or New Harmony. His entire aim was to convert Chicksauga
into the reminiscence of Italy. Unlike Robert Dale, as he was a
happily fictitious character in a happily fictitious world, he was
able to introduce many Italian relics and to institute, in spite of
backward elements, a sewage system. Also, though opposed by
conservatives and die-hards, he built a canal to connect Church
and Brewery Streets with the Wabash, the outer world. There
were a few wandering fools. There were many inferior characters. Amos Clair, a dishonest lawyer in Chicksauga, had been
Amos Cranstoun, a dishonest lawyer in New Harmony. Elisha
Embree, or Elisha Emberly, was a Republican and a scoundrel
in both towns. The good horse Marmaluke was the good horse
Marmaluke. There was a hunter of exotic insects and shells, none
other than Thomas Say, devoid of Thomas Say. There was a faint
suspicion of old Neef blowing a trumpet at the borderline. There
were a few characters who had got to Chicksauga by accident.
A Quaker martyr to luxury stood under the golden rain trees of
Chicksauga or New Harmony—a still unhappy citizen, as wherever he went, he always arrived too late or too early for Utopia.
Life in Chicksauga was a perpetual English Sunday, a division of
the wheat from the tares.

    Beyond the Breakers was but a diversion from the greater task
at hand. Though in Chicksauga there were few miracles, and

perhaps none in New Harmony, there were miracles elsewhere. *The Debatable Land between this World and the Next* recorded them.

The book was a sensation in the publishing world. Nothing like this had dawned on the national horizon before. Every thoughtful reader should own a copy. It blew away the dust of ages. There were numerous wild advertisements. *The Debatable Land*, according to Mrs. Harriet Beecher Stowe, was the spiritual counterpart to Darwin's materialistic *Voyage of a Naturalist*. It dealt with the soul, as Darwin had dealt with bodies. Whereas Darwin had written of sea rocks whitened by dung of white sea birds, and colonies of seals, and butterflies blown on a gale five hundred miles out to sea, Robert Dale had added the missing half, that was to say, man's immortal nature. Facts more far-reaching in their consequence to man on the eternal quest than Darwin's citation of flowers which have a rudimentary sense of memory. Instances in proof of angelic guardianship more wonderful than old baboons who never yet had swung between two stars, more wonderful than cherry-colored spiders. And every miracle, someone had been eye witness to! Herein was shown, also, the significance of dreams in history—the dreams of Abimelech, Pharaoh, Saul, Solomon, Nebuchadnezzar, and all those who had broken out with sweat like cold dew—the testimony of Elihu, that "In slumbering upon the bed, God openeth the eyes of men and sealeth their instructions." On what occasions did spiritual beings return to earth? Instances of these. A man returned to earth to warn his son against extravagance. A servant girl returned to obtain her letters to her lover. Many returned to lament the decay of old houses.

Robert Dale might have been a great student of the supernatural natural, had it not been for his enthusiasm, his desire for the immediate revelation. Wanting the empirical evidence for each metempirical event, he went to mediums. None were so feather-brained as they seemed. He paid two dollars for every revelation that man might exist in a bodiless state. Such a spiritualism was very different from the philosophy of spirit he thought he was arriving at—perhaps Bishop Berkeley's contention that all things, all the furnitures of earth and choirs of heaven, are ideas upheld in the mind of God. Robert Dale paid two dollars to see the table upheld by nothing. What he required was a sudden disjoining of the events in God's mind—and the mediums, with their concealed ropes and pulleys, were ideally situated for that transaction, the deceiving him to believe what he saw. His particular craft was destined, like his father's before him, to be wrecked upon the shoals and rocks of human nature.

At séances in the home of the American mediums, Mr. and Mrs. Holmes, there was much ribald joking among the spirits, none of whom seemed to have approximated the nature of divinity—they were drunks in a seaman's tavern or traders in explosives. One recited poems ascribed to the posthumous spirit of Edgar Allan Poe. He had not changed his style. However, had not Robert Dale always believed that man's character accompanies him, from sphere to shining sphere—like sin itself? The spirits were sensationalists, though out of their senses. One rode on a scared horse. Another planned to lay an Atlantic cable, whereby to connect the voice of London with the voice of New York—though this should certainly contribute to the world's madness. The spirit was planning to do something that had already been done. Still another, a diamond-studded gambler, was stalking his prey throughout eternity. Every once in a while, he belched. There was a gentleman whose invisible body could be apprehended by the fact of his visible watch and chain. This gentleman stood perfectly still in space.

A most active spirit, Katie King, habituée of cosmic seamen, made her appearance on both sides of the Atlantic, depending on Robert Dale's location, for they were remarkably fond of each other. Portraits, the works of cynics, showed that her English face was quite different from the one she presented in America. In fact, Katie had no harmony at the center, was not one Katie, but two, both fat and lean, both fair and dark. There was no way, evidently, to reconcile the two as one, ever in time and space. She was an abused servant girl in London, and she was an abused servant girl in New York. Alas, for the best of plans! Holmes, who had so often produced Katie at will, was unable to produce a much less miraculous matter, a bank account. Having counterfeited the true spiritual being, he proceeded to manufacture the coin of the realm, but much less successfully, for the United States Treasury was not gullible. Holmes was thrown into jail, where the spirit of Katie doubtless twittered. Robert Dale, who had publicized Katie in the columns of *The Atlantic Monthly*, found it hard to give her up to nothingness. Katie was Katie, whose manifestations he had so often reported. Katie was a leaping flame, to whom no ordinary standards of measurement could apply. If she had crossed the gulf between the living and dead, what obstacle was the Atlantic? Wherever there was a luminous soul, he would find his lodging in Katie. Why should she not be both fair and dark? Spontaneity was ever the chief characteristic of spiritual beings. In a perfectly empty room, he had felt her hand brushing against his knee.

The nation was profoundly shocked by the credulity of a man who had been a leader in public affairs of the greatest importance to its history. Suppose that, while advising others, he himself had been advised by Katie. There was a little song which went the rounds among his political enemies in Washington and nonbelievers everywhere—

> *Said Robert Dale to Katie King,*
> *I think I hear an angel's wing.*
> *Said Katie King to Robert Dale,*
> *It's nothing but an old man's wail.*

Utopia in Bedlam

More and more, Robert Dale gave himself up to the hypothesis that the mind dwells separately from the body, even in this lifetime. More and more, wherever he went, spiritual beings accosted him. He could hardly step out into his garden at New Harmony, to take the evening air, without finding some new visitant. The spirits, when unconfined by such parties as the Holmeses, were almost a torment too great to bear.

The air was so thick with spirits, Robert Dale could have cut it with a knife. Where others saw only a few yellowed lilies in the waning light, he saw his mother or her embroidery needles. The wind was a sadness. More than once, Jessie emerged from the weeping willows, although, in less inspired moments, it occurred to Robert Dale that she must be a hallucination, for the dear lady was putting on flesh at Glasgow, and quite unaware that she had joined the ranks of the immortals. The dead, however, were insistent—impossible to reason into nothingness. Even after evening, between the oleanders and the garden pump emerged a quiet, sad gentleman, and what was very strange, he wore only one glove, as his right hand was completely missing, perhaps as a result of friction in the infinite. He was an Austrian with a

Spanish accent. Benjamin Franklin, who always appeared between the church bells ringing, confessed that he, too, was being worn down, although he showed no evidence of any loss but appeared to have all his properties, including a coonskin hat. Perhaps it was because, even as a spirit, he had exercised a certain amount of prudence, and had avoided whirlwinds. Not all were so fortunate. There was no harmony at all in the universe, no center but whirlwinds, evidently. Time and again, wherever Robert Dale was, there was a lovely, snow-white mulatto girl, who confessed that she had not attained the freedom she had expected to find. She had longed to make the acquaintance of Abraham Lincoln, but had hardly crossed his path as yet, in the confusion of so many whirling stars, blind spots, immense holes, whirlwinds of ether and cosmic dust. She clasped, oddly enough, an emptyheaded, yellow-haired doll in her hands. So almost every spirit seemed, in his own way, pitiful. An English poetess, who had died on the wild coast of Guinea, emerged from a bed of violets along the back fence, in the company of a white-bearded monkey, Diana, who gaped. She said that now, if she chose, she could write the most beautiful poem that was ever written, an elegy for Diana, for the sense of death had never been lost by those who enjoyed a life beyond this life—there was always something missing. Always a space outside of God.

Robert Dale, more and more melancholy, drank whisky in large quantities, though it gave him no relief from horrors and grotesque shapes, though it multiplied the number of their visitations. Where was the truth, where was the light, where was the kingdom of God? Jessie would always put on weight in Glasgow. Fanny Wright's old party would always laugh at him. Gradually, he began to feel that his senses were numbed. That numbness was all he wished for. Visions, like dogs chained to a sled, drew him over the Arctic waste of nonexistence, toward no goal he knew of. At any moment, his hands might drop off like golden rain tree leaves in autumn. By and by, he would be much happier, the Marquis de Lafayette assured him. By and by, he would be himself a visitation in a garden. This expectation was his only hope in life.

In moments of lesser clarity, he saw himself as others saw him—and was amused. He remarked, in one of these rare moments, that the best way to inspire the tolerance of one's political enemies is to lose one's mind—that by such an extreme measure only, a Republican can be brought to understand a Democrat.

From his great height, wrapped by clouds and girt around by stars thick as the sands of the sea, he saw the world for what it was, a series of illusions of grandeur. The universe was all a lie, from beginning to end—not even a straw of truth to be found there. The Fool of Nature rose like Triton from the waves and turned into an octopus, carrying in every hand a golden book, in every book a different writing. The great joker in the philosophic pack was God, was man, was everything, was cancer, was chemistry, was an octoroon, was a golden rose, was a pig's snout, was Jessie, was a billiard ball, was a maze, was an empty-headed doll, was ostrich eggs, was Napoleon, was a cherry tree, was a rectangle, was mountains, was nature, was human nature, was Fanny Wright's old party, was a table, was a chair, was Saint Ursula, was Chicksauga, was a brain fever, was happiness, was an acorn, was blocks of populace, was an albatross on the banks of the Wabash far away, was Marmaluke.

How his father had lost his shirt in Utopia.

Farewell to New Harmony

The primary and necessary object of all existence is to be happy. . . . But happiness cannot be obtained individually, it is useless to expect isolated happiness; all men must partake of it, or the few can never enjoy it; man can therefore have but one real and genuine interest, which is, to make all his race as peaceful in character and happy in feeling as the original organization or nature of each will admit . . . and the only contest among men then will be, who shall the most succeed in extending happiness to his fellows. . . . No animal will be wantonly destroyed. The whole animal creation will lose its fear of man. . . . Thus will a terrestrial paradise be formed, in which harmony will pervade all that will exist upon the earth, and there will be none to hurt or destroy throughout the whole extent of its boundaries. . . .

The practice of the rational religion will consist in promoting, to the utmost of our power, the happiness and well-being of every man, woman, and child, without regard to their sect, class, party, or color, and its worship, in those inexpressible feelings of wonder, admiration, and delight, which, when man is surrounded by superior circumstances only, will naturally arise from the contemplation of the infinity of space, of the eternity of duration, of

the order of the universe, and of that Incomprehensible Power by
which the atom is moved and the aggregate of nature is governed.
—FROM THE WRITING OF ROBERT OWEN

On the graveyard hill outside New Harmony, this summer day in 1940, overlooking all time and space, sits Fuzzy Wuzzy with her children around her, and cherubim, too. Under the blowing smoke trees, high above the wide-sweeping river and its islands, Fuzzy Wuzzy and her children are eating raw hamburgers out of a paper sack. Down in the valley, the old hogs grunt and the pigs squeal. Here in the graveyard it is beautiful. Nobody will hurt you. Fuzzy Wuzzy sits with her head against the tomb of a Greek—inscribed "Ephemera! All die at sunset"—and Fuzzy Wuzzy's children toss their ball above a fence of tombs inscribed with other words—"The spirit of man is immortal." The baby turns in Fuzzy Wuzzy's stomach. There is a dead, naked sparrow at Fuzzy Wuzzy's feet. There is an old tin wreath that Fuzzy Wuzzy puts on her head. It is their picnic, high above the river where it don't matter if they don't have no breeches on. For nobody can see them. Pretty soon, it will be time to go down the graveyard hill, hand in hand.

The waitress at the saloon says she wishes she could get outside New Harmony. She was born where Feiba Peveli used to be. All the good people, the waitress says, are up on the hill. It has always been that way since the world began.

The barber, sharpening his hone, says that he does not wish to leave New Harmony, a place for the planting of peach trees when the world has ended. What would Shakespeare have to write about, if everything were as it should be? The barber would be unhappy in a perfect world—it is the world's imperfection that keeps him going, from day to day.

The theater owner says—well, it was like this. When he came to New Harmony, he was so discouraged, he just sat down, and

his wife cried. They had heard it was the scene of two Utopias—
and what did they find but a dead town, exactly what they had
experienced all the way through Kentucky? The seats in the show
sagged. There were cobwebs woven over the screen. A spider
focused bigger than Charlie Chaplin with his shoes on. There
were bats flying overhead, just like in a Kentucky cave town.
Honestly, it was awful. At that point, the theater owner says,
the undertaker stepped in—God knows why. The undertaker
said that things were never so bad as they seemed. He said to
cheer up. He lent them enough paint to make a decent appearance. They built a glass cage in front for the ticket seller. They
made all kinds of improvements in the interior, too. They added
a lobby with velvet curtains. The undertaker lent them some
paper roses in green urns he might have to borrow back. They
put up paper stalactites, for they had come here from the cave
country. Pretty soon, they felt at home. Everything looked so
real. People expressed their appreciation. In New Harmony, a
strange thing has happened. They are happy. They don't know
how it happened. But all of a sudden, they began to be interested in human nature. This is the biggest show on earth—old
human nature, and free to everybody! The theater owner says
he feels like somebody now. He is watching the show outside
on the streets, and everybody wants to come inside. The show
is out there, milling. He feels like a preacher under a big tent.
Still, although he has his job, which is to bring the outside in,
he can't run pictures about far-away subjects, such as a preacher
does. Highbrow things don't go over in a small town. The week
he played *Lost Horizon* was a hell on earth for him. The farmers
saw no sense in the damned thing, Shangri-la, how there could be
snow one minute and warm sunlight with green leaves the next,
just by turning a corner—or how a man eighty-five years old
could have all his teeth in his head, like that lama in a monastery,
Sam Jaffe. Such things simply could not happen, they say—and

would rather see something that is at least possible, like Shirley Temple. Greta Garbo is Shangri-la to them.

Oh, this theater has its troubles, all right. The boy who runs the machine in the booth cannot figure out how so many cowboys get killed every Saturday night, and yet they keep on coming back. He would think they would not be so dumb. A fellow he saw hanged by the noose one Saturday night turned up broad and smiling the very next, helping to hang someone else, who had already helped to hang him, which don't seem quite reasonable. The boy in the booth said it made his head roar, trying to figure out why Hollywood would do such a thing or think people could be so dumb. The same way, he could see that the film was on one disk and the voice on the other—but not how they got together away out on the screen. Someday he was going to get the tracks mixed up, just to see what would happen. He was going to make women crow like roosters, just for the hell of it. Another thing, he wants to know how there could have been Hollywood photographers away back there at the burning of Sodom, photographing Cleopatra, especially when he saw her just the other day in Arizona, pushing a couple of cowboys over a banister.

Oh, this theater owner has his troubles, all right—you can tell the world. Besides the boy in the booth, who has a glass eye, there is always taxation. There is a tax on the seat, there is a tax on the screen. He has got to the point where he cannot absorb any more taxes, though that is what he has always done so far. His wife says he is public-spirited. But when a poor farmer with a family makes seven dollars a week, and has to pay rent, a penny looks mighty big to him. See? So far, the theater owner has paid all the pennies and has done everything he could think of to keep business from dying. Sweetheart Night is two for a dime. Of course, his wife says that as long as he has his worries, he will be happy, which is probably the God's truth. Sure, he's a Republican. There was a fire in the booth last year and a flood the year before, or almost a flood. Nature was complaining against the Department of Agriculture.

The old Irish sailor says that he would be glad to say farewell to New Harmony—that is, if he was in his right senses, but he isn't, and that is the way he got here. Sure, he's a Democrat. It was like this, see? In Buenos Aires, he heard New Harmony was the scene of two Utopias. It was one night in a hot gambling joint. What a fool he was, not to know that Buenos Aires, with butterflies measuring six feet from wingtip to wingtip, had more nature and human nature than New Harmony will ever dream of. Well, he was rounding the Cape of Good Hope in a storm one day when the idea, which had been in the back of his mind, struck him full in the face—maybe he would be a lot better off in New Harmony, a place where there would be plenty of peaches. And a country churchyard. So nothing happened. He drifted. He went around the world with a mad millionaire in a padded cell in a private yacht. The millionaire had killed his sweetheart and got himself declared insane. It was easy. The millionaire never saw the world at all, though he went around it. At every meal, he put out a plate of crumbs for invisible birds. He thought they were his girl, see? After a while, he got himself declared sane. So that was the end of a good job. Then one night in New Orleans, this sailor on a holiday knocked out a fellow who, just as he was passing out like a light, looked up out of one eye and said out of the corner of his mouth—he heard New Harmony was the scene of two Utopias. Honestly, it was enough to make his blood run cold. Then one night in Corpus Christi he ran into a woman who owned a lot of real estate, so he dragged her to the altar, not asking where—for he was getting too old to plow the ocean any longer. Where should it be but New Harmony, of all the places on God's green earth? Why did not somebody tell him? So here he stands, high and dry. He has a tattoo of the Western Hemisphere on his chest, a tattoo of the Eastern Hemisphere on his back. He's covered all over with the words "Remember the Marne." He goes out behind the gooseberry bush with his bottle when he wants to forget. He can't drink in the house because his wife is a Christian woman. He would like to sell the old Rappite house, where the rats are as big as dogs, and buy a trailer, and see America first. But what's the use of wishing? His wife says it would be just the same old seventy-six, another filling station, another gooseberry bush, and she as heavy on her feet as ever. The guy he knocked out in New Orleans must have known this would happen. His wife used to fly the trapezes for Barnum and Bailey, before she fell. That was before he knew her, though. That was when he was buying wild animals for Hagenbeck.

An old lady says she is nobody. Aristocracy looks out from her eyes. No, she has not a pot to cook her dinner in. That is the sad story. All she has is the collected works of Ruskin. It was this way. When she was a young girl, she worked for a drunken sad-dler. Punching holes in leather, she made a design of lilies with burnished thread. Her saddles were famous—though nobody knew her name, for she was nobody. The drunken saddler was educated. A socialist. When she got tired, he quoted Ruskin at her. Her eyes went blind, and only recently has she been able to get her sight back—the cobwebs, like Ruskin, are blown away. It was a hard youth. She could not go a-nutting with the other boys and girls. Oh, what an empty nutshell Ruskin was. The leather that covers the books is lovely. There is nothing to remember. She went to the state fair once in Indianapolis. She rode up with a carload of dappled ponies, their eyes as big as moons. She caught a ride back with a corpse. That was a long time ago. Well, she can see no difference between the New Jerusalem and the New Moral World. She wants her immortality to be violets in the wet ground. She has asked not to have geometry put under her head. Geometry is so confusing. If she could have an urn, she would be happy. She approves of all the housing projects.

Old farmer says it is a long, hard row to hoe. No, happiness don't seem to him like the instinct of the universe—as he wipes his brow with a red handkerchief. That is just some more of the Secretary of Agriculture's propaganda, he would trust no farther than you can throw a bull by the tail. Those gentlemen in the White House are always manufacturing ideas. By the way, his best bull up and died—if that's what you call the happiness of the universe. The government kills all your hogs and says you can't plant corn in the corn fields. Then your wife falls out of a tree at cherry-picking time. Has this administration ever so much as sent up a prayer for rain?

An effete old gentleman, bearded like a patriarch, taps with his cane on the sidewalk, pushing a golden rain tree leaf which has fallen. He has traveled everywhere, he says, with pride that he is not provincial. Twice a year, for nearly thirty years, he made a trip to Chicago. That's where he gets all his handmade shoes and gloves. He has found no place, however, so rare as New Harmony, the golden rose which marked his soul from childhood up and gave him his sense of values and human dignity. Chicago ought to be ashamed of itself. Human life is cheap up there. He still thinks New Harmony has it all over Chicago. That was the way it was in the beginning, and that is the way it will be in the end. It seems to him that, when all is said and done, New Harmony is still a good place for Utopia. It has never been spoiled by smoke, grime, and factories. There are no industries of death here. Oh, it is the gate to paradise! A free hospital might be located on Indian Mound. Those suffering from disease of the lungs would enjoy a salubrious air and a fine view of the river. There never was a better pasture land. New Harmony is a great place for longevity, as he himself is the living proof, having a sound chest and all his own teeth in his own head at the age of sweet sixteen and never been kissed. New Harmony is just as old Father Rapp would have had it. A place for the keeping of things. Robert Owen was the great windbag, always making false promises. It is God's earth. So tapping with his cane upon the walk, stopping to peer at every drain—leaves clog, the water never runs off quite right, and though the farmers say not, there has been quite a shower here—he goes on his way. He is the voice that keeps the Negroes out of New Harmony.

It don't make any difference what that old Croesus tells you, his fellow traveler says. Ragged at the elbow, with dust of pollen on his beard, and a bundle of daisies in his arms, he looks as mad as King Lear in a dry season. If you want to know anything about New Harmony, here's the only man who won't make it prettier than it is. "I am the true Owenite," he announces, "the last leaf on the tree." He pauses, profoundly, trying to organize his thoughts. "They've made an aristocrat and an ancestor out of Robert Owen. It is a rotten shame. I am going to put these flowers on the grave of Judith, my wife. He was not an Episcopalian. He never cared about that harpsichord or that pearl-handled riding whip. All he ever cared about was the workers of the world. All he ever owned was a three-legged stool. He left here with his pockets empty. He loved little children, and so do I. These daisies are for Judith. Let the dead bury the dead, I say." He worked for an undertaker when he was a lad. He could do everything but cut the jugular. He didn't have a license to cut the jugular. If he had had a license, he would have cut it. "I never went much to school. My mother beat me with a pearl-handled riding whip. I have picked up quite a bit of information. There was a little man sitting in the British Museum. He was under the bust of Queen Anne. His name was Karl Marx. All the while that Robert Owen was working for the workers of the world, there sat Karl Marx. The workers of the world will be united. Robert Owen didn't have a license. Marx cut the jugular. Robert Owen was like me. He loved the world. When the workers of the world are united, it is Robert Owen who will resurrect them. I always spit at Hitler when his face comes on the screen. You can't get away with murder, I tell him. Maybe you think this world is a concentration camp, I tell him. I would like to join with Judith, my wife, wherever she is. She is not anywhere."

The storekeeper says, and he has Father Rapp's statue in the window, over the fly-swatters and bottles of wild bee honey, "Well, aren't we all looking for greener pastures? That's why I came here. The people are so much friendlier than those in Little Rock, Arkansas." They are so much more public-spirited, too. They live with history in their blood. He is always kicking against history in the dark. He found a pair of Father Rapp's old spectacles, they must have been his, up under the eaves at the Tavern. When he put them on his nose, everything looked bigger than it was. By God, he almost saw an angel. His wife said that maybe it was that automobile accident giving him trouble again. Another time, he was pulling down a house when he came on Father Rapp's old strongbox—it must have been his. It was empty—not even a scrap of paper—but what was it doing in the ground? So he passed it on to the museum down the road. "That's the genuine beauty of this place," the storekeeper concludes. "You don't have to do anything to get into history. You are just there. They can put me in among the Indian skulls and conch shells. I won't complain."

The town philosopher sits on the porch behind dusty moon-vines, asleep with a fly on his nose. He is the oldest man around here. Practically a centenarian. A tree that blossomed once in a hundred years. Aroused from helpless slumbers, he is glad to express an opinion of the world.

There are those who would give no more votes to a controlled society than they would give to the world's end. They scoff at it, they say it is a dream. They say that nobody wants it, that human nature is not ready for it. Who would be happy in a world purged completely of error, suppose such a world possible, they say—and not one horse thief in the entire creation, and not even a chance for graft? They say it would last no longer than prohibition did. They say that competition has no limits, not even the sky. They say that the rule of the strongest is the only rule, that without it business must sicken and die. They oppose the union of labor and the emancipation of the slave. They oppose every attempt to reorient the world on rational principles. They point out the divergence thus far between the dream and the achievement, not as the present world crisis but as the crisis of the world in eternity. Their conception of life is an exclusive one. They substitute words for things. They purchase space in newspapers. The ideal of a common good is at war with all their vested interests, their privileges, their powers. The ideal is at war with all the experience of the past, they say, and with that of the future. They are the dictators, to whom the great mass of mankind seems like a poor cattle. They do not believe in human nature. The only collectivism, from their point of view, is the collectivism of war. Yet in spite of their primitive soothsaying and their strange argument that men can be protected by destroying them, or that the union of labor can grow only through its death, the many are not deceived. The many know that the dream of a controlled society is not a dream—though the symbolic life of man will have to be considered.

Over at the museum, the geologist says, there is a collection of stones bearing human footprints. The stone which was rejected, he says, will be the chief cornerstone of the new moral world. Perhaps that world can come only after a great catastrophe to shake man out of his slothfulness and the falsehood of partial security.

The miller says that no two millers can make the same flour—even though they be father and son, and even though they try throughout eternity. The wheat and the bread may be the same, but there will be an inscrutable difference between one flour and another, as long as time lasts—because of a difference in the millers, though both are shrouded from head to foot, and many a man will think they are one and the same miller. The flour from one miller will seem like the flour from another, but a chemical test will always show that there is a great chasm, caused by something so slight that nobody can name it, nobody can catch hold of it. That is life. The flour bears the impression of the miller's thumb and the miller's soul. There will always be as many flours as there are millers. Could man but realize this difference between one flour and another, the miller says, as between one soul and another, then he might stop thinking about flour, which was never important in itself, and think more about bread, which is the only true test of flour. If the bread is all right, and if the flour is excellent, nobody ought to ask unnecessary questions. God's is excellent flour.

Women stand in the clothing store. They have come in from the outlying fields. They are sunbonneted, and their aprons are the color of dust. Yardgoods, bright blue and green and yellow, are draped on every counter. They wet the yardgoods with their tongues, chewing a little piece to see if the pattern will fade in weekly wash. They are glad when patterns fade, so they can look till closing time, seeming remote and not satisfied. They will carry away the colors in their minds. The times are still so hard in New Harmony, every woman knows. There are only turnips to give to the doctor when the baby comes—or maybe some old, rain-rotted walnuts, or maybe a beet or two. He never complains. He acts grateful. He says it will be the President of the United States if it's a boy. He says Abraham Lincoln rose from nothing. Maybe when you want him most, though, and there isn't even a kettle of hot water on the stove, and the baby's head is coming through, and you wish to God you had never been born—maybe he's far away, out shooting birds down from the sky, more than likely, and that is just the way life goes. So when you die, the undertaker is out bringing lambs into the world.

Marguerite Young (1908–1995), born and reared in Indiana, moved to New York City in the 1940s, where she lived for the rest of her life. She is the author of two books of poetry, a collection of essays entitled *Inviting the Muses*, and two novels, *Miss MacIntosh, My Darling* (also a Dalkey Archive Essential) and *Harp Song for a Radical*.